Finance, Governance and Economic Performance
in Pacific and South East Asia

Dedicated to Maxwell J. Fry

Finance, Governance and Economic Performance in Pacific and South East Asia

Edited by

D.G. Dickinson

Director of Money, Banking and Finance and Senior Lecturer, Department of Economics, University of Birmingham, UK

J.L. Ford

Professor Emeritus, Department of Economics, University of Birmingham, UK

M.J. Fry

Formerly Department of Accounting and Finance, University of Birmingham, UK

A.W. Mullineux

Professor of Money and Banking, Department of Economics, University of Birmingham, UK

S. Sen

Professor of Development Economics and Head, Department of Economics, University of Birmingham, UK

Edward Elgar

Cheltenham, UK • Northampton, MA, USA

Published by
Edward Elgar Publishing Limited
Glensanda House
Montpellier Parade
Cheltenham
Glos GL50 1UA
UK

Edward Elgar Publishing, Inc.
136 West Street
Suite 202
Northampton
Massachusetts 01060
USA

A catalogue record for this book is available from the British Library

Library of Congress Cataloging in Publication Data
Finance, governance and economic performance in Pacific and South East Asia / edited by David G. Dickinson ... [et al.].
   p. cm.
   Papers presented in a conference held Dec. 16–17, 1997 in Bangkok which was jointly sponsored by the Central Bank of Thailand and by the University of the Thai Chamber of Commerce.
   Includes index.
   1. Fiscal policy—East Asia—Congresses. 2. Fiscal policy—Asia, Southeastern—Congresses. 3. Monetary policy—East Asia—Congresses. 4. Monetary policy—Asia, Southeastern—Congresses. 5. East Asia—Economic conditions—Congresses. 6. Asia, Southeastern—Economic conditions—Congresses.
I. Dickinson, David G. II. Thanakhan hæng Prathet Thai. III. University of the Thai Chamber of Commerce.

HJ1390.5 .F56 2001
330.959—dc21

                                                      00–047646

ISBN 1 85898 973 6
Printed and bound in Great Britain by MPG Books Ltd, Bodmin, Cornwall

Contents

Contributors

A. Bende-Nabende is Post-Doctoral Fellow in the Birmingham Business School, University of Birmingham, UK.

D.G. Dickinson is Director of Money, Banking and Finance and Senior Lecturer in Economics in the Department of Economics, University of Birmingham, UK.

J.L. Ford is Professor Emeritus of Economics in the Department of Economics, University of Birmingham, UK.

Maxwell J. Fry was formerly Tokai Professor of International Money and Finance in the Department of Accounting and Finance, University of Birmingham, UK.

Kenjiro Hirayama is Professor of Economics in the Department of Economics, Kwansei Gakuin University, Hyogo, Japan.

Shin'ichi Hirota is Professor of Economics in the School of Commerce, Waseda University, Tokyo, Japan.

Andy Mullineux is Professor of Money and Banking in the Department of Economics, University of Birmingham, UK.

Hitoshi Osaka, a former doctoral student of the Department of Economics, University of Birmingham, is Assistant Professor of Economics in the Department of Economics, Kyushu University, Fukuoka, Japan.

Somnath Sen is Professor of Development Economics and Head, Department of Economics, University of Birmingham, UK.

J.R. Slater is Director of the Graduate School of Business Administration, University of Birmingham, UK.

N. Suppakitjarak is Research Associate in the Department of Accounting and Finance, University of Birmingham, UK.

M.F. Theobald is Professor of Finance in the Department of Accounting and Finance, University of Birmingham, UK.

Yos Vajragupta is an economist in the Thailand Development Institute, Bangkok, Thailand.

Pakorn Vichyanond is an economist in the Thailand Development Institute, Bangkok, Thailand.

Jiann-Chyuan Wang is an economist in the Central Bank of China, Taiwan District, Taipei, Taiwan.

Norman Yin is Professor of Banking, National Chengchi University, Taipei, Taiwan.

Preface

By the mid-1990s governments in Western economies, envious of, while full of admiration for, the exceptional economic success of the countries of Pacific and South East Asia, were anxious to learn the secrets of their achievement. In October 1995 the United Kingdom's Economic and Social Science Research Council (ESRC) launched its Pacific Asia Programme, which was a major initiative designed to study the economic, political and social aspects of the economically successful economies of that region with the aim of unscrambling some of the lessons that could be learnt by other countries. Of 19 projects funded under the initiative, two were wholly economics-based, of which one was our project at the University of Birmingham. Each project was to be of three years' duration, with the programme being completed by the end of 1998.

Our project (L324253010) was entitled 'Capital formation, financial development and good governance: lessons from Pacific Asia'. It included, amongst other means of dissemination of results at various stages of our work, a conference (with the same title) held in Bangkok on 16 and 17 December 1997 at the end of the second year of the project. Participants included academic, government and central bank economists, together with doctoral students from the University of Birmingham and from universities in the area who were part of our networking. The audience included representatives of government agencies in the region, other academics and members of corporate enterprises.

The intention was to publish the papers in a conference volume, as agreed with Edward Elgar, as soon as possible after the conference, as a set of interim results. The June prior to the conference, of course, saw the start of the Asian financial crisis, with the financial crisis in Thailand. Some authors of papers on financial systems and governance changed tack to accommodate the events that were beginning to engulf the region, as subsequent developments were to demonstrate. Others chose to do so by revising their papers and others again, during the gestation period, abandoned their conference papers in favour of others with a different slant. In the editors' case, some of their contributions have been altered to impart more breadth to the subjects covered, as well as to provide an indication of the variety of issues that have been investigated in our project.

We would like to make a number of acknowledgments. In addition to being partly funded by the ESRC, the Bangkok conference was jointly sponsored by the Central Bank of Thailand and by the University of the Thai Chamber of Commerce. To those institutions we express our profound thanks. The burden of organization was undertaken by Sirivan Chomjumroone and Prasit Mahamad of the University of the Thai Chamber of Commerce, assisted by Adisorn Pinijkulviwat the deputy governor of the Bank of Thailand. The president of the university, Professor Krirkkiat Phipatseritham, gave the opening address to the conference. Dr Tarisa Watanagase, then director of the department of financial institutions supervision and development and now an assistant governor, also addressed the conference. To all these individuals we say a special thank you for their part in helping to ensure the success of the conference. Lastly, we thank the staff of the Regent Hotel in Bangkok, the venue for the conference. They assumed charge of the daily arrangements of the proceedings, doing so with courtesy and unobtrusive efficiency.

In regard to the execution of our project, we extend our thanks to Dr Hitoshi Osaka and Dr Juda Agung who acted as our research associate in the first and second halves, respectively, of our programme. We are also grateful to all those in the Pacific Rim who contributed to our research output; some of their names appear on the contributions to this volume.

Our final thank you is one that is very special and concerns our colleague and friend, Max Fry. Max, acknowledged internationally as an expert in the area of our research, naturally played the major role in generating publications and thereby bringing the project to (what we hope is a successful) fruition. In the last few months of the project Max suffered a bout of illness that saw the return of the cancer that had afflicted him at the outset of the project, and from which he seemed to have recovered. Throughout his struggle, Max has shown his customary ebullience, determination and boyish enthusiasm, ever wanting still to discuss economics without a thought for the morrow. We would like to pay our tribute to that fortitude and to his inspirational example, as well as to his outstanding gifts as scholar, researcher and teacher. It is to that end that we dedicate this volume to him.

David Dickinson, Jim Ford, Andy Mullineux and Somnath Sen
1 November 1999

1. Introduction

David Dickinson, Jim Ford, Max Fry,
Andy Mullineux and Somnath Sen

As we have noted in the Preface, as a major initiative to evaluate the economic success of the countries in Pacific and South East Asia, the ESRC established a special programme of research. We were awarded one of the 19 grants allocated within that programme. Our particular project was entitled '*Capital formation, financial development and good governance: lessons from Pacific Asia*'. As part of our introduction to the papers collected here, we thought that it might be instructive if we were to provide a summary of what the objectives of our project were, and to give some idea of what we discovered. This we do in the following paragraphs before we proceed to outline the papers that are published here.

Our broad theme was the impact of 'governance' on the economic development and growth of the Pacific–Asia region. Three countries were to be studied in depth: Japan, Taiwan and Thailand (often replaced by Indonesia because of lack of data: hence the reference to South East Asia), to cover the range of economic development. Other countries were to be included for comparative studies in many aspects of the research (some of which again were in South East Asia). The objective was to evaluate the part played by the stance of 'governance' in capital formation, financial development and economic development (in terms of gross domestic product (GDP) per capita) and economic growth. Both the microeconomic and the macroeconomic dimension of government policies were to be explored.

The microeconomic aspects of government policy and strategy encompass their impact on the activities of individuals/households, commercial firms (both private and state-owned) and financial firms. Government can influence the behaviour of individuals in labour and goods markets through a variety of channels; for example: tax rates, wages–incomes policies, interest rate structures, the degree of state ownership of commercial and financial enterprises, investment in the infrastructure, and the degree of regulation of markets.

The macroeconomic aspects of governance are likewise manifold. These involve such considerations as the structure of domestic financial and monetary policy, the kind of fiscal stance adopted in regard to the budget, the nature of international monetary and financial policy, particularly in regard to the exchange rate and international capital flows, and the structure of taxation, which together with monetary policy can have substantial impacts on the saving of both the household and the corporate sector.

As a consequence we addressed many issues and, as illustrations, we list below some of the kinds of questions that we sought to answer.

- To what extent did the fiscal stance of the government contribute to the absolute and comparative economic success of the various countries?
- Did any such success arise though the combination of 'good' monetary and fiscal policies, which encouraged saving and investment, without creating inflationary pressures?
- How has government capital formation, particularly in the infrastructure and education, affected the economy?
- Was financial repression instrumental in limiting economic progress and, hence, financial liberalization beneficial to its enhancement?
- Did the Asia–Pacific governments outperform other governments in developing countries elsewhere in the world, by ending financial repression and distortions with subsequent benefits to the economy?
- Did the degree of economic liberalization in general engendered by the government in the economic system and its relationship with the international community (in respect, for example, of foreign direct investment) play a part in stimulating economic advance?
- Were successful monetary policies aided by good governance, in the sense that the government altered the constitutions of the central banks to make them independent of political considerations? Were the consequent central bank policies and preferences a positive influence on the macroeconomic environment?

A flavour of the findings on these and on other related issues that we studied is provided in the following illustrative examples.

1. *Macro-governance, macroeconomic policy and economic performance: why Pacific–Asia performs better.*
The size of the government's deficit and the methods by which it is financed are strongly related to the monetary policy reactions to increases in both government credit and net foreign assets. In turn, such policies are associated not only with higher inflation but also with lower economic growth. Several of the countries in the Pacific–Asian region exhibit considerably greater monetary control than a control group of 15 other developing countries.

2. *Saving, growth, and financial distortions in Pacific Asia and comparisons with other developing countries.*

We discover that financial distortions reduce investment and export growth, thereby cutting output growth rates. Because a major determinant of saving is the output growth rate, we conclude that saving is influenced substantially, albeit *indirectly*, by financial distortions through their effects on investment, export growth and output growth. Simulations indicate that differences in the average values of the financial distortion variables explain 75 per cent of the difference in output between five Pacific Basin and South East Asian countries (Indonesia, Korea, Malaysia, the Philippines and Thailand) and 11 countries in other developing areas (Argentina, Brazil, Chile, Egypt, India, Mexico, Nigeria, Pakistan, Sri Lanka, Turkey and Venezuela).

3. *Financing economic reform: domestic and external resources, government deficits and saving.*

To develop, newly emerging market economies need to increase the resources they have available for investment. We show that government deficits reduce national saving, hence investment and, subsequently, growth. However, financing deficits through voluntary private sector purchases of government debt appears to reduce the damaging effects of any given deficit. Should deficit reduction be infeasible, any deficit should be financed by selling government debt in voluntary domestic markets. Financial distortions should be removed and the climate improved to facilitate foreign direct investment (FDI).

4. *External funds, capital accumulation and growth: the role of FDI.*

FDI is shown, in fact, for our case studies of the ASEAN-5 countries (Indonesia, Malaysia, the Philippines, Singapore and Thailand) and Taiwan, to be conducive to growth in ways that were denied some years ago. It has stimulated economic growth through human capital followed by technology transfer, international trade and learning-by-doing.

5. *Infrastructural investment, liberalization, the openness of the economy and growth.*

For the ASEAN countries and Taiwan, significant governance effects on growth as well as those emanating from FDI were found to operate. Of special significance, since its effect has been doubted, is the direct and indirect impact over time on growth of investment in the infrastructure, accompanied by that in education. Investment in human capital and in the infrastructure had the greatest long-run effects on growth. Additionally, the research highlighted the importance of 'liberalization' epitomized by the switch from financial repression to financial liberalization. For the ASEAN-5 group of countries, in addition, the impact on growth of the Preferential Trading Agreement for the region was investigated. This was found to increase the effectiveness of the countries in attracting FDI with its subsequent beneficial impact upon their growth rates.

6. *Governance: central bank independence.*

Measuring central bank independence by the central bank's reaction to increased credit demands by the central government, we estimated policy reaction functions that show that larger deficits and greater reliance by governments on the inflation tax and financial repression are associated with less central bank independence. Considerable central bank independence is detected in the high-growth economies of Pacific Asia.

A detailed study was undertaken of central bank activity for Taiwan. Illustrative estimates of the weights that the central bank might attach to its targets point to the paramount importance attached to the control of inflation and, therefore, to the prudent governance of the central bank, which was instrumental in the economy's success.

7.   *The link between economic and financial development: deregulation and liberalization.*

Detailed results for Japan, Taiwan and Indonesia over 40 years or so, embracing pre- and post-liberalization periods, indicate that for Taiwan and Indonesia it is financial development that causes economic development. The opposite is the case in Japan. For Japan also there is clearer and more substantive evidence of a long-run relationship between economic and financial development. That carries an interesting implication for Japanese reforms.

A variety of mathematical, statistical and econometric techniques were used in our investigations. Statistical techniques employed included principal components and factor analysis. The predominant econometric approaches used were those of integration, cointegration and ECM (error correction mechanism) modelling. In addition, general VAR (vector auto-regressive) systems were estimated, as were small simultaneous equations systems of structural equations for which three stage least squares was the most frequently used estimator. Panel data techniques were used where appropriate. Full details of the publications that have arisen from the project, in addition to those appearing here, can be found on the Regard Website (*www.regard.ac.uk*), which is run on behalf of the ESRC.

Some of the techniques mentioned above are in evidence in the papers that appear in the ensuing chapters of this volume, to which we now turn our attention. The papers are best taken seriatim since they do not fall naturally into sub-groups, the majority of them focusing on issues of money and finance. Sen's opening paper (Chapter 2) is particularly apposite. It provides an overview of the nature of the still-disputed relationship between financial development in the broad sense and economic development. In doing so it encapsulates the key elements of the intuitive and analytical discussion that has taken place over the years in this debate.

Ford's paper (Chapter 3) focuses on the kind of issues raised in Sen's introductory essay. It evaluates the link between financial and economic development over 35 years in Taiwan. It does so by using alternative indicators of financial development, including some experimental measures of what are labelled 'quantitative measures' of that development. The econometric techniques employed are integration, cointegration and causality. The relationship between financial and economic development is tested against the background of liberalization; and tests of the link between real interest rates, which are the immediate target of liberalization, and measures of financial development are examined, albeit at a superficial level.

Opening domestic fixed-income markets to foreign participation requires, first and foremost, the existence of such markets. Fry (Chapter 4) argues that experience suggests that development of these markets may be best achieved by starting with the market for government debt because a buoyant domestic market for government debt is a key prerequisite for the development of private fixed-income markets. Voluntary domestic markets for government debt provide opportunities for learning-by-doing in market price determination of relatively simple financial claims. The skills aquired in domestic markets for government debt can then spill over into markets for private sector claims, in which the additional complication of credit risk arises. Before such markets can be opened to foreign investors with any realistic expectation of foreign participation, they must meet international standards with respect to the market microstructure, such as trading practices, registry, transfer and settlements systems, and have established a track record.

Fry's essay concludes with three suggestions to countries on the threshold of opening up their markets:

1. Promote interest rate flexibility through monetary control and ensure that the central bank is never the 'lender of first resort'.
2. Ensure that there is in place an adequate system of regulatory control: extend the risk-weighted capital adequacy standard.
3. Abolish reserve and liquid asset requirements on financial institutions. Proper capital adequacy requirements render these otiose.

Hirayama's paper (Chapter 5) evaluates the Japanese experience with financial liberalization over the past two decades and analyses its link with the bubble economy in the 1980s. It also examines the consequences of the bursting of the bubble and attempts to draw lessons for financial institutions. A main conclusion is that the financial liberalization deprived the banks of their traditional clientele, since firms could now gain access to the liberalized capital market. Banks increased their lending to the real estate sector, a crucial sector in the bubble. The lending to that sector seemed justifiable in view of the Japanese banks' tradition of relying on collateral, given the boom in the real estate prices. Absence of adequate corporate governance of the banks at the time aggravated the effects of this lending policy.

Hirota's paper (Chapter 6) investigates how bank–firm relationships in Japan affect corporate performance, an issue that is complementary to the evaluation of the 'bank lending' channel of monetary policy. Using the data from large manufacturing firms for the 1960s, the 1980s, and the 1990s, it is found that the close *lending ties* between the bank (or the main bank) and the firm increase the productive efficiency of the firm. On the other hand, the *shareholding relations* between the bank and the firm do not play such a role; rather they may lower corporate productivity. These results suggest that bank lending is the only governance mechanism to have monitored and disciplined the firm in Japanese financial markets for the past 30 years.

The contribution from Wang (Chapter 7) takes us back to Taiwan. He considers the interaction between the financial sector and the real economy over the past 40 years. The paper offers a different perspective from that provided by Ford, and its main purpose is to describe the recent reforms that have taken place in the financial sector and to analyse its contribution to economic growth. At the same time, the paper moves on to recent events and it assesses the reaction of the CBC, Taipei, to the Asian financial crisis. It suggests that several things can be learnt, the main ones being that a flexible exchange rate should be established, simultaneous with a strengthening of discipline within the financial sector; the capital market should be developed further and on a sound basis; and savings should be promoted to raise capital to maintain financial market stability.

Yin's essay (Chapter 8) complements that of Wang. It concentrates on the impact of the monetary crisis that began in May 1997 as it affected Taiwan, which the author believes is the least affected of the Asian tigers. This is simply attributed to the sounder financial structure and regulatory system operating in Taiwan.

Our attention is switched to Thailand in the paper (Chapter 9) by Vajragupta and Vichyanond. They review the economic history of Thailand's financial sector over the past 25 years, as a preamble to an examination of the 1997 crisis. The authors conclude that 'in retrospect the crisis can be largely attributed to three policy errors: liberalizing foreign capital flows while keeping exchange rates rigid; liberalizing financial institutions when they were not ready; and failing to supervise financial institutions prudently'.

The paper by Suppakitjarak and Theobald (Chapter 10) is a technical study that embraces several countries in the region. A number of currency hedging strategies are evaluated at both the individual country and portfolio level. The countries used in the study were Australia, Hong Kong, Indonesia, Japan, Malaysia, the Philippines, Singapore, Taiwan and Thailand. Currency hedging strategies which incorporate stock market/currency co-movements led to reductions in position risk, but Sharpe ratios were not statistically significantly greater than simple minimum variance currency hedges or reverse hedges. Forward positions deriving from maximizing quadratic utility functions did not lead to statistically significant increases in Sharpe ratios for investors with high risk tolerances. Currency hedging in portfolios did not lead to statistically significant improvements in risk-return space as measured by Sharpe ratios.

The two broad papers by Mullineux that follow (Chapters 11 and 12) provide a general summing-up of several of the issues that have been discussed in the preceding papers in relation to the Asia financial crisis and the role of financial institutions in the macroeconomic sphere. Chapter 11 argues for better supervisory and regulatory controls of financial institutions to prevent recurrences of the financial crises. Chapter 12 considers the meaning of good governance in general terms and then proceeds to discuss the role of the banking and the wider financial sector in generating good governance. Experience in Germany and the UK is used as the benchmark for the discussion of good governance. In addition, the experience in the transition economies is brought to bear on the prescriptions for the Pacific and South East Asian countries, in the light of their recent and continuing financial crises.

The theme of 'good governance' is pursued further, in macroeconomic terms, by Bende-Nabende, Ford and Sen (Chapter 13). 'Good governance' is frequently cited as the key factor in the economic success of the tiger economies. This embraces the many facets of government, but especially in terms of the government's finances: the budgetary stance, the level of expenditure, the level and type of taxes collected, and the composition of expenditure, across infra-structural activities for example, including the creation of human capital. This paper provides a pilot study of the influence of such factors on the economic growth of the ASEAN-5 countries. Using an endogenous growth model, the findings indicate that governance has differential impacts on the GDP of the five countries. The influence, for example, of physical capital depends upon the GDP of the country. In line with that outcome, it is noted that governments benefit from taxation when the tax base is large. The results for human capital were disappointing, however; they tend to show that countries at the lower and moderate levels of economic development do not derive benefits from higher levels of human capital.

Osaka's contribution (Chapter 14) evaluates a controversial and important facet of the growth process in the tiger economies: aside from such issues as what role governance might have played, can the success achieved so far be at least partly attributable to increased productivity? It is Krugman's contention that the answer is an emphatic no. Consequentially, Krugman draws the pessimistic conclusion that the Asian tigers' rapid economic success will be a once-and-for-all phenomenon. To compete in the world, and hence to be able to maintain future economic success, will be impossible. Osaka's paper tests this hypothesis for Japan, South Korea, the Philippines and Thailand, for 1960–91. Using growth accounting methodology, cointegration tests and a dynamic version of the logarithmic Cobb–Douglas production function, the paper finds that the hypothesis cannot be substantiated. For example: for South Korea and Thailand there is evidence of an increasing trend in total factor productivity. The decreasing trend for the Philippines disappears once the economy recovers from the political turmoil of the mid-1980s. In regard to production function analysis, the proxy for productivity growth has the largest impact of all supplementary inputs in the long run for all countries save Japan.

Domestic investment is not, other things being equal, the only engine of growth, as we know. Foreign direct investment (FDI) can have a major impact on growth: some would contend not always for the better. The general consensus now has moved away from that scepticism to one where FDI is looked on with more favour. FDI can also, of course, be a reflection of both special micro-economic policies (special tax and location incentives) of the government and of its macroeconomic policies (good infrastructure, for example). The paper by Bende-Nabende, Ford and Slater (Chapter 15, which concerns the key area discussed under (5) above) investigates empirically the dynamic impact of policy variables on FDI and its spillover effects on variables and consequently the economic growth process of the ASEAN-5 economies (1970–94). A small dynamic simultaneous equation endogenous growth system is used. Unlike previous studies which either assumed the linkage was one-way from FDI to growth or vice versa, this paper allows for two-way interaction. The paper assesses the effect of one form of governance, in the form of liberalization in terms of increasing the openness of the economies, on economic growth.

The results demonstrate that, whereas the impact is immediate in the more developed, politically stable and 'foreign investment-friendly' countries, there is a time lag (resulting from 'wait and see' strategies) in those economies which are less developed, politically unstable and have an element of hostility to foreign investment. They further suggest that the magnitude of the multiplier effects and the degree of the relocation of production increase as the level of economic development increases; while the speed of the spillover process slows down as the level of economic development increases.

The final paper, by Dickinson (Chapter 16), focuses on company investment and its behaviour in the period prior to the financial crisis. Dickinson argues that firms overinvested in pursuit of growth rather than of value maximization. He attributes this to agency problems exacerbated by an undeveloped financial structure and by the economic environment. The paper considers data on manufacturing industry in Indonesia, Korea, Malaysia, Thailand and Taiwan and examines interactions between variables at a sectoral level as well as undertaking formal econometric modelling of an investment function to consider the evidence for the overinvestment hypothesis. His paper concludes with policy recommendations.

2. Finance, development and growth: an overview

Somnath Sen

INTRODUCTORY IDEAS

During the last two decades world economic growth has been relatively high, fuelled by spectacular growth rates in Pacific Asia and creditable growth performances in both the EU and the USA. At the same time, there has been a huge increase in global financial flows and a rapid rise in the size of the international financial sector. Within this international framework, there has been increasing discussion about the relationship between financial development and economic growth. Specifically, the question has been asked whether finance causes growth, or their relative growths are coterminous and rapid growth essentially forces the financial sector to respond to the 'real' economy's needs and therefore expand.

Financial sectors and institutions, as well as services of financial intermediaries, together define the size and scope of financial development. It is proxied by empirical measures such as financial depth (ratio of liquid liability stock to real output flow) which measures the overall size of the financial intermediary sector of the economy. It is important to note at the outset the similarity of such empirical measures of financial development to that of the physical capital–output ratio – so vital to growth theory. Essentially, the measures represent *financial* capital stock to real output.

Financial *intermediation* does not imply that this service is an intermediate good used up in the production process; rather, it is an essential input into aggregate output and vital for production of gross domestic product (GDP). The financial sector, small or large, is as much a part of the real economy as steel, manufacturing or construction. The role of finance in growth can be best appreciated if the artificial distinction between financial (monetary) and real sectors of the economy are eradicated. The stress should be on finance sector output being a part of aggregate real output, as well as being an intermediate input (like oil) in the aggregate macroeconomic production function.

9

The purpose of this chapter is to ask and answer the question: does financial development affect growth and, more importantly, does it increase the rate of growth of GDP of the non-financial sector's output? It provides a critical overview of the literature and attempts to demonstrate the importance of finance in causing growth. The conclusion is simple: much theory and evidence shows that financial development is crucial for growth and should have a beneficial effect. Thus the recent turmoil in financial markets and its negative impact in Pacific Asia, which form the backdrop to this book, should not be exaggerated. The short and medium-term instability of the financial system, as we have been observing in Pacific Asia, should not detract from a long-run perspective. If the financial sector is treated as a separate independent sector, producing an essential input into the aggregate production process and needing regulation to preserve the quality of its products, then its impact on growth must be favourable.

SOME REFLECTIONS ON THEORY

The impact of financial variables and factors on economic growth and the real capital stock (physical assets) of the economy has always been of interest to macroeconomists (Fry, 1997). The seminal work by Tobin (1965) analysed the impact of finance on growth by focusing on monetary growth. Tobin showed that an increase in the growth rate of money stock could increase real capital formation by reducing real interest rates and increasing the value of physical assets through inflation. Others working in the same genre, such as Shaw (1973) and McKinnon (1973), increased the menu of assets that could be called 'money' (emphasizing the distinction between inside and outside money), but once again showed how financial widening via monetization could have a favourable impact on growth. The influence of such work was profound because it showed that the Walrasian division between the real and the monetary economy could be breached (as Wicksell had claimed many years back); that 'money', representing the width, depth and strength of the financial system, was not necessarily neutral and could have effects on the physical assets and welfare in the steady state; and that the transition path towards the steady state could be dramatically affected by the presence or increase of monetary and financial variables.

These models had at least three types of deficiencies, but which were corrected only in the late 1980s and early 1990s – testifying to the resilience of such models. First, the attempt to mimic financial development by the variable 'money' was rather restrictive. Clearly, model tractability required simplification and in the more wider representation these pioneers like Tobin were clearly discussing the whole financial system and its impact on growth.

However, the formal models looked at money and monetary variables as inputs into a production function and/or state variables in the felicity function and thereby looked at their real effects on the rest of the economy (such as on physical capital or social welfare); alternatively, the existence or proliferation of such monetary variables reduced transaction costs and thereby reduced the real rate of interest increasing the price of bonds and attracting more investment capital. According to the earlier models, whatever the monetary system looks like (and clearly institutions are vital here), it is essentially a transmission mechanism whereby the 'real' economy benefits. This is clearly a narrow and restrictive view. The financial and monetary system is as much part of the aggregate economy as consumption, physical asset creation or the government. The optimum way to deal with the financial system in the context of capital formation is to treat it as a special and unique sector which has its own production function but is also an input into the aggregate production process.

A second problem common to all the growth models of this genre was that the long-run steady-state rate of growth was exogenously given by the growth rate of efficiency labour. The growth rate of any reproducible factor of production, such as physical capital created through saving or forgone consumption, would have zero impact in the long-run steady state on the growth rate of aggregate output. This is because sustained accumulation of an endogenous factor of production, without bound, would reduce the marginal product of such a factor to zero, and therefore its contribution to long-run growth of output would be null too. This 'iron law' could only be broken by an exogenous factor of production, that is, manpower or labour or technical progress which fell as 'manna from heaven', and so long-run growth is circumscribed by these variables. Clearly, all factors must be essential to production; otherwise, non-labour factors could continue on their own forever. In such models we have exogenous growth.

The alternative, as first formally proposed by Romer (1986) but having roots in the Harrodian model of growth with fixed output–capital coefficients, is to have 'endogenous growth'. Here reproducible factors of production such as physical capital, human capital, technical progress embodied in capital assets and so forth can indeed raise the economy's long-run steady-state rate of growth even if the exogenously determined growth of efficiency labour is zero. Essentially, an economy with a Cobb–Douglas technology (that is, where all factors are vital for production) can have a positive long-run steady-state rate of growth (which can be increased by policy) even if the supply of efficiency labour (physical labour augmented by technical progress) is constant. This is endogenous growth (Aghion and Hewitt, 1998).

A final issue that the old models failed to take account of is that of the open economy. With terms of trade (real exchange rates) as a major macroeconomic variable, domestic growth issues will have spillovers for the overseas sector which in turn will feed back into the domestic macroeconomy. The interrelationships between financial variables (such as the rate of interest), macroeconomic variables (such as the saving rate) and the foreign sector (through influencing the terms of trade or ratio of export to import prices) become vital.

Growth crucially depends on domestic savings complemented by external savings. How the terms of trade affects domestic saving is obviously a matter of major importance. A seminal discussion of this was given by Laursen and Metzler (1950) who showed that a rise in the terms of trade (an increase in competitiveness or a real devaluation) would increase expenditure in terms of the home good; thus aggregate demand creation within the domestic economy would increase aggregate output via a Keynesian open economy multiplier. However, unlike the Laursen–Metzler claim, a real devaluation could cause the saving rate to fall, thus causing long-term growth to decline. It is clear that, once the foreign sector is introduced into the model of saving and growth, the results become more problematic.

Consider the earlier discussion on endogenous versus exogenous growth. Suppose we assume for simplicity that efficiency labour is constant (that is, it does not grow). It is still possible to generate endogenous growth by increasing the productivity of physical capital. The evidence surveyed in the next two sections demonstrates that an effectively functioning large financial system can increase the output–capital ratio and thereby increase the long-run steady-state rate of growth. However, this also increases the real rate of interest domestically. A capital inflow from abroad will put pressure on the domestic currency to appreciate, thereby reducing international competitiveness. This could have growth-dampening effects. Thus financial development in an open economy could reverse the positive relationship between finance and growth stressed earlier. However, the story does not finish here. If the Laursen–Metzler effect holds then domestic saving will rise consequent to a fall in the terms of trade and a reduction in competitiveness. A rise in saving (decline in expenditure) could offset the growth-dampening effect. The final outcome is unclear.

We may be observing the opposite effect in South East Asia. The failure of the financial system reduces the real return on physical capital, causing capital outflows. Growth will suffer because the real interest rate has fallen. Nevertheless, the devaluation will increase competitiveness, thus mitigating the negative effects. On the other hand, better terms of trade will increase domestic expenditures, reducing savings and causing harm to long-term growth prospects. Clearly, we hope that the weakness of the financial system will not cause long-term damage, but economic theory cannot make such a clear-cut judgment. We need to look at the functional role of financial development and what it does; in addition, a brief survey of the empirical literature is required to see the impact of finance and growth.

The various roles that financial development can play are exemplified in a strongly stylized form in the Pagano (1993) model, where growth of output, g (assuming labour force growth is zero) is given by:

$$g = Azs$$

where A is the social marginal product of capital (if a distinction needs to be made between private and social productivity); z is the proportion of savings channelled to productive investment through financial intermediation; s is the economy's rate of saving. Financial development raises A (through improved allocation), raises z (through more efficient intermediation and less moral hazard and adverse selection) and also possibly increases s (at least at the household level owing to a reduction in risk).

Increases in the coefficient A work as an output-augmenting technical change or a shift in the fixed output capital. Financial development collects and disseminates information which allows investors to evaluate alternative investment projects. Secondly, it induces economic agents to invest a higher proportion of their wealth in high-return, but also high-risk, assets because there is less need, under efficient financial intermediation, to keep wealth in liquid assets (Rajan and Zingales, 1998). Thirdly, where there are transaction and sunk costs to individual investment, or lumpiness and other constraints prevent some individuals investing immediately, economic agents with surplus funds can lend to others who can make productive investments. There are clearly asymmetric information issues to be resolved here. However, under plausible circumstances, total productivity can rise since the borrowers do not suffer from the same constraints as lenders.

What about the other two parameters, z, s, in the simple formulation. First, it is clear that, the more advanced is the financial sector, and the more competitive with lower margins are the financial houses, the greater will be parameter z. A greater proportion of saving will be channelled towards investment (and growth) with less slippage, lower spread between borrowers and lenders and lower margins for brokers and dealers (all leading to a decline in $(1 - z)$ and hence to an increase in z.

As regards the relationship between financial development and the savings rate s, the jury is still out. If financial intermediation increases risk sharing between lenders and borrowers, allows households to smooth their consumption patterns so that long-term potential savings may be diverted towards investment rather than maintained to balance consumption flows, and makes saving elastic to interest rate rises, clearly the rate of savings will rise. However, these are relatively strong assumptions and the impact effect on saving is ambiguous.

Building formal models to show the impact of finance and growth must satisfy certain criteria. First, there should be endogenous growth such that the long-run steady-state rate of growth can be made dependent on financial development *independent* of growth of capital and efficiency labour. Secondly, the model should have wider generality than the earlier models of monetary growth (by Tobin, for example) where the monetary/financial system is essentially and only a transmission mechanism whereby the 'real' economy benefits. This is clearly a narrow and restrictive view. A more general model should avoid this problem. Thirdly, the financial and monetary system is as much part of the aggregate economy as consumption, physical asset creation or the government. The optimum way to deal with the financial system in the context of capital formation is to treat it as a special and unique sector which has its own production function but is also an input into the aggregate production process.

The Appendix to this paper constructs a model, emphasizing a two-sector framework, for analysing the impact of financial development and the effect of expansion of the financial sector on the growth of GDP (or even GDP minus the financial sector output). The conclusion is the following: financial expansion is crucial for improving endogenously the economy's rate of growth; a stylized economy, with capital and efficiency labour having zero growth, can still produce growth in aggregate output with financial development. Although an 'extreme' result, this demonstrates analytically that financial development is vital for growth and not just an intermediate facilitator of growth.

WHAT DOES FINANCIAL DEVELOPMENT ACTUALLY DO FOR GROWTH?

Traditionally, the most important role attached to the financial system in fostering growth was in terms of uncertainty and risk. With Knightian uncertainty (where probabilities of investment projects succeeding or failing are not known) a well-developed financial system reduces variability and unpredictability of asset prices. The cost of fluctuations in asset prices around the mean could mean lower investment and hence lower growth; clearly, a reduction in the standard deviation or variance of the price of assets would be helpful in stimulating higher asset accumulation. With the additional element of risk (that is, with known probabilities), financial development helps to trade, hedge, diversify and pool risk.

Although these factors are important, their long-run growth implications are small. The main impact of reducing uncertainty and diversifying risk is on short-run fluctuations. As the parallel literature on exchange rates shows, the reduction in variability and fluctuations of international asset prices increases trade and transactions, but the impact effects are of a second order of magnitude. A similar conclusion can be drawn for financial markets reducing fluctuations.

A second channel by which the financial sector can make an impact on growth is via market frictions as well as the existence of imperfect or incomplete markets, which all create information costs. Financial development reduces such costs to individuals. The gathering and processing of investment opportunities and funding is done better by financial houses rather than individuals, yet these are institutional features which may differ from country to country and could also link up with the structure of corporate governance. For example, if banks are major shareholders in large companies then the regulation is often easier than dispersed or non-financial shareholding. In Germany and South Korea, for example, the specific form of corporate governance has allowed information costs to be minimized without necessarily a large expansion of the financial system as in the UK or USA. An alternative model is that of Taiwan, where informal funding through family finances has allowed small and medium-sized enterprises to expand and grow fast without a consequent expansion of the formal financial system. Once again, the growth implications of information costs are not profound.

In principle, the most important effect of financial development on economic growth is via the reduction of transactions costs. Market imperfections, incomplete markets and frictions in trade all produce transaction costs. These costs are reduced by financial sector expansion even in a certain world. This has a major impact on investment and therefore on growth. When transaction costs in investing in riskier assets (but with higher returns) are reduced, investors move towards these investments with greater growth potential. Secondly, there is also less need to keep a large proportion of assets in liquid form because the transaction costs of borrowing have been reduced. Thirdly, agents who have surplus funds which they cannot invest can rapidly lend to others, through the financial sector, provided the transactions costs of such transfers are low. In Figure 2.1 we show a stylized representation of these effects.

SOME REFLECTIONS ON EVIDENCE

Formal empirical and econometrics evidence has increased in recent years on how financial development affects growth. First, let us look at some more informal evidence and then mention the econometric results. The first obvious candidate for explanation is *causality*. All the theoretical models build the postulated relationships in such a way that causality runs from financial development to economic growth. But is this appropriate?

Joan Robinson (1952) has said: 'where enterprise leads, finance follows'; in other words, growth causes the financial sector to expand, rather than vice versa. There are essentially three types of evidence to demonstrate the validity of what we have postulated – that finance causes growth: (a) history of economic

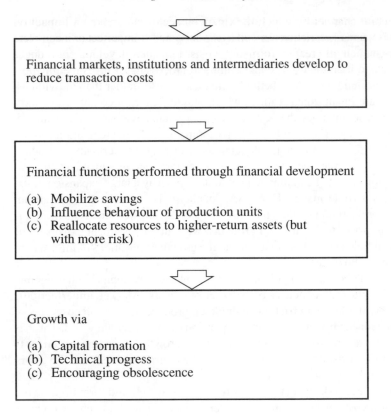

Figure 2.1   Stylized picture of financial development causing economic growth

analysis, (b) economic history, and (c) statistical methods. Consider evidence
from the history of economic ideas or thought. Schumpeter claims (1911): 'The
banker is *not* so much as a *middleman*. He authorises people to *innovate*.' Thus
finance represented by the 'banker' is not just an intermediary but also a supplier
or facilitator of innovation. Innovation is only partly benign. It constitutes
'creative destruction' in the sense that older vintage machines are destroyed
while new vintages produce 100 per cent depreciation. But this can only be
done if there is sufficient finance available to replace older machines (which
may still be making profits, that is, with prices above marginal costs) and the
financier induces the owner of the new machine to replace the old.

   Economic history tells many stories in a similar vein. When the East India
Company wanted to introduce the output of new European technology (such as
machine-made textiles produced after the Industrial Revolution in Britain) in
India, it first had to change the source of financial capital. This was done through

the destruction of indigenous financial houses by increasing risk (through tax or plunder) of financial intermediation conducted by well-established local families and castes. At the same time the British administration made land a secure and profitable asset, so that the 'moneylenders' or financiers and bankers decided to change their portfolio towards land rather than towards borrowing and lending. A change in the financial structure allowed British financial houses and banks to take over and introduce new technology (including transport such as railways).

Prior to the arrival of European traders, economic growth and prosperity in India was high (Frank, 1998); indeed, this was one of the main reasons for attempts from the late 15th century to early 16th century to find alternative sea-routes to the Indies. India was initially, during the 12th to 16th centuries, relatively well endowed with precious metals as a source of currency. A high stock of money relative to GDP allowed productivity to increase and high growth to take place. However, relative scarcity of precious metals, by the 16th and 17th centuries, allowed more elaborate and complex financial structures to grow up. This in turn supported trade, specialization, innovation, productivity and growth. India's banking system

> was efficient and well organised throughout the country, and the hundis and bills of exchange issued by the great business and financial houses were honoured everywhere in India, as well as in Iran, and Kabul, and Herat and Tashkent and other places in Central Asia – there was an elaborate network of agents, jobbers, brokers and middlemen – a very rapid and indigenous system of communicating new and market processes had been evolved. (Nehru, 1960, p. 192)

Clearly, the high growth rates observed in mediaeval India owed much to a highly developed financial system.

Economic historians have pointed to the causal links flowing from finance to growth. In other words, a well-developed financial intermediary system increased productivity growth through the ability to finance innovation and enterprise and/or through the power to expand specialization and trade. An Indian author, discussing economic institutions prior to the arrival of the Portuguese (the first foreign traders to arrive via the Cape of Good Hope discovered by Vasco da Gama) says the following:

> there is evidence of a highly developed class (the shroff or sarafs) dealing with currency, commercial credit, loans, insurance of goods – [which] were undoubtedly closely connected with the rural petty bourgeoisie – [which was] an important link in the transmission of a definite share of the agrarian surplus to the commercial classes. (Ganguli, 1964, p. 57)

Historical evidence is quite definitive about the importance of finance in Asia (see Frank, 1998) in fostering economic growth during the mediaeval and early modern periods of its history; India is one example, but there are others.

A third source of empirical evidence is that of Granger causality tests which show that, after a minimum level of development, finance 'causes' growth. Choosing countries which have attained some infrastructural growth around 1970, a set of Granger causality tests (conducted by the author) for 24 developing countries, for the period 1970–90, showed that financial development Granger-caused growth of GDP for 19 of these countries.

Another set of econometric evidence looks at data-based results regarding the *long-term impact*. Interpreting the econometric relationship between indicators of economic growth and indicators of financial development depends on how one defines the former and the latter (Levine, 1997). King and Levine (1993) estimate three alternative measures of growth: real per capita GDP growth (GY), real per capita capital stock growth (GK), and productivity growth (GP).

They also estimate four alternative measures of financial development. These are given by:

DEPTH (FD1): a measure of financial depth given by the ratio of liquid liabilities (currency held outside the banking system plus demand and interest-bearing liabilities of the banks and non-banking financial intermediaries) of the financial system to GDP;

BANK (FD2): a measure of banking sector output in domestic credit given by the ratio of deposit bank domestic money asset to central bank domestic asset plus deposit bank domestic money asset;

PRIVATE (FD3): a measure of lending to private enterprises by the financial sector given by the ratio of claims on the non-financial private sector to total domestic credit (excluding credit to money banks);

PRIVY (FD4): a measure of private non-financial borrowing, for the production of output, from the financial sector given by the ratio of claims on the non-financial private sector to aggregate output or GDP.

Using cross-section data from a large country-based data set the authors estimate 'long-run' relationships since a large cross-section gives results for a wide variety of countries replicating the behaviour of development from poor to rich. After controlling for various other variables that are independently affecting growth, they find that these measures of financial development all positively affect growth. Thus the expansion of the financial sector has a beneficial impact on economic growth. Table 2.1 summarizes these results.

The final empirical question is whether there is time-series evidence that, for some countries, the initial level of financial development has a positive impact on future growth. In other words, there should be not only contemporaneous evidence, as shown in Table 2.1, but also some causal evidence that today's financial expansion will help tomorrow's growth rate. It needs to be demonstrated that current growth is related positively to *initial* or past financial depth. King and Levine (1993) show precisely that. The growth rates averaged over the 1960s, 1970s and 1980s are made dependent on the initial values of the relevant financial development indicators for 1960, 1970 and 1980. The panel data (pooled cross-section and time series taken together) also show that the various decadal growth rates (of output, capital and productivity) are generally positively related to the initial values of the financial indicators (financial depth given by the ratio of liquid liabilities of the financial system to GDP, commercial banking sector output towards domestic credit, a measure of lending to private enterprises by the financial sector as well as a measure of private non-financial borrowing, for the production of output, from the financial sector). In other words, countries with reasonably developed financial sectors in the early 1960s grew faster than those with more backward financial sectors during the 1960s; and so on, for the 1970s and the 1980s. Coupled with the empirical fact that financial development is often associated with financial liberalization, and that the domestic saving ratio rises with interest rate rises consequent to financial liberalization, it is evident that the expansion of the financial sector (adequately handled) is good for growth.

Table 2.1 *Impact of financial development on economic growth for a cross-section of 77 developing countries, 1960–89*

Dependent variable	FD1	FD2	FD3	FD4
GY	0.024	0.032	0.034	0.032
GK	0.022	0.022	0.020	0.025
GP	0.018	0.026	0.027	0.025

Note: All FD (financial development) variables have a positive, significant and relatively large impact on various indicators of economic growth. Although the level of significance varies, they are all statistically significant.

Source: King and Levine (1993).

CONCLUSION AND MACROECONOMIC GOVERNANCE

The lessons from macroeconomic modelling, empirical evidence and historical events all demonstrate that finance is good for growth. In other words, liberalization of the financial system, expansion of financial intermediation and overall financial development tend to have a positive impact on growth. Yet the experience of Pacific–Asian economies since the summer of 1997 seems to say the opposite. Even leaving out the teething troubles faced by emerging markets, the developmental and growth problems of the High Performing Asian Economies (HPAEs) seem to have stemmed from the weaknesses of the financial sector itself. In spite of large-scale financial expansion, the system's collapse has heralded economic decline – albeit in the short and medium term. Is this a contradiction to the hypothesis emphasized in this chapter?

There are at least three arguments in support of our central concept. First, in a perverse way, the difficulties of Pacific–Asian economies could be construed as showing that adverse financial sector shocks create growth problems; just as financial expansion is helpful, so also is the fact that financial collapse and contraction is inimical to growth. The second reason is familiar: the underlying strengths of these economies are still significant and long-run growth will recover. Although the jury is still out about the so-called 'myth of the Asian miracle', there is enough evidence to show that numerous long-run factors are still helping growth in these countries.

A third reason is the argument that the quality of financial development is as important and even more important than the quantity of financial development (Stiglitz, 1994). As the model in the Appendix emphasizes, the various parameters that channel the impact of financial development towards economic growth are quality-adjusted; in other words the level of the parameters must take into account quality indicators. Hence growth is enhanced when financial development is of high quality and growth is reduced when such financial development is of inferior quality. In many ways, the failure of the economies in the Pacific–Asian region is as much due to the failure of governance and regulation as it is to the size of the financial system per se.

It may be instructive to look briefly at the features of the so-called 'Asian crisis'. Recent experience of these economies shows a number of major characteristics or features which may help to define the framework of the crisis. We discuss six of these stylized facts. Note that the objective here is to not to get at the roots of the problems of the Pacific–Asian economies, but rather to see whether the concepts and ideas postulated in this chapter have wider relevance to these economies which have generally had high economic growth and major expansion of the financial sector prior to the crisis in the late 1990s. We first look at the six crucial stylized facts and then consider their implications:

1. large current account deficits for many (though not all affected) countries;
2. reduction in growth rates from the double-digit figures common in the 1980s to more 'reasonable' rates;
3. high private sector corporate debt, much of this in unhedged foreign currencies;
4. in other regions (such as in Latin America), financial and currency crises often reflect fundamental disequilibria such as the 'twin deficit' where

budget and trade deficits coexist; policy measures, involving austerity programmes, are designed to alleviate such classical macroeconomic problems; in Pacific Asia policy measures were more difficult because there was no twin deficit, government budgets were often in surplus and inflation was relatively low; therefore austerity measures (for example, cutting government expenditure, increasing interest rates) were inappropriate;

5. although fundamentals were fine, speculative bubbles created a 'bubble economy' which had a vicious cycle impact on the economy;
6. there was large-scale political contamination of economic problems so that political governance issues were as important as problems of economic fundamentals.

The impact of these stylized facts on the financial system had complex repercussions. First, the current account deficits were caused by private sector macro imbalances; in other words, the macroeconomic accounts of the households and firms in aggregate were responsible (government budgets were generally healthy and mostly in modest surplus). Overall private sector saving was less than investment and this was reflected in current account deficits (foreign borrowing). In most other countries, the saving–investment gap is due to a reduction in household or corporate savings. However, in the Pacific–Asian economies, the national private sector saving rate was extremely high by international standards, so the so-called 'problem' was excessive investment. Overinvestment as opposed to overconsumption created the excess domestic demand. The financial sector may have been less than successful in curbing excess investment, but certainly cannot be blamed for its existence. In some ways, the economy was a victim of its own success.

Secondly, much of this high level of investment was financed by foreign borrowing, but this inflow was not necessarily based on FDI and equity investment, but rather on borrowing from the international commercial banking sectors. So the capital account showed excessive transfers of capital inflow but these only increased corporate debt and exposure to foreign currency risk. A devaluation was particularly harmful because it caused insolvency and then bankruptcy. The fact that much of borrowing was unhedged (given the stability of foreign exchange relative prices over the previous decades) implied greater instability and a faster downward spiral.

Thirdly, a set of exogenous changes took place, quite independent of domestic financial development, but which nevertheless had dramatic adverse consequences. International financial investors and market participants began moving into US and European investments where the ratio of corporate earnings to equity values started rising from the mid-1990s. Regional integration elsewhere (European Union, NAFTA) slowed down Asian exports. Some exchange rate adjustment (for example, a strengthening of the dollar, with which some currencies were pegged, as in Taiwan, Thailand and Hong Kong) caused a loss in competitiveness.

Fourthly, there was a huge growth of credit to the private sector from the financial sector. Asymmetric information problems arose, but lack of corporate governance within the financial sector allowed these issues to be swept under the carpet. So long as growth rates remained at double digit figures, it was easy to borrow to finance investment since the returns from growth exceeded borrowing costs and risk premia. When the downturn appeared in growth rates, the boom became a bust and the downward spiral mirrored the earlier upward spirals. In many ways, these economies were faced with a 'Ponzi game' where intertemporal and terminal constraints on borrowing were not obeyed.

Fifthly, weaknesses in the financial system, such as lack of transparency, bad corporate governance and lax financial regulation, all caused problems. These are issues that need to be incorporated into quality indicators of financial development so that empirical evidence and country studies can pick up such quality failures as compared to expansion of quantity indicators of financial growth.

Finally, political problems, including macro governance problems, exacerbated the core problems. Needless to say, crony capitalism, for example in Indonesia (under Suharto) or the Philippines (under Marcos), makes it very difficult for the financial system to fulfil its obligations adequately. Once again we may observe the standard indicators of financial development show an expansion, but the type and quality of services provided will be inappropriate for growth to take place at a sustainable level.

The conclusion, even if somewhat weakened by the negative case study of Pacific Asia, is clear. High-quality financial expansion and development is a vital input towards economic growth. In this respect, 'finance' is no different from other forms of 'physical' capital. Just as roads or infrastructure are 'good for growth' provided they are of high quality and not excessive in terms of needs, so also is financial expansion good for growth.

APPENDIX

In this Appendix we construct a two sector model of the economy where the endogenous behaviour of the financial sector affects the long-run rate of growth in steady state. The impact of financial development on long-run endogenous growth depends on the crucial parameters involved, but the model is constructed to show the positive impact in general.

Consider a macroeconomy with an aggregate production function:

$$Y = K^{\alpha} F^{\beta} L^{1-\alpha-\beta} \tag{2A.1}$$

The Cobb–Douglas formulation ensures that all inputs (factors of production) are essential for output.

Here Y is output, K is physical capital, L is efficiency labour and F is a measure of financial capital or, more broadly, of financial development. Note that Y is output of the 'rest of the economy'; that is, aggregate GDP minus the financial sector. The reason for keeping Y and F separate is to clarify the nature of causality and the impact effect *from* finance *to* growth.

The growth rate of Y from (2A.1) is

$$g_Y = \alpha g_K + \beta g_F + (1 - \alpha - \beta) g_L \tag{2A.2}$$

where $g_Y = (dY/dt)/Y$ and so on.

Consider a simple proportional saving function where s_1 is the proportion of GDP invested for physical capital formation (K) and s_2 is the proportion invested in the financial sector (F). Then

$$g_K = (dK/dt)/K = s_1 \, Y/K \tag{2A.3}$$

$$g_F = (dF/dt)F = s_2 \, Y/F \tag{2A.4}$$

It is clear from the nature of the production function (2A.1) that, as K increases without bound, Y/K tends to zero; thus g_K tends to zero. In the same way, as F increases over time, Y/F becomes smaller and tends to zero.

In such an exogenous growth model, therefore, the long-run steady-state rate of growth must be independent of g_k and g_F. In other words, neither physical nor financial capital is very relevant for long-term growth which is 'exogenously' given by the growth of efficiency labour – a 'manna from heaven'.

Now think of an endogenous growth model where economic behaviour, such as human capital formation, can actually affect the rate of growth in steady-state equilibrium (that is, where all variables grow at the same rate). The analysis concentrates on financial capital formation, that is, the growth of the financial sector.

Consider a *two*-sector model of an economy. The first sector produces output Y, as defined earlier. The second sector produces a financial capital 'good' F. This F can represent the size of the financial sector or be measured as an index of financial development. The sector F also has a production function, but it does not use physical capital or labour as inputs. The only input required to produce *new* financial capital (or investment) is some stock of existing F. Let there be a constant return to scale production function which relates inputs of F to the output of flows of new financial capital goods or financial capital *investment*. Thus

$$(dF/dt) = \lambda F_f \tag{2A.5}$$

where F_f is the amount of F required to produce incremental value added or investment in financial capital.

Total stock of F is divided into two parts, one used as inputs in the production of Y and the other as inputs into the production of financial investment goods (as in (2A.5)). Thus

$$F = F_y + F_f \tag{2A.6}$$

Let there be a constant proportion of each element in (2A.6) such that

$$F_f = \phi F \tag{2A.7}$$

$$F_y = (1 - \phi)F \tag{2A.8}$$

The production function for Y is

$$Y = K^\alpha F^\beta_y L^{1-\alpha-\beta} \tag{2A.9}$$

Since we concentrate on the impact of F on Y, let us assume that K and L are constant. Hence K and L can have no impact on long-run growth. The question is whether resource allocation towards the finance sector can create growth in the 'rest of the economy', that is, can affect growth of Y. From (2A.9)

$$g_y = (dY/dt)/Y = \beta(dF_y/dt)/F_y \tag{2A.10}$$

Given (2.A7) and (2A.8), (2A.10) can be written as:

$$g_y = \beta(dF/dt)/F \tag{2A.11}$$

and, substituting (2A.5) in (2A.11),

$$g_y = \beta\lambda F_f/F \tag{2A.12}$$

or

$$g_y = \beta\lambda\phi$$

It is clear that, in such an endogenous growth framework, the growth of output in the rest of the economy (outside the financial sector) can be made to depend on the three parameters β, λ, ϕ relevant to the financial sector. In particular, the resource allocated to the financial system to produce new investment goods emanating from such a sector is crucial in enhancing growth, as also is the 'technology' associated with the sector given by the productivity coefficient.

REFERENCES

Aghion P. and P. Hewitt (1998), *Endogenous Growth Theory*, Cambridge, MA: MIT Press.

Frank. A.G. (1998), *ReOrient: Global Economy in the Asian Age*, Berkeley: University of California Press.

Fry, M.J. (1997), *Emancipating the Banking System and Developing Markets for Government Debt*, London: Routledge.

Ganguli, B.N. (1964), *Readings in Indian Economic History*, Bombay: Asia Publishing House.

King, R.G. and R. Levine (1993), 'Finance and growth: Schumpeter might be right', *Quarterly Journal of Economics*, 108, 513–42.

Laursen, S. and L. Metzler (1950), 'Flexible exchange rates and the theory of employment', *Review of Economics and Statistics*, 32, 281–99.

Levine, R. (1997), 'Financial development and economic growth: Views and agendas', *Journal of Economic Literature*, 35, 688–726.

McKinnon, R.I. (1973), *Money and Capital in Economic Development*, Washington, DC: Brookings Institution.

Nehru, J. (1960), *The Discovery of India*, ed. R.I. Crane, New York: Anchor Press.

Pagano, M. (1993), 'Financial markets and growth: An overview', *European Economic Review*, 37, 613–22.

Rajan R.G. and L. Zingales (1998), 'Financial dependence and growth', *American Economic Review*, 88, 559–86.

Robinson, J. (1952), 'The generalisation of the general theory', *The Rate of Interest and Other Essays*, London: Macmillan.

Romer, P.M. (1986), 'Increasing returns and long-run growth', *Journal of Political Economy*, 94, 1002–37.

Schumpeter, J.A. (1911), *A Theory of Economic Development*, Cambridge, MA: Harvard University Press.

Shaw, E.S. (1973), *Financial Deepening in Economic Development*, New York: Oxford University Press.

Stiglitz, J.E. (1994), 'The role of the state in financial markets', in *Proceedings of the Annual World Bank Conference on Development Economics 1993*, Washington, DC: World Bank.

Tobin, J. (1965), 'Money and economic growth', *Econometrica*, 33(4), 671–84.

3. Economic development, financial development and liberalization: Taiwan, 1960–95

J.L. Ford

INTRODUCTION

The question of whether or not financial development plays a key role in economic development has long been debated, ever since Schumpeter (1934: first edition, 1911) argued that financial services are crucial for technological innovation, and therefore for economic development.[1] Modern growth theory lends support to that contention, pointing to the importance of the growth of financial intermediaries in affecting the steady-state rate of growth.[2] In sum, endogenous growth theory suggests that financial development can increase, first, steady-state per capita income, and accordingly medium-term growth, by raising saving and investment; second, short-term growth by raising production as a consequence of generating improvements to the quality of investment (capital) that enters the aggregate production function; and, third, the long-run rate of growth, since it channels greater resources than hitherto to innovating entrepreneurs, at the same time opening up the possibility of a greater quantity of learning-by-doing at higher levels of real investment.

This modern research echoes the findings of earlier theoretical constructs devised by Gurley and Shaw (1955), McKinnon (1973) and Shaw (1973). Both McKinnon (1973) and Shaw (1973) set out to challenge the prevailing orthodoxy that economic development is founded upon low, controlled, nominal interest rates and financial repression generally. They developed theoretical paradigms that demonstrated the contrary conclusion:[3] low or negative real interest rates (commonly) associated with low nominal rates and financial repression reduce financial saving, hence investment and, thereby, economic growth. The McKinnon–Shaw hypothesis has influenced many policy makers in both developed and developing countries; and the IMF and the World Bank have encouraged financial liberalization in developing countries as a part of a more broad agenda of economic reform.

The case for financial liberalization, naturally, has not gone unchallenged on theoretical and empirical grounds. On theoretical grounds, Stiglitz (1994) demonstrates that the higher interest rates consequent upon financial liberalization generate adverse selection and incentive problems in financial markets. Gertler and Rose (1996) also point out that, in a world of imperfect information, the rise of interest rates in the aftermath of financial liberalization leads to a drop in the firms' net worth and, hence, increases the premium for external finance, even for 'good' borrowers. Therefore, at least in the short run, the economy's real investment could be below the optimal level. This market failure due to informational asymmetry calls for government intervention to make the markets function better and leads to the suggestion that there should be a 'mild' financial repression (Stiglitz, 1994). On empirical grounds, doubts have been raised as to whether any benefits of financial liberalization are likely to exceed the costs that might be engendered as a result of (possible subsequent) crises and financial failures in many countries, bearing in mind the experiences of those Latin American countries (and now, recently, those of South East Asia) that had implemented financial liberalization. So, though a well-functioning financial market has been recognized to be an important factor in promoting economic growth, perhaps the choice in fact is not between the regimes of financial liberalization and repression, but lies in having a competitive financial sector monitored and controlled by prudential regulation designed to ensure that it operates in a sound and safe manner (Honohan, 1992; Fry, 1997). Yet here, too, the issues are problematic, since it is frequently claimed that financial liberalization will reduce the volume of kerb-market activity and this might reduce the volume of deposits created (and hence of loans granted) in the system since the banks have to comply with liquidity and other constraints whilst those involved in kerb-market activities do not have to do so by definition.

In this chapter we provide findings obtained from an inquiry into the connection between financial and economic development in Taiwan, acknowledging the attempt to deregulate and liberalize the money and financial markets that began, ostensibly, in the late 1970s (see later). We do so by using the techniques of integration, cointegration and ECM (error correction mechanism) modelling, which are only just beginning to be used to study this issue (for example, Demetriades and Hussein, 1996; Agung and Ford, 1999; Arestis and Demetriades, 1997). In addition, we will report results obtained (where there is no evidence of cointegration) by the more conventionally used vector autoregressive (VAR) and Granger causality techniques.[4]

In the next section we provide a synopsis, and nothing more than that, on liberalization in Taiwan. This is followed by the presentation of some basic statistics on the pattern of various measures of financial development, introducing some quantitative measures of that development to supplement the traditional 'financial' ones based upon the pioneering study of Goldsmith

(1969). Their connection with measures of economic development, bearing in mind the observations made in the present section, is covered in the fourth section, together with the order of integration of the variables used in this study.

The fifth section begins the reporting of the econometric investigations into the relationship between the two forms of development and offers an initial answer to the question of causality. Those initial investigations were conducted by means of tests of cointegration, and of ECM modelling (where this was apposite), which is the subject of the sixth section. The presence of cointegration over pre- and post-liberalization periods and over the whole sample period, with the cointegrating vectors differing only by (or because of) an intercept term, would be prima facie evidence against the liberalization thesis. However, the existence of cointegration in the two sub-periods with no (or very divergent) cointegration over the whole sample period would imply that the link between the two forms of development did depend upon liberalization or repression; and any change in the direction of causality (from economic development to financial development in the repression period to the reverse causality under liberalization) would offer further information on the importance of the McKinnon–Shaw hypotheses. Where there is no evidence of cointegration or where this is rather problematic (which it can be despite the statistical criterion's being satisfied) the links between the two forms of development have to be explored (as they have been almost invariably in the published literature) by means of VARs, Granger causality (and even simple correlations).

Granger causality is considered in the seventh section. In the ensuing section we examine the possible connection between a physical measure of financial development and the broadest Goldsmithian financial measure of that development, which is perhaps marginally the better of the two financial measures upon which we focus. The ninth section considers the link between the end of financial repression, with concomitant changes in real rates of interest, and measures of financial development. The last section offers some concluding remarks as well as some observations on further work in this area.

Our broad findings can be summarized as follows. The evidence from cointegration and ECM modelling is that a measure of both monetization and of financial assets to gross national product (GNP) 'cause' economic development, represented by GNP per capita. Since cointegration could only be discovered for lag length 1 for both indicators of financial development, VARs were formed to test for Granger 'causality'; and these corroborated the findings of the integration and ECM modelling. 'Causality' was found to exist from one of the quantitative measures of financial development and the broad measure of financial development, by means of integration and Granger causality. These linkages held over the entirety of our data period; no acceptable cointegration was discerned for our pre- and post-liberalization periods. What we have called our 'quantitative' measures of financial development appear to have limited value. Additionally, although the reported results are based on annual data, it was found that quarterly data convey the same picture.

A BRIEF OVERVIEW OF REPRESSION AND LIBERALIZATION IN TAIWAN

From the start of our sample in 1960, the central bank and the Ministry of Finance exercised strong control of the banking and financial system and it was not until the 1970s that any formal relaxation of the controls was announced, and even later before they became effective. Apart from those controls that were imposed for prudential reasons in the form of liquid assets' constraints (though these could, of course, be varied for reasons connected with economic management),[5] the central bank issued directives that affected the maximum rates of interest rates on all of the numerous types of bank deposits and minimum limits on the costs of loans. Simultaneously, implicit quantity controls were imposed on loans through the use of required ratios of reserves to deposits,[6] and the central bank issued directives to the banks on the sectoral allocation of loans (to support the state sector and the export industries). Ceilings were imposed upon the (large) variety of time and savings deposits.

The intention of rescinding the ceilings on interest rates was voiced in 1976 (according to the Ministry of Finance (see, MOF, 1996a) with the inauguration of a formal money market,[7] but this does not appear to have been widespread until the end of that decade. It was not until the revised Banking Law was promulgated in July 1989 that all controls on interest rates were completely abolished.[8] The required ratios remain both in principle and in actuality.

The Banking Law of 1989 also contained the intention of opening up the banking system to increased competition from both domestic and foreign sources. As part of this process the government's stake in the commercial banking sector was to be further reduced, with the aim of eradicating it altogether. However, even until the 1990s the government maintained a substantial stake in the dominant commercial banks, with the heralded disposal of its remaining stock being postponed owing to the downturn on the stock market in 1991. That year did, nevertheless, see the creation of some 16 domestically owned commercial banks (so doubling the number of parent banks at that time) consequent upon the implementation by the Ministry of Finance of the revised Banking Law of July 1989 (see Shea, 1994; Yang, 1994; MOF, 1996b). More investment and securities firms were also established and existing ones expanded.

The reform of the foreign exchange market also occurred gradually, with a shift from a fixed rate regime to a managed floating regime; but it was not until

April 1989 that a more flexible regime in regard to movements of foreign exchange was introduced on the basis of negotiations between customers and the banks. In February of the following year the reference exchange rate regime for inter-bank trading was abandoned; and so the market, in the form of customers and bankers, was (apparently) given some potential for influencing exchange rates. The changes in the foreign exchange market and in the relaxation of capital controls mirrored the globalization process and were in part a consequence of the role of foreign direct investment (FDI) in the Taiwanese economy.

In regard to the exchange rate (taken here, as in the official publications of the monetary authorities, to be the (New Taiwanese) NT$ price of 1US$), exchange controls and liberalization, we note that the foreign exchange market and hence the rate of foreign exchange were for most of the period from the end of 1959 to the early 1980s either fixed or subject to a managed float, despite the alleged freeing of the market (officially, the floating rate was introduced in August 1978). Capital account control began to be relaxed in July 1987 for local residents; for corporations important relaxation occurred only in January 1994. So, for the years up to the 1980s, the rate of exchange was fixed by the central bank and thereafter for the remainder of our data period (up to 1995) it was effectively determined by it and the Ministry of Finance.[9]

Some of the 'physical' developments in the banking and financial sector to which we have alluded in the preceding paragraphs are referred to in more explicit fashion in the following section, where, in fact, we provide an overview of that sector (see Appendix I).

CONVENTIONAL AND 'QUANTITATIVE' MEASURES OF FINANCIAL DEVELOPMENT AND LIBERALIZATION

The main indicators of financial development that have been employed in the applied econometric work on the links between that development and economic progress are derivatives of that proposed, as we have noted above, by Goldsmith (1969). He makes the point that, since financial structure is an amalgam of financial instruments and institutions, no one indicator of financial development can be adequate. He proposed that financial development be measured by the financial interrelations ratio (FIR). This is defined as the ratio of 'the market value of all financial assets in existence at one date [to] the total value of tangible assets plus net foreign balance, i.e ... national wealth'. A related measure that he proposed is the financial intermediation ratio: the value of the assets of the financial institutions as a proportion of the value of all financial assets. Goldsmith (1969) had a predilection for the demand-leading hypothesis, but his empirical results for several countries (developed and developing) over many years could not substantiate that leaning.[10]

Estimates of financial wealth have been problematic, so that the common approach has been to replace those estimates with GDP or GNP figures. Further, several financial ratios have been calculated, using a measure of 'national income' as the denominator. These have frequently replaced the assets of key financial institutions with data on the alternative measures of the money supply, beginning with money supply narrowly defined but including bank current accounts, through the addition to that measure of money supply of all types of deposits, to a very broad measure that further incorporates the deposits of non-banking deposit-taking institutions, such as building societies (savings and loans associations).

In sum, the range of 'monetary' measures of financial development are these:

(i)   Some measure of monetization, which is the ratio of currency to alternative wider measure of moneyness; frequently, the broadest of the central bank measures is adopted. In the case of Taiwan it would be M2.

(ii)   A measure of financial assets varying from a narrow definition to a wider one, so that we might commence with the assets of the money deposit-taking institutions, gradually extending the coverage of the institutions until we had included the last institution in the form of the central bank's assets.

(iii)   Measures based on the ratio of those financial asset aggregates to an indicator of national income, such as GNP.

As it happens, if we take each of these in turn, it makes a barely perceptible difference:

(i)   If we take any other measure of monetization than the one given by the ratio of currency in circulation to M2. For Taiwan the latter consists of currency, netchecking accounts, passbook accounts, passbook savings accounts; time deposits, deposits in savings accounts (which include deposits replaced by the postal savings system); short-term foreign currency funds and some short-term assets.[11] The non-currency items are held in domestic banks, local branches of foreign banks, medium business banks (which prior to 1979 were savings and loans associations), credit cooperative associations, credit departments of farmers' associations and credit departments of fishermen's associations.

(ii)   If we use a narrow or a wide aggregate of financial assets, and we choose to utilize the widest, so that the financial assets of monetary institutions (central bank and the banks just listed) are added to those of other financial institutions, as they are labelled by the central bank, namely, investment

and trust companies, postal savings system and the life insurance companies.
(iii)   Whichever ratio of an aggregate of financial assets to GNP that we take. Again, we take the one that is based upon the widest measure of financial assets.

Figure 3.1 (a) depicts the monetization ratio (currency to M2) which we abbreviate to monet and the broadest measure of total financial assets to GNP which we denote by TFA1GNP; so too does Figure 3.1 (b) which also includes GNP per capita at 1991 prices (GNPPH91).

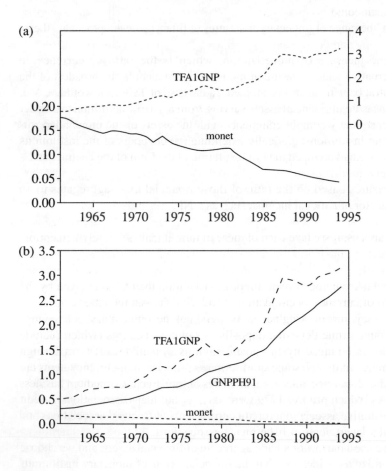

Figure 3.1

All of these findings hold, of course, because of the high, almost perfect, degree of correlation between the alternatives within a category or indicator of financial development. Accordingly, we concentrate in what follows on the findings that we obtained from using the currency to M2 ratio and the ratio of the widest aggregate of financial assets to GNP. These two ratios themselves are sufficiently correlated to make it feasible that the one will be conveying the same information as the other; they are, in effect, almost two sides of the same coin.[12]

We mentioned above that up to the present (as far as we are aware) all measures or indicators of financial development have been of a monetary nature, even though, of course, as ratios they become real magnitudes since the currency unit cancels out in the formation of the ratio. Alternative measures of a quantitative form could be imagined; one basis for the calculation of perhaps a variety of measures is the physical structure of the banking/monetary system in terms of the number of banks by type and their branch networks, including details on the geographical dispersion of networks or their density in terms of population.

It is a platitude (though this is less self-evident in the modern age of computer banking) that without physical banks and other deposit-taking institutions there would be no money and other liquid assets as we know them (discounting the impact of a Giro system). While the recent electronic revolution has begun to alter the concept of money and to reduce the physical number of bank branches, this cannot alter this platitude, and the 'electronification' represents a further stage in the evolution of the banking system rather than presaging its demise (see, Ford, 1994). An increase in the number and type of banks, of course, will increase the customer-catchment potential of the banks, but the actual demand for banking services will influence the physical composition of the banking system itself. So the possibility of two-way causality underlies any attempt to obtain a quantitative measure of financial development. There is the opportunity to examine any cointegration between the two types of measures of financial development and to deduce the direction of causality between them.

We have experimented with the construction of measures of the development of the banking system, two of which we refer to in this chapter: the evaluation of an index based upon giving equal weight to all bank branches, no matter what their origin; that is, whether they were commercial banks, credit associations, medium-sized banks and so on;[13] and the construction of indices founded upon principal components and factor analyses. The latter were employed to see if there could be different factors operating in the banking system, so as to suggest that some of the institutions constituted one group while the others constituted another. In fact, that study produced two indices for the whole of our data period and two for each of the sub-periods that we used, as mentioned above, to endeavour to capture any impacts of liberalization on the relationships between financial and economic development.

Let us consider those indices now, and link them to the process of liberalization and innovation in the banking system. After a slow, gradual, start at the beginning of the 1960s, the physical nature and size of the banking system began to expand, growing at an increasing pace from the early 1970s. The number of branches of established monetary institutions, such as the commercial banks and the various credit associations, increased *pari passu* with the emergence and growth of other banks, particularly the medium business banks (introduced in 1979). The liberalization induced a number of new banks, including foreign-owned banks, to be established. That process was accelerated following the enactment of the revised Banking Law of July 1989, as we noted in the preceding section.

The number of foreign banks, for example, rose from none in 1960 to six in 1970, to 21 in 1980, to 43 in 1990, and to 59 in 1995. Although the number (by parent) of medium business banks remained at eight over the whole of our sample period, the number of branches increased gradually from 76 to just over 500. Investment trusts grew steadily from the beginning of the 1970s, even though the number of head offices only expanded from 1989. From that year life companies also expanded. The fishermen's associations began in 1976 and grew at a low level over the period. By contrast, both the farmers' and the credit associations experienced a steady decline over the period (see Appendix I).

Figures that illustrate these patterns are provided in Appendix III. From the data on networks a bank index (Bkindex, when we use its abbreviated form), referred to as the first measure above, was calculated. This is an index derived from giving each of the banking and other financial institutions mentioned above a weight of one and normalizing on one for 1991 (which is the base year for prices and output). The bank index and its rate of growth are shown in Figure 3.2.

An alternative approach to the construction of an index is to use principal components aided by information conveyed by principal factor analysis. This takes us to the second approach mentioned above. Using those forms of analysis makes it possible to gauge whether the networks of the various institutions are giving the same information. If they are, any one of them can be used to epitomize that banking sector. Alternatively, since the one eigenvector to the principal component will give them equal (or just about equal) weights, an index can be calculated by taking a weighted average of the institutions' networks.

In using principal components the objective, then, was to construct an index number (or numbers) that could be used to encapsulate the elements (maybe different elements) in the development of the banking system.[14] The principal components analysis, summarized in Table AII.1, Appendix II, indicates that we can accept the presence of two eigenvalues; the loadings of the various institutions in the two concomitant factors are provided in Table AII.2.[15]

One of the features of the banking system that might suggest that the different institutions might be conveying different information over time to one another,

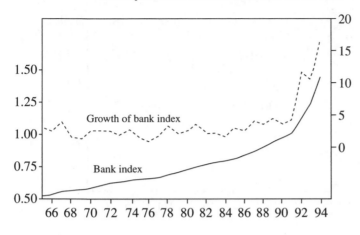

Figure 3.2

or that they might all be conveying the same, but different, information across time, is the issue of liberalization of the system. From what we have said by way of summary of events that occurred in that respect in Taiwan over the recent past, we can see that we might select two or three potential 'liberalization break-points'. However, it would appear that, if one such break is effectively what occurred, this is more than likely to have happened at the end of the 1970s. We experimented with various break-points and ultimately settled on the year 1979 as the one that seemed to be capturing what amounted to a structural break. Hence the two sub-periods in Tables AII.1 and AII.2.

Two index numbers were calculated for each of the sub-periods. These are denoted in Figures 3.3 (a) and (b) simply as Index1 and Index2.

The companions to these indices, for the whole period, are depicted in Figure 3.4, labelled Qindex1 and Qindex2. It will be seen that Qindex1 tracks the bank index (Figure 3.2). Of the Qindex1 and Qindex2, the former produced the better results; but Qindex1 itself could only provide results as good as those obtained from utilizing the bank index, so that they are now omitted from this paper. That outcome follows immediately from the fact that the information contained in Qindex1 and the bank index for the entire period is effectively identical. The correlation between the two series is 0.9992. Accordingly, we make no further reference to these Qindices.

Before we proceed, we should perhaps pause to consider the possible interpretations of Tables AII.1 and AII.2. Table AII.2 suggests that the composition of the banking sector matters between the two sub-periods. Prior to liberalization, all the banking institutions were loaded in the first factor, which could reflect the repression of their activities as a whole, whilst the second factor was

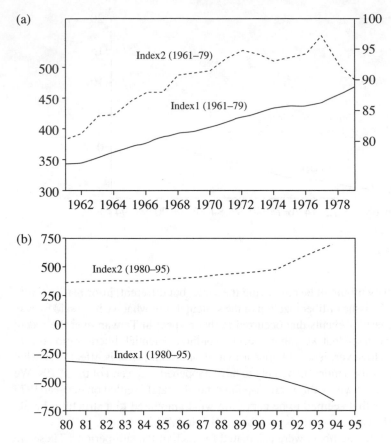

Figure 3.3

loaded in the other financial institutions. The pattern changes in the post-lib-eralization period: now the commercial banks and the credit institutions are loaded together in the second factor with all the other institutions (with farmers' associations) being heavily loaded in factor 1. That, too, is the picture for the entire period of our sample.

We might contend that the switch between the two sub-periods would be consistent with there being a break at 1979. Why? Because after liberalization the banks could expand by virtue of the freeing of interest rates, the general move to a lessening of controls, and the gradual removal of restrictions on the establishment of new banks and branches. As a consequence, they would expand and (partly as a result of the freedom to expand credit that the liberalization

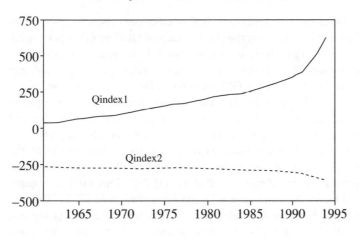

Figure 3.4

conferred upon the commercial banks) the credit associations decline. The only apparent anomaly in the period 1980–95 is the foreign banks.

All of these considerations would suggest that we should experiment by using two indices for each sub-period and two for the entire sample period, to capture financial development. However, as for the entire period, only Index2 for 1980–95 gives anything like reasonable empirical results; and for 1961–79, the better results were obtained by using Index1. This is essentially due to the fact that the two principal components for each sub-period and for the entire sample are not orthogonal, as they should be. In effect, we find these covariances and correlations, respectively: (1) entire period: between Qindex1 and Qindex2, –2923.8 and –0.9681; (2) 1961–79, between Index1 and Index2, 150.11392 and 0.853; and (3) 1980–95, between Index1 and Index2, –9054.4, and –0.987. Effectively, we have indeed one principal component for every period. Furthermore, as we remarked above, for the entire period we can utilize the bank index rather than Qindex1 or Qindex2.

MEASURES OF ECONOMIC DEVELOPMENT: THE ORDER OF INTEGRATION OF THE VARIOUS MEASURES OF FINANCIAL AND ECONOMIC DEVELOPMENT AND THEIR CORRELATIONS

Economic development can self-evidently be measured in several ways, but in the literature the link between that development and that of the financial structure of the economy has been explored by using one of four measures:[16]

(1) GDP or GNP in real terms, (2) real GDP or GNP per capita, (3) the growth rate of GDP or of GNP and, (4) the growth rate of GDP or GNP per capita. Strictly, we might argue that, if any measure is to represent economic development, it should be one that is based upon a per capita magnitude, and this should be the level of GDP or GNP per capita. However, various measures have been employed. In part, the usage will depend upon whether cointegration studies are being attempted, since the order of integration of the variables will generally differ as we move from data on levels to data on rates of growth.

So we now summarize the findings on the order of integration of the variables. We take the whole of our data period first of all. Our findings are as follows: monet (cash to broad money), all of TFA1GNP, GNP, GDP and output (real GDP and GNP) per capita are I(1); the growth rates of GNP, GNP per head, monet and TFA1 are I(0); all three quantitative measures (Bkindex, QIndex1 and QIndex2) are I(2) variables. In testing for unit roots the usual panoply of equations was run for each variable, that is, with varying lag lengths: without a constant, with a constant, with a constant and a time trend, with a constant and seasonals (for the quarterly data sets); with a constant, seasonals and a time trend (again obviously for the quarterly data sets); and use was made of the Dickey–Pantula (1987) procedure. Almost invariably, the 'most statistically significant' results were obtained without a constant and with no lags.

For our first sub-period, 1961–79, the unit roots revealed the following. I(1) variables were found to be: monet, TFA1GNP and both measures of output; the I(0) variables again were the rates of growth, per capita or otherwise, of real GNP (and GDP) and the rates of growth of the 'monetary'indicators. The three indices, Bkindex, Index1 and Index2 were found to be I(2). For 1980–95, all the 'monetary' indicators of financial development appeared to be at least I(2), as did the quantitative measure Bkindex; the two principal components indices, Index1 and Index2, were found to be I(3). The growth variables were all I(1).

COINTEGRATION

Tests for the potential linkages between economic and financial development have until very recently been founded on measures of correlations or evidence of Granger causality between the two variables (as noted earlier and in note 4). In this study we have supplemented those methods with tests of integration, cointegration and the consequent ECM modelling. Whilst the application of those modern statistical and econometric techniques to this topic is new, some might argue that it is problematic whether they should be utilized to tackle the issues at hand. We make that observation for the following reasons, to which, no doubt, others could be added: (a) often the sample period will encompass a time when liberalization was introduced into financial markets to terminate a period of so-called financial repression, (b) that process itself might be amplified by the wider deregulation of markets that emanates from the sort of phenomena that we have observed across the world economy in the last few years, and, (c) it might be suggested that we can only expect to observe any cointegration between indicators of financial and economic development once the system is in (or around) a long-run equilibrium.

These are important considerations. However, they could be surmounted effectively if any process described under (a) and (b) could be pinpointed exactly in time and if it did not have any diffusion mechanism. Then the answer to point (c) is the obvious one that we would only be testing for the presence of cointegration, and the causality that it, and its ECM equations, imply. If it is not found to be present, then we can always resort to correlation and Granger causality tests.[17]

Monet and TFA1GNP portray a somewhat similar picture, with the fall in the former reflecting the increasingly sophisticated nature of the financial system that is measured by the other. Nevertheless, they are sufficiently different to suggest that they could impart different information about economic development and about causal links between the two types of development. Table 3.1 provides a summary of the cointegration results. We note that, in obtaining those results, we made use of Johansen (1992) for accommodation of trends in the data, doing so by what he calls the Pantula principle: that is, testing from the most restrictive to the least restrictive form of the VARs in respect of the trend. So, when a trend appears in a cointegrating vector, this is because the more restrictive models in which a constant does not appear in the short-run dynamics and a trend does not appear in the cointegrating vector do not exhibit cointegration by the trace and eigenvalue tests. It will be noticed that Table 3.1 omits any reference to our quantitative indices for the two sub-periods: no cointegration could be discerned between any index and economic development. However, this was, in principle at least, not the case for (change in) the bank index (and effectively, for Qindex1) over the entire sample period. That index had a more reliable role to play in the cointegration studies, as we will see in a later section.

A glance at Table 3.1(a) reveals, that according to the tests statistics,[18] TFA1GNP only cointegrates with GNP per capita at lag length 1. The monetization variable and the bank index suggest that cointegration is present across more lag lengths.

Despite the indications of the test statistics on the trace and the maximum eigenvalue of the stochastic matrix (and a satisfactory value of the Reimers 'small sample' test), cointegration between the bank index and economic development could not be accepted. The cointegrating vectors were not, in fact, stationary and the recursive eigenvalues demonstrated too much volatility; and the test statistics corresponding to the significant eigenvalues should grow linearly with time (see Hansen and Johansen, 1993). On this basis all lag lengths in excess of 1 for the monetisation variable were ignored.

Table 3.1   Summary of cointegration findings for the financial development and GNPPH

(a)   Whole sample

| Lag | Rank of the stochastic matrix[*] | | |
	Monet[**]	TFA1GNP[***]	ΔBkindex[***]
8	1	2	1
7	0	2	1
6	1	2	2
5	1	2	1
4	2	0	2
3	0	2	2
2	1	2	2
1	1	1	2

(b) Sub-period: 1961–79

| Lag | Rank of the stochastic matrix[*] | |
	Monet[***]	TFA1GNP[***]
4	2	2
3	2	0
2	0	0
1	1	1

(c)   Sub-period: 1980–95

| Lag | Rank of the stochastic matrix | |
	Monet[**]	TFA1GNP[**]
4	2	1
3	1	1: Trace only at 5%
2	2	0
1	2	2

Note:[*]   The maximal eigenvalue and the trace tests here produce the same value of the rank; [**] for all lags the time trend was significant in both the unrestricted reduced form (URF) and the CVector; and, [***] the time trend was not significant in the URF and in the CVector.

So, in sum, for the whole data period, cointegration was accepted between financial and economic development for both measures of financial development but not for the quantitative measure of financial development. This cointegration was with one lag in the unrestricted reduced form system. Before we move on to consider the cointegration findings, which are contained in Tables 3.2 and 3.3, we pause to comment upon the findings for the two sub-periods.

Table 3.2   Cointegration tests: monet and GNPPH

(a)   Rank of the stochastic matrix: with one lag[*]

Rank	Max. λ_i	T-nm	95%	Trace	T-nm	95%
0	49.35[**]	46.36[**]	19.0	55.13[**]	51.79[**]	25.3
≤ 1	5.788	5.437	12.2	5.788	5.437	12.2

[*] In the unrestricted reduced form equations, the F-tests on the retained regressors (one-period lags of both variables and the trend) showed that their impacts were significantly different from zero at the 1% level or better. The correlations of actual with fitted values were for monet and GNPPH, respectively, 0.9921 and 0.995.
[**] Significant at the 1% level or better.

(b)   Cointegrating vectors (β_i) and standardized α_i coefficients: monet and GNPPH[*]

	β_1	β_2	α_1	α_2
Monet	1.0000	8287	–0.08155	–0.00003778
GNPPH	0.000061	1.0000	–296.7	–0.0005392
Trend	0.002217	29.05		

[*] χ^2 (2) test that the coefficient on the trend is zero, 8.5254 (0.0141), so that the hypothesis can be rejected at the 5% level or better.

(c)   Long-run matrix: monet and GNPPH

	Monet	GNPPH	Trend
Monet	–0.3946	–0.00004275	–0.001278
GNPPH	–301.1	–0.01863	–0.6733

Tables 3.1 (b) and (c) do not contain any quantitative index since, as mentioned above, we could locate no cointegration between it for the two sub-

periods (in first difference and second difference form for the two respective sub-periods). Ostensibly, there appears to be evidence again of cointegration between monetization and economic development in both sub-periods.

However, on closer inspection of the cointegrating vectors and the recursive eigenvalues, as well as of the significance of the variables in the unrestricted reduced form of the system, cointegration had to be ruled out.

Therefore, we turn to the cointegration results given in detail in Tables 3.2 and 3.3. The salient cointegrating vector for monet is, naturally, that given in the β_1 column of Table 3.2(b). Recall that the monetization variable has a downward trend and so the negative sign on output per head when we take it

Table 3.3　Cointegration tests: TFA1GNP and GNPPH

(a)　Rank of the stochastic matrix: with one lag[*]

Rank	Max. λ_i	T-nm	95%	Trace	T-nm	95%
0	52.67[**]	49.48[**]	19.0	56.62[**]	53.19[**]	25.3
≤ 1	3.948	3.708	12.2	3.948	3.708	12.2

[*] In the unrestricted reduced form equations, the F-tests on the retained regressors (one period lag of both variables) showed that their impacts were significantly different from zero at the 1% level or better. The correlations between actual and fitted values for TFA1GNP and GNPPH, respectively, were 0.9896 and 0.9993.
[**] Significant at the 1% level or better.

(b)　Cointegrating vectors (β_i) and standardized α_i coefficients: TFA1GNP and GNPPH[*]

	β_1	β_2	α_1	α_2
Monet	1.0000	−7.195E-6	0.02218	1.172E-6
GNPPH	−7.704E4	1.0000	1.162E4	0.01632

[*] χ^2 (2) test that the coefficient on the trend is set correctly at zero, 0.183.

(c)　Long-run matrix: TFA1GNP and GNPPH

	TFA1GNP	GNPPH
TFA1GNP	−0.06812	1.013E-6
GNPPH	1.037E4	−0.06732

across the equals sign to produce the cointegrating equation satisfies prior expectations. As monet declines there is financial development. The standardized a-coefficients (column a_1) indicate that there is a large (or fast) response of output per head to the lagged cointegrating vector (or the lagged error correction term), evidence of 'causality' from financial to economic development. This is confirmed, of course, by the long-run coefficients matrix in Table 3.2 (c). The same picture emerges when we examine Tables 3.3 (b) and (c) for the wider definition of financial development. Again, we note that, when output per head is taken across the equals sign in vector β_1, it will have the correct, positive, sign. 'Causality' is unidirectional from financial development to economic development.

ECM MODELLING

The question of 'causality' can be investigated further by means of Engle-Granger ECM modelling. ECM equations for monetization and total financial assets to output are summarized in Table 3.4. As can be seen, the lag structure of these best equations is very limited. The optimal lag structure was reached by applying the Hendry general-to-specific methodology. This has been shown to be superior to the Akaike final prediction error (FPE) criterion (see DeSerres and Guay, 1995).

Table 3.4   ECM equations for monet and TFA1GNP with GNPPH

Dep. variable	Indep. variables	EC(–1)	Adjusted R^2	LM($\chi^2(1)$)
(1) Δmonet	Constant(C)	1.7736E-07 (0.3117): No	–0.03	–
(2) ΔGNPPH	C, Δmonet(–1)	–320858 (–7.68698): Yes	0.66	1.63 (0.8)
(3) ΔTFA1GNP	ΔGNPPH (0,–1)	1.102E-05 (0.8797): No	0.249	2.34165 (0.6732)
(4) ΔGNPPH	ΔTFA1GNP (0,–1)	9306.61 (12.7477): Yes	0.689	1.96773 (0.7417)

Notes: EC(–1) denotes the one-period lagged error correction term (cointegrating vector); the figures in column 3 denote the coefficients on EC(–1) together with their t-statistics in parentheses; the No/Yes indicates that the EC(–1) term is not/is statistically different from 0 at the 5% level or better; the LM test is based on 4 lags (and is not given for equation (1), in view of its overall properties); and the residuals from equations (2)–(4) are normally distributed, and there is no evidence of ARCH.

These findings show that the error correction term is significantly different from zero in the dynamic equation for output per capita equations for both measures of financial development; and that it is insignificant in the dyanamic equations for those measures themselves. These results are given further import by the poor overall explanatory power of the dynamic equations for the financial measures. Marginally, the performance of TFA1GNP is superior to that of monet. The two ECM equations for output per capita are depicted in Figure 3.5.

Whilst we have relied upon annual data in this chapter, we reiterate that the same findings occur with respect to the order of integration of the variables and the presence or otherwise of cointegration between the economic development and the financial and quantitative indicators of financial development. So,

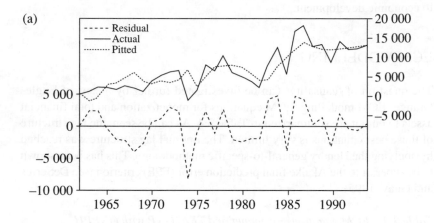

Figure 3.5(a)   ECM equation for monet

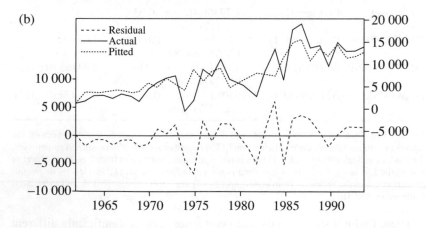

Figure 3.5(b)   ECM equation for TFA1GNP

despite the possibility that there is a break-point due to the impact and diffusion of the liberalization process, effective, and differing, cointegration (despite the fourfold increase in the number of observations) could not be accepted for each of the two sub-periods.

THE VAR GRANGER CAUSALITY FINDINGS

The evidence, at least for the two sub-periods, leads us to pursue the matter of the direction of causality between financial and economic development by means of VARs or Granger causality, with the possibility that a change in the direction might be detected between sub-periods. Furthermore, the results obtained from the cointegration studies are such that we are justified in exploring Granger causality tests for the whole data period. Again, we note that the results that we now report are qualitatively reproduced when quarterly data are used.

The Granger causality results are presented in the tables in Appendix III. We include the links between economic development and the bank index. Each table is split into three sections: the first is for 1961–95, the second for 1961–79 and the third for 1980–95. We take the tables in sequence.

Table AIII.1 shows evidence of causality; but at the 10 per cent level or better this is unidirectional causality from the monetization variable to output per capita. Thus the second and third columns indicate that monetization is not Granger-caused by economic development for every period, while the fourth and fifth columns indicate that the absence of causality from monetization to output per capita can be rejected (except for lag lengths of 8 and 10 for the entire period: though it is questionable as to what such lags mean, since they begin to reduce the overall data set to one approaching that of the second sub-period). Similar results are obtained for TFA1GNP (Table AIII.2) for the entire period and for the first sub-period; but the evidence is less strongly in favour of causality from financial development to economic development than it is for the monetization variable. Indeed, in the second sub-period no clear picture of the direction of causality exists for the wider financial measure. The bank index (Table AIII.3) mainly offers evidence that there is no causality either way between it and output per head.

We turn now to the other three tables, which are concerned with the rate of growth of output per capita. A comparison of Tables AIII.4 and AIII.5 reveals a clearer picture for the growth of TFA1GNP than for the growth of monetization. Apart from one instance, however, Table AIII.4 tells us that the latter is not caused by the growth of output per head. Economic growth is caused at low lag levels by monetization growth. Except for lag 1 over 1961–79, the growth of TFA1GNP is not caused by economic growth; the latter is seen to be caused by the growth of TFA1GNP at low lags over the entire period and at lag 1 over

1961–79 and lags 1 and 2 over 1980–95. Table AIII.6 again suggests the absence of any causality between the bank index and economic growth.

COINTEGRATION BETWEEN THE BANK INDEX AND TFA1GNP

The bank index promised on occasions above to offer us something useful, though the separate quantitative indices for the sub-periods could not. However, the bank index might have a part to play in economic development and in capturing the effects of liberalization that provides incentives to the expansion of real investment in the banking sector.

Over the whole sample we find that there is evidence of cointegration between TFA1GNP and (changes in) the bank index. Bearing in mind all the criteria for selecting the appropriate lag length by reference to the properties of the VARs and the attributes of the cointegrating vectors, lag length 2 offers the best cointegrating vector. The results for a lag of 2 periods are given in Tables AIV.1 (a), (b) and (c) in Appendix IV. They indicate that an acceleration in the physical measure of the banking sector, no matter what its composition of institutions happens to be, will be accompanied by an increase in the broad measure of, as it were, 'financial' financial development. The evidence, from the standardized a-coefficients and the long-run matrix, as to which (if either) of the two variables is 'weakly exogenous' is mixed; the first cointegrating vector (which we must use, of course) suggests that it is TFA1GNP that attracts that epithet. The second vector suggests that is should be assigned to the bank index. ECM modelling does, in fact, corroborate these likelihoods.

On reflection, this is not that surprising, since we might reasonably expect that these two (endogenous) variables are, in fact, likely to 'cause' each other. The liberalization of interest rates, if it does lead to an expansion of financial assets within the banking industry, is, other things being equal (for example, given that profitability has increased), likely to engender expansion of branch networks, which is now permitted under the liberalization programme. Alternatively, permitting the physical expansion of the banking sector could produce an actual expansion, in view of the knowledge of the bankers that there is an excess demand for loans which can now be serviced owing to the freedom of the banks to gather in funds under the more liberal regime. Since the expansion is likely to lead (and did so) to an increase in the geographical dispersion of the banking network, this will provide the extra catchment areas for those funds.

So measures that permit the expansion of branch networks, or which allow the establishment of new banks or financial institutions, will, of themselves, not provide the central bank with a unique and certain means of predicting the future financial development of the economy. Obviously, in particular economic circumstances, when any permitted expansion is responded to positively by the financial sector, it will be worthwhile for the central bank to use the (suitably adjusted) bank index to construct a forecast of financial development as captured by TFA1GNP. For we recall that, moving outside the framework of cointegration and ECM modelling, the zero-order correlation coefficient between the bank index and TFA1GNP for the entire period was 0.9223.

It is feasible that the motive force in the development of the banking system and in the subsequent financial ratios is, indeed, the liberalization of the level and structure of interest rates on deposits and loans. The unravelling of the link between financial and economic development is not different in kind from evaluating the connection between the end of financial repression and subsequent economic development. Some insight might be obtained on the impact of liberalization of interest rates on the economy by considering how such liberalization might have influenced the various measures of financial development (which themselves depend upon savings, the focus of most studies of interest rate liberalization). A glance at that issue is provided in the following section.

LIBERALIZATION, REAL RATES OF INTEREST AND FINANCIAL DEVELOPMENT

Appendix V provides details of principal components and principal factors analysis of (a) monetization with two real rates of interest, in Tables AV.1 and AV.2; (b) TFA1GNP with two real rates of interest, in Tables AV.3 and AV.4; and, in Figure AV.1 monet and the two real rates of interest are graphed for illustrative purposes. The money rates of interest are that on six months' bank deposits and that on savings deposits of one year maturity; the rate of inflation is the implicit deflator of GNP, and we note that only in the last five years does this begin to diverge from the implicit deflator of GDP, which itself is tracked almost perfectly by the consumer price index. In effect, the results are independent of the measure of inflation that is used.

Before we consider the material in the tables of Appendix V, we concentrate on Figure AV.1 and the zero-order correlations between the variables. The figure shows that the real rates (effectively, of course, the money rates) are almost perfectly collinear over the whole period, but that the degree of association increases even further after the 'liberalization break-point'. The interest rate correlations are (1961–95) 0.9722374, (1961–79) 0.9923819 and (1980–95) 0.9813099. The real rates have become consistently positive subsequent to the liberalization, though they were not negative for the whole of the period of 'repression'.

What about the zero-order correlations between the measures of financial development and the real rates of interest? These are, with the real six months rate and the real one year rate, respectively: (1) for monetization: (a) 1961–95: –0.1536, 0.02722, (b) for 1961–79: 0.24796, 0.27594, and (c) for 1980–95: –0.5229, –0.50564, and (2) for TFA1GNP: (a) 1961–95: 0.15714, –0.01621, (b) for 1961–79: –0.2920, –0.30008, and (c) for 1980–95: 0.383036, 0.341068. The figures for 1980 onwards exhibit the a priori expected signs between the interest rates and the financial measures, contrasting with the evidence for 1961–79, suggesting that liberalization did affect financial development, though it must have been liberalization in the wider sense in the banking sector and not just liberalization working through interest rate effects.

We consider now the information contained in Tables AV.1 to AV.4 in Appendix V. Taking Tables AV.1 and AV.2 first, we point out that we have only listed two factors when we might have validly listed three for the entire period and probably also for the two sub-periods. On that basis, if we refer to that period, we can conclude that the three variables are loaded in different factors; and even if we do take only the two factors given in the tables, the monetization variable and the real six months rate of interest are in principle representing differing aspects of the financial system. The pattern diverges from this for 1980–95, where we might accept that there are only two factors and that the interest rates are loaded in the one and the monetization variable in the other. This is similar to the situation for 1961–79, but is sufficiently different from it to counterbalance the situation for 1980–95 to make the results for the entire period suggestive of the existence of the three factors as noted above. There is again, therefore, some hint that the liberalization was indeed a liberalization and had some discernible impact on the system, but this is not powerful enough to result in the three variables capturing the same influence, such as 'a competitive market'.

The data supplied in Tables AV.3 and AV.4 tell a broadly similar story. Any potential for differences between the two financial measures is contained in the principal factors for the sub-period 1961–79. It is clear that the second factor, however we might choose to interpret it, is loaded in the one year real rate of interest. On a strict basis the first factor is loaded (but only by a fraction) in the financial variable; but we could fairly claim that it is loaded in the one year real rate of interest and to a substantial degree in the six months real rate of interest. This is a problematic set of findings, but it comes closest to suggesting that, in the period (as delineated here) of repression, the three variables were conveying similar if not identical information. They reflected the 'price' and 'quantity' controls on the size and structure of the financial system.

SOME CONCLUDING OBSERVATIONS

We now summarize our various findings and arguments expeditiously despite the extent of our experimentation, findings which are replicated for quarterly data. The major conclusion is that for the last 35 years there is evidence of cointegration between a measure of monetization and a very broad measure of financial development and output per head. The cointegration, buttressed by ECM modelling, suggests that there is unidirectional 'causality' between financial development and economic development; with the 'causality' operating from the financial to the economic. Granger causality tests corroborated those contentions; in some instances, for the quantitative measures of financial development, for example, where the apparent cointegration could not be accepted, such tests are apposite. In the case of the two 'financial' indicators of financial development, we suggested that this was so since only in one instance could we, on further inspection of the cointegrating vectors, feel confident about accepting the existence of cointegration.

Of the possible range of quantitative indicators of financial development that have been constructed, the best turned out to be an index of the size of the banking system and an index that applied to the whole data period. That index, by its construction, does not reflect the changing composition of the banking sector. The other indices that did so were discovered to offer no assistance in unscrambling the link between financial and economic development, either over the entire data period or when the two sub-periods were used in an endeavour to encapsulate the effects of repression and liberalization. The bank index, though it did ultimately prove sterile for cointegration and VAR, Granger-causality, analysis, did offer some information in that it was found to be cointegrated with the broad measure of financial development; and though the direction of causality between them was rather ambiguous, the one did appear to 'cause' the other.

Causality could not be said to have switched direction between the financial development variables and economic development at the liberalization break point. Both the level of economic development and the rate of economic growth seemed to respond positively to financial development. The principal components and principal factors analysis gave an inkling of a change in the information that the institutions in the banking system were conveying before and after liberalization. The evidence on the link between 'financial' measures of financial development and the real rates of interest likewise conveyed the impression that those measures and the real rates of interest were not always representing the same aspects of the financial system; and for the broad measure of financial development in particular, the evidence conveys the impression that under repression it and the real rates of interest were encapsulating a single characteristic of the banking system, and that, following liberalization, this was not so. However, the evidence is not consistent and strong enough to enable a firmer conclusion to be drawn.

This points the way to the need for further work to be undertaken on the comparison between the so-called repression and liberalization episodes to determine whether real rates of interest did affect the financial measures of development (maybe through savings which are channelled into the range of financial assets in the banking and other financial institutions) and did so differentially in the two episodes. The link between financial and economic development might then be explored on a wider basis that embraces a detailed study of the loan allocations across sectors and by types of loans (for example, for investment) made by the banks from 1960 onwards, ascertaining how they relate to real rates of interest and how they influence, through investment and the productivity of that investment, the level and rate of economic development. In that way, and by relating in more detail the quantitative indices, such as the bank index, to the real rate of interest and to the volume and types of investment, we will be able to accomplish the task of discriminating between the McKinnon and Shaw versions of the supply-side hypothesis.

APPENDIX I: DEVELOPMENT OF THE BANKING SYSTEM

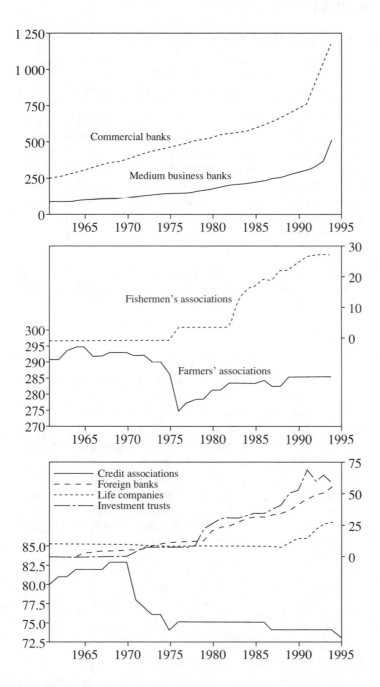

APPENDIX II: 'QUANTITATIVE' FINANCIAL DEVELOPMENT

Table AII.1   Principal components

Variable	Factor	1961–95		1961–79		1980–95	
		Eigenval	% of var	Eigenval	% of var	Eigenval	% of var
Combs	1	6.71677	84.0	6.77569	84.7	5.60056	70.0
Cred	2	1.08382	13.5	1.06033	13.3	1.59825	20.0
Farm	3	0.15283	1.9	0.14876	1.9	0.50032	6.3
Fish	4	0.03775	0.5	0.01403	0.2	0.23964	3.0
Forbs	5	0.00802	0.1	0.00077	0.0	0.05501	0.7
Invtrust	6	0.00064	0.0	0.00028	0.0	0.00619	0.1
Lifeco	7	0.00010	0.0	0.00011	0.0	0.00002	0.0
Meds	8	0.00008	0.0	0.00002	0.0	0.00000	0.0

Notes: *Combs*, commercial banks; *Credit*, credit associations; *Farm*, credit departments of farmers' associations; *Fish*, credit departments of fishermen's associations; *forbs*, foreign banks; *invtrust*, investment and trust companies; *lifeco*, life companies; *Meds*, medium business banks.

Table AII.2   Principal factors after varimax rotation using the Kaiser normalization

Variable	1961–95		1961–79		1980–95	
	Factor 1	Factor 2	Factor 1	Factor 2	Factor 1	Factor 2
Combs	0.34797	0.93741	0.94897	0.29849	0.19004	0.97503
Cred	0.29564	0.95468	0.94984	0.30342	0.17778	0.97542
Farm	0.91109	0.36394	0.94818	0.31043	0.65116	0.40789
Fish	0.91569	0.35960	0.93805	0.33893	0.91409	0.26163
Forbs	0.93705	0.32502	0.93699	0.34158	0.96068	0.18654
Invtrust	0.94013	0.32186	0.78205	0.51195	0.96508	0.18460
Lifeco	0.93715	0.28164	0.32445	0.94416	0.94165	0.13121
Meds	0.93287	0.26952	0.31973	0.94586	0.94342	0.13211

Notes: As for Table AII.1.

APPENDIX III: GRANGER 'CAUSALITY'

Table AIII.1

Lag	Δmonet not G-caused by ΔGNPPH		ΔGNPPH not G-caused by Δmonet	
	F	Probability	F	Probability
10	0.090333	0.9971	1.466252	0.4724
8	0.199251	0.9826	1.839087	0.2035
4	0.139587	0.9655	4.067447	0.0143
2	0.278136	0.7594	6.652248	0.0046
4	0.436936	0.7787	3.857064	0.0856
2	0.760504	0.4905	3.745545	0.0575
1	3.124894	0.0989	8.622897	0.0108
4	0.700913	0.6190	5.300562	0.0358
2	2.295551	0.1512	4.570883	0.0389
1	0.317190	0.5837	1.011676	0.3344

Table AIII.2

Lag	ΔTFA1GNP not G-caused by ΔGNPPH		ΔGNPPH not G-caused by ΔTFA1GNP	
	F	Probability	F	Probability
10	3.664676	0.2333	3.634880	0.2349
8	1.168529	0.4155	2.242888	0.1371
4	0.532731	0.7132	3.153531	0.0366
2	0.617669	0.5469	5.450525	0.0105
4	1.994625	0.2337	3.071860	0.1249
2	0.495135	0.6224	3.669257	0.0601
1	1.036918	0.3258	7.661620	0.0151
4	6.957664	0.0193	2.302015	0.1730
2	0.300605	0.7468	2.396301	0.1412
1	2.197714	0.1640	3.462221	0.0875

Table AIII.3

Lag	Δ^2Bkindex not G-caused by ΔGNPPH		ΔGNPPH not G-caused by Δ^2Bkindex	
	F	Probability	F	Probability
10	0.300440	0.9019	89.21710	0.0822
8	2.234570	0.1529	3.761920	0.0488
4	0.702055	0.6002	0.370357	0.8268
2	2.052809	0.1495	0.103107	0.92024
4	1.464352	0.3604	0.268499	0.8846
2	0.926238	0.4275	0.231967	0.7971
1	0.215318	0.6503	0.029834	0.8655
4	0.423941	0.7872	0.285913	0.8771
2	1.028303	0.3925	0.068570	0.9342
1	1.555127	0.2362	0.024393	0.8785

Table AIII.4

Lag	Grmonet not G-caused by GrGNPPH		GrGNPPH not G-caused by Grmonet	
	F	Probability	F	Probability
10	0.659980	0.7338	0.296319	0.9241
8	0.792104	0.6252	0.870263	0.5755
4	0.841180	0.5153	1.746025	0.1795
2	1.001379	0.3811	2.742970	0.0830
4	0.597689	0.6809	2.600257	0.1615
2	0.813677	0.4682	5.802940	0.0190
1	3.012728	0.1046	11.41520	0.0045
4	1.840807	0.2401	1.520486	0.3074
2	4.385335	0.0429	4.790727	0.0347
1	0.025920	0.8748	1.310297	0.2747

Table AIII.5

Lag	GrTFA1GNP not G-caused by GrGNPPH		GrGNPPH not G-caused by GrTFA1GNP	
	F	Probability	F	Probability
10	2.221525	0.3502	1.143484	0.5533
8	1.160920	0.4190	1.216179	0.3943
4	2.072815	0.1225	2.593035	0.0677
2	1.909898	0.1683	8.027954	0.0019
4	3.012728	0.1046	2.439886	0.1772
2	1.785609	0.2130	2.611728	0.1180
1	4.187912	0.0600	9.396377	0.0084
4	2.742714	0.1299	3.114126	0.1039
2	0.048443	0.9529	7.626708	0.0097
1	1.292244	0.2778	11.29038	0.0057

Table AIII.6

Lag	Δ^2Bkindex not G-caused by GrGNPPH		GrGNPPH not G-caused by Δ^2Bkindex	
	F	Probability	F	Probability
10	0.885187	0.6872	5.373712	0.3247
8	2.816378	0.0951	2.114064	0.1700
4	1.092312	0.3886	0.785712	0.5485
2	0.324804	0.7257	0.216873	0.8065
4	1.807229	0.2903	0.475585	0.7553
2	1.184901	0.3453	0.244775	0.7874
1	0.110137	0.7453	0.289198	0.5998
4	0.360829	0.8285	0.438836	0.7775
2	0.666562	0.5349	0.102735	0.9033
1	0.002265	0.9628	0.141121	0.7137

APPENDIX IV: COINTEGRATION BETWEEN TFA1GNP AND THE CHANGE IN THE BANK INDEX

Table AIV.1

(a)   Rank of the stochastic matrix: with two lags[*]

Rank	Max.λ_i	T-nm	95%	Trace	T-nm	95%
0	24.48[**]	21.1[**]	19.0	32.21[**]	27.76[**]	25.3
≤ 1	5.788	7.728	12.2	6.662	7.728	12.2

[*] In the unrestricted reduced form equations, the F-tests on the retained regressors showed that the impacts of the one-period lags of the variables and of the two-period lag of ΔBkindex were significantly different from zero at the 1% level or better; the two-period lag of TFA1GNP was significant at the 3.87% level and the trend was significant at the 5.31% level. The correlations of actual with fitted values were, for TFA1GNP and ΔBkindex, respectively, 0.9918 and 0.9407.
[**] Significant at the 1% level or better.

(b)   Cointegrating vectors (β_i) and standardized α_i coefficients[*]

	β_i	β_2	α_1	α_2
TFA1GNP	1.0000	−0.9838	−0.00001051	0.2617
ΔBkindex	−1.808E+004	1.0000	−0.00004349	0.002306
Trend	−4.33	0.0951		

[*] χ^2 (2) test that the coefficient on the trend is zero, 7.7402 (0.0209), so that the hypothesis can be rejected at the 5% level or better.

(c)   Long-run matrix

	TFA1GNP	ΔBkindex	Trend
TFA1GNP	−0.2575	0.4517	0.02493
ΔBkindex	−0.002312	0.7887	0.0004076

APPENDIX V: FINANCIAL DEVELOPMENT AND REAL RATES OF INTEREST; PRINCIPAL COMPONENTS AND PRINCIPAL FACTORS; TIME SERIES

Monetization and Real Rates of Interest

Table AV.1   Principal components

Variable	Factor	1961–95		1961–79		1980–95	
		Eigenval	% of var	Eigenval	% of var	Eigenval	% of var
Monet	1	1.0471	34.9	1.24397	41.5	1.48784	49.6
Real 6m	2	1.0301	34.3	1.02222	34.1	0.95963	32.0
Real 1yr	3	0.92276	30.8	0.73381	24.5	0.55253	18.4

Table AV.2   Principal factors for Table AV.1 for the two sub-periods, based upon the varimax rotation using the Kaiser normalization for 1961–79

Variable	1961–95		1961–79		1980–95	
	Factor 1	Factor 2	Factor 1	Factor 2	Factor 1	Factor 2
Monet	0.81975	–0.20039	0.01292	0.96136	–0.05854	0.99813
Real 6m	–0.18457	0.82506	0.76605	0.25526	0.84699	–0.06655
Real 1yr	–0.57705	–0.56331	0.80503	–0.20429	0.85138	–0.03332

TFA1GNP and Real Rates of Interest

Table AV.3   Principal components

Variable	Factor	1961–95		1961–79		1980–95	
		Eigenval	% of var	Eigenval	% of var	Eigenval	% of var
TFA1GNP	1	1.04760	34.9	1.73559	57.9	1.46547	48.8
Real 6m	2	1.02884	34.3	0.93024	31.0	0.99235	33.1
Real 1yr	3	0.92356	30.8	0.33417	11.1	0.54218	18.1

Table AV.4   Principal factors for Table AV.3, based upon varimax rotation using the Kaiser normalization

Variable	1961–95		1961–79		1980–95	
	Factor 1	Factor 2	Factor 1	Factor 2	Factor 1	Factor 2
TFA1GNP	0.82178	–0.19705	0.91918	–0.00577	–0.3636	0.99307
Real 6m	–0.18321	0.82650	0.88972	0.18963	0.84063	–0.1425
Real 1yr	–0.57422	–0.56203	0.9183	0.99242	0.85917	0.07231

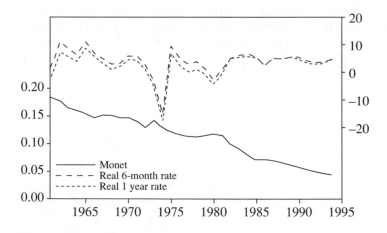

Figure AV.1   The real rates of interest and monet

NOTES

1. For a recent survey, see Levine (1997).
2. For example, see Greenwood and Jovanovic (1990), Bencivenga and Smith (1991), King and Levine (1993a, 1993b) and Roubini and Sala-i-Martin (1991, 1992).
3. An excellent overview of the McKinnon and Shaw models is provided in Fry (1998, chapter 2). The McKinnon model is based on outside money and on Keynes's finance motive to explain the holding of money by entrepreneurs. In effect, it is assumed that (at low levels of development) entrepreneurs have to rely upon accumulating funds themselves in order to effect investment in physical capital. Improving the real return on bank deposits will increase their financial savings with consequent effects upon the level of investment. Money and physical capital are complements. By contrast, Shaw's model is based upon inside money and on the advantages of financial intermediation emphasized in his earlier classic work with Gurley (Gurley and Shaw, 1960).
4. Apart from the papers mentioned in the text, empirical work has tended to rely on the application of those techniques. Thus Bhatia and Khatkhate (1975) and Abdi (1977) used correlations; Gupta (1984), Jung (1986) and Murinde and Eng (1994) rely on Granger causality tests.
5. As it happens, the liquidity ratio has not been employed as an instrument of monetary policy since July 1978, when it was set at 7 per cent. An analysis of the instruments and targets of monetary policy in Taiwan is the subject of Ford (1997).
6. Reserves have to be held against all types of accounts: current, passbook deposits, savings deposits, time deposits; and all balances deposited in domestic currency in respect of foreign currency certificates of deposit.
7. The 'money market' began to be formed in Taiwan in the 1970s. This is a market in which funds and money market instruments of less than one year's maturity can be traded. In 1973, the central bank disposed of the first issue of treasury bills. In June 1984, the Republic of China granted permission for government bonds with a maturity of less than one year to be traded on the market. These items of government stock are small in the context of the banking system and, of course, have a narrow impact on the structure of interest rates and quantities. Nevertheless, in some years the *proportion* of treasury bills issued to the total of new issues on the money market has been substantial: for example, 1976 (41.48 per cent), 1977 (22.49 per cent), 1978 (15.68 per cent), dropping to low figures (for example, 1981 (0.84 per cent)) until beginning to climb again in the mid-1980s: 1985 (25.26 per cent), 1986 (31.54 per cent), 1987 (28.6 per cent), 1988 (41.05 per cent), falling away again to very low figures (with the exception of the 15.13 per cent rate that was recorded in 1991).
8. The introduction of a money market inevitably led to some rates being market-determined, and these were used by the central bank as indicators of the levels of the rates of interest that it regulated. Further relaxation of interest occurred consequent upon the issuance in November 1980 of the central bank's 'Essentials of Interest Rate Adjustment' which, amongst other things, widened the differential between the maximum and the minimum (regulated) lending rates, a move that was extended further in 1985. For example, in March 1985, banks were required to set a prime rate and the differential of (regulated) lending rates was widened; and in September 1985 the central bank rescinded its edict preventing the maximum deposit rate from exceeding the minimum lending rate. In January 1986, the types of deposits that were subject to interest rate ceilings were reduced from 13 to four. The Banking Law of July 1989 itself revoked the regulations on maximum deposit rates, and the upper and lower limits on loan rates were abolished.
9. Foreign exchange regulation was introduced in April 1951, as was a multiple exchange rate system, which was abandoned in 1958. Prior to February 1979, a fixed exchange rate system was adopted, with the currency pegged to the US dollar. From that date a floating rate was notionally introduced. Foreign exchange controls were not even removed in principle, however, until 1987, following the amendment to the Statute Governing the Foreign Exchange (promulgated on 11 January 1949). Controls on foreign exchange to fund capital movements have still not been totally rescinded.

   Details on these matters, and on the development of the financial system in general, can be found in, for example, the Bureau of Monetary Affairs (MOF, 1996a, b) and Shea (1994).

10. Amongst his conclusions (these are covered in, for example, Drake, 1980, who provides an excellent summary of the issues and of the early empirical evidence thereon) were (1) the FIR rises with economic growth, (2) that ratio eventually declines, levelling off between 1 and 1.5, (3) the ratio reflects the economy's degree of specialization in both finance and production, (4) the share of financial institutions in the ownership of financial assets is positively related to economic development, and (5) financial development begins with the banking system, depending on the diffusion of scriptural money that the system provides, with the ratio of money to national wealth initially increasing with economic growth, but it eventually levels off or declines.

11. In regard to foreign currency funds, these items are included in the broad money measure by the central bank: foreign currency deposits, foreign exchange proceeds deposits, foreign exchange trust funds and foreign currency certificates of deposit of enterprises and individuals that are held in monetary institutions. In respect of 'short-term' assets we have bank debentures issued, savings bonds issued by the central bank and held by enterprises or individuals, and treasury bills-B issued by the central bank and held by enterprises or individuals. From January 1991, the latter items held by the postal savings system are included in the definition of broad money, as are other claims by the postal savings system, namely, (negotiable) certificates of deposits and time deposits redeposited in the commercial banks.

12. The correlation between them for the whole period is − 0.9725. In principle, naturally, the numerator of this monetization variable can be taken to be the ratio of currency to GNP, and the denominator can be seen as the ratio of total financial assets to GNP.

13. We exclude the postal savings system since its outlets have increased enormously in recent years and therefore it would dominate and distort any index constructed to include it – all the more so when we recall that the postal savings system has been effectively incorporated into the deposit-taking banking system for the greater part of our sample period.

14. In writing about principal components, and their possible usage in the derivation of index numbers, Kendall (1975), referring to his own work (Kendall, 1939) on the yield from ten crops in 48 counties in England taken over four years, found that one principal component (one factor) was responsible for about 50 per cent of the total variation; identified this with productivity, suggesting that the eigenvector from that principal component (eigenvalue) might be interpreted as determining an *index* of productivity.

15. The conventional approach seems to be to identify the number of principal components by the number of eigenvalues that are 1 or higher. There is no intrinsic reason for this, but in the case of Tables AII.1 and AII.2 it is apparent that the application of that criterion is apposite. Tests can be performed to determine whether the eigenvalues are identical (see, Bartlett, 1951, 1954) and then if the k largest should be different, tests can be conducted to decide whether the remaining eigenvalues also differ from one another (Bartlett, 1951).

16. So that, for example, the Friedmanite approach of measuring it by industrial development is not used.

17. There is, naturally, a more general issue that is germane to all econometric studies of the link between financial and economic development. That is that, if economic development is sustained once there is a take-off, the only appropriate point(s) at which to test the causality between the two forms of development is at (or around) the time that economic development commences.

18. All tests were conducted by PCFiml 8.0. So, the maximal eigenvalue and trace test statistics are based on Osterwald-Lenum (1992) and the 'small' sample test statistics are based on Reimers (1992).

REFERENCES

Abdi, A.I. (1977), *Commercial Banks and Economic Development: The Experience of East Africa*, New York: Praeger.

Agung, J. and J.L. Ford (1999), 'Economic development, financial development and deregulation: Japan, 1960 to 1996', Discussion Paper 99–04, Department of Economics, University of Birmingham.

Akaike, H. (1969), 'Fitting autoregressive models for prediction', *Annals of the Institute of Statistics and Mathematics*, 3, 243–7.

Arestis, P. and P. Demetriades (1997), 'Financial development and economic growth: assessing the evidence', *Economic Journal*, 107, 783–99.

Bartlett, M.S. (1951), 'The effect of standardisation on an approximation in factor analysis', *Biometrika*, 50, 337.

Bartlett, M.S. (1954), 'A note on the multiplying factors for various approximations', *Journal of the Royal Statistical Society*, Series B, 16, 296.

Bencivenga, V.R. and B.D. Smith (1991), 'Financial intermediation and endogenous growth', *Review of Economic Studies*, 58, 195–209.

Bhatia, R.J. and D.R. Khatkhate (1975), 'Financial intermediation, savings mobilisation and entrepreneurial development: The African experience', *IMF Staff Papers*, March.

Demetriades, P. and K. Hussein (1996), 'Financial development and economic growth: cointegration and causality tests for 16 countries', *Journal of Development Economics*, 51 (December), 387–411.

DeSerres, A. and A. Guay (1995), 'Selection of the truncation lag in structural VARs (or VECMs) with long-run restrictions', Working Paper 95–9, Bank of Canada.

Dickey, A. and S.G. Pantula (1987), 'Determining the order of differencing in autoregressive processes', *Journal of Business and Economic Statistics*, 5(4), 455–61.

Drake, P.J. (1980), *Money, Finance and Development*, Oxford: Martin Robertson (Basil Blackwell).

Ford, J.L. (1994), 'Financial innovation and evolution', *Advances in Austrian Economics*, 1, 175–96.

Ford, J.L. (1997), 'The targets and instruments of monetary policy: long-run trade-offs, multiplier effects and central bank preferences, Taiwan, 1955–1995', Discussion Paper 97–21, Department of Economics, University of Birmingham.

Fry, M.J. (1997), 'In favour of financial liberalisation', *Economic Journal*, 107 (May), 754–77.

Fry, M.J. (1998), *Money, Interest and Banking in Economic Development*, Baltimore and London: Johns Hopkins University Press.

Gertler, M. and A. Rose (1996), 'Finance, public policy and growth', in J.G. Caprio, I. Atiyas and J.A. Hanson (eds), *Financial Reform: Theory and Experience*, Cambridge: Cambridge University Press.

Goldsmith, R. (1969), *Financial Structure and Development*, New Haven: Yale University Press.

Greenwood, J. and B. Jovanovic (1990), 'Financial development, growth and the distribution of income', *Journal of Political Economy*, 88, 1076–1107.

Gupta, K. (1984), *Finance and Economic Growth in Developing Countries*, London: Croom Helm.

Gurley, J.G. and E.S. Shaw (1955), 'Financial aspects of economic development', *American Economic Review*, 45(4), 515–38.

Gurley, J.G. and E.S. Shaw (1960), *Money in a Theory of Finance*, Washington, DC: The Brookings Institution.

Hansen, H. and S. Johansen (1993), 'Recursive estimation in cointegrated VAR models', Discussion Paper, Institute of Mathematical Statistics, University of Copenhagen.

Honohan, P. (1992), 'Financial repression', in J. Eatwell (ed.), *The New Palgrave Dictionary of Money and Finance*, London: Macmillan.

Johansen, S. (1992), 'Determination of cointegration rank in the presence of a linear trend', *Oxford Bulletin of Economics and Statistics*, 54, 383–97.

Jung, W.S. (1986), 'Financial development and economic growth: international evidence', *Economic Development and Cultural Change*, 32, 429–39.

Kendall, M.G. (1939), 'The geographical distribution of crop productivity in England', *Journal of the Royal Statistical Society*, **102**, 21–32.

Kendall, M.G. (1975), *Multivariate Analysis*, London: Griffin and Co.

King, R.G. and R. Levine (1993a), 'Finance and growth: Schumpeter might be right', *Quarterly Journal of Economics*, 108, 717–37.

King, R.G. and R. Levine (1993b), 'Finance, entrepreneurship and growth: theory and evidence', *Journal of Monetary Economics*, 32, 513–42.

Levine, R. (1997) 'Financial development and economic growth: views and agenda', *Journal of Economic Literature*, **35**, 688–726.

McKinnon, R.I. (1973), *Money and Capital in Economic Development*, Washington, DC: The Brookings Institution.

Ministry of Finance (1996a), *The ROC Financial Market Regulation*, Taipei: Bureau of Monetary Affairs, April.

Ministry of Finance (1996b), *The Financial System in the ROC*, Taipei: Bureau of Monetary Affairs, July.

Murinde, V. and F. Eng (1994), 'Financial development and economic growth in Singapore: Demand-following or supply-leading?', *Applied Financial Economics*, 4, 391–404.

Osterwald-Lenum, M. (1992), 'A note with quantiles of the asymptotic distribution of the ML cointegration rank test statistics', *Oxford Bulletin of Economics and Statistics*, 54, 461–72.

Reimers, H.-E. (1992), 'Comparisons of tests for multivariate cointegration', *Statistical Papers*, 33, 335–59.

Roubini, N. and X. Sala-i-Martin (1991), 'Financial development, the trade regime and economic growth', NBER Working Paper, 3876.

Roubini, N. and X. Sala-i-Martin (1992), 'A growth model of inflation, tax evasion and economic growth', NBER Working Paper, 4062.

Schumpeter, J.A. (1934), *The Theory of Economic Development*, Cambridge, MA: Harvard University Press.

Shaw, E.S. (1973), *Financial Deepening in Economic Activity*, Oxford: Oxford University Press.

Shea, Ji-Dong (1994), 'Taiwan: development and structural change of the financial system', in H.T. Patrick and Yung Churl Park (eds), *The Financial Development of Japan, Korea and Taiwan*, Oxford: Oxford University Press.

Stiglitz, J. (1994), 'The role of the state in financial markets', *Proceedings of World Bank Annual Conference on Development Economics*, 1993, 19–52.

Yang, Ya-Hwei (1994), 'Taiwan: development and structural change of the banking system', in H.T. Patrick and Yung Churl Park (eds), *The Financial Development of Japan, Korea and Taiwan*, Oxford: Oxford University Press.

4. Financial market opening in developing countries

Maxwell J. Fry[1]

INTRODUCTION

In 1993, total capital flows to developing countries of $159.2 billion consisted of $66.6 billion foreign direct investment (FDI), $89.0 billion in portfolio investment (of which equity acquisitions accounted for $46.9 billion and bond purchases for $42.1 billion) and $3.6 billion in loans and other debt-creating flows (World Bank, 1995a, Table 4.1, 50). Evidently, portfolio investment, of which bonds represented almost 50 per cent, constituted the largest component of these capital flows. However, much of the recorded bond finance flowed through international bond issues rather than through foreign participation in domestic bond markets.

By convention, bonds are classified as domestic, foreign or Euro. A Euro-bond is issued through an international syndicate of securities houses; the securities houses could be located in the same city but some would have foreign parents. Bonds are domestic if the issuer's country of residence corresponds to the bond's currency of denomination; otherwise, they are foreign or international bonds.[2] This three-way distinction is of practical importance in that, for example, Euro-bonds need not be registered with the Securities and Exchange Commission. In some markets, domestic bonds are subject to withholding tax, whereas international bonds denominated in the domestic currency may not be. Distinctions also occur in terms of clearing systems, collateral and so on (Benzie, 1992, pp. 15–18).

While these distinctions are extremely important for various purposes, they are important here only for the purpose of delineating the focus of this chapter, which is not concerned with Euro-bonds or international bonds. Rather, it concentrates on the development of domestic markets for domestic bonds and the further issue of restrictions on the purchase of such bonds by foreign investors. Here the internationalization of domestic bond markets means the process of permitting and perhaps encouraging foreign investors to participate in domestic bond markets.

Of particular relevance is the fact that two countries – Korea and Taiwan – possess large bond markets to which foreign access is relatively restricted. Despite being the second-largest fixed-income market in Asia (Japan's is the largest), Korea's bond market is dominated by captive buyers who hold their securities until maturity. Foreign participation in the Korean bond market is severely restricted (Banks, 1994, p. 227; Emery, 1997). Foreign investors were excluded entirely from the primary bond market until 1994, but could obtain approval to buy securities in the secondary market. Internationalization of Korea's domestic bond market is proceeding gradually (Banks, 1994, p. 228), although the current plans envisage only limited access to foreign investment in the domestic bond market (International Monetary Fund, 1995d, p. 52).

Taiwan's bond market, consisting predominantly of government bonds, is also dominated by captive buyers (Emery, 1997; Semkow, 1994, 238). Foreign investors may participate in the domestic bond market after becoming 'qualified investors'. However, each investor faces a ceiling as well as a global foreign-investor ceiling. Qualified investors are obliged to bring funds into Taiwan within six months, must hold securities for at least three months, and may repatriate proceeds only once a year (Banks, 1994, p. 280). Not surprisingly, therefore, foreign investors are not active in the Taiwanese fixed-income securities market (Lynch, 1995, p. 356).

Opening domestic debt markets to foreign participation requires, first and foremost, the existence of such markets. Experience suggests that development of these markets may be best achieved by focusing attention in the first instance on the market for government debt. Voluntary domestic markets for government debt provide opportunities for learning-by-doing in market price determination of relatively simple financial claims. The skills acquired in domestic markets for government debt can and do spill over into markets for private sector claims, in which the additional complication of credit risk arises. As exemplified by Hong Kong's experience, a buoyant domestic market for government debt is a key prerequisite for the development of private fixed-income securities markets. Indonesia corroborates this point, in that the prohibition of domestic government debt issue there has kept the Indonesian bond market, the smallest bond market in East Asia, at a size equal to only 5 per cent of the country's stock market valuation (Emery, 1997; International Monetary Fund, 1995c, p. 82).

At the outset, developing a voluntary market for government debt involves a fundamental change in the approach to financing the government deficit. Typically, the change occurs from a system in which most institutional interest rates are fixed and the government is financed at favourable fixed rates by unwilling captive buyers of its debt. Privileged access and captive buyers are now eschewed in favour of a level playing-field philosophy. Government now competes on the same terms and conditions as private agents for available saving. The economic principle behind the change is that a level playing field maximizes the efficiency with which scarce resources are allocated throughout the economy.

While macroeconomists may be convinced of the efficacy of financial liberalization and related economic reforms directed at producing a more market-based economy, central bankers, ministers of finance and civil servants may have reservations which are typically expressed with vigour at the first signs of trouble. The reluctance to let go and to rely on market forces is pervasive. Hence one cynical question, when confronted by a liberalization programme is, Have these leopards really changed their spots?

Maintaining the old system of ratio controls on bank balance sheets as a safeguard or fallback should things go wrong with the indirect market-based approach to implementing monetary policy typically damages or retards market development. For example, high liquid asset ratio requirements in Jamaica have distorted the pricing mechanism, particularly when the volume of government debt eligible as liquid assets fell short of the volume needed to satisfy the requirement.

Vested interests created under controlled market conditions are bound to oppose reform. Financial restriction involves protecting the commercial banks from which government can expropriate significant seigniorage and discouraging direct markets. Not too surprisingly, when the government develops direct markets not only for its own debt but for private debt as well, commercial banks face a competitive threat. Non-bank investors can be dissuaded to some extent from participating in direct markets by fear of reprisals in some form or another from their banks. Aggressive competition among banks should prevent such behaviour, so measures to ensure vigorous competition may be needed at the start of the market development programme. At the same time, prudential supervision and regulation can play a vital role in maintaining stable rather than unstable competitive conditions.

To enhance competition, measures to broaden the investor base are crucial. These may include advertising as well as improving access for non-bank participants at treasury bill auctions. Indeed, if the major investors remain commercial banks, portfolio adjustments by the banking system as a whole in response to changing business conditions may be constrained or disruptive. If there are no other holders of treasury bills, the banking system will perforce have to hold the same volume even though it would now prefer to reduce such holdings in favour of loans to the private sector. In such case, treasury bill yields must adjust, by possibly large amounts. With a broad and deep market for treasury bills, however, banks can use these assets as shock absorbers against fluctuations in both deposits and loan demand. Under such conditions, it is typical to find that banks decrease their holdings of government securities and increase their loans during economic upswings (Fry and Williams, 1984, pp. 92–3).

If the banking system holds the lion's share of government securities, secondary market development is inevitably retarded, if not stifled completely, because of the lack of diversity amongst the holders of government debt. The homogeneity of banks implies that they will frequently all be on the same side of the market. Hence trading remains thin and yield fluctuations excessive.

Before domestic debt markets can be opened to foreign investors with any realistic expectation of foreign participation, they must meet international standards with respect to the market microstructure, such as trading practices, registry, transfer and settlements systems, and must have established a track record. Some of the issues involved in developing voluntary markets for domestic debt are examined elsewhere (Fry, 1997). Hence this section focuses on specific issues involved in internationalizing these markets.

While no foreign demand exists for some government bonds because of their low yields and high risk, some governments (for example, Korea) restrict foreign acquisition of bonds that yield rates above the world level. Whether due to lack of demand for unattractive fixed-income securities offering yields below the world level or government restrictions on supply, the general pattern of capital account liberalization over the past two decades exhibits a preference for opening the equities market to foreign investors before the debt market. This preference may reflect, in part, a belief that foreign equity participation does not involve payment of a country risk premium to foreigners and, in part, a belief that capital flows into and out of equity markets are less speculative or destabilizing than capital flows into and out of debt markets. In fact, destabilizing capital flows tend to use bank deposits denominated in both local and foreign currency and may be generated just as much, if not more, by residents than by non-residents.

On the one hand, restrictions on foreign participation in fixed-income securities markets are unlikely to counteract speculative surges. First, speculators can use bank deposits rather than fixed-income securities. Second, restrictions can only make foreign participation more difficult rather than impossible. Indeed, foreign participation can be rather easily arranged where financial institutions offer custodial ('nominee') accounts to their clients. In the United Kingdom, for example, nominee accounts constitute a large proportion of holdings of government securities and identifying categories of beneficial. owners is possible only through periodic questionnaires (Gray, 1996, p. 16).

On the other hand, foreign participation in domestic government bond markets broadens the investor base, permits foreign investors greater diversification than is possible through international bonds, stabilizes aggregate capital flows since more portfolio reallocation can occur among bonds of the same country, supports bond issuers that are too small for the international market, improves depth and liquidity, improves risk management for investors which simultaneously benefits issuers, increases market sophistication through the transfer of technology and imposes additional fiscal discipline on the government through the threat of capital withdrawal. In the vast majority of developing countries, the main problem is not a potential oversupply of foreign investment into domestic bond markets but rather the lack of a well-functioning bond market into which foreign investment can flow. Examining the specific cases of Mexico and Korea leads to the conclusion that opening domestic fixed-income markets is unlikely to produce destabilizing capital inflows.

FOREIGN INVESTORS AND CAPITAL FLOWS

In the absence of domestic distortions, foreign capital inflows can augment domestic resources available for capital formation and hence can accelerate economic growth. When relative domestic prices differ substantially from relative world prices, however, foreign capital inflows even in the form of foreign direct investment, can be immiserizing (Fry, 1993, 1994). Here it is assumed that the development of a voluntary domestic market for fixed-income securities has been accompanied by financial sector and foreign trade liberalization to remove such domestic distortions. Hence the specific issue I addressed here is that of opening domestic debt markets to foreign investors, rather than the broader issue of opening the capital account. Therefore the analysis is based on the assumption that other capital flows, including short-term capital inflows into bank deposits, are already permitted.

Given these basic prerequisites, there are two cases where the opening of domestic fixed-income markets is likely to have no impact and hence could produce no cause for concern. The first is where the market for government securities is still dominated by captive buyers and hence yields are artificially depressed. The second is where the country is so small that foreign investors will not find it worth the set-up costs to enter the local market. For example, Mauritius suspended all foreign exchange controls in 1994 during a period of tight monetary and loose fiscal policy, a policy combination that produced high real interest rates and hence attractive returns to foreign investors. Nevertheless, no measurable capital inflow occurred, largely because the market was just too small. The same phenomenon has been observed in the smaller transitional economies in which even higher real yields on domestic fixed-income assets have been observed.

One source of reluctance to permit foreign investors to participate in domestic fixed-income securities markets emanates from a concern that the country will pay an unnecessary and expensive currency risk premium. To the extent that foreign investors are already permitted to participate in equity markets as well as to undertake FDI, the relevant comparison is between returns that foreign investors are obtaining in these two markets and returns in the bond market.

Given the typical incentive package encouraging FDI, the cost to the host country of this form of capital flow may well exceed the cost of funding through domestic bond markets by a considerable margin.

As David Folkerts-Landau and Takatoshi Ito (1995, p. 115) point out, 'preferences for liquidity have limited foreign participation in emerging bond markets; corporate bond markets are underdeveloped in most developing countries, and in most cases foreign investors can satisfy their demand for sovereign risk in international bond markets'.[3] Again this suggests that large flows of unwanted foreign capital into domestic currency fixed-income securities are unlikely. To illustrate differential liquidity in emerging and Organization for Economic Cooperation and Development (OECD) bond markets, David Lynch (1995, p. 305) presents data on the ratio of turnover to total outstanding government debt in various countries. While this liquidity ratio is 14.2 in Australia, 13.1 in the United States, 6.3 in the United Kingdom and 5.2 in Japan, it is only 0.5 in China and 0.2 in India, Malaysia and Nepal.[4] While futures and options markets for government bonds exist in these four OECD countries, they do not in the four developing countries. Finally, bid–ask spreads are far lower in highly liquid markets, such as Australia (0.03 per cent) and Japan (0.02 per cent), than they are in illiquid markets, such as India (1 per cent), Indonesia (1.5 per cent), Malaysia (0.25 per cent) and Thailand (0.75 per cent) (ibid., p. 330).

Given the relatively small size of fixed-income markets in most developing countries, foreign inflows would in any case be limited by their negative impact on yields.[5] While bubbles and herd instincts can produce large stock price rallies under illusions that future dividends will rise, too, higher bond prices are necessarily *always* accompanied by the sobering reality of lower yields because coupon payments remain constant.

As a general principle, the World Bank advocates foreign participation in domestic bond markets to broaden the investor base, permit foreign investors greater diversification than is possible through international bonds, stabilize aggregate capital flows since more portfolio reallocation can occur among bonds of the same country, support bond issuers that are too small for the international market, improve depth and liquidity, improve risk management for investors, which simultaneously benefits issuers, and increase market sophistication through the transfer of technology (World Bank, 1995a, p. 56). One might add that foreign participants may also impose additional fiscal discipline on the government through the threat of capital withdrawal. This would strengthen local confidence, so deterring capital flight and reducing the cost of government borrowing.

For developing countries to reap these benefits, the World Bank (ibid.) lists the measures needed to develop voluntary domestic bond markets, that is, to emancipate captive buyers and allow bond prices to be freely determined by market forces, build market-based benchmark issues and provide transparent and efficient legal, regulatory, clearing and settlement systems. To this list can be added the importance of the macroeconomic policy mix. On the one hand, to deter any excessive or disruptive capital inflow, the market opening should occur when fiscal policy is relatively tight and monetary policy neutral or relatively loose. To encourage foreign participation, on the other hand, particular attention should be focused on strengthening money markets, lengthening maturities and providing benchmark issues and a central depository.

The fiscal prerequisite is emphasized by several country experiences. For example, India's continued sizable fiscal deficit has been held responsible for high real interest rates. These led to strong capital inflows in 1993/94 and 1994/95. In order to prevent a real appreciation of the rupee, the Reserve Bank of India intervened to buy foreign exchange and sterilized the monetary consequences through open-market operations. With the slowdown in capital inflows in 1995/96, however, it has become increasingly expensive to fund the government's borrowing requirements. The result has been a further rise in real interest rates. As Mexico can also attest, sudden and sizable swings in capital flows increase volatility in both domestic interest rates and exchange rates. In New Zealand, foreign capital inflows produced an overvaluation of the real exchange rate after the 1984 liberalization, which may have raised the costs of disinflation. Sri Lanka's continued high government deficit also led to high real interest rates that crowded out domestic investment and encouraged excessive capital inflows.

A view prevails that foreign investments in fixed-income securities tend to be volatile (World Bank, 1995b, p. 138). Particularly where real interest rates are high, as in Russia, concern is expressed that 'hot money' will be attracted. In the process, the capital inflow will appreciate the real exchange rate, so reducing the competitiveness of exports and, at the same time, lower real rates. When real rates are reduced sufficiently by the surge of foreign capital, foreign investors will remove their funds. The disruption and instability achieve no long-term benefits.[6]

In most developing countries, existing volatility of domestic returns already deters foreign participation in domestic currency fixed-income securities. Jeanne Feldhusen (1994) shows just how volatile, dollar-equivalent returns on domestic currency-denominated government bonds over three-month holding periods can be. Over the year ending October 1994, annualized yields ranged from −0.9 to 2.7 per cent in Indonesia, −9.2 to 7.8 percent in Malaysia, −5.3 to 9.2 per cent in Mexico, 1.7 to 9.5 per cent in the Philippines, −2.0 to 5.0 per cent in Singapore and −0.5 to 3.7 per cent in Thailand. In fact, of course, exchange-rate volatility deters all types of foreign capital. Since such volatility generates risk premia, we now examine this issue in more detail.

CURRENCY PREMIA

Data on treasury bill yields for developing countries are scarce. In part, this simply reflects the absence of market-determined yields in many of these countries. Nevertheless, the available data demonstrate clearly that the dispersion in yields is much greater among the developing countries than among the OECD countries. Over the period 1989–93, the highest depreciation-adjusted dollar return on treasury bills over a single year was provided by France (17.7 per cent), while the lowest dollar yield was posted by Brazil (–112.5 per cent). The data also show that dispersion and volatility were both extremely low among small countries, such as Bahamas, Barbados, Belize, Netherlands Antilles, St Kitts & Nevis, St Lucia and St Vincent & the Grenadines, whose currencies are pegged to the dollar.

Jeffrey Frankel and Alan MacArthur (1988) find that, in a sample of 24 countries possessing forward foreign exchange markets, an exchange risk premium is statistically significant in only one (Saudi Arabia) over the period September 1982 to December 1986. However, forward markets did not exist in 35 of 90 sample developing countries at the end of 1993; a much larger

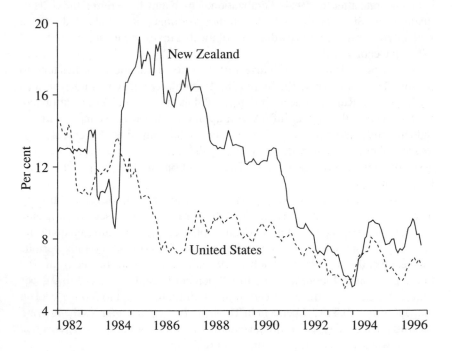

Figure 4.1   Nominal yields on New Zealand and US government bonds

proportion of developing countries did not possess such markets in the mid-1980s. Clearly, therefore, there is a considerable self-selection bias in the choice of developing countries in the Frankel–MacArthur study.

Case study evidence indicates that exchange risk premia are almost inevitable in the early stages of the market-opening process. In New Zealand, for example, depreciation-adjusted treasury bill yields averaged 14.1 per cent during 1984–8, the first five years of its market-opening experiment. This represented a premium of 7.2 percentage points over the US treasury bill yield of 6.9 per cent. New Zealand's treasury bill yield was halved to 7 per cent over the period 1989–93, providing a premium of 1.7 percentage points over the 5.3 per cent US yield. Argentina provided a comparable differential of 1.5 percentage points in mid-1994, when a five-year peso-denominated bond yielded 1.5 percentage points more than a five-year dollar-denominated bond (Blauer and West, 1994, p. 16).

Figure 4.1 shows the initial rise in New Zealand government bond yields after its 1984 liberalization. This was followed by gradual convergence over the subsequent nine years, until New Zealand domestic currency-denominated government bond yields had declined to the level of US government bond yields by the end of 1993.

TAXATION

Rather than prohibition, another way of deterring unwanted capital inflows is to impose taxes on interest earned on domestic currency debt by foreigners. A general deterrent to speculative capital movements takes the form of the Tobin tax on foreign exchange transactions. While such a general tax is impracticable, a more specific tax on capital account transactions could be applied. Other variants, such as pre-deposits with the central bank and reserve requirements against foreign borrowing, have also been employed.

Brazil has experimented to a substantial extent with such deterrents. While real interest rates were averaging about 2 per cent a month in 1993 and 1994, Brazil established a Fixed-Income Fund in December 1993 through which all foreign investment in fixed-income securities had to be channelled. This fund was subject to various special taxes designed to deter any excessive inflow of speculative capital. Among these taxes were (a) a 5 per cent financial transaction tax on the initial capital or new money converted from foreign exchange to domestic currency; (b) a 0.25 per cent tax on the transfer of reals into the fund; (c) a 15 per cent income tax on all income earned by the fund; (d) a 0.25 per cent tax on the sale of domestic currency for foreign exchange; and (e) an additional financial transaction tax for short-term investments with redemption within 16 days (Sutter, 1994, p. 20). In the wake of the Mexican crisis, Brazil removed some restrictions on and deterrents to capital inflows in March 1995

(Folkerts-Landau and Ito, 1995, pp. 96, 100). The financial transaction tax which had previously been raised to 9 per cent was lowered back to 5 per cent.

Chile also experienced unwanted capital flows during the 1990s. Over the period 1990–95, capital account surpluses averaged 7 per cent of GDP. Some of these capital inflows were absorbed through central bank reserve accumulation with partial sterilization; real yields on long-term Central Bank Promissory Notes averaged 6 per cent in mid-1995, compared with an indexed yield of 5.5 percent on 3–12 month time deposits (International Monetary Fund, 1995a, pp. 118–19). Another response was revaluation of the peso; the real exchange rate appreciated by 23 per cent over this period.

To deter excessive capital inflows, the Chilean authorities used all the standard devices: fiscal restraint, sterilized intervention, controls on capital inflows and high reserve requirements on foreign currency deposits, liberalization of capital outflows and trade liberalization. Portfolio inflows are subject to prior authorization by the central bank and to a minimum one-year holding period (five years for investment through the foreign capital investment funds). In 1992, for example, the central bank imposed a 30 per cent reserve requirement on foreign currency-denominated deposits. In 1995, this reserve requirement was extended to cover all investment flows that did not represent increases in domestic capital formation but only ownership transfers. The International Monetary Fund (ibid., p. 32) reports that the attempts to discriminate between short- and long-term capital flows were difficult.

> Controls on capital inflows may help in temporarily insulating the economy from destabilising short-term capital inflows. However, these controls become progressively ineffective [for example, as market participants find ways of circumventing the reserve requirement] and eventually have to be intensified; controls on capital inflows make speculative attacks more costly but they cannot stop them. They also have an efficiency cost. (Ibid., p. 33)

Of relevance to this study, none of Chile's capital inflow difficulties has been related to foreign access to its domestic fixed-income securities markets.

Registered foreign institutional investors (FIIS) in India are subject to a 20 per cent tax on their interest and dividend earnings, while capital gains are taxed at 30 per cent if realized on investments held for less than a year and 10 per cent otherwise (International Monetary Fund, 1995b, p. 3).[7] In fact, although India has experienced considerable inflows of portfolio investment in the 1990s, there has been little foreign interest in domestic fixed-income securities, in part because of their illiquidity and in part because of the exposure of malpractices in the trading of public sector bonds (ibid., p. 9).

Elsewhere in Asia, withholding taxes on interest range from 10 to 20 per cent, transaction taxes from 0.1 to 1 per cent, and capital gains taxes from 0 to

25 per cent in Indonesia, Korea, Malaysia, the Philippines and Thailand (World Bank, 1995a, 29). The World Bank's (ibid., p. 30) assessment of these taxes is:

> The slow development of Asian bond markets has translated into scant attention to tax definition and interpretation, presenting both domestic and foreign investors with legal and administrative uncertainty and complexity, frustrating engagement and spawning loopholes bringing domestic revenue seepage. Importantly these complications have often driven activity off-shore both in the region and globally, where taxes, when they exist at all, are lower and the associated framework is far better defined.

John Campbell and Kenneth Froot (1993) also find that transaction taxes cause shifts to trading in foreign markets and to untaxed assets, and to reduced trading volumes.

Carmen Reinhart and Todd Smith (1996) examine the effects of taxes on capital inflows. Many of the measures examined were either used counter-cyclically, announced as temporary, or became temporary because they were circumvented in the long run. Reinhart and Smith conclude that, in most cases, the measures did reduce the overall capital inflow, altered its composition in terms of maturity, or did both in the short run. However, these measures had little or no measurable impact on consumption, the current account, or the real exchange rate in the longer run.

INDEXATION

When financial opening forms part of a broader strategy of financial stabilization and liberalization, indexation may prove a useful device to deter unwanted capital inflows. At the start of the stabilization process, real interest rates are typically high. If part of the cause of high real interest rates is an inflation-risk premium, this can be avoided through inflation indexation. While this can be particularly attractive to residents, it may not appeal so much to foreign investors. Provided the initial inflation rate lies under 20 per cent, deviations from purchasing power parity are typically so large as to divorce inflation indexation entirely from exchange indexation. In other words, real rates can be reduced by making assets more attractive to residents without their becoming more attractive, that is, less risky, to foreigners.

Conversely, if foreign participation is desired for any reason, the government may choose to issue currency-indexed bonds as a compromise between issuing foreign currency debt and domestic currency debt. If the government succeeds in maintaining the exchange rate, such indexation may prove a cheap form of borrowing. If it fails, however, the unplanned devaluation could make it very expensive. Furthermore, currency-indexed bonds may not be as useful as conventional securities in promoting the market development process. They represent just one more instance of deliberate market segmentation. At worst, they may encourage currency substitution, that is, dollarization (Gray, 1996, p. 23).

New Zealand's experience is particularly noteworthy in the existence of a high-risk premium after its 1984 reforms. Part of the reform package consisted of making price stability the only objective of monetary policy and in giving the Reserve Bank full independence to achieve this single objective. Furthermore, the governor's emoluments are dependent on the achievement of this objective. Although these measures undoubtedly contributed to building credibility for low inflation and therefore facilitated the development of the voluntary domestic market for government debt, the erosion of this risk premium occurred only gradually. From levels of 18 to 19 per cent in the mid-1980s, yields on ten-year domestic currency government bonds have fallen to around 8.5 per cent. For a few months in 1994, the New Zealand government was able to sell ten-year bonds at a slightly lower yield than the US government.

One of the important lessons learnt from New Zealand's reform experience was that consumer price index (CPI) index-linked debt could have been issued to great benefit at the start of the reforms in 1984. If one of the legacies of past inflation is a high-risk premium embedded in nominal yields, indexed bonds can offer large savings for the government in terms of lower interest costs, so reducing the likelihood of igniting a Ponzi game, provided its new commitment to fiscal discipline and price stability is effective. An issue of CPI index-linked debt can also enhance credibility in the new regime: the government can no longer benefit from surprise inflation to erode the real value of its debt. Consequently, it has less incentive to renege in this way.

CAPITAL INFLOWS AND MONETARY CONTROL IN NEW ZEALAND

Foreign participation in the New Zealand bond market became significant after withholding taxes were removed; 50 per cent of New Zealand government securities are now held by foreigners. That there would be such a large shift in the government's borrowing from abroad to domestic currency-denominated debt had not been anticipated at the outset of the liberalization programme in 1984. While it reduced the fiscal cost of government debt, this capital inflow appreciated the real exchange rate. Clearly, if inflationary pressure is intense in the non-tradables sector and non-existent in the tradables sector, this downward pressure on interest rates and upward pressure on the exchange rate may be harmful. This was New Zealand's primary monetary policy dilemma in the mid-1990s.

A switch from foreign to domestic borrowing may have unintended signalling effects. When New Zealand tightened monetary policy to achieve its announced policy target of low inflation, this implied an expected appreciation in the exchange rate. In fact, however, uncertainty about the government's commitment and ability to achieve this target kept domestic currency yields much higher than yields on the New Zealand government's foreign currency-denominated debt. Under such conditions, a policy of switching from foreign to domestic currency-denominated debt could have been interpreted by the market as a lack of belief in its inflation target on the part of the government itself. With a low inflation outcome, the government would be paying higher real rates to borrow in domestic currency than it would pay to borrow in foreign currency. Therefore a policy of reducing both domestic and foreign currency-denominated debt together with sales of shorter-maturity domestic debt might have been interpreted by the market as more consistent with a belief in its own inflation target. Indeed, the New Zealand government's funding strategy was revised in the light of this signalling problem.

THE MEXICAN EXPERIENCE

Foreign participation in emerging fixed-income securities markets has been considerably greater in Mexico than in any other developing country. By 1994, one-third of Mexican government securities (about $23 billion) was held by foreign investors. There has therefore been a strong temptation to blame this large foreign presence in its domestic financial markets for the Mexican currency crisis of December 1994 and the first quarter of 1995. The facts tend to refute this premise.

The origins of the Mexican crisis of December 1994 can be traced back to the 0.25 per cent rise in the US federal funds rate in February 1994. As the markets anticipated, this was followed by four more interest rate increases which raised the Federal funds rate to 5.5 per cent by the end of November 1994. Despite political unrest (including two political assassinations), the Banco de México sterilized the capital outflows that occurred, partly in response to political uncertainty but also in response to rising interest rates in the OECD countries. Hence Mexican interest rates remained relatively low and stable throughout 1994.

As a result of increasing fiscal pressures in 1994, the Mexican government decreased its reliance on domestic currency-denominated debt, mainly *Cetes*, and increased the issue of dollar-indexed debt, *Tesobonos*, which are short-term debt paid in pesos but indexed to the US dollar. From 6 per cent in

February, *Tesobonos* constituted over 50 per cent of all Mexican government debt outstanding in November 1994. The evidence indicates that foreign holdings of *Cetes* declined considerably in December 1994, but 65 per cent of this decline was offset by an increase in foreign holdings of *Tesobonos* (Folkerts-Landau and Ito, 1995, p. 60). Because of the 15 per cent devaluation of the peso on 20 December, *Tesobonos* constituted 66 per cent of total domestic government debt by the end of December 1994.

In fact, *Tesobonos* did incur currency risk because repayment in pesos occurred two days after maturity and after the conversion rate was fixed. This practice was discontinued in February 1995, when direct settlement of *Tesobonos* in dollars at the option of the investor was permitted. As the currency crisis continued, concern over the volume of maturing *Tesobonos* in early 1995 increased. Despite these negative factors, foreign holdings of *Tesobonos* remained stable before, and actually increased after, the devaluation.

After the auction of *Tesobonos* on 27 December 1994 at which $600 million was offered but only $28 million was sold, holdings by non-residents, but more markedly by residents, declined (ibid., p. 61). From a yield of 8.6 per cent at the 20 December auction, auction yields on *Tesobonos* rose to 10.2 per cent at the 27 December 1994 auction and peaked at 25 per cent at the 31 January 1995 auction. Yields on *Cetes* rose far more dramatically, from 15 per cent on 15 December 1994 to 83 per cent on 15 March 1995. These large interest rate hikes caused a crisis for both the commercial banks and their borrowers (ibid., p. 63).

In retrospect, it is not at all evident that the financial market disruptions in Mexico were magnified by foreign participants in Mexico's fixed-income securities markets. Folkerts-Landau and Ito (ibid., pp. 7–8) infer:

> The available data show that the pressure on Mexico's foreign exchange reserves during 1994, and in particular just prior to the devaluation, came not from the flight of foreign investors or from speculative position-taking by these investors, but from Mexican residents. ... Indeed, foreign investors did not start to sell their Mexican equity holdings in any sizable quantities until February 1995.

Supporting this view, Jeffrey Frankel and Sergio Schmukler (1996) find that, just before the December 1994 devaluation, 'Mexican country fund Net Asset Values (driven mainly by Mexican investors) dropped faster than their prices (driven mainly by foreign investors). Moreover, we find that Mexican NAVs tend to Granger-cause the country fund prices.' Hence they conclude that 'causality, in some sense, flows from the Mexico City investor community to the Wall Street investor community'.

An alternative explanation is that easy monetary policy at the start of 1994, combined with government debt management policy, were responsible for the crisis; the volume of short-term dollar-indexed debt maturing in early 1995 exceeded by a large margin Mexico's foreign exchange reserves. Again, Folkerts-Landau and Ito (1995, p. 8) conclude: 'the general message emerging from these developments is that the room for policy slippage has been significantly reduced, because the disciplining mechanism of capital flight can be expected to be applied sooner and to be more potent in the future'. The underlying problem resulted from the escalating value of short-term dollar-indexed government debt caused by the December 1994 devaluation and the subsequent market fear that the government would be unable to service its *Tesobono* obligations. Longer maturities of government debt might have prevented an exchange rate crisis from becoming a debt-service crisis (ibid., p. 16).

THE KOREAN CASE

With a bond market of $161 billion, equal to 43 per cent of GDP at the end of 1994, Korea constitutes a special case in terms of the sequencing of foreign participation. Were foreign participation in the Korean bond market to be permitted and to result in 50 per cent foreign ownership over a five-year period, this would involve annual capital inflows averaging over 8 per cent of GDP. That this might indeed occur is supported by the fact that real yields on Korean bonds have been and still are relatively high.

Because rapid economic growth increases prices of non-traded goods in fixed supply, consumer price inflation in Korea has been considerably higher than wholesale or producer price inflation (Balassa, 1964). Over the period 1982–96, for example, the average inflation rate measured by the annual rate of change in consumer prices was 5.3 per cent, compared with 2.1 per cent for wholesale price inflation. Ronald McKinnon (1973, pp. 96–7; 1979, pp. 234–6; 1993, pp. 31–8) argues that the wholesale or producers' price index is a far better measure of inflation for the assessment and measurement of real interest rates.

On this basis, Figure 4.2 shows real bond yields in Korea and the United States over the period 1982–96. For both real interest rates, nominal yields are adjusted by the rates of change in the appropriate wholesale or producer price indices over the past 12 months, using the formula $r = 100[(1 + i/100)/(1 + \pi/100) - 1]$, where r is the real interest rate, i is the nominal rate, and π is the inflation rate. Figure 4.2 shows quite clearly that real yields on Korean bonds exceeded real yields on US bonds throughout a period of 15 years. Summary statistics for January 1982–July 1996 and August 1991–July 1996 are presented in Table 4.1. Evidently, over the five years 1991–6 real yields on Korean bonds were about five percentage points higher than real yields on US bonds; standard deviations on these yields have been almost identical.

However, a comparison of real yields is inappropriate from the viewpoint of potential foreign investors. What is relevant for them is the comparison between

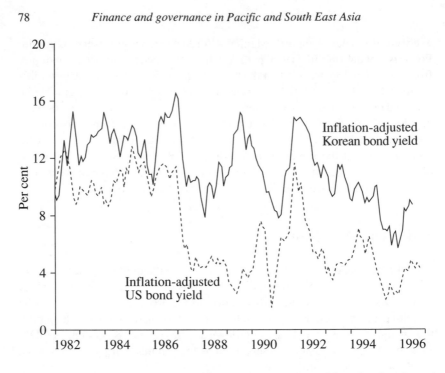

*Figure 4.2   Inflation-adjusted yields on Korean national housing bonds and
ten-year US government bonds*

depreciation-adjusted Korean bond yields and nominal US bond yields,
illustrated in Figure 4.3. As shown in Table 4.1, not only is the gap between
Korean and US bond reals reduced, particularly when based on the median
yield, but the standard deviation of the depreciation-adjusted Korean bond yield
is now far higher than the standard deviation of the nominal US bond yield. In
other words, it is far from evident on an exchange rate-adjusted basis that foreign
investors would flood the Korean bond market, given the substantially higher
risk created by exchange rate fluctuations.

   Indeed, to the extent that the prerequisites for the development of voluntary
domestic fixed-income markets are still lacking in Korea, relevant sequencing
might focus on the market development process rather than on the particular
issue of foreign participation (Noland, 1996). Following James Stock and Mark
Watson (1989) and Zuli Hu (1993), Lynch (1995, pp. 318–25) tests the
efficiency of the Korean bond market by using the yield curve to predict
economic growth. Theory suggests that the term structure will be upward-
sloping if economic growth is expected to accelerate and downward-sloping if
growth is expected to decline. Using lags of one and three years, Lynch finds

significant positive relationships in Australia, Japan and Singapore, but a significantly negative relationship in Korea. Negative relationships are also detected in other financially repressed economies, such as New Zealand prior to liberalization in 1984 and Pakistan.

Table 4.1   Bond yields in Korea and the United States, 1982–96 and 1991–6

Statistic	Korean real		US real		Korean ex. adj.		US nominal	
	82–96	91–96	82–96	91–96	82–96	91–96	82–96	91–96
Mean	11.3	10.0	6.9	5.2	12.8	11.2	8.7	6.7
Median	11.3	9.8	6.0	4.7	10.5	10.0	8.2	6.7
Maximum	16.4	14.7	12.7	11.6	31.1	20.4	14.6	8.1
Minimum	5.6	5.6	1.5	2.0	2.9	3.3	5.3	5.3
S.D.	2.4	2.4	3.1	2.2	6.9	4.0	2.2	0.7

Source: *International Financial Statistics*, CD-ROM, December 1996.

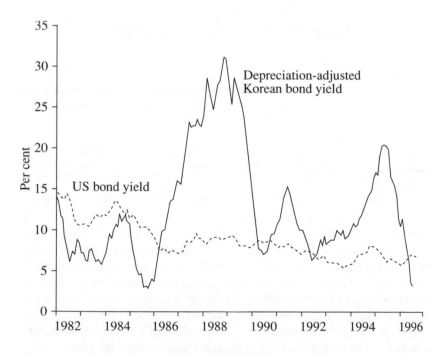

Figure 4.3   Depreciation-adjusted yields on Korean national housing bonds and nominal yields on ten-year US government bonds

Lynch (1995, p. 348) concludes that 'captive market constraints stymie market development' in Korea. Were Korean banks emancipated, not only would they be able and willing to lend more to current bond issuers, but they would also demand bonds themselves. Hence, financial liberalization in the banking sector would reduce real bond yields in Korea by shifting both the supply and demand curves in the appropriate directions. Indeed, Marcus Noland (1996) suggests that, not only would faster financial and capital account liberalization in Korea be beneficial, but also it need not be accompanied by any macroeconomic destabilization.

SEQUENCING

Permitting foreign participation in equity markets has tended to precede the opening of domestic fixed-income markets in most developing countries. Ironically, this sequencing appears to be motivated by reluctance to share real returns on fixed-income claims that exceed worldwide real returns with foreigners. In practice, however, real yields gained by equity holders have often exceeded by large multiple real yields on fixed-income securities. Indeed, as Roger Gordon and Lans Bovenberg (1996, p. 1060) suggest,

> Given foreigners' informational disadvantage when buying domestic equity, one might expect that capital flows instead take the form of purchases of domestic government bonds. Asymmetric information about future interest rates, inflation rates and tax policy would still put foreign investors at somewhat of a disadvantage, but perhaps less so when purchasing domestic bonds than domestic equity.

In such case, foreign participants would be willing to invest in domestic fixed-income claims for a smaller risk premium than they would be willing to invest in domestic equities.

One sequencing pattern that appears to have had the opposite result to that intended is relaxing capital outflow controls before capital inflow controls. Experience suggests that liberalizing outflows induce greater capital inflows (Labán and Larrain, 1997). While Folkerts-Landau and Ito (1995, p. 101) interpret this phenomenon in terms of sending 'a positive signal that increases the confidence of foreign investors', another interpretation is that a substantial proportion of foreign capital inflows to developing countries takes the form of recycled domestic capital that was previously removed in the form of flight capital. When outflow restrictions are relaxed, confidence of *residents*, who now have an increased incentive to repatriate their savings, increases.

One approach is to relax controls on long-term capital inflows before controls on short-term capital. Applied to foreign participation in domestic fixed-income markets, this would involve relaxing restrictions on foreign acquisition of long-term before short-term fixed-income securities. However, such sequencing cannot be confined to domestic fixed-income securities because of the existence of close substitutes such as bank deposits. Clearly, deterrents to short-term capital inflows must cover all potential avenues that include not only domestic currency-denominated claims but also short-term foreign borrowing on the part of residents. Given this requirement, the only appropriate measure would appear to be some form of transaction tax on all capital account foreign exchange transactions. A fixed transaction tax necessarily imposes a greater proportional cost on short-term than on long-term capital movements. The main drawback lies in evasion and hence ineffectiveness: capital inflows can be routed through the current account by overinvoicing exports and underinvoicing imports. Indeed, this is the standard route used in reverse, that is, underinvoicing exports and overinvoicing imports, for capital flight (Cuddington, 1986, p. 38; Dooley, 1986; Khan and Haque, 1985; Watson *et al.*, 1986).[8] Over the shorter term, the same effect can be achieved through leads and lags. Dooley, Donald Mathieson and Rojas-Suárez (1996) estimate that the cost of disguising capital flows of this kind declined by nearly 70 per cent between the early 1970s and the late 1980s.

In fact, foreign exchange transaction costs, that is, the bid–ask spread, deter short-term international capital flows. It is noteworthy that overnight money market rates in both Singapore and Switzerland have reached triple digits on occasions. The monetary authorities in both countries chose not to meet the reserve demands of the commercial banks over and above predetermined levels. In both cases, however, the monetary authorities managed the exchange rate. Hence the only way that commercial banks collectively could obtain reserves was to borrow abroad and sell the foreign exchange to the monetary authorities. Transaction costs ensured that overnight rates rose to about 120 per cent before borrowing abroad for 24 hours became as cheap as domestic borrowing. In other words, the foreign exchange transaction cost translated into an annualized rate exceeding 100 per cent.

In conclusion, little purpose can be served by restricting foreign participation to segments of the domestic fixed-income market. On the one hand, any benefit from deterring short-term capital inflows can be achieved effectively only through a broad measure such as a transaction tax on foreign exchange transactions related to the capital account. On the other hand, benefits of foreign participation in terms of increasing competition and liquidity may well be greatest at the short end of the maturity spectrum. Given that market development may well start with treasury bill auctions and the concomitant development of secondary trading, the transfer of technology from abroad as well as the other benefits mentioned above could be particularly useful at just this early stage.

TRIUMPHALISM

Ronald McKinnon and Huw Pill (1996) examine the 'overborrowing syndrome' that has plagued capital-account liberalization, particularly in Latin America. The authors motivate their analysis with data showing surges of capital inflows to Chile, Colombia, Mexico, Spain and Thailand. The overborrowing syndrome has also occurred in Argentina, Estonia, Egypt, India, Malaysia, Sri Lanka, Turkey and Uruguay.

The basic problem is that a credible domestic reform leads to overoptimistic forecasts of future economic growth and 'excessive' capital inflows to finance consumption smoothing in the light of anticipated higher future incomes. McKinnon and Pill use an extended Fisherian two-period model of production, consumption, borrowing and lending to illustrate three cases: the financially repressed economy in which all agents are borrowing-constrained so that they can invest only in traditional technology, the domestically liberalized economy in which some agents can now borrow from the banking system at high real interest rates to invest in high-return modern technology, and the internationally liberalized economy in which all agents can now borrow through the domestic banking system at the world real interest rate to invest in the new technology.

In most countries, the main constraint to higher growth lies in their modest saving ratio. However, if the government convinces the population that the growth rate will accelerate in the near future to double digits, the rational individual may well react by consuming more now, anticipating that he or she will also be able to consume more in the future as well. This is simply consumption smoothing. The result is a reduction in the present saving ratio, exactly the opposite of what is needed for the higher growth rate to be achieved.

Saving ratios in the market-based developing economies of East Asia typically range between 30 and 40 per cent. Elsewhere, saving ratios are typically under 20 per cent. One can detect a virtuous circle in which high growth causes high saving, so financing higher investment that in turn causes higher growth in output and exports. Export growth itself stimulates growth in other parts of the economy. Before anticipating accelerated economic growth outside East Asia, therefore, signs of substantial increases in both the quantity and quality of investment are generally required.

Market failure arises as a result of overoptimistic, albeit rational, beliefs about returns to the new technology, combined with implicit or explicit deposit insurance. Under these conditions, capital inflows into insured deposits with the domestic banks will prove to have been excessive when lower than anticipated returns to investments are realized. If the first-best solution of removing deposit insurance is not feasible, McKinnon and Pill recommend the imposition of reserve requirements on foreign as well as domestic deposits combined with some discouragement of consumer credit, as the best practical solution.

If the predicted growth acceleration fails to materialize, in part because of lower saving induced by triumphalistic pronouncements on the economic front by government, the country may well find that it has overborrowed in international capital markets. If the triumphalism has convinced both residents and non-residents, it may have produced capital inflows that are unsustainable, and reversible as soon as the euphoria ends. Large capital inflows appreciate the real exchange rate, so deterring exports which are invariably a strong engine of growth. When reality strikes, large capital outflows then cause a balance of payments crisis.

CONCLUSION

A majority of countries exhibiting positive double-digit real interest rates possess fragile financial systems that lack adequate prudential supervision and regulation and face extensive distress borrowing. The basic cause of the problem often lies in large and unsustainable government deficits. Capital inflows of any kind into such countries may well produce more harm than good. A fundamental prerequisite for smooth capital account liberalization and the avoidance of disruptive capital inflows is fiscal discipline (Schadler *et al.*, 1993).

In two countries, Korea and Taiwan, the explanation is quite different. In these countries, rates of return to capital are well above the world average. Given the relatively similar investment ratios between geographic regions of the developing world, the relatively high growth rates in Korea and Taiwan cannot be explained by higher saving and investment ratios. What these economies have achieved is more efficient use of the factors of production, labour and capital. While the additional output produced by an extra unit of investment fell in all other developing regions of the world between 1976–81 and 1982–88, it rose from 0.20 to 0.26 on average in the Asia–Pacific developing countries. In Korea, the incremental output/capital ratio (IOCR) rose from 0.21 to 0.31 between 1976–81 and 1982–8, while in Taiwan the IOCR rose from 0.30 to 0.44 between 1976–81 and 1982–7. Elsewhere, it is suggested that these higher IOCRs are associated with higher returns to investment or to the capital stock in both Korea and Taiwan (Fry, 1991).

It is also suggested that maximizing the efficiency of resource allocation on a worldwide basis involves continued capital inflows to Korea and Taiwan until all their above-average investment returns have been exploited. Provided that such increased capital inflows are accompanied by increased domestic capital formation, there would be no reason to expect any exchange rate impact, except the inevitable Balassa effect due to the more rapidly rising prices of non-traded goods caused by faster economic growth. Indeed, Marcus Noland (1996) suggests that not only would faster financial and capital account liberalization in Korea be beneficial, but also it need not be accompanied by any macroeconomic destabilization. For this reason, this chapter examined some issues involved in opening domestic financial markets to foreign investors.

We conclude by offering three tentative suggestions that may be relevant to an economy on the threshold of opening its financial markets to foreign participation.

Promoting Interest Rate Flexibility through Monetary Control

Financial liberalization is necessarily accompanied by a switch from direct to indirect market-based techniques of monetary control, yet central banks and their governments in developing countries appear distrustful of market mechanisms that produce interest rate volatility. While excessively high real interest rates are clearly inimical to economic development, volatile interest rates may be more beneficial than many developing country central banks and governments seem to acknowledge. Indeed, it is difficult to envisage how the adoption of indirect market-based methods of monetary control can be achieved without greater reliance on interest rate movements.

If there are costs to such volatility, the next question to be addressed is whether or not there are any benefits. Perhaps volatility is particularly low in the United States because the United States does not pursue any exchange rate target. For countries adopting any form of exchange rate target, however, volatility in overnight interest rates may be essential to enable the monetary authorities to counter speculative attacks. Volatility may also be necessary to maintain central bank credibility over the implementation of non-inflationary monetary policy.

If the central bank fails to control the level of excess reserves continuously, short-term interest rates may be excessively volatile. On the other hand, central bank rediscount practices can deter market development if virtually unlimited access at a fixed non-penal rate is available. Under such conditions, there will be no volatility in short-term interest rates. In this case, the central bank can encourage the process of developing treasury management capabilities by being less accommodative.

To ensure that interest rates fluctuate to some extent, a penal rate or limited rediscount tranches may be appropriate. Under one system which has worked well, each bank has access to its first rediscount tranche calculated as the coefficient of variation of daily deposit values over the preceding six months at 1 per cent over the latest treasury bill auction rate, a second rediscount tranche equal in size to the first at a rate 50 percentage points above the first tranche's rate, and a third unlimited tranche at 500 percentage points above the rate on first-tranche rediscounts. This system also constitutes part of a defence mechanism against turbulence on the foreign exchange market. Obviously, the authorities expect the second- and third-tranche facilities to be used only very occasionally and then only overnight.

Whatever rediscount system is adopted, one principle consistent with the development of financial markets is crucial: ensure that the central bank is never the lender of first resort, that is, that it never presents profitable arbitrage opportunities for commercial bank borrowing. This necessarily involves access limits or costs of access continuously above market rates.

An Extension of the Risk-weighted Capital-adequacy Standard

In several countries, rapid expansion of lending by newly liberalized banks has resulted in just as high levels of non-performing assets as did directed credit policies under financial repression. Most banking systems simply lack the expertise needed to make good commercial judgments. In any case, they cannot acquire more of such expertise at the moment financial liberalization occurs. Hence prudential regulation and supervision are doubly imperative at the outset of financial liberalization to curtail the worst excesses of inexperienced and untrained bankers (Villanueva and Mirakhor, 1990; Vittas, 1992).

A new and simplified, if not immediately liberalized, interest rate structure must ensure that banks can increase their profits by aggressively competing for deposits and lending these funds at their own discretion and at their own risk to sound borrowers. In this situation, good bank management would ensure the soundness of the bank. However, the burden of previous directed and unprofitable lending must be also be removed.

Once banks have been restructured so that non-performing policy loans are removed from their balance sheets, prudential supervision and regulation must ensure that banks are prevented and protected from returning to a state of insolvency. In other words, banks must be effectively deterred from lending to insolvent borrowers. Clearly, this necessitates the abolition of any policy-imposed requirements on the banks to extend loans to particular borrowers. The banks must be responsible for their own lending decisions. Prudential regulation and supervision can also be applied to assist banks in their task of establishing safe and sound banking practices.

Experience indicates that interest rate liberalization typically raises at least two major questions. The first is how to curb or counter an explosion in consumer lending after financial liberalization, particularly when it takes the form of the abolition of credit ceilings. The second is how to confront the herd instinct possessed by bankers throughout the world.

International evidence suggests that easier access to consumer credit lowers private saving ratios in the medium term (Jappelli and Pagano, 1994; Liu and Woo, 1994; Patrick, 1994). A burst of consumer lending following financial liberalization may also jeopardize monetary control or squeeze out investment lending. Perhaps the pragmatic answer lies in imposing high downpayment requirements for mortgages and loans for durable consumer goods at the outset of the liberalization programme. Subsequently, such requirements can be gradually reduced, particularly when the economy is in no danger of overheating.

Many newly liberalized banking systems have become overly enthusiastic about property development, credit card lending and housing finance, only to find that expected returns failed to materialize. Loan officers have an incentive to follow others when it comes to sectoral lending decisions. To be wrong in the company of most other loan officers is excusable. To be wrong in isolation may not be forgiven so readily.

Loan officers can be compared to a herd of wildebeest moving from one watering hole to another. As one hole runs dry and the surrounding grass is overgrazed, the herd moves on to a new source of water and pastures. The first to arrive at the new watering hole do well, the laggards struggle to survive. Competition conditions the behaviour of members of the herd.[9] This herd instinct among bankers takes the form of bank lending surging into particular sectors or activities only to withdraw again after delinquency and default rates rise. With deregulation, there seems to be an increasing incidence of such lending concentration into specific fields (for example, in Malaysia, Hong Kong and China).

Occasionally, this herd instinct degenerates into lemming-like behaviour, when bankers all rush into a new activity with virtually no consideration of the risks involved. The macroeconomic problem is that such credit surges produce bubbles in which prices are increased solely as a result of the credit injections. When the bubbles burst banks are left with collateral worth considerably less than the loans that are now non-performing. The end result is financial crisis.

One way of containing systemic risk inherent in overexuberant financial sector growth, the herd instinct, and herd or lemming-like lending behaviour involves deterring excessive lending concentration to (a) a single sector of the economy, such as construction or real estate, (b) a single region of the country, such as the coastal areas, or (c) a single borrower through the application of risk-weighted capital-adequacy requirements. These would be aimed at gradually raising the marginal cost of excessive growth in loans of all particular types. Thus a bank that increased risk through rapid expansion of any loan category by either changing the composition of its portfolio or increasing its total portfolio size would incur increased risk weighting on all loans in its high-growth categories.

Such a system could start with an increased risk weighting on all loans in any category whose annual growth exceeded, say, 20 per cent in real terms by the actual percentage growth of this loan category For example, a 30 per cent growth of loans in any specific category would involve an increase in risk weighting of 30 percentage points on each loan.

In this way the price mechanism can be used, for example, to increase the financial institutions' marginal cost of property lending, so raising interest rates on such loans and deterring speculative real estate booms. A more sophisticated version of this proposal would be to assess a bank's portfolio in terms of the covariance of individual loan default probabilities. The score in this exercise would then produce an adjusted capital adequacy requirement. Hong Kong appears to be the only territory that has attempted to impose an informal risk-weighted capital adequacy requirement on portfolio concentration as opposed to individual items in the portfolio.

The main problem is that the internationally agreed system of risk-weighted capital adequacy assessment is already too complicated for most developing economies to implement effectively. Adding yet more complexity may have to wait. Meanwhile, the central bank may simply have to resort to the tried and true technique of moral suasion. Given the moral hazard problem created by deposit insurance, the central bank might kill two birds with one stone by introducing risk-weighted deposit insurance premia. These would not only address the moral hazard problem, but could also deter excessive lending concentration or excessively risky lending.

Abolishing Reserve and Liquid Asset Requirements

Given the substantial increase in banks' off-balance sheet activities, combined with the introduction of a capital-adequacy requirement, the retention of reserve and liquid asset ratio requirements appears redundant as well as damaging. My final suggestion, therefore, would be to lower any such ratio requirements in steps of 5 percentage points until they reach zero.

NOTES

1. My thanks go to Simon Gray, Nigel Jenkinson and Lionel Price for comments on an earlier draft.
2. Ecu-denominated bonds issued by the EC governments are exceptions, as these are classified as domestic bonds.
3. Mexico provides an obvious exception to this general conclusion.
4. In contrast, Hong Kong Exchange Fund bills achieve a liquidity score of 119. 1.
5. The World Bank (1995a, p. iii) notes that total market capitalization of East Asian bond markets equalled $338 billion, that is, 22 per cent of GDP or one-third of the size of equity markets, at the end of 1994.
6. This argument was used by the Russian commercial banks to justify restricting foreign access. One of the beneficial side-effects of such restriction from their viewpoint was the continued high yield on Russian treasury bills in 1995–6.
7. However, capital gains tax is not levied on investment funds registered in Mauritius, which has a double taxation treaty with India.
8. An exporter submits an invoice for a smaller sum than that actually received for the exports when surrendering foreign exchange to the central bank; the difference can then be deposited in the

exporter's bank account abroad. Conversely, an importer submits an invoice for an amount exceeding the true cost of the imports in order to siphon the difference into his foreign bank account.
9. I am grateful to Andy Mullineux for providing this analogy.

REFERENCES

Balassa, Bela (1964), 'The Purchasing-Power Parity Doctrine: A Reappraisal', *Journal of Political Economy*, 72(6), December, 584–96.

Banks, Erik (1994), *Emerging Asian Fixed Income Markets*, Basingstoke: Macmillan.

Benzie, Richard (1992), *The Development of the International Bond Market*, BIS Economic Papers No. 32, January, Basle: Bank for International Settlements.

Blauer, Ingrid and John West (1994), 'Solid State: Argentina's Bond Market Continues to Offer Opportunity', *Latin Finance Supplement: Latin Bonds 1994*, July/August, 14–16.

Campbell, John Y and Kenneth A. Froot (1993), 'International Experiences with Securities Transaction Taxes', Working Paper 4586, December, National Bureau of Economic Research, Cambridge, MA.

Cuddington, John T. (1986), 'Capital Flight: Estimates, Issues and Explanations', *Princeton Studies in International Finance*, 58, December.

Dooley, Michael P. (1986), 'Country-Specific Risk Premiums, Capital Flight and Net Investment Income Payments in Selected Developing Countries', DM/86/17, March, Washington, DC: International Monetary Fund.

Dooley, Michael R, Donald J. Mathieson and Liliana Rojas-Suárez (1996), 'Capital Mobility and Exchange Market Intervention in Developing Countries', IMF Working Paper, WP/96/131, November, Washington, DC: International Monetary Fund.

Emery, Robert F. (1997), *The Bond Markets of Developing East Asia*, Boulder, CO: Westview Press.

Feldhusen, Jeanne (1994), *Overview of Fixed Income in the Pacific Rim*, New York: JP Morgan.

Folkerts-Landau, David and Takatoshi Ito (1995), *International Capital Markets: Developments, Prospects and Policy Issues*, World Economic and Financial Surveys, August, Washington, DC: International Monetary Fund.

Frankel, Jeffrey A. and Alan T. MacArthur (1988), 'Political vs. Currency Premia in International Real Interest Rate Differentials: A Study of Forward Rates for 24 Countries', *European Economic Review*, 32(5), June, 1083–1114.

Frankel, Jeffrey A. and Sergio Schmukler (1996), 'Country Fund Discounts and the Mexican Crisis of December 1994: Did Local Residents Turn Pessimistic before International Investors?', International Finance Discussion Paper No. 563, September, Washington, DC: Board of Governors of the Federal Reserve System.

Fry, Maxwell J. (1991), 'Domestic Resource Mobilization in Developing Asia: Four Policy Issues', *Asian Development Review*, 9(1), 15–39.

Fry, Maxwell J. (1993), *Foreign Direct Investment in Southeast Asia: Differential Impacts*, Singapore: Institute of Southeast Asian Studies.

Fry, Maxwell J. (1994), 'Foreign Direct Investment, Financing and Growth', in Bernhard Fischer (ed.), *Investment and Financing in Developing Countries*, Baden-Baden: Nomos Verlagsgesellschaft.

Fry, Maxwell J. (1997), *Emancipating the Banking System and Developing Markets for Government Debt*, London: Routledge.

Fry, Maxwell J. and Raburn M. Williams (1984), *American Money and Banking*, New York: John Wiley.

Gordon, Roger H. and A. Lans Bovenberg (1996), 'Why Is Capital So Immobile Internationally? Possible Explanations and Implications for Capital Income Taxation', *American Economic Review*, 86(5), December, 1057–75.

Gray, Simon (1996), 'The Management of Government Debt', Handbooks in Central Banking 5, May, London: Bank of England, Centre for Central Banking Studies.

Hu, Zuliu (1993), 'The Yield Curve and Real Activity', *International Monetary Fund Staff Papers*, 40(4), December, 781–806.

International Monetary Fund (1995a), 'Chile – Recent Economic Developments', IMF Staff Country Report No. 95/102, October, Washington, DC: International Monetary Fund.

International Monetary Fund (1995b), 'India – Background Papers', IMF Staff Country Report No. 95/87, September, Washington, DC: International Monetary Fund.

International Monetary Fund (1995c), 'Indonesia – Recent Economic Developments', IMF Staff Country Report No. 95/83, September, Washington, DC: International Monetary Fund.

International Monetary Fund (1995d), 'Korea – Background Papers', IMF Staff Country Report No. 95/136, December, Washington, DC: International Monetary Fund.

Jappelli, Tullio and Marco Pagano (1994), 'Saving, Growth and Liquidity Constraints', *Quarterly Journal of Economics*, 109(1), February, 83–109.

Khan, Mohsin S. and Nadeem Ul Haque (1985), 'Foreign Borrowing and Capital Flight: A Formal Analysis', *International Monetary Fund Staff Papers*, 32(4), December, 606–28.

Labán, Raúl M. and Felipe B. Larrain (1997), 'Can a Liberalization of Capital Outflows Increase Net Capital Inflows?', *Journal of International Money and Finance*, 16(3), June, 415–31.

Liu, Liang-Yn and Wing Thye Woo (1994), 'Saving Behaviour under Imperfect Financial Markets and the Current Account Consequences', *Economic Journal*, 104(424), May, 512–27.

Lynch, David (1995), 'Links between Asia–Pacific Financial Sector Development and Economic Performance', PhD. thesis, October, Macquarie University, Sydney.

McKinnon, Ronald I. (1973), *Money and Capital in Economic Development*, Washington, DC: Brookings Institution.

McKinnon, Ronald I. (1979), *Money in International Exchange: The Convertible Currency System*, New York: Oxford University Press.

McKinnon, Ronald I. (1993), *The Order of Economic Liberalization: Financial Control in the Transition to a Market Economy*, 2nd edn, Baltimore, MD: Johns Hopkins University Press.

McKinnon, Ronald I. and Huw Pill (1996), 'Credible Liberalizations and International Capital Flows: The "Overborrowing Syndrome"', in Takatoshi Ito and Anne O. Krueger (eds), *Financial Deregulation and Integration in East Asia*, Chicago: University of Chicago Press for the National Bureau of Economic Research, 1996.

Noland, Marcus (1996), 'Restructuring Korea's Financial Sector for Greater Competitiveness', Asia Pacific Economic Cooperation Working Paper Series No. 96–14, Washington, DC: Institute for International Economics.

Patrick, Hugh T. (1994), 'Comparisons, Contrasts and Implications', in Hugh T. Patrick and Yung Chul Park (eds), *Financial Development of Japan, Korea and Taiwan: Growth, Repression and Liberalization*, New York: Oxford University Press.

Reinhart, Carmen M. and R. Todd Smith (1996), 'Too Much of a Good Thing: The Macroeconomic Effects of Taxing Capital Inflows', September, University of Maryland, College Park, MD.

Schadler, Susan M., Maria Carkovic, Adam Bennett and Robert Khan (1993), 'Recent Experiences with Surges in Capital Inflows', Occasional Paper 108, December, Washington, DC: International Monetary Fund.

Semkow, Brian Wallace (1994), *Taiwan's Capital Market Reform: The Financial and Legal Issues*, Oxford: Clarendon Press.

Stock, James H. and Watson, Mark W. (1989), 'New Indexes of Coincident and Leading Indicators', in Olivier J. Blanchard and Stanley Fischer (eds), *NBER Macroeconomic Annual*, Cambridge, MA: MIT Press.

Sutter, Pedro Archer (1994), 'On the Right Track: The Pursuit of Stability Influences Brazil's Fixed-Income Market', *LatinFinance Supplement: Latin Bonds 1994*, July/August, 18–22.

Villanueva, Delano P. and Abbas Mirakhor (1990), 'Strategies for Financial Reforms: Interest Rate Policies, Stabilization and Bank Supervision in Developing Countries', *International Monetary Fund Staff Papers*, 37(3), September, 509–36.

Vittas, Dimitri (ed.) (1992), *Financial Regulation: Changing the Rules of the Game*, EDI Development Studies, Washington, DC: World Bank.

Watson, C. Maxwell, G. Russell Kincaid, Caroline Atkinson, Eliot Kalter and David Folkerts-Landau (1986), *International Capital Markets: Developments and Prospects*, World Economic and Financial Surveys, December, Washington, DC: International Monetary Fund.

World Bank (1995a), *The Emerging Asian Bond Market*, Washington, DC: World Bank, June.

World Bank (1995b), *China: The Emerging Capital Market. Volume II: Detailed Technical Analysis*, Washington, DC: World Bank, November.

5. Japanese financial markets in turmoil: liberalization and consequences

Kenjiro Hirayama

INTRODUCTION

Japanese financial markets are in turmoil. After failures of a few smallish credit unions and banks in 1995 and 1996, one life-insurance company (Nissan Life) was liquidated in May 1997, Hokkaido Takushoku Bank, one of the 'city' banks, went bust in October, and Yamaichi Securities, one of the 'big four' securities companies,[1] decided to discontinue its business in November. The reason for all this is the collapse of the bubble economy. There is a growing suspicion that there will be more failures of financial institutions in the years ahead.

We need to take stock of what happened in the Japanese financial markets. In this chapter, it will be argued that financial liberalization in the 1980s is one of the causes of the bubble, which is a view shared by many economists in Japan. One salient feature of Japanese finance was a predominant position held by banks. During the high economic growth of the 1950s and 1960s, the capital market was inaccessible to many firms. This was a deliberate policy decision on the part of the monetary authorities. The Bank of Japan, for example, used to rely on the so-called 'window guidance' which would instruct banks to restrain their lending at the time of monetary policy tightening.[2] Bank lending was more easily manipulated than flows of funds through the capital market.

The advent of financial liberalization in the 1980s started to change this structure. Massive flotation of government bonds after the first oil crisis gave rise to an active secondary market in these bonds in which interest rates were free from regulation. With the exchange rate floating freely since February 1973 and the current account balance in surplus, the authorities found less reason to restrict international capital flows. Large firms increasingly procured funds from the capital market, both domestic and overseas. Banks which lost the traditional clientele of these large firms turned to small businesses in real estate industry and fledgling non-banks. The funds thus provided were directed to property investment and drove up land prices. Requiring properties as collateral only aggravated this process, as will be shown below.

When the bubble collapsed in the early 1990s, it inflicted deep wounds on the financial sector. The practice of cross-shareholdings among *keiretsu* firms was also called into question, as the stock prices stagnated. However, the direction of change aimed at by the planned Japanese Big Bang is for greater 'securitization'. Hence the nature of corporate governance will also undergo substantial changes, if the traditional predominance of banks is eroded by securitization.

The next section is a brief overview of financial regulations in Japan up to the 1970s. The third section reviews the process of financial liberalization that began in the 1980s. The fourth section will describe the link between financial liberalization and the emergence of a bubble, and draw some lessons from this experience. Issues of the post-bubble malaise are addressed in the fifth section, and a final section presents conclusions.

FEATURES BEFORE FINANCIAL LIBERALIZATION

This section will briefly summarize characteristics of financial regulation up to the liberalization in the 1970s.[3] After the defeat in World War II, the Japanese government designed financial institutions and markets so as to promote swift reconstruction from the devastation of the war. They were characterized by three features: (a) interest rate regulation, (b) market segmentation, and (c) restrictions on international capital flows.

Interest rates on bank deposits were regulated by the Ministry of Finance and they were revised only when the official discount rate was altered. Interest rates were set below market-clearing level in order to make low-cost funds available to industrial development. Second, financial markets and institutions were segmented: banking was separated from securities business as in the USA,[4] long-term banking and short-term (commercial) banking were distinguished, financial institutions dedicated to small- and medium-sized businesses were set up, and life insurance and non-life insurance companies were also differentiated. The rationale behind this segmentation was to restrain 'excessive' competition among financial institutions. Competition was feared likely to make the financial system unstable. If a financial institution ran into difficulties, the Ministry of Finance would intervene and arrange a relief plan, such as finding a partner for merger. It utilized the authority not to approve a new financial product or service such that smaller institutions should not lag behind larger, more efficient ones.

Market segmentation coupled with interest rate regulation implied a comfortable life for financial institutions. Incentives to innovate were minimal, but the appetite for size was insatiable, because a larger volume of funds meant larger profits due to a profit margin guaranteed by the interest rate regulation.

Hence Japanese banks are huge by international standards, and yet the instruments they sell are largely US-made: for example, certificates of deposit, money market certificates and so on. Absence of competition led to little innovation in Japan's financial sector. This is in sharp contrast with its manufacturing sector, where competitive pressure prompted manufacturing firms to invest in research and development and to introduce ever more improved products.

In the third place, domestic financial regulation needed to be complemented by control of foreign exchange transactions. International capital outflows were strictly regulated, because foreign exchange was a scarce commodity. Regulation was also necessary from the viewpoint of maintaining the fixed exchange rate.

Table 5.1   Structure of corporate finance in selected countries

			Japan	USA	UK	Germany
Internal Funds		1965–69	49.7	68.2	74.5	69.3
		1970–74	42.8	55.2	34.5	61.1
		1975–79	49.5	67.2	79.5	64.8
		1980–84	59.0	73.3	80.4	75.2
		1985–89	51.7	82.9	63.6	78.7
		1990–94	70.2	80.8	58.0	57.9
External funds	Borrowing	1965–69	43.8	18.2	14.0	20.1
		1970–74	48.8	24.7	31.0	23.4
		1975–79	42.5	19.0	15.3	27.8
		1980–84	35.1	16.6	17.3	21.3
		1985–89	33.2	13.9	31.0	16.2
		1990–94	26.3	−1.3	5.5	27.0
	Securities	1965–69	5.2	13.6	11.5	4.1
		1970–74	5.6	19.2	4.5	3.5
		1975–79	7.7	13.8	5.2	1.4
		1980–84	6.1	10.1	2.3	3.6
		1985–89	10.8	1.6	7.4	5.1
		1990–94	7.5	9.8	25.5	8.6

Source: Bank of Japan, *Comparative Economic and Financial Statistics.*

Within the above institutional framework, noticeable features of financial structure can be pointed out. First and foremost, the predominance of banks stands out. Table 5.1 compares the structure of fund raising by non-financial firms in selected countries. The proportion of borrowing was especially high in Japan in the 1960s and 1970s. Over 40 per cent of the total funds raised by non-financial firms was bank borrowings. Even in Germany, where the banking sector also plays a substantial role, that proportion is much less than 30 per cent. A favourable tax treatment of bank deposits for households, known as *maruyu*, which exempted tax on interest income from deposit accounts for a small saver,[5] also helped banks to obtain necessary funding.

The second feature, which is closely related to the first point, is insignificance of capital markets. The use of equity shares and bonds was of small magnitude relative to borrowing (see Figure 5.1). Issuing bonds was costly owing to regulation which allowed banks to levy 'a large toll charge (in the form of collateral management fees) from anyone who used the bond market' (Ramseyer, 1994, p. 253). Furthermore, there was an explicit system of controlling the issuance of bonds by non-financial corporations: the *hachi-ko-kai*, a group of eight banks headed by the Industrial Bank of Japan, would decide who would issue bonds at what price (Ueda, 1994, pp. 98–9). The idea behind this was not to impede sales of bank debentures which long-term credit banks issue to raise funds.

To summarize, up to the early 1970s the banks dominated the financial markets. However, the situation started to change in the mid-1970s.

DEREGULATION IN THE 1980s

The Japanese economy was hit hard by the first oil crisis of 1973. Average growth rate of real GDP between 1955 and 1973 was 9.2 per cent per annum. However, real GDP registered a negative growth in 1974 for the first time in many years, and the era of 'high economic growth' came to an end.[6] This recession caused an enormous deficiency in government revenues, since the corporate profits tax declined sharply in 1975. Massive flotation of government bonds started in 1975 and it kept increasing in the next decade. Figure 5.2 shows a rapid pile-up of government debt from 1975 until the late 1980s. At the early stage of this period, the Ministry of Finance (MOF) sold government bonds to a syndicate of financial institutions at interest rates below the market-clearing level. However, when these bonds were traded in the secondary market, their prices would reflect market forces, resulting in a drop in price from their issue price. Having suffered from capital losses, private financial institutions demanded that the MOF auction new government bond issues. The MOF had to concede, because it needed cooperation from the financial institutions for issuing a large amount of government bonds each year. Emergence of an active secondary market for government bonds signified that there is now a market segment where interest rates are determined freely by market forces.

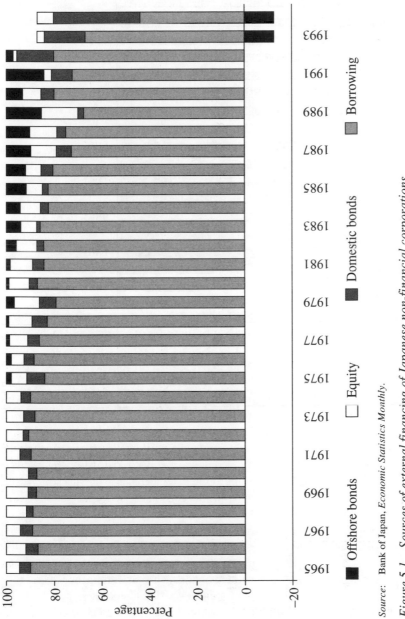

Source: Bank of Japan, *Economic Statistics Monthly.*

Figure 5.1 Sources of external financing of Japanese non-financial corporations

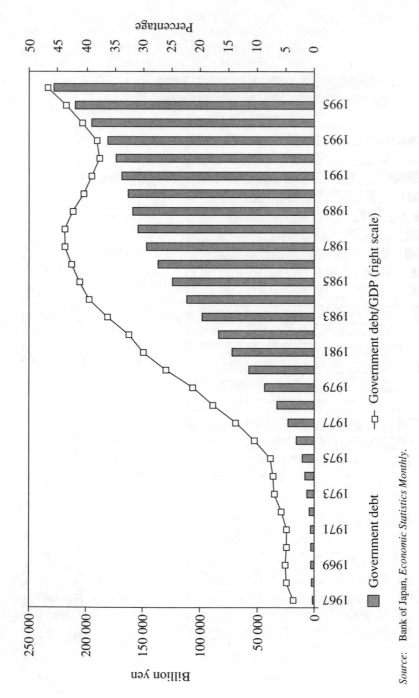

Source: Bank of Japan, *Economic Statistics Monthly.*

Figure 5.2 Outstanding government debt and ratio to GDP

Financial instruments that are derived from this market can offer market interest rates. Noticing this imminent danger, banks asked the MOF to permit issuing certificates of deposit (CDs) at market interest rates. This was the first deposit instrument without interest rate regulation. *Chuki kokusai* (medium-term government bond) funds were started in 1980 by the securities companies in return for banks' CDs. Other financial institutions also offered new products: trust banks marketed 'big' trusts and long-term credit banks introduced 'wide' accounts. These offered a higher yield than previously regulated accounts. Furthermore, banks launched large-denomination time deposits without interest regulation and money market certificates (MMCs) with market-related interest rates in 1985. The minimum denominations for these deposits/accounts were also gradually reduced.[7]

The emergence of a secondary market for government bonds ushered in the age of financial liberalization. There was another force that promoted the process of liberalization: *gaiatsu* (foreign pressure), from the US government in particular. When President Reagan visited Japan in November 1983, the Working Group on the Yen–Dollar Exchange Rate was organized and it produced a report in May 1984 which recommended measures to liberalize financial markets (Frankel, 1984). They included the following:

1. the liberalization of issues of Euroyen bonds,
2. establishment of new short-term financial markets (in banker's acceptances (BA), June 1985,[8] short-term bonds, November 1986, and commercial paper, November 1987),
3. further liberalization regarding the Euromarket (such as allowing foreign companies to lead-manage Eurobond issues in December 1986, and introducing rating systems for Euro-bonds in 1987),
4. establishment of an offshore market in Japan (December 1986), and
5. liberalization by the Ministry of Finance of restrictions on what share of their portfolios Japanese insurance companies and trust banks could hold in the form of foreign securities (in 1986 and 1987).[9]

The Japanese yen started floating in February 1973. The flexible exchange rate system discharged the Bank of Japan from obligations to defend a fixed exchange rate. There was much less need for restricting international capital flows. Volatile as cross-border capital flows are, the flexible rate would absorb and mitigate the disturbances. The new Foreign Exchange and Foreign Trade Control Law was implemented in December 1980. Capital flows between Japan and the rest of the world were in principle prohibited up to that point. Now they became generally free.[10] This allowed Japanese firms to raise funds abroad. Offshore bond issues by Japanese firms increased rapidly in the 1980s (Figure 5.3). They exceeded domestic issues as early as 1983 and stayed above them until 1986. In the peak year (1989), they were close to 12 trillion yen.

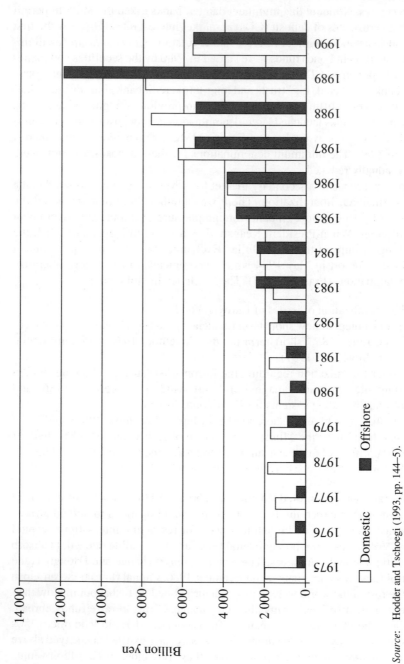

Source: Hodder and Tschoegi (1993, pp. 144–5).

Figure 5.3 Domestic and offshore bond issues by Japanese firms

In the meantime, capital markets were also gradually liberalized. Japanese corporate bonds were required by law to be collateralized since the 1930s. Firms had to pay high management fees and underwriting commissions for secured debt, as noted in the previous section. However, unsecured debt was first issued in 1979. In January 1983, the restrictions on convertible bonds were relaxed so that some 30 firms became eligible to issue such bonds without collateral. Restrictions for both convertibles and straight bonds were relaxed in stages until several hundred firms were eligible for unsecured issues by November 1988. These steps led to an upsurge in domestic bond issues in the late 1980s (Figure 5.3).

EMERGENCE OF A BUBBLE

The previous section outlined the process of financial liberalization in Japan in the 1980s. This section will describe how financial liberalization is related to the emergence of a financial bubble in the late 1980s. Figure 5.4 depicts the 40-year history of land and stock prices as well as the consumer price index. We cannot but observe a huge bulge in the late 1980s. The stock price index rose by 26.4 per cent a year on the average between 1984 and 1989. The comparable figure for land price (commercial land in the six largest cities) was 26.9 per cent a year for the period from 1984 to 1990. In the same six-year period, real GDP grew at an average rate of 4.6 per cent. Given the subsequent fall in these prices, we could safely conclude that Japan was flying high with 'excessive exuberance' during the late 1980s.

It is a popular view in Japan that an easy-money policy during the second half of the 1980s was to blame for the speculative bubble. In an attempt to avert a downturn that the rapid appreciation of the yen after the Plaza Accord of September 1985 might have caused, monetary policy was loosened in 1986. The official discount rate remained at 2.5 per cent, a historical low at the time,[11] from February 1987 to May 1989. The incidence of Black Monday which saw a 22.3 per cent decline in the New York Dow Jones Industrial Average on 19 October 1987 was unfortunate, in that the Bank of Japan could not change its policy stance towards tight money for fear of a stock market crash in Tokyo. Commercial land prices rose by 44 per cent between 1986 and 1987, and there was naturally a grave concern about this property price inflation. However, the consumer price index was declining in 1987 (−0.2 per cent from the previous year) as a result of cheaper imports and increased productivity in manufacturing industries, while real GDP was growing at 4.1 per cent. Macroeconomic conditions seemed to be flawless, except for rising stock and land prices.

If an asset price is determined by the present discounted value of future income stream, it is inversely related to the discount (interest) rate. The formula

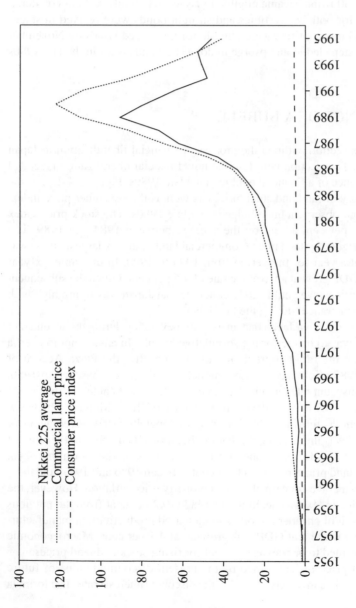

Sources: Bank of Japan, *Economic Statistics Monthly* (consumer and stock prices); Japan Real Estate Research Institute, *National Urban Land Price Index* (land price).

Figure 5.4 Land and stock prices (1955 = 1.0)

is: $P = D/(r - g)$, where P is the asset price, D annual income from the underlying asset, r the discount rate, and g the constant annual growth rate of D. When r drops from 6 per cent to 4 per cent with g supposed to be 3 per cent, the asset price will triple, representing a 200 per cent increase in price. However, this drop in the interest rate cannot be expected to be permanent. If the decline in r from 6 per cent to 4 per cent is expected to last for the first five years and if the interest rate is expected to go back to the original level of 6 per cent after five years, the rise in the discounted present value is only 9.4 per cent. Likewise, a temporary acceleration in D cannot produce a large increase in price. Low interest rates were certainly one factor in the bubble, but the expectation of ever-higher asset prices was probably the true underlying cause of this process, implying that it was indeed a speculative bubble.

There are some studies (Yoshikawa, 1996, ch. 6, Ito and Iwaisako, 1996) that focus on the role bank lending played in the formation of a bubble in the second half of the 1980s. They maintain that the increased lending by banks to real estate industry in the 1980s was one determinant of rapidly rising property prices. Figure 5.5 plots the share of bank lending to real estate industry and non-banks and the rate of change in commercial land prices. The real estate industry obtains funds from banks to embark on property developments. Non-banks are a group of financial institutions that procure funds mainly from banks and lend them for various purposes: consumer credit, mortgage loan, leasing and so on. According to Yoshino (1992), close to 40 per cent of their lending (as of 1991)[12] is to the real estate industry. As banks increased their lending to these two sectors in the second half of the 1980s, the commercial land price accelerated its rise (Figure 5.5). We notice a close link between the two.

Why did the Japanese banks increase their lending to the real estate industry and non-banks to such an extent in the 1980s? When we examine the sectoral shares of bank lending, we notice that a structural change was taking place. Figure 5.6 clearly shows that manufacturing and wholesale and retail sectors took the lion's share in bank lending at the beginning of the 1970s. But their share declined throughout the 1970s and the pace of decline accelerated in the 1980s. We notice that real estate industry and non-banks seem to have filled the vacuum left by the declining importance of these sectors. The picture becomes more evident when we compute sectoral shares on the basis of annual increases in lending (Figure 5.7). As the combined share of manufacturing and wholesale and retail declined in the 1980s, the share of real estate and non-banks increased concurrently.

Large firms in manufacturing and wholesale and retail industries were the ones that benefited from financial liberalization in the 1980s. Liberalization of the capital market led to increased issuance, both domestic and offshore, of bonds as Figure 5.3 shows. Access to the capital market is typically open to

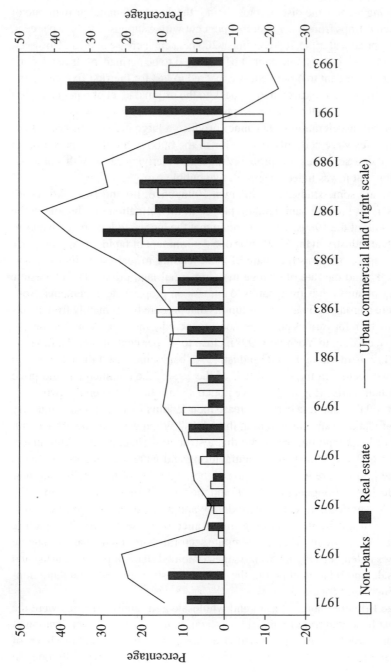

Sources: Bank of Japan, *Economic Statistics Monthly*; for land price, see Figure 5.4.

Figure 5.5 Share of bank lending and land price inflation

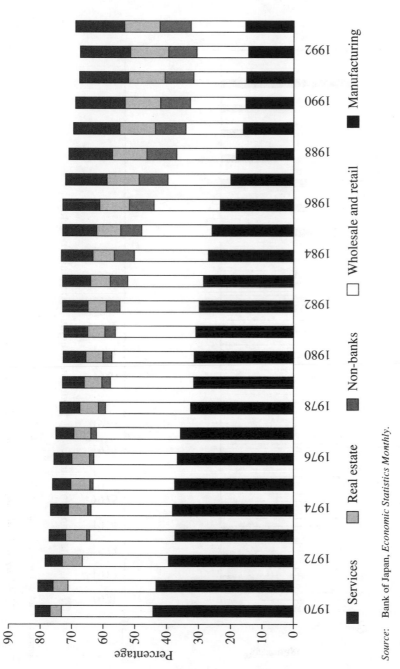

Source: Bank of Japan, *Economic Statistics Monthly.*

Figure 5.6 Sectoral share of bank loans (outstanding balances)

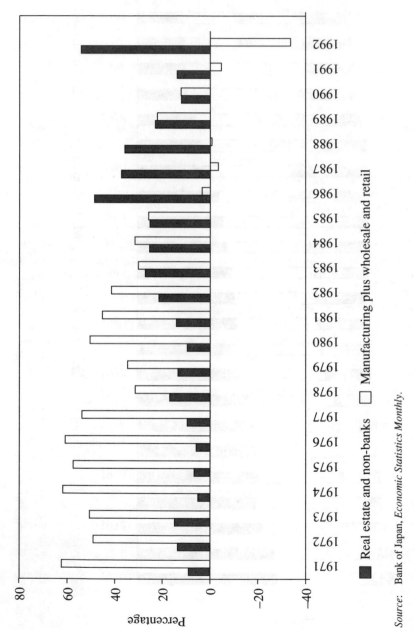

Source: Bank of Japan, *Economic Statistics Monthly.*

Figure 5.7 Share of bank lending to selected industries (annual flows)

large, well-known firms, which naturally decreased their traditional dependence on bank loans. Small or new firms in the real estate industry and non-banks did not have recourse to the capital market. They turned to banks for funds, and the banks found a convenient clientele in them.

Increased bank lending to the real estate industry was aggravated, in retrospect, by a traditional practice of requiring collateral. The experience of a severe financial panic in the early 1930s resulted in the practice of requiring collateral for either bank loans or corporate bonds. When the property prices were continuously rising, as in post-war Japan, this practice made good sense. If a borrower defaulted on a loan, the collateral could be disposed of at a higher price than the face value of the loan, since property prices were rising generally. Lending to the real estate industry was thus regarded as quite safe in the late 1980s, when property prices were rapidly rising. However, when these prices decline continuously, the collateralized property diminishes in value and the defaulted loans can never be recovered in full. This is the root cause of the 'bad debt' problem in Japan.

Another lesson we can draw from this experience is that monitoring of borrowers by the bank loan officers became lax because of rising property prices. Instead of examining carefully the prospect for success of a given investment project that a firm proposed to the bank, loan officers tended to pay more attention to the value of collateral. Criticism of lax monitoring by banks is put forward forcibly by Yamanaka (1997) and Kikuchi (1997), both of whom are former bank employees. Banks were also captive to seeking larger size, as noted previously. With a profit margin guaranteed by interest rate regulation, banks could automatically increase profits by seeking larger volume. Branch managers competed to expand bank assets (Yamanaka, 1997, pp. 136–7). This also tended to make the monitoring less strict.

Rising property prices had effects on stock prices as well. Japanese accounting rules do not call for evaluating assets at market prices. Large firms that had acquired properties early in the post-war period (or even before the war) came to enjoy sizable unrealized capital gains on these holdings. Investors in stocks directed their attention to these capital gains. A report by Wakasugi *et al.* (1988) claimed that high stock prices at the time can be explained by capital gains on property holdings by the Japanese firms. This view was shared by institutional investors and securities analysts. According to a questionnaire survey of these professionals, conducted in 1989 by Kon'ya and Tsutsui (1990), 62.6 per cent of them regarded Japanese stocks as appropriately priced, because firms' property holdings were of greater value. However, the same people (84.5 per cent of them) answered that Japanese land prices were too high![13]

COLLAPSE OF THE BUBBLE AND ITS CONSEQUENCES

We have delineated above the possible linkage between financial liberalization in the 1980s and the increased bank lending to real estate industry and non-banks, which led to rapidly rising property prices. The Bank of Japan raised its official discount rate in May, October and December 1989 and further in March and August 1990. In March 1990, the Ministry of Finance also issued a ministerial ordinance requiring banks to limit the growth of lending to firms in real estate and construction and non-banks within the average growth of total lending (*soryo kisei*).[14] The Nikkei 225 average peaked at 38 916 yen on 29 December 1989. A year later it dropped to 23 849 yen. At the time of writing (April 1998), it is hovering around 16 000 yen. Land prices peaked in 1990 and have plummeted even faster than stock prices (Figure 5.4). The total value of national wealth in the form of non-reproducible fixed capital, most of which is land, dropped from 2420 trillion yen (at current cost) in 1990 to 1840 trillion yen in 1995 – a loss of 580 trillion yen, which is greater than Japan's annual GDP (around 500 trillion).

Soon after the collapse of the bubble, people expected stock and land prices to come back up in a few years. Their expectation turned out to be completely unfounded. The fiasco of seven *jusen* (mortgage loan companies) which prompted the government to inject 685 billion yen of tax money in 1996 exemplifies this. But use of public money was strongly criticized by the news media.[15]

The Ministry of Finance has in the past not allowed any financial institution to go bust; it would arrange a rescue package, such as arranging a merger for the failing bank. However, moral suasion does not work any longer, because every other bank is also struggling to write off mounting bad debt. Two small credit unions based in Tokyo (Tokyo Kyowa and Anzen) failed in 1995, and another credit union in Osaka (Kizu) went bust and one of the largest second regional banks (Hyogo) also went under. In 1997, a life insurance company (Nissan Life) became insolvent and was liquidated. More recently, one of the city banks (Hokkaido Takushoku), with more than 6 trillion yen in deposits, failed and Yamaichi Securities, one of the 'big four' securities companies, decided to discontinue its operations. In many of these failures, the Ministry of Finance attempted to organize bail-out schemes, but to no avail. The so-called 'convoy system' (*goso sendan hoshiki*) that the Ministry of Finance would bail out a failing financial institution is not sustainable.

The collapse of the bubble has many far-reaching implications. Concerning the emergence of a bubble, the behaviour of banks should have been more closely monitored. The well-known Japanese main bank system was being eroded by financial liberalization. As large firms found new sources of funds in the capital market, Japanese banks turned to smaller businesses in real estate or non-banks. Screening and monitoring by banks was becoming degenerate owing to blind dependence on collateral. In short, the 'corporate governance' of banks was absent.

Stagnant stock prices have cast doubt on the efficacy of the Japanese cross-shareholdings, the centrepiece of *keiretsu* relationships. Unlike banks in Anglo-Saxon countries, Japanese banks are permitted to hold up to 5 per cent of a non-financial corporation's shares. The cross-shareholdings were mutually beneficial as long as stock prices kept going up. Now that they have stagnated for the past eight years, funds locked in shareholdings are yielding too little to be justified. The capital adequacy rules drawn up by the Bank for International Settlements allow Japanese banks to include 45 per cent of unrealized capital gains on stocks in capital. This allowance was a boon in the late 1980s, when stock prices were soaring, but became a nuisance in the 1990s. This is precisely the problem posed by holding risky assets. Stocks naturally fluctuate in market value and financial institutions that take in deposits should not rely on such assets excessively.

There are many studies which give positive appraisals of the Japanese main bank system. This line of research culminated in publication of the Aoki and Patrick (1994) volume. However, there are also studies that question the efficiency of the main bank system and the cross-shareholdings. For example, Lichtenberg and Pushner (1994) conclude that cross-shareholdings among *keiretsu* firms (including financial institutions) do not improve management efficiency. Hirota (1996) conveys a similar message.[16] The Japanese main bank system has served some important purposes, but its eclipse has already started and will continue for some time to come.

In November 1996, Prime Minister Hashimoto unveiled a plan for a Japanese Big Bang by the 21st century which would liberalize remaining regulations altogether. This would accelerate the trend for securitization which had begun with the advent of financial liberalization in the 1980s. Firms would increasingly procure funds from the capital market, but the problem remains with the household sector, which has traditionally preferred bank deposits. Table 5.2 is a breakdown of households' financial assets by category in selected countries. The sum of currency, demand deposits and time deposits for Japanese households exceeds 60 per cent, whereas in the USA or the UK the figure is around 20 per cent. It is also quite small, relative to Japan, in Germany (42.5 per cent) and France (36.0 per cent) where the structure of corporate finance and corporate governance is considered more similar to that of Japan than to that of Anglo-Saxon countries (Moerland, 1995).

The Japanese public's enthusiasm (or even obsession) for deposits underlies the huge size of Japanese banks. When large firms started obtaining funds in the capital market, it was not individuals but other financial institutions such as life insurance companies that bought those securities domestically and abroad. (1 wonder what would have happened to bank lending in the late 1980s, if the households had reduced their deposits with banks.) To put it differently, the Japanese public is not ready for securitization. The recent failure of Sanyo and Yamaichi Securities[17] only aggravates the situation. The financial institutions in Japan are faced with the challenge of how best to woo individuals into holding more securities.

Table 5.2   Financial assets of the household sector (%) in selected countries, 1996

	Currency & demand deposits	Time deposits	Insurance & pension funds	Securities	Total assets
Japan	11.3	52.0	25.1	11.7	1 209tn yen
US	2.0	17.1	30.3	36.2	22 768bn dollars
UK	23.4		51.4	19.6	2 177bn pounds
Germany	8.9	33.6	21.5	29.5	4 955bn DM
France	9.8	26.2	16.5	42.7	13 149bn FF

Source: Bank of Japan, *Comparative Economic and Financial Statistics*.

As Japanese finance becomes more securitized, the structure of financial markets and the form of corporate governance will undergo substantial changes. Since cross-shareholdings as well as the main bank system are gradually fading away, firms will have to pay closer attention to their own stock prices. Their profitability will be constantly checked by the stock market. Japanese corporate governance, hitherto delegated to the main bank,[18] has to transform itself into one that relies more on equity markets, as in Anglo-Saxon countries, if the 'securitization' of Japanese finance is to succeed.

CONCLUSIONS

We have outlined above the link between financial liberalization and the bubble economy in the second half of the 1980s in Japan. Increased bank lending to the real estate industry and non-banks was one crucial factor in forming the bubble. The change in the structure of bank lending was partly an outcome of financial liberalization. As large firms decreased their bank borrowing by procuring funds from the liberalized capital market, banks had to find a new clientele. In this sense, financial liberalization indirectly caused the bubble.

Banks' traditional reliance on collateral was also justifiable insofar as property prices were rising. In fact, they were too dependent on collateral and their screening of borrowers seems to have become lax. One of the most important functions of financial institutions is to transfer the public's savings into productive investments. Japanese banks failed to accomplish this function by betting on properties rather than on firms of tomorrow. Absence of corporate governance of Japanese banks (monitoring the monitor) is the acute problem which may be dealt with by the greater competition that the Big Bang is expected to introduce.

Sluggish stock prices have made cross-shareholdings among *keiretsu* firms less attractive in terms of financial returns. Some banks and firms have already started disposing of their long-term holdings of stocks. As the ownership structure of stocks becomes more widely dispersed, the corporate takeover activities may become more the norm than before. As securitization of Japanese financial markets progresses, the role of banks as a delegated monitor will also diminish and the Anglo-Saxon type of corporate governance needs to be implemented. However, the Japanese household sector still prefers bank deposits to stocks and bonds. How to lure this sector into holding more securities is a challenge for the future Japanese financial institutions.

NOTES

1. The other three are: Nomura, Daiwa and Nikko.
2. Private banks concurred, because they enjoyed a subsidy from heavy borrowing from the central bank at an official discount rate lower than the inter-bank money market rate (call rate). For example, the call rate was around 5.8 per cent, but the discount rate was 1.5–1.6 per cent in 1966.
3. For a more detailed description, see Suzuki (1987). Ito (1992, ch. 4) is a good introduction to Japanese financial markets and institutions.
4. The influence of the US federal securities laws is evident because Japan's Securities and Exchange Law was enacted when Japan was still occupied and governed by the Allied Forces, mainly staffed by US nationals (Kanda, 1993).
5. *Maruyu* was abolished in 1987.
6. Average annual growth in the subsequent 18-year period (1973–9 1) was 3.9 per cent. It grew even less between 1991 and 1994, averaging a paltry 0.5 per cent.
7. More detailed accounts of financial liberalization in Japan can be found, for example, in Hirota (1996) and Aoki and Patrick (1994).
8. The BA market vanished by November 1989, because it was subject to heavy stamp duty.
9. This list is based on Frankel (1993).
10. The right to require prior approval for some transactions was retained for emergencies.
11. The discount rate was reduced to 0.5 per cent in September 1995 and remains at this lowest level as of April 1998.
12. Statistics of their lending are not available, except for questionnaire surveys conducted by the MOF in 1990 and 199 1. See Yoshino (1992, p. 249).
13. The land price to rent ratio (equivalent to the price earnings ratio for stocks) for commercial land reached 500 in 199 1. It was 125 in 1979. See Nishimura (1995, p. 29).
14. This ordinance was terminated in January 1992.
15. Agricultural cooperatives were heavily involved in lending to *jusen*, and the members of the ruling Liberal Democratic Party are quite susceptible to the agricultural lobby. It is widely

believed in Japan that the government bailed out agricultural cooperatives by using public money.
16.	Furthermore, Okumura has been a staunch critic of cross-shareholdings among Japanese firms. See, for example, Okumura (1975).
17.	Unlike Yamaichi, which was jettisoned by the Ministry of Finance, Sanyo Securities appealed under the Stock Company Reorganization and Rehabilitation Act, which was approved by the court.
18.	Aoki (1997, ch. 12) even doubts whether there was such close monitoring by the main bank. In a series of interviews with corporate managers, he concludes that the main bank does not normally intervene in a firm's management except at times of financial distress.

REFERENCES

Aoki, Masahiko and Hugh Patrick (eds) (1994), *The Japanese Main Bank System: Its Relevance for Developing and Transforming Economies*, Oxford and New York: Oxford University Press.

Aoki, Shigeo (1997), *Kigyo Zaimu no Nichibei Hikaku (Comparison of Corporate Finance in the USA and Japan)*, Tokyo: Moriyama Shoten.

Frankel, Jeffrey A. (1984), 'The Yen/Dollar Agreement: Liberalizing Japanese Capital Markets', *Policy Analyses in International Economics*, 9, Washington, DC: Institute for International Economics.

Frankel, Jeffrey A. (1993), 'The Japanese Financial System and the Cost of Capital', in Shinji Takagi (ed.), *Japanese Capital Markets: New Developments in Regulations and Institutions*, Oxford: Blackwell.

Hirota, Shin'ichi (1996), 'Nihon no Kin'yu Shoken Shijo to Koporeto Gabanansu' (The Japanese Financial and Securities Markets and Corporate Governance), in T. Tachibanaki and Y. Tsutsui (eds), *Nihon no Shihon Shijo (The Japanese Capital Markets)*, Tokyo: Nihon Hyoronsha.

Hodder, James E. and Adrian E. Tschoegl (1993), 'Corporate Finance in Japan', in Shinji Takagi (ed.), *Japanese Capital Markets: New Developments in Regulations and Institutions*, Oxford: Blackwell.

Ito, Takatoshi (1992), *The Japanese Economy*, Cambridge, MA: MIT Press.

Ito, Takatoshi and Tokuo Iwaisako (1996), 'Explaining Asset Bubbles in Japan', *Bank of Japan Monetary and Economic Studies*, 14 (1), 143–93.

Kanda, Hideki (1993), 'The Regulatory Environment for Japanese Capital Markets', in Shinji Takagi (ed.), *Japanese Capital Markets: New Developments in Regulations and Institutions*, Oxford: Blackwell.

Kikuchi, Hidehiro (1997), *Ginko Biggu Ban (Big Bang for Banks)*, Tokyo: Toyo Keizai Shimposha.

Kon'ya, Fumiko and Yoshiro Tsutsui (1990), 'Japanese and U.S. Investors' Market Forecasts and Their Investing Behavior: Results from Questionnaire Surveys', mimeo, Osaka University.

Lichtenberg, Frank R. and George M. Pushner (1994), 'Ownership Structure and Corporate Performance in Japan', *Japan and the World Economy*, 6 (October), 239–64.

Moerland, Pieter W. (1995), 'Alternative Disciplinary Mechanism in Different Corporate Systems,' *Journal of Economic Behavior and Organization*, 26 (January), 17–34.

Nishimura, Kiyohiko (1995), *Nihon no Chika no Kimari-kata (Determinants of Land Prices in Japan)*, Tokyo: Chikuma Shobo.

Okumura, Hiroshi (1975), *Hojin Shihon Shugi no Kozo (The Structure of Corporate Capitalism)*, Tokyo: Nihon Hyoronsha.

Ramseyer, J. Mark (1994), 'Explicit Reasons for Implicit Contracts: The Legal Logic to the Japanese Main Bank System', in M. Aoki and H. Patrick (eds), *The Japanese Main Bank System*.

Suzuki, Yoshio (1987), *The Japanese Financial System*, Oxford: Clarendon Press.

Ueda, Kazuo (1994), 'Institutional and Regulatory Frameworks for the Main Bank System', in M. Aoki and H. Patrick (eds), *The Japanese Main Bank System*.

Wakasugi, Takaaki, Fumiko Kon'ya, Junko Maru, Yasuhiro Yonezawa *et al.* (1988), *Nihon no Kabuka Suijun Kenkyu Gurupu Hokokusho (Report of the Research Group on Japanese Stock Price Level)*, Tokyo: Nihon Shoken Keizai Kenkyusho.

Yamanaka, Hiroshi (1997), *Mein Banku no Shinsa Kino (Monitoring Functions of the Main Bank)*, Tokyo: Zeimu Keiri Kyokai.

Yoshikawa, Hiroshi (1996), *Kin'yu Seisaku to Nihon Keizai (Monetary Policy and the Japanese Economy)*, Tokyo: Nihon Keizai Shimbunsha.

Yoshino, Naoyuki (1992), 'Non Banku no Kino to Kin'yu Seisaku' (Functions of Non-banks and Monetary Policy), in Akiyoshi Horiuchi and Naoyuki Yoshino (eds), *Gendai Nihon no Kin'yu, Bunseki (Financial Analyses of Contemporary Japan)*, Tokyo: The University of Tokyo Press.

6. Bank–firm relationships and corporate governance in Japan: evidence for the 1960s to the 1990s

Shin'ichi Hirota

INTRODUCTION

This chapter explores how bank–firm relationships work as a corporate governance mechanism in Japan. It is well known that the Japanese financial system is bank-oriented and it is considered that banks have played an important role in corporate finance and governance. In particular, in recent years, increasing attention has focused on the corporate governance roles of banks.

In Japan, banks have relationships with their client firms in two ways; lending and shareholding. Through these relations, banks are said to monitor and discipline the firm and to realize efficient operations of the firm. Also it should be pointed out that each firm has a close relationship with a particular bank, called the main bank. The main bank, usually the largest lender and a major shareholder in the firm, is usually considered to play the central role in the corporate governance system in Japan (Aoki and Patrick, 1994; Sheard, 1994).

This chapter investigates empirically how and to what extent bank–firm relationships (or main bank relationships) affect corporate performance in Japan, using data from large manufacturing firms for the high growth era of the 1960s, the stable growth era of the 1980s, and the low growth era of the 1990s. Also, it distinguishes the effect of bank lending from that of bank shareholding and sees whether there is any difference between them.

The following results on the role of banks in Japanese corporate governance were obtained. First, the close lending ties between the bank (or the main bank) and the firm increase the productive efficiency of the firm. On the other hand, shareholding relations between them do not play such a role; rather, the bank shareholding may lower corporate productivity. These results suggest that bank lending has been the only governance mechanism to monitor and discipline the firm in Japanese financial markets for the past 30 years. However, as will be shown later, the firm's dependence on the bank (or main bank) borrowing declined sharply during the financial liberalization and globalization of Japanese capital markets in the 1980s. Hence governance through bank lending must have played a lesser role for recent periods. Therefore, in the 1990s, it is possible that there are few mechanisms for corporate governance in Japanese financial markets and that Japanese firms may tend to lose corporate efficiency.

The remainder of the chapter is organized as follows. The next section describes bank–firm relationships in Japan for the past 30 years. The third section investigates the effects of these relationships on corporate productivity, and the fourth section discusses the implications of the results for Japanese corporate governance.

BANK–FIRM RELATIONSHIPS FROM THE 1960s TO THE 1990s

Before analysing the effects of bank–firm relations on corporate efficiency, a brief overview indicates how these relationships have changed over the past 30 years.

Figure 6.1 plots the bank borrowing ratio (*BLOAN*; borrowings /(borrowings + bonds)) of Japanese large companies for the past 30 years. The sample firms are the companies listed in the *Kigyo Keiei no Bunseki*, published by Mitsubishi Research Institute. This book is published once a year and is famous for including financial statements of major (about 500) Japanese companies (both in manufacturing and non-manufacturing sectors). Figures are sample means of *BLOAN*. We observe that firms had depended mostly on bank borrowing in their finance until 1983. The bank borrowing ratio over this period had been over 85 per cent.

However, in the 1980s, dependence on bank loans dropped drastically. This was due to the financial liberalization and globalization of Japanese capital markets which provided firms with several methods of finance, such as public bonds. In addition, the bubble economy in the late 1980s made firms issue equity-related bonds (convertible bonds and bonds with warrant) intensively. This accelerated the trend towards less dependence of the firm on bank borrowings.

Figure 6.2 indicates how much the firm borrows from its main bank. Each firm's main bank is identified through *Kaisha-shikiho (Japan Company Handbook)* published by Toyokeizai-shinposha. *Kaisha-shikiho* reports the names of five or six transaction banks for each firm, depending on the results of an interview with the firm. Among them, the first listed bank is generally regarded among practitioners as the firm's main bank. This chapter follows this definition in specifying each firm's main bank. The data about relation-

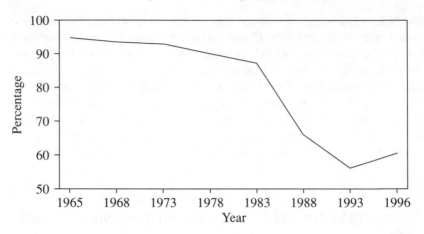

Figure 6.1   Bank borrowing ratio

ships between a firm and its main bank are taken from *Kigyo Keiretsu Soran*, published by Toyokeizai-shinposha.

The main bank borrowing ratio (*MLOAN*; borrowings from the main bank/(total borrowings and bonds)) for the sample firms have been calculated and their means have been taken. We observe that the mean of *MLOAN* declines from the 1960s to the 1970s and decreases more sharply in the 1980s as the bank borrowings ratio (*BLOAN*) does in Figure 6.1. Both Figure 6.1 and 6.2 show that (a) Japanese firms had depended heavily on bank borrowings in their financing in the 1960s and the 1970s, and (b) after the 1980s, they drastically

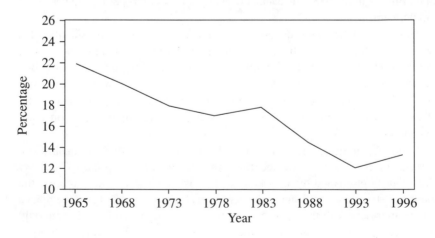

Figure 6.2   Main bank borrowing ratio

reduced borrowings from banks since they had other methods of finance provided by the financial liberalization and globalization of the capital markets.

Figure 6.3 shows the shareholdings of the main bank for a period of 30 years. *MSTOCK* is the main bank stockholding ratio (shareholdings by the main bank/total stock outstanding of the firm), and its sample means are plotted. Looking at the figures, we find that in the 1960s the main bank stockholding is relatively low (3–4 per cent). In the 1970s, it rises to about 5 per cent, and in the 1980s it declines again to about 4 per cent. The fall in the main bank shareholdings in the 1980s reflects the reform of the antitrust act which restricted shareholding by banks to less than 5 per cent of total outstanding stock of the firm. We observe, however, that the degree of decline in *MSTOCK* in the 1980s is not as large as that in *BLOAN* or *MLOAN*. Therefore, we judge that bank–firm relations through shareholdings have not changed much over the last 20 years, and banks and the firm still have close ties in shareholdings in the 1990s.

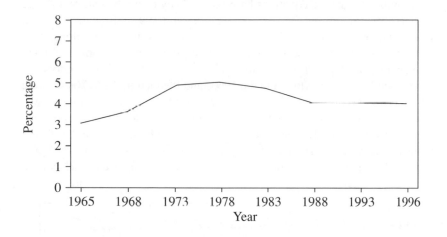

Figure 6.3   Main bank stockholding ratio

BANK–FIRM RELATIONSHIPS AND CORPORATE PERFORMANCE: AN EMPIRICAL ANALYSIS

Basic Strategy and the Data

This section explores how bank–firm relationships affect the corporate efficiency of Japanese firms. To examine this issue, we use a Cobb–Douglas production function, that is,

$$Y = A\, K^{\alpha}\, L^{\beta}, \tag{6.1}$$

where Y denotes output, A is a parameter representing productivity, and K and L are capital stock and employment, respectively (α and β are parameters). In this framework, we assume that bank–firm relationships affect the productivity parameter A and suppose that

$$A = \exp\,(a_0 + a_1 X_1 + a_2 X_2 + \ldots\ldots\ldots\ldots) \tag{6.2}$$

where X_1, X_2, ... are variables representing bank–firm relations and other control variables. Taking logarithms of (6.1), we get:

$$\ln Y = a_0 + a_1 X_1 + a_2 X_2 + \ldots\ldots\ldots + \alpha \ln K + \beta \ln L \tag{6.3}$$

We will estimate the equations based on (6.3) by using the data from large Japanese manufacturing firms for 1968, 1983 and 1993 (all years are fiscal years). The reason for choosing these three years is that each belongs to a different growth era in the Japanese economy. Figure 6.4 presents real GDP growth rate in Japan for a period of 30 years. The Japanese economy experienced a high growth era in the 1960s and it ended in the 1970s with the first and second oil shocks. The early 1980s are known as the stable growth era, when GDP growth was 3–5 per cent. After the bubble economy of the late 1980s, however, the Japanese economy has had a hard time: as the figure indicates, growth rate declined sharply in the 1990s. It would be interesting to examine how bank–firm relations affect corporate performance in each era and

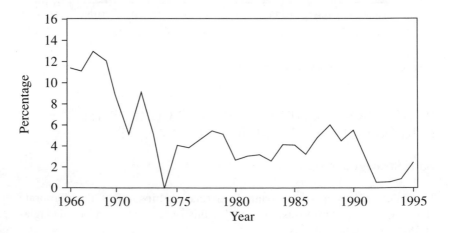

Figure 6.4   GDP growth in Japan, 1966–95

see whether there are any differences in the bank effects among these periods. For that reason, 1968 is taken as the year in the high growth era of the 1960s, 1983 as that in the stable growth era of the 1980s, and 1993 as that in the post-bubble low growth era.

In each year, the manufacturing companies listed in the *Kigyo Keiei no Bunseki* were chosen. Sample firms were then restricted by two conditions. First, any firms for which all the data necessary for our study were not available were dropped. Secondly, if a firm had changed the month in which its accounting year ended during a sample year or the following two years, it was omitted from the sample. This procedure is needed for the estimation of the model with lagged financial variables which will be explained later. For example, if one firm changed the ending month from September to March in fiscal 1984, this firm was dropped from the sample for 1983. As a result, the numbers of sample firms are 333 for 1968, 357 for 1983 and 409 for 1993. For these sample firms, most of the data were extracted from *Kigyo Keiei no Bunseki* and *Kaigin Kigyo Zaimu Data Bank (The JDB Corporate Finance Data Bank)*.

Estimation Procedure

As a beginning, we estimate the following equation:

$$\ln Y = a_0 + a_1 BLOAN + a_2 BSTOCK + a_3 DEBT$$
$$+ \alpha \ln K + \beta \ln L + \text{industrial dummies} + u, \qquad (6.4)$$

where Y is output, *BLOAN* is the bank borrowings ratio (borrowings/ (borrowings + bonds)), BSTOCK is the bank stockholding ratio (shareholdings by banks and other financial institutions/total stock outstanding of the firm), *DEBT* is debt ratio (total liabilities/total assets), K is the capital stock, L is labour, and u is error term.

Following Jones and Kato (1995), output is measured by value added deflated by the wholesale price index (WPI) for manufacturing products. The capital stock is the (tangible plus intangible) fixed assets deflated by the WPI for capital goods. Labour is measured by the number of workers of the firm. For both capital and labour, we use the average of beginning and ending values of the year.

BLOAN and *BSTOCK* are variables for bank–firm relationships. *BLOAN* represents the strength of lender–borrower relations between the firm and the banks, whereas *BSTOCK* represents shareholding relations between them. If banks play some roles in monitoring and disciplining the firm through these relationships, these variables have positive effects on the firm's output (a_1 and a_2 are positive). In contrast, if bank–firm relations generate slack in managing the firm, their effects should be negative (a_1 and a_2 are negative).

Debt ratio (*DEBT*) is the control variable to capture the effect of the firm's debt on corporate efficiency. Jensen (1986) suggests debt reduces free cash flow in the firm and keeps the management from investing in unprofitable projects. In addition, high debt payments provide an incentive for managers and workers to raise their effort in order to avoid bankruptcy. From these arguments, *DEBT* is predicted to have positive effects on productivity (a_3 is positive). For financial variables, *BLOAN*, *BSTOCK* and *DEBT*, we use the beginning values of the sample year. Industrial dummies in the equation are defined by three-digit industry codes. These dummies remove industrial specific effects on productivity.

As was explained in the first section of this chapter, it is said that the main bank plays the most important role in monitoring and disciplining the firm among all the banks. Therefore, in addition to the *bank effect*, it is interesting to see the *main bank effect*, that is, how the main bank affects corporate efficiency. Hence two variables are used for the relationships between the firm and its main bank: *MLOAN* (borrowings from the main bank/(total borrowings and bonds)) and *MSTOCK* (shareholdings by the main bank/total stock outstanding of the firm) as independent variables instead of *BLOAN* and *BSTOCK*. The estimation equation to examine the main bank effect is

$$\ln Y = b_0 + b_1 MLOAN + b_2 MSTOCK + b_3 DEBT$$
$$+ \alpha \ln K + \beta \ln L + \text{industrial dummies} + u \qquad (6.5)$$

Means and standard deviations of variables in (6.4) and (6.5) are summarized in Table 6.1.

In estimating (6.4) and (6.5), we should notice that the capital stock (*K*) and labour (*L*) may be endogenous variables. *DEBT* is also known as an endogenous variable as several capital structure studies suggest that the firm determines debt ratio, based on real factors such as assets type, profitability and firm size. To cope with possible endogeneity of these variables, we take an instrumental variables approach. In addition to predetermined variables included in equations (6.4) and (6.5), we use as instruments the one-year lags of the following variables: the tangible assets ratio (tangible assets/total assets), advertising and R&D ratio (advertising plus R&D expenditures/sales), profit rate (operating income plus depreciation/total assets), log of real sales and wage rate (total labour cost/the number of workers) deflated by WPI.

Regression Results

We perform a cross-sectional regression of equations (6.4) and (6.5) for each sample year (1968, 1983, 1993) respectively by the instrumental variables

Table 6.1   Summary statistics: means (standard deviations)

	1968	1983	1993
BLOAN	0.934	0.863	0.531
	(0.109)	(0.215)	(0.348)
BSTOCK		0.353	0.423
		(0.147)	(0.150)
MLOAN	0.204	0.176	0.120
	(0.159)	(0.128)	(0.120)
MSTOCK	0.039	0.050	0.042
	(0.028)	(0.022)	(0.012)
DEBT	0.727	0.741	0.625
	(0.107)	(0.158)	(0.166)
Y	29 917	47 323	64 610
	(47 720)	(89 714)	(109 590)
K	25 356	54 310	91 546
	(45 447)	(136 928)	(160 204)
L	5 979	5 385	5 055
	(9 774)	(9 664)	(8 933)

Note: The table presents sample means and standard deviations of dependent and explanatory variables in regression equations (6.4) and (6.5). The figures are sample means, and standard deviations are in parentheses. The definition for each variable is as follows: BLOAN is the bank borrowings ratio, BSTOCK the bank stockholding ratio, MLOAN the main bank borrowings ratio, MSTOCK, the main bank stockholding ratio, DEBT debt ratio; Y is value added in millions of 1980 yen, K is the fixed assets in millions of 1980 yen, L is the number of workers. We use the beginning values of the sample year for BLOAN, BSTOCK, MLOAN, MSTOCK, and DEBT, and the average of beginning and ending values of the year for K and L.

method. For 1968, JDB data bank does not provide the bank shareholdings ratio (BSTOCK), so BSTOCK was omitted from the regression equation (6.4).

Table 6.2 presents the estimation results of equation (6.4). The results of each year's regression are reported in each column (to save space, the coefficients of industrial dummies and constant terms are not reported). Looking at the table, we find that BLOAN has positive coefficients that are significant at at least the 5 per cent level in all regressions (1968, 1983 and 1993). This indicates that, the more the firm depends on bank borrowings, the higher its productivity will be. This is consistent with the notion that bank lending plays an important role in monitoring and disciplining the firm. In contrast, BSTOCK shows negative signs and in the 1983 regression this is significant. This shows that shareholding by banks does not raise corporate efficiency; rather, it may lower the productivity level of the firm. This result contrasts with that of Lichtenberg and Pushner (1994) which suggests that equity ownership by financial institutions increases corporate productivity.

Table 6.2 Bank–firm relationships and corporate productivity

	1968	1983	1993	1983 and 1993	All sample
BLOAN	0.41**	0.18*	0.58**	0.47**	0.53**
	(2.78)	(2.08)	(3.22)	(4.95)	(5.96)
BSTOCK	–	0.31*	–0.26	–0.42**	
		(–2.29)	(–1.24)	(–2.96)	
DEBT	–2.42*	–1.92**	–2.97	–2.88**	–2.94**
	(–8.32)	(–6.90)	(–4.23)	(–7.81)	(–9.09)
ln$K$	0.26**	0.26**	0.40**	0.27**	0.18**
	(3.89)	(3.88)	(3.57)	(3.85)	(2.86)
ln$L$	0.88**	0.78**	0.66**	0.80**	0.90**
	(10.47)	(9.88)	(5.26)	(9.91)	(12.75)
YEAR83					0.53**
					(8.84)
YEAR93				0.07	0.66**
				(1.07)	(6.11)
Number of observations	333	357	409	766	1099
Adj. R^2	0.947	0.960	0.898	0.912	0.908

Note: The table reports regression results for equation (6.4): ln$Y = a_0 + a_1BLOAN + a_2BSTOCK$ $+ a_3DEBT + \alpha$ln$K + \beta$ln$L$ + industrial dummies + u, where Y is output, $BLOAN$ is the bank borrowings ratio, $BSTOCK$ is the bank stockholding ratio, $DEBT$ is debt ratio, K is the capital stock, L is labour and u is error term. YEAR83 and YEAR93 are year dummies. Cross-sectional regression results for each year are reported in the columns, 1968, 1983 and 1993. Pooling regression results are presented in the columns, 1983 and 1993 and All sample. Figures in parentheses are t values calculated using White's (1980) heteroscedastic-consistent standard errors. ** and * indicate that the coefficient is significant at the 1,5 per cent levels, respectively. The estimated results for an intercept and industrial dummies are not reported to save space. The regression is estimated using the instrumental variables method, assuming that $DEBT$, ln$K$, and ln$L$ are endogenous variables.

DEBT has significant negative coefficients in all regressions. This result does not support the hypothesis presented by Jensen (1986) that leverage increases corporate efficiency. We also find that the sums of coefficients of ln$K$ and ln$L$ ($\alpha + \beta$) are over one in all regressions, suggesting increasing returns to scale technology over our sample periods.

Pooling regressions for 1983 and 1993 (which include *BSTOCK*) and All sample of the above three years (which does not include *BSTOCK* because its data cannot be obtained for 1968, as was explained above) we also estimated. Year dummies (YEAR83 YEAR93) are also added to capture the unobserved effects of macroeconomic shocks. Regression results of the pooling sample are presented in the columns of 1983 and 1993 and All sample. We observe that the results do not change those of cross-sectional regressions; the bank lending ratio (*BLOAN*) has positive effects on productivity, whereas the bank share-holding ratio (*BSTOCK*) has negative effects.

Table 6.3 documents how the main bank lending and shareholding ratios affect corporate performance. In each cross-sectional regression (1968, 1983 and 1993) and the pooling regression (All sample), we see that the main bank borrowings ratio (*MLOAN*) shows significant positive signs. On the other hand, the main bank stockholding ratio (*MSTOCK*) does not have any significant coefficients. That is, the main bank lendings increase corporate productivity while the main bank stockholding does not. These observations for the main bank effect are similar to those for the bank effect we saw in Table 6.2, in the sense that the bank–firm relationships raise corporate efficiency only through lender–borrower relations, not through shareholdings.

The possibility that there are one or two-year lags in the productivity effects of bank–firm relations was also considered. Regressions were performed in which $Y(+1), K(+1), L(+1)$ or $Y(+2), K(+2), L(+2)$ are used instead of Y, K, L in (6.4) and (6.5). These regressions do not change the basic results obtained above.

From these results, it is conjectured that bank lending is very different from bank shareholding in corporate governance in Japan. The former plays an important role in corporate governance; lending banks monitor the firm and discipline the management and this behaviour leads to high efficiency of the firm. In contrast, the latter has no role in governance; the bank as a shareholder does not seem to monitor the firm or to contribute in raising corporate performance. Rather, it is possible that bank shareholdings may lower the efficiency of the firm.

Finally, we examine the sizes of the productivity effects of the bank lending and the main bank lending. We calculate how much productivity A (or output Y) rises when the bank (or main bank) borrowing ratio increases by one standard deviation in each year. This can be computed as [exp $\{a1(\text{or } b1) \times$ one standard deviation of bank (or main bank) borrowing ratio$\} - 1] \times 100$. Table 6.4 represents the results. In 1968 and 1983, we observe that an increase in the bank borrowing ratio by one standard deviation leads to a rise in productivity by 4.57 per cent and 4.02 per cent, respectively. The productivity effects of an increase in the main bank borrowing ratio are 3.94 per cent and 3.58 per cent. These figures are almost as large as the productivity effects of employee stock-ownership plans which Jones and Kato (1995) estimated. On the other hand, in 1993, we see that bank (or main bank) relations have prominently large effects on productivity (22.33 per cent and 15.80 per cent). In other words, in the 1990s, there may have been considerable differences in productivity between firms with close bank ties and those without them. This indicates that bank's (or main bank's) monitoring and disciplinary roles were more efficient in the 1990s than

Table 6.3   *Main bank relationships and corporate productivity*

	1968	1983	1993	All sample
MLOAN	0.24*	0.27*	1.23**	0.59**
	(1.87)	(2.28)	(2.56)	(4.17)
MSTOCK	0.33	0.53	–0.001	0.61
	(0.52)	(0.75)	(–0.001)	(1.01)
DEBT	–2.41	–1.94**	–2.78*	–2.84**
	(–8.59)	(–6.87)	(–4.16)	(–9.04)
lnK	0.26**	0.27**	0.41**	0.19**
	(4.06)	(3.97)	(3.68)	(2.98)
lnL	0.87**	0.75**	0.63**	0.87**
	(11.08)	(9.45)	(5.21)	(11.84)
YEAR83				0.48**
				(8.03)
YEAR93				0.47*
				(4.20)
Number of observations	333	357	409	1099
Adj. R^2	0.947	0.959	0.898	0.908

Note: The table reports regression results for equation (6.5): $\ln Y = b_0 + b_1 MLOAN + b_2 MSTOCK + b_3 DEBT + \alpha \ln K + \beta \ln L$ + industrial dummies + u, where Y is output, $MLOAN$ is the main bank borrowings ratio, $MSTOCK$ is the main bank stockholding ratio, $DEBT$ is debt ratio, K is the capital stock, L is labour and u is error term. YEAR83 and YEAR93 are year dummies. Cross-sectional regression results for each year are reported in the columns, 1968, 1983 and 1993. Pooling regression results are presented in the All sample column. Figures in parentheses are t values calculated using White's (1980) heteroscedastic-consistent standard errors. ** and * indicate that the coefficient is significant at the 1,5 per cent level, respectively. The estimated results for an intercept and industrial dummies are not reported to save space. The regression is estimated using the instrumental variables method, assuming that $DEBT$, $\ln K$ and $\ln L$ are endogenous variables.

Table 6.4   *Productivity effects (per cent) of bank–firm relationships*

	1968	1983	1993
Productivity effect of the bank	4.57	4.02	22.23
Productivity effect of the main bank	3.94	3.58	15.80

Note: The table shows the sizes of the productivity effects of bank lending (or main bank lending). I calculate how much productivity A rises when the bank (or main bank) borrowing ratio increases by one standard deviation in each year. The estimated effect is computed as $[\exp \{a_1 (\text{or } b_1) \times$ one standard deviation of the bank (or main bank) borrowing ratio$\} - 1] \times 100$.

in the period before the 1980s. This may imply that the low growth economy of the 1990s has increased the necessity of corporate governance and assigned bank monitoring (through lending) a more important role than before, in an environment in which there are no other corporate governance mechanisms in Japanese financial markets.

IMPLICATIONS FOR CORPORATE GOVERNANCE

This chapter investigates how and to what extent bank–firm relationships affect corporate performance in Japan for the 1960s to the 1990s. We find two main results: (a) bank (or main bank) lending has positive effects on corporate productivity and (b) bank (or main bank) shareholding does not have such effects; rather it may decrease corporate productivity. Considering that take-over bids (TOB) have hardly been seen in Japan, these results suggest that bank lending is the only corporate governance mechanism which has worked in Japanese financial markets for the past 30 years.

As we saw in Figures 6.1 and 6.2, in the 1960s and 1970s, the firm relied heavily on bank borrowing for corporate finance. Therefore we may consider that bank monitoring and governance are effective in disciplining the firm's management. After the late 1980s, however, we observed that the firm's dependence on bank (or main bank) borrowings declined sharply. Hence we conclude predict that governance through bank lending plays a lesser role for the more recent periods than in those before.

What mechanism, then, disciplines the firm in Japanese financial markets? Although bank shareholding has not decreased recently (see Figure 6.3), the results of this chapter have shown that it is not expected to play any governance roles. Also the TOB mechanism does not work well owing to interlocking share-holdings in the capital market. From these facts, it may be said that there have been few mechanisms for corporate governance in Japanese financial markets since the late 1980s. If this is so, it is possible that the corporate efficiency of Japanese firms tends to diminish, insofar as governance mechanisms other than financial markets (such as employee stock-ownership plans – see Jones and Kato, 1995) do not work fully to discipline the management.

ACKNOWLEDGMENTS

I would like to thank the conference participants for valuable comments and discussions. This research is supported by a grant from Zengin Foundation for Studies on Economics and Finance.

REFERENCES

Aoki, M. and H. Patrick (eds) (1994), *The Japanese Main Bank System: Its Relevance for Developing and Transforming Economies*, Oxford: Oxford University Press.

Jensen, M.C. (1986), 'Agency Costs of Free Cash Flow, Corporate Finance and Takeovers', *American Economic Review*, 76, 323–9.

Jones, D.C. and T. Kato (1995), 'The Productivity Effects of Employee Stock-Ownership Plans and Bonuses: Evidence from Japanese Panel Data', *American Economic Review*, 85, 391–414.

Lichtenberg, F.R. and G.M. Pushner (1994), 'Ownership Structure and Corporate Performance in Japan', *Japan and the World Economy*, 6 October, 239–61.

Sheard, P. (1994), 'Main banks and the governance of financial distress', in M. Aoki and H. Patrick (eds), *The Japanese Main Bank System: Its Relevance for Developing and Transforming Economies*, Oxford: Oxford University Press, pp. 188–230.

White, H. (1980), 'Heteroskedasticity-consistent Covariance Matrix Estimator and a Direct Test for Heteroskedasticity', *Econometrica*, 48, 817–38.

7. The performance of Taiwan's financial sector

Jiann-Chyuan Wang

INTRODUCTION

Taiwan has performed relatively well over the past 40 years, in terms of economic development and income distribution, when compared with other developing countries. The well-functioning financial sector and related policies formulated by the government are considered to be amongst the influential factors behind such successful development. In particular, Taiwan's recent financial reform has not only prepared it for accession to the World Trade Organization (WTO), but has also give Taiwan increased momentum for further economic development. As a consequence, the interactions between the financial sector and growth in the real economy deserve attention.

In addition, in recent months the financial turmoil which has affected Asian currencies has swept across the region. Faced with such a financial crisis, how does Taiwan's monetary authority – the Central Bank of China (CBC) – react to the impact of such a crisis on its financial sector as well as real sector? This is also a focal point of the chapter.

The purpose of this chapter, then, is to outline the recent reforms that have taken place in Taiwan's financial sector and analyse the contribution of the financial sector to the growth of the real economy.

The chapter is divided into five sections. The next section briefly reviews the recent development of Taiwan's financial sector, and the third section analyses the interaction between Taiwan's financial sector and the growth of the real economy. The fourth section describes how financial bubbles that have spread all over Asia have affected Taiwan, and what their resulting impacts have been. The last section contains the concluding remarks.

THE RECENT REFORMS IN TAIWAN'S FINANCIAL SECTOR

As the Taiwan economy has kept on going, recording an average 8.4 per cent economic growth rate over the past ten years, the need for financial services has significantly increased. In response to these needs, the government has implemented a policy of financial liberalization and internationalization since the early 1980s. Recent financial reforms in Taiwan may be summarized as follows.

Interest Rate Deregulation

Prior to 1980, bank interest rates in Taiwan had been controlled for a long time. However, beginning in 1980, the central bank adopted a series of policy measures to gradually remove controls over interest rates. For instance, interest rates in the cases of bank debentures and negotiable certificates of deposit were allowed to fluctuate freely in 1980. From 1985 onwards, banks were allowed to set their own interest rates on loans within ceiling and floor limits prescribed by the CBC. In July 1989, the Banking Law was revised and interest rate controls were completely eliminated.

The Relaxation of Foreign Exchange Control

Between 1969 and 1978, the New Taiwan (NT) dollar exchange rate was pegged to the US dollar. However, in February 1979, following the establishment of the foreign exchange market, the exchange rate (that is, the 'central rate') was determined by the market forces of supply and demand based on the previous day's transactions. Finally, in April 1989, the 'central rate' was abolished, and a flexible exchange rate system has been in operation ever since. At the same time, the restrictions pertaining to the capital account have been gradually relaxed.

Privatization of the Banking Industry

Before the implementation of the revised Banking Law in 1989, most of the banks were state-owned, except for a few private ones which are owned by overseas Chinese on the basis of certain considerations. Following the revision of the Banking Law, 15 new private banks were allowed to be set up in 1991. By the end of 1996, 18 new private banks had been established and had begun operations. Since these newcomers entered the banking industry, competition has been fierce, but better service has been created and capital is allocated more efficiently.

Financial Internationalization

In addition to domestic financial reforms, Taiwan has also implemented financial internationalization. First, new private banks have been given the right of establishment and both foreign financial institutions and domestic banks have been allowed to engage in offshore banking.

Second, there has been deregulation in the money market. The establishment of new bill-financing companies was deregulated, boosting the number of local bill companies to 14 in 1997 from three in 1994.

Third, controls on capital movements have been greatly relaxed. The upper limit in respect of both capital inflows and outflows for each individual was raised to US$5 million, while, in the case of a company, the limit was raised to US$50 million per year. It is planned that, during the year 2000, restrictions on capital movements will be fully lifted. Foreign institutional investors had been permitted to invest in the local stock market since January 1991. The maximum investment by a foreign institutional investor was raised to US$600 million from the previous US$400 million. Another reforming measure took effect in March 1996 whereby a foreign individual or a corporate investor was allowed for the first time to invest in the domestic stock market. The total foreign investment in a local listed company was raised to 30 per cent of the company's capital; and that by one foreign entity was relaxed to 10 per cent.

Fourth, Taiwan is being developed into an Asia–Pacific regional financial centre. According to the plan drawn up by the Executive Yuan, the central bank is the agent responsible for promoting the development of the financial centre. In order to implement this plan, 14 laws and more than 60 regulations are in the process of being revised or newly introduced. The plan is based on the principle of 'completely opening offshore financial markets, while gradually liberalizing domestic financial markets'.

In the foreign exchange market, foreign currency-related derivatives transactions have been fully liberalized, and those related to domestic currency are also being relaxed step by step.

In the offshore banking market, currently, a new revision is being made to the Offshore Banking Act to allow offshore banking units (OBUs) to deal with residents and to engage in offshore securities business. At the end of March 1997, 68 OBUs were operating in Taiwan, with total assets of US$318 billion, seven times the figure of a decade earlier, when OBUs had just been established.

In the equities markets, further liberalization will expand the international scope of these markets, and the ceiling on foreign ownership will be raised step by step as market conditions allow. Currently, up to 25 per cent of the shares of a single listed local company may be held by foreign investors. This restriction has been substantially liberalized during the year 2000. In addition, the state-owned financial institutions are also on the way to being privatized, which will provide the financial sector with more efficiency.

THE CONTRIBUTION OF THE FINANCIAL SECTOR TO THE REAL ECONOMY

As we look back at Taiwan's early stage of development, it will be seen that the adoption of a deliberate monetary policy to maintain stable prices as well as a well-functioning financial system have paved the way for the country's remarkable economic growth. In the 1950s and 1960s, there were two major reforms in the financial sector which contributed significantly to Taiwan's economic take-off: adopting a high-interest rate policy to curb inflation and maintaining an undervalued exchange rate to encourage exports.

In the early 1950s, there was not much difference between Taiwan's industrial policy and that of other developing countries of the time. Quota restrictions and tariff barriers were used to protect the domestic market in order to promote import-substituting industries. In the banking sector, in order to encourage local investment, interest rates were set at a very low level, which not only created inflationary pressure but discouraged domestic saving. As a result of this import-substitution strategy, Taiwan's exports were limited to a few traditional products like sugar, rice and so on, and no new export industries could be established.

In the mid-1950s, however, Taiwan began to adopt an export-promotion strategy and to implement fundamental reforms in terms of its trade policy. To this end, it liberalized trade restraints and promoted trade at an undervalued exchange rate. As a result, Taiwan rapidly entered a new era of export expansion; Taiwan's foreign trade increased by more than 200 times between 1954 and 1980. The undervalued currency and export-oriented strategy had a tremendous impact on Taiwan's industrial structure. The share of the manufacturing sector in Taiwan's GDP grew rapidly, increasing from 15.6 per cent in 1955 to as high as 37.6 per cent in 1985 (see Table 7.1). On the other hand, the share of the agricultural sector shrank from 29.1 per cent in 1955 to 3.6 per cent in 1994. In addition, in order to encourage private saving and curb domestic inflation, the government gave up its low interest rate policy and interest rates were subsequently adjusted several times. As a consequence, the consumer price index fell from 18.8 per cent in 1953 to 1.7 per cent in 1954.

In addition to the above courageous financial policy reforms, the financial sector has also played an important role in Taiwan's fast economic growth. The financial sector can be considered the lubricant of economic activities. Domestic savings are channelled through financial intermediaries to be used for investments. However, before the 1970s, since state-owned banks tend to operate conservatively, the long-regulated banking system could not meet the market demand for funds. Usually, big firms have easier access to credit compared to small- and medium-sized businesses, who have difficulty obtaining funds from government commercial banks. Those businesses have to seek underground capital, and an informal financial market has grown accordingly. As a result, formal and informal financial markets coexist. This is a major characteristic of Taiwan's financial market. After the 1970s, savings accumulated quickly, and excess savings have persisted. And the function of the financial system is to act as the channel between savings and investments.

Table 7.1   Composition of Taiwan's GDP by sector, 1955–94 (percent)

Year	Agriculture	Manufacturing	Services
1955	29.1	15.6	47.7
1960	28.5	19.1	47.7
1965	23.6	22.3	44.6
1970	15.5	29.2	47.7
1975	12.7	30.9	47.4
1980	7.7	36.0	46.6
1985	5.8	37.6	47.9
1990	4 1?	33.3	54.6
1991	3.8	33.3	55.1
1992	3.6	31.7	56.5
1993	3.7	30.5	57.3
1994	3.6	29.0	59.1

Source: Council for Economic Planning and Development (1995), *Taiwan Statistical Data Book*, Taiwan, ROC: Executive Yuan.

Firms are considered as the financial deficit sector, while households are a financial surplus sector. The government sector has retained a budget surplus most of the time. With a very high saving level from households and budget surplus from the government, these excess savings are led into investments through the financial sector. As a consequence, investments, exports and economic growth are all promoted accordingly.

Since the main objective of Taiwan's industrial policy during the 1960s was to promote infant industries (Wade, 1990), the government selected several such (strategic) industries and the central bank provided the funds needed for their development. Moreover, a special fund for medium- and long-term credit was established to finance major infrastructure projects. In the late 1980s, the central bank also allocated NT$30 billion in loans to strategic industries as well as small- and medium-sized enterprises for investment and development projects, respectively. Such financial assistance certainly helped local industries to build up their competitive strength.

In the 1990s, Taiwan has been pushing for greater economic liberalization because of its desire to become a member of the WTO. Formerly well-protected service sectors such as banking, insurance and the money market have all been opened for new domestic entrants as well as foreign investors. As a result of these reforms and the strong economic growth of the 1990s, the share of the financial sector has increased sharply. According to Liang (1996), finance, insurance and real estate services measured in terms of value added have increased on average by 11.7 per cent annually over the past ten years. In 1996, the value added of the above services accounted for a fifth of gross domestic product (GDP), a proportion similar to that of advanced economies.

The opening up of the money and capital markets has made it easier for firms to raise funds for investment. In the capital market, the restrictions on firms' shares to be listed have been greatly relaxed. Taiwan companies' listed shares have also been allowed to be listed and traded in the foreign stock markets. As a result, the number of registered firms in the listed and over-the-counter (OTC) market has expanded quickly. In addition, foreign institutional investors have been allowed to invest in the local stock market since 1991. A ban on private individuals investing in the stock market was also lifted in 1996. In the money market, private firms have issued commercial paper and corporate bonds to obtain short-term and long-term loans, respectively, thereby replacing bank loans.

Following stock market liberalization, the size of Taiwan's stock market has expanded quickly. The number of listed and OTC companies over the years increased from about 200 to 490 in July 1997. Market capitalization also increased from about NT$100 billion to NT$350 billion over the same period. In addition, several other financial instruments have emerged consequent upon the government's financial reform. These financial tools, such as American Depository Receipts (ADRs) and stock warrants, are attractive investments and funding vehicles, which offer low-cost equity for firms. When US residents buy foreign equity shares, they are given ADRs instead of actual foreign securities. Thus, when a company is registered on the New York Stock Exchange, its ADRs are bought and sold.

Thanks to the above liberalization measures, more and more enterprises can now easily raise funds in the capital market, which has thus become an important source of company long-term capital. Furthermore, according to central bank statistics, the annual rate of borrowing from major financial institutions has been steadily decreasing since 1994. In 1994, it was 17.36 per cent, but it dropped to 9.07 per cent in 1995, and declined further, to 3.72 per cent, in 1996. The ratio of borrowing from financial institutions to total capital sources has declined since 1994. According to Schive (1997), the ratio of the annual bank loans to enterprises to the annual issuance of stocks and bonds by enterprises was more than 10:1 before 1994. However, the ratio has now shrunk to about 1:4. Intermediation through financial markets has increased in importance relative to intermediation through banks. This new trend allows firms to leverage their financial resources, giving them more flexibility to expand their business.

Since the late 1980s, information and electronics companies have adopted a more aggressive stance in investing overseas. Through foreign investment, Taiwanese firms have established operations based on an international division of labour, reaping economies of scale in the process. As a result, firms now have a considerable lead over their competitors from other developing countries. The value of output in the information and electronics industry has increased exponentially, from US$3 million in 1966 to US$27.4 billion in 1996. In 1996, Taiwan's electrical and information industry was the third-largest such industry in the world, being surpassed by only the United States and Japan. Taiwan's sales of keyboards, mice and monitors all accounted for more than 50 per cent of the global market and Taiwan is now number one in the world in terms of sales of these products as well as of notebook computers. The reason for the recent boom in Taiwan's information and electronic industry has something to do with financial liberalization and internationalization, which has allowed firms to raise funds more easily in the capital market.

Moreover, since 1995, there have been several announcements of firms investing, or intending to invest, in Dynamic Random Access Memory (DRAM) production in Taiwan. Such investments are expected to amount to US$80 billion for 30 or more DRAM firms over the next ten years, which will enable Taiwan to become a big player in the global semiconductor industry. The rapid development of Taiwan's information industry will in turn induce demand for financial services, as well as boosting the further development of the financial market (Schive, 1997).

THE IMPACT OF THE ASIAN FINANCIAL CRISIS ON TAIWAN AND THE RESPONSE OF THE MONETARY AUTHORITIES

The recent currency turmoil in South East Asia arose as a result of current account deficits, and bad loans caused by declining real estate prices and falling stock prices. Even though Taiwan has sound economic fundamentals, it cannot prevent speculative attacks against the NT dollar (see Table 7.2). Generally speaking, there has been a need for the central bank to intervene to maintain confidence in the local currency, especially for an export-oriented country like Taiwan. Therefore it is understandable for the central bank to make exchange rate stability a top priority. In August and September 1997, the exchange rate

Table 7.2 The comparisons of economic indicators among Asian countries (billion US dollars)

Item	Taiwan	Singapore	Hong Kong	South Korea	Thailand	Malaysia	Philippines	Indonesia
Foreign exchange reserves	82.9	77.4	91.8	24	28.6	24.7	10.9	20.3
Foreign debts	1	0	0	110.3	89.2	42.4	41.9	109.3
Current account balance (1996)	10.97	19.9	–1.6	–23.7%	–14.4	–5.16%	–3.8	–7.7
Current account balance/GDP (1996) (%)	4	21.40	–1.00	–4.90	–8.20	–4.60	–3.20	–3.60
Economic growth rate (1996) (%)	5.71	7.00	4.70	7.10	6.70	8.20	5.50	7.80
Inflation rate (1996) (%)	3.07	1.40	6.00	5.00	5.80	3.50	5.20	7.90
The ratio of non-performing loans (1996) (%)	3.08	N.A.	2.70%	7.00	8.00	3.90	N.A.	8.80

Source: The Central Bank of China (1999, p. 12).

of the NT dollar to the US dollar fluctuated between 28.7 and 28.4. In early October, influenced by media reports about expectations of the NT dollar's depreciation, speculation became rampant, and daily foreign exchange transactions at one point reached US$1.5 billion. The central bank responded by raising short-term interest rates to dampen devaluation expectations, and the foreign exchange market then returned to normal. During this period, short-term interest rates increased sharply and the central bank not only engaged in open market operations but lowered deposit reserve ratios to alleviate the pressures of a capital shortage.

However, on 17 October, the central bank decided to allow market forces to operate freely, on the basis of the following considerations. First, persistently managing the exchange rate was not regarded as normal, and higher interest rates only hurt local investment. Second, the pressure of depreciation speculation was too huge to dissipate. In late October, the NT dollar exchange rate declined to 30.23, having depreciated by about 8 per cent against the US dollar. The inter-bank interest rate rose to between 8.6 per cent and 11.47 per cent, and then declined to 6.43 per cent after the NT dollar exchange rate stabilized. On 1 December, affected by the wide appreciation of the Korean won, the NT dollar exchange rate further declined to 32.11 (see Table 7.3).With regard to the stock market, the stock price index plunged 18.05 per cent from the end of June onwards, which was not too bad compared with other Asian countries.

However, the major reasons for the declining share prices included the fall in the international stock prices, lower turnover and profits in the electronics industry, readjustment of the overheated share prices and investors' lack of confidence. Exchange rate fluctuations should not become a scapegoat for the sluggish performance of the stock market.[1]

For an export-oriented country like Taiwan, how the ASEAN currency turmoil affects Taiwan's real economy is another area deserving attention. Intuitively, the NT dollar is slightly stronger when compared to the ASEAN-4 countries, which places Taiwan at a competitive disadvantage relative to ASEAN-4 countries. This deduction may be true for traditional industries with very limited profit margins such as plastics, textiles and petrochemicals. However, in the information and electronics industry, the impact may be different.

The strength of Taiwan's electronics sector lies in its flexibility, economies of scale resulting from mass-production and as the establishment of an international division of labour. Most Taiwanese companies have invested heavily overseas both in ASEAN-4 countries and in Mainland China. Additionally, Taiwan's total sales of PC hardware in ASEAN countries were less than 8 per cent of the total exports of the electronics sector. Over two-thirds consisted of semi-finished goods or re-exports, which basically remained intact when faced with the recent Asian financial crisis (SBC Warburg, 1997). As a corollary, the relatively stronger Taiwanese dollar may harm Taiwan's export competitiveness *vis-à-vis* ASEAN-4 countries, but only to a limited extent in the electronics sector. Nevertheless, the falling asset prices in the South East Asia countries resulting from the financial crises may harm Taiwan's exports to this region.

Table 7.3 Fluctuations in exchange rates and stock prices in major Asian countries

| Item | Exchange rate | | | Stock price index | | |
| | Asian currency/dollar | | % | index | | % |
Country	End of June	1 Dec.		End of June	1 Dec.	
Singapore	1.4305	1.5965	−10.40	1 987.95	1 665.47	−16.22
Hong Kong	7.7470	7.7380	0.21	15 196.79	10 750.88	−29.26
Taiwan ROC	24.8120	32.1100	−13.39	9 030.28	7 400.64	−18.05
South Korea	888.0000	1 185.0000	−25.06	745.50	393.16	−47.26
Thailand	24.7000	40.8500	−39.53	527.28	389.33	−26.16
Philippines	26.3760	35.0000	−24.64	2 809.21	1 777.04	−36.74
Malaysia	2.5245	3.5360	−28.61	1 077.30	531.46	−50.67

Source: The Central Bank of China, 1997.

However, since the crisis spread across the region, the problems in ASEAN-4 have, to differing degrees, been shared by all Asian developing economies. Taiwan may learn some valuable lessons from the Asian financial crisis and the resulting speculative pressure on the local currency. Important considerations included the following. First, *it is necessary to establish an exchange rate mechanism with more flexibility, while at the same time strengthening financial discipline*. The main reasons for the Asian currency turmoil are the rigid exchange rate mechanisms (pegged to the US dollar), the malfunctioning of the financial sector and large external borrowing. Under such circumstances, should governments allow their currencies to float with more flexibility, speculation may to a certain extent be reduced. Moreover, bad loans caused by overinvestment in the property and stock markets, which damage the real sector of the economy, may cause expectations of currency depreciation to increase. As a result, foreign investors will withdraw their investments to protect their profits, and thus a financial crisis will occur. For this reason, enforcing law and discipline in terms of supervising the financial sector to maintain the soundness of economic fundamentals is extremely important.

Second, *it is understandable for the central bank to intervene in the foreign exchange market*. In late September 1997, there was a serious debate as to whether the government should intervene aggressively in the foreign exchange market. Arguments opposing government intervention claimed that the exchange rate represented price in the market, and that should be determined by market supply and demand. According to this view, even under speculative pressure, an overshooting exchange rate will be adjusted by market forces. However, opinions that favour government intervention argue that, unlike commodity prices, the exchange rate exerts an extensive and profound effect on the economy. A widely fluctuating exchange rate will have an adverse impact, not only on commodity prices and foreign trade, but also on inward and outward investments. Moreover, an overshooting exchange rate may not be corrected by the market mechanism, since it is characterized by rigidity. Even if there may be a rebound, it will take time. Therefore, as a result, an overvalued or undervalued currency will result in tremendous adjustment costs to the real economy. For these reasons, it is not inappropriate for the central bank to intervene in the foreign exchange market even under a floating rate regime. However, the central bank should implement a mechanism whereby it intervenes in accordance with economic fundamentals and other monitoring indicators.

Third, *there is an urgent need to develop a healthy, well-functioning capital market*. A sound capital market can provide firms with needed long-term capital without their having to obtain loans from a bank. This will enhance the allocative efficiency of capital. In particular, when the central bank is faced with sporadic speculation and decides to stabilize the exchange rate, the reduction in money supply will push up short-term interest rates, resulting in a shortage of capital. This in turn will put pressure on the central bank to stick to its foreign exchange policy. Should a country have a sound bond market, firms can still obtain stable long-term capital. This will not only alleviate capital shortage, thus preventing firms' investments from being damaged, but will also lessen the pressure on the central bank to defend the local currency.

Fourth, *the government needs to continue to pursue financial liberalization*. Recently, there have been arguments for and against financial liberalization. Since the Asian currency turmoil, many people have lost confidence in financial liberalization. They believe that foreign capital tends to opt for short-term financial investment but not long-term productive investment. In this way, damage will be done to the local economy. However, a liberal financial market can in fact provide firms and government with better risk management and is thus a beneficial means of preventing a financial crisis. For a developing economy, too much regulation is inefficient and costly. However, since financial liberalization often takes place very suddenly, the government must implement policy measures to pursue liberalization in a more cautious manner by first gradually expanding the domestic capital market, and then lifting investment restrictions. At the same time, the lesson of the Asian currency turmoil is that a developing economy should not liberalize capital account transactions prematurely when a risk appraisal of the financial sector is still inadequate and monetary control is difficult.

Fifth, *promoting saving to raise domestic capital is a better way of maintaining the stability of the financial market*. Capital inflows can facilitate economic growth only if they are put to productive use, rather than being directed towards speculative activities. In that sense, capital inflows are risky if they stay in the financial market for a speculative purpose. Therefore providing incentives to channel foreign investment into productive activities is important. However, it is better to encourage local saving, thereby transferring funds into productive capital for economic development. At the same time, funds so used can also reduce the risk of volatile foreign capital damaging the stability of the financial market.

Sixth, *cooperation among Asian monetary authorities should be enhanced to prepare for possible future crises*. There was controversy over Japan's proposal of an Asian Fund to bail out the region's faltering economies. In addition to political concerns, the argument against the proposal was that it might encourage more speculators to attack Asian currencies. In such circumstances, if global investors destabilize a small economy, they can always bail out once things turn sour. This may lower the risks for the speculators, inviting even more serious speculative fever. In the meantime, governments may be tempted to take soft options and avoid the rigorous economic programmes that require IMF assistance. However, after the crisis swept from Thailand to the whole of Asia, even to the USA, a coordinated effort in the region to prepare for future crises does not appear to be a far-fetched idea.

CONCLUDING REMARKS

Taiwan has transformed itself from a poor. agriculture-dominated, closed society into a high-income, newly industrializing and open society within a period of only 40 years. A well-functioning financial sector and a stable monetary policy that has kept prices stable are major factors that have contributed to Taiwan's rapid economic growth.

As the economy has continued to grow, the need for financial services has greatly increased. Since the 1980s, the financial authorities in Taiwan have persistently pursued the goals of financial liberalization and internationalization. Among these, interest rate deregulation, foreign exchange control deregulation and the privatization of banking industry are well-known examples. These efforts have given Taiwan's financial sector the flexibility and efficiency to face new challenges and promote further economic growth. With regard to financial internationalization, banks have, since 1984, been allowed to engage in offshore banking, and controls over capital movements will be fully lifted by the year 2000. Moreover, in order to develop Taiwan into an Asia–Pacific regional financial centre, both the tax and regulatory systems as well as affiliated financial services are being improved. Through these efforts, it is hoped that the goal of developing Taiwan into a financial centre in the Asia–Pacific region can be accomplished.

As a result of these efforts in the areas of financial liberalization and internationalization, more and more enterprises have been able to raise funds in the capital market, which has contributed greatly to the rapid development of Taiwan's information and electronics industry. The booming information industry has, in turn, increased demand for financial services and promoted the further development of financial markets.

The recent Asian financial crisis, which began in Thailand, spread across Asia. Taiwan was not able to avoid the financial storm, even though it has healthy economic fundamentals. At the time, there were arguments for and against the central bank intervening to stabilize the exchange rate. After careful thought, the central bank finally allowed market forces to boost export competitiveness, thereby avoiding sharply raising the interest rate and damaging the real sector.

On the whole, the decline in the NT dollar exchange rate resulting from the Asian currency turmoil has not brought serious damage to the Taiwan economy so far. In the traditional industries, the relatively weak ASEAN currencies may damage Taiwan's exports, However, with regard to Taiwan's information and electronics industry, the largest industry, that is characterized by flexibility and which operates on the basis of an international division of labour, we are not unduly worried about a strong NT dollar harming Taiwan's export competitiveness in the electronics sector in the long run.

However, there are several lessons we can learn from this Asian financial crisis, which can be summarized as follows:

- a flexible exchange rate mechanism should be established, but discipline within the financial sector should be strengthened;
- a sound, well-functioning capital market should be developed;
- adherence to the goal of financial liberalization should be pursued;
- savings should be promoted as a means of raising domestic capital in order to maintain the stability of financial markets;
- cooperation among Asian monetary authorities should be enhanced to prepare for the possibility of crises in the future.

After the financial crisis, the Asian economic growth model has been seriously challenged , which makes us realize that fast economic growth could not continue without limit. Slow economic growth will be inevitable in the coming two or three years. However, I do believe, after this precious lesson, that the region will again find its way to more appropriate currency flexibility, fiscal restraint and other reforms needed to restore international competitiveness. It could then regain investors' confidence quickly and resume growth soon after.

NOTE

1. The responsible authority for the stock market in Taiwan is the Securities Exchange Commission under the purview of the Ministry of Finance.

BIBLIOGRAPHY

The Central Bank of China (1997), 'The Contribution of the Central Bank of China to Taiwan's Economic Development', in *The Central Bank of China*, Central Banking Publications Ltd.

Chan, K.K. and C.H. Kwan (1997), 'Weaker Asian Currencies – a Double-EdgedSword', *Asia Pacific Economic Outlook*, September, 4–10.

Chung, LW. (1997) 'A Study on Direct and Indirect Finance', paper presented at the Money and Finance Policy Conference, Taipei, Taiwan, 27 September (in Chinese).

Krugman, Paul (1997), 'Wrong, It Never Existed', *Time*, 29 September, p. 37.

Liang, Y. (1996), 'The Central Bank and the Economic Miracle in Taiwan', *Euromoney*.

SBC Warburg Dillon Read (1997), 'The ASEAN Currency Crisis and the Implications for Taiwan's Electronics Industry', *SBC Warburg Dillon Read*, October, 1–5.

Schive, Chi (1995), 'Industrial Policies in a Maturing Taiwan Economy', *Journal of Industry Studies*, 2(1), 5–26.

Schive, Chi (1997), 'Asian Financial Centers in the 21st century', XXII Annual Conference of the International Organization of Securities Commissions, Taipei, 2–7 November.

Sheu, Yuan Dong (1997), 'Deregulation and Expansion of the Banking Sector', *Global Banking and Financial Policy Review*, 98, 162–66.

Wade, R. (1990), *Governing the Market: Economic Theory and the Role of Government in East Asian Industrialization*, Princeton: Princeton University Press.

Wang, Jiann-Chyuan (1996), 'The Industrial Policy of Taiwan, ROC', *Industrial Policies in East Asia*, Singapore: Institute of Southeast Asian Studies.

Yang, Ya-Hwei (1997), 'An Overview of Taiwan's Financial System and Financial Policy', mimeo.

8. Financial reform and Asian turmoil: Taiwan's experience

Norman Yin

SHOCKS OF THE ASIAN TURMOIL

From May 1997 the monetary crisis swept through most of East Asia. Most East Asian countries had gone through the 1980s with a brilliant economic record. The fast economic growth led to the accumulation of huge financial assets in their private sectors. Primitive financial markets were thrown out of balance by an excess demand for funds. With financial innovations aggravating the problem, obsolescent financial regulations could not constrain the growing financial activities. In financial institutions loans were piling up, and banks were becoming insolvent and failing. Falling currency values triggered panic capital outflows and drained reserves became inadequate. The burst bubbles in the real estate markets aggravated the financial crisis, prompting falls on stock markets.

The failure of the financial system has afflicted most economies and such failure has been exacerbated by political crises. So far, the Philippines, Thailand, Indonesia and South Korea have scrambled for assistance from the IMF. The East Asian miracle has been questioned by some economists. Is it an economic phantom? Where are those dragons or tigers? What may happen after the Asian turmoil? There are too many questions left to be answered.

Taiwan has been the least affected of the Asian economies. As in most emerging economies, the financial sector has been used as a policy tool for economic growth. Over the past 45 years the average GNP growth rate of Taiwan has been 7.6 per cent and the annual average growth rate of M1 exceeds 20 per cent; but the average inflation rate has been kept at around 6 per cent.

THE UNDERDEVELOPED FINANCIAL MARKET, 1965–1987

Up to the mid-1980s, more than 50 per cent of the financial uses of funds of households and non-profit institutions were channelled to regulated financial market intermediaries, notably banks. The saving ratio was high while the interest rates were kept at a lower level in order to provide low-cost funding for designated key industries. The financial market was quite shallow and undeveloped. In the period 1980–85, companies listed on the stock market accounted for only 16 per cent of total capital of Taiwan enterprises, and households allocated as little as 3 per cent of their funds to the stock market during that period.[1] Financial sector regulations tended to segment financial markets and reduced the allocation of funds outside the regulated financial sector. Entry barriers and interest rate limits were deregulated after 1989 and branching restrictions were also gradually eased. Until 1987, capital control curbed capital outflows but did not effectively control capital inflows. Subsequently, the policy turned around, with liberalized capital outflows and restricted inflows, but the new policy was equally ineffective. The exchange rate was influenced by the discretion of policy makers to preserve the competitiveness of the export sector and, before being forced to change to the regular bid and offer trading mechanism, fluctuations in the exchange rate were limited to 2.25 per cent from the average central rate of the previous trading day, which induced a persistent expectation of NT dollar depreciation.

Taiwan's economy exhibited a general shortage of capital before 1980. A tight foreign exchange control, restricted interest rate levels, market entry barriers with a strictly regulated financial sector, all served as a means to achieve the end of economic development. The market mechanism played a limited role prior to 1980.

However, the system helped to build one of the most successful economies in the world. With an export-oriented economic policy, Taiwan experienced her first trade surplus in 1965, but this soon turned into deficit as imports grew the next year. Only after 1971 did the trend of continued expansion of trade surplus gain momentum, but expanding domestic investment demands kept Taiwanese businesses ploughing their surplus back into their businesses. In the end, capital shortage still prevailed.

THE FINANCIAL BUBBLES

After the 1985 Plaza Accord, the depreciation of the US dollar further fuelled the Taiwanese economy. The trade surplus jumped to US$15.6 billion in 1986 and US$18.6 billion in 1987, after the NT dollar appreciated sharply from NT$39.8 against the US dollar in 1985, and to NT$26.12 in 1989. The central bank's foreign exchange reserves increased from the level of US$2.2 billion in 1980 to US$76.7 billion in 1987. The build-up of reserves not only forced the NT dollar to appreciate sharply, but also caused a rapid growth in money supply. The growth rate of money supply M1b reached 51.42 per cent in 1986 and 37.82 per cent in 1987, but it did not generate inflation, since the NT dollar appreciation and the drops in the import prices minimized the price effect, and the average annual increase of the consumer price index for the 1980s was only 3.3 per cent per annum.

The high saving ratio, which once provided capital to meet the requirements for economic growth, turned out to be a negative factor for the financial sector in the 1980s. Annual gross savings accounted for 30 to 40 per cent of the gross national product (GNP) in the 1980s. As personal incomes and money supply rose, the bank deposits were fattened and the banking system was deluged with cash. Huge excess reserves therefore forced most banks to turn down large deposits or to lower their interest rates, and money market rates hit their lowest level of 2.1 percent in 1985. As a result, all the excess liquidity in the private sector was floating around seeking higher returns. Real estate prices were driven sky high. According to one of the statistics, the average real estate price in metropolitan Taipei increased by 2.7 times during January 1987 to July 1988. The Taiwan Stock Exchange (TAIEX) Composite Index went wild, soaring from 648 points in April 1985 to 12 460 points in February 1990, but plunged to 2400 points at the end of 1990 as the investment bubble burst.

FINANCIAL DEPTH

The private sector started to accumulate its financial assets after 1980 in Taiwan. Such a development has led to significant changes in the financial structure, the expanded volume of financial transactions and changes in the flow of fund patterns. In *Financial Reform*,[2] Gerard Caprio, Izak Atiyas and James Hanson use a country's M2 minus M1 then divided by GDP to measure its financial depth – in other words, the size of the quasi-money stocks measured by GDP – since they considered that quasi-money reflects the component of intermediation that is more likely to be driven by lending and borrowing considerations than by the demand for a transactions medium, divided by GDP so that it can be compared internationally. They found that, by comparing the financial depth of different countries, they can tell how the pressures of financial reform have been built up in a country. In their book they computed financial deepening measures of Chile (30 per cent), Korea (25 per cent) and Malaysia (40 per cent) in the early 1990s. Using the same measure, Taiwan has a remarkable result for the 1980s: the ratio (see Figure 8.1) increased from 43 per cent in 1980 to 72 per cent in 1985, indicating that financial assets have accumulated enough pressure to enlarge the scope of financial markets, but the pace of change was very slow. In 1988, the financial deepening ratio was over 100 per cent. The excess liquidity reached a critical point; financial bubbles appeared and the pressure for financial reform was so high that the authorities quickly reacted by revising stock transaction law, banking law and insurance

law, and enacting futures transaction law. The financial deepening ratio rose
still further, to 165 per cent in 1996, which means that the financial market
had not expanded enough to accommodate all this excess liquidity. In *Financial
Reform*, the authors suggested measuring it by adding the value of capital
market capitalization to quasi-money in order to have a real measure of the
financial deepening of a country, but there is no available data for them to
compare. If we add the value of capital market capitalization to it, the ratio
becomes more interesting. The ratio (see Figure 8.2) was 104 per cent in 1985,

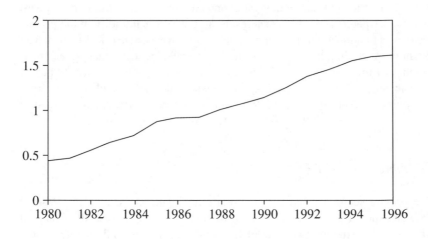

Figure 8.1   Financial depth ratio I

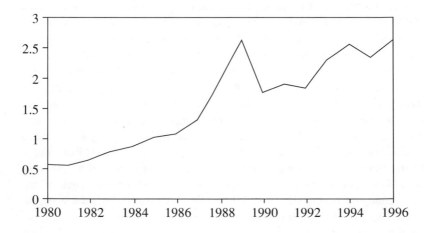

Figure 8.2   Financial depth ratio II

and went straight up to 265 per cent in 1989, then fell back to 187 per cent in 1992, which showed that the stock bubble expanded and then burst because the financial market failed to expand further. After 1994, the market diversified and more financial instruments were introduced into the market. For instance, the listing stocks increased to 300 and the financial futures and options were unofficially introduced into the market. Even with these efforts, the financial depth of the market has still yet to expand, since the ratio had risen again to 265 per cent in 1996.

CAPITAL SPILLOVER TO EAST ASIA

Because the shallow financial market could not hold the excess liquidity, Taiwanese capital spilled over to East Asia in the late 1980s. In the meantime, higher labour costs and appreciated currency value forced Taiwanese manu-facturers to upgrade their products into higher value-added areas or seek lower labour costs elsewhere. Labour-intensive industries, having lost their comparative advantage, had to migrate to other Asian countries, such as Thailand, Malaysia, Indonesia, Vietnam, the Philippines and China. Obviously, part of the excess capital did not stay in Taiwan waiting for the financial market deepening process, but, rather, found its way out through external investment. It is estimated that the direct investment in East Asia has exceeded US$50 billion, half of the investment being in China. Eventually, Taiwan has turned out to be one of the most important capital export countries in East Asia.

FINANCIAL DEREGULATION

The government was forced into financial reregulation by encouraging financial deepening in Taiwan's financial market. Foreign exchange control has been loosened since 1987 and the mid-rate trading system was abandoned in the foreign exchange market in 1989. The revised Securities Transaction Law of 1988, permitting new entrants to the brokerage business, contributed greatly to the buoyancy of the stock market in 1989 and the early part of 1990. The number of brokerage houses grew from 28 to 335 and effective customer accounts increased from 634 000 to 4.8 million, averaging one account per four persons. Subsequently, the stock market expanded dramatically in the 1990s, with listing stock increasing from 130 to more than 300. The TAIEX index stood at 7000 points, and over-the-counter (OTC) markets opened with more than 200 stocks trading. In July 1995, the market was rocked by financial scandals and a crisis of confidence, caused by missile tests conducted on the

Chinese mainland. The TAIEX index plummeted to 5180 points. The authorities took several measures to pull the market out of its tailspin. The central bank removed the US$7.5 billion cap on foreign investment in the stock market for all foreign institutional investors. On 11 August 1995, the Securities Futures and Exchanges Commission (SFEC) further raised the ceiling on total foreign holdings of individual stock from 12 per cent to 15 per cent. Recently, this was raised to 20 per cent. In August 1997, the East Asia monetary crisis hit Taiwan, speculative capital outflows increased the depreciation pressure on NT dollars, pulled up interest rates by draining liquidity in the market, and pushed the stock market down. While the monetary trouble was deepening in Korea and Japan in December 1997, TAIEX rallied and bounced back. In terms of annual turnover, Taiwan stock market ranks as the fourth largest in the world. Whether it maintains its position or not will depend on the interaction of Taiwan's financial market and the other Asian markets.

Interest Rate Deregulation

Taiwan has gradually liberalized its interest rates since 1980. More precisely, the central bank deregulated the discount rates on certificates of deposit (CDs) and bank debentures, and let the Bankers' Association set the range of the maximum and minimum lending rates. In September 1984, the central bank informed individual banks that they could set their own prime rate based on their cost of funds. In January 1986, the deposit interest rate ceilings were simplified, being reduced from 12 rates to four, and the spread of maxi-mini lending rates was enlarged. Finally, in July 1989, the revised banking law lifted all restrictions on interest rates, bringing the long history of interest rate control in Taiwan to an end. The reason for the continuous loosening of interest rate control after 1985 was the pressure from the fast-growing money supply and the high saving ratio that flooded banks with excess liquidity. The banking rate was then forced to adjust, in line with the money market interest rates.

While price liberalization has made considerable progress, it is still premature to say that interest rates are principally determined by market mechanisms in Taiwan, since the government has dominant influence over financial sectors. Entry barriers are still found in this oligopolistic structure of the banking industry, although the privatization of state-owned banks and market entry has been permitted.

The Money Market

In addition to the liberalization of interest rates, an important requirement for the market forces to play a greater role in determining the market rate is the development of a short-term money market and a long-term capital market where market forces can adjust their surpluses or shortages through the pricing mechanism.

Taiwan set up its money market in 1975. The central bank engaged heavily in the open market operation with treasury bills, CDs and saving bonds to counter the money supply pressure from the foreign exchange reserves accumulated in the 1980s. During the peak period of open market operation in 1987, total short-term instruments issued by the central bank reached NT$1.1 trillion, 3.47 times larger than the total currencies outstanding. It created a NT$47 trillion market in 1996, with market segregation among the inter-bank loans and other short-term foreign exchange instruments.

The Bond Market

As to the bond market, the heavy issuing of government bonds has enlarged the scale of the market. Total turnover of debt securities in 1996 amounted to NT$28.3 trillion. Trading was dominated by repurchase agreement transactions which made up 94 per cent of the total value of transactions. Interest rate-related derivatives have not been officially introduced into the market. However, an interest rate future has been brought in as a margin plus reverse-repo. Taiwan's futures market was due to open up for business in January 1998, with government bond futures and options being the major instruments for trading.

Tibor Market

In August 1989, Taiwan established a US dollar inter-bank call loan market to provide domestic financial institutions with a market to adjust their foreign currencies' excesses or shortages. It expanded dramatically in the mid-1990s, with the Japanese yen and the DeutschMark being added.

FINANCIAL CRISIS FROM JULY 1995 TO MARCH 1996

In late July 1995, the Chinese mainland missile tests and navy manoeuvres in the East China Sea to the north of Taiwan triggered a massive financial confidence crisis. The total amount of capital outflow topped US$15 billion, while the central bank pegged the US dollar at NT$27.5. To make things worse, a series of bank runs started. The Fourth Credit Cooperative of Changhua was taken over by the Cooperative Bank of Taiwan because its general manager allegedly embezzled NT$2.9 billion of the cooperative's money. Panicking depositors withdrew NT$32 billion from the institution, sparking the bank run. During the long last 10 months of tension over the Taiwan Strait situation, there were 29 bank runs from the credit cooperatives and farmers' associations, but the authorities did successfully isolate each case to avoid systemic risk. About the same time, another scandal at one of Taiwan's leading underwriters for commercial paper, the International Bill Finance Company (MFC) shook the money market when a dealer allegedly defrauded NT$10.6 billion in CPs from the company. Keeping the scandal from spreading into systemic risk was an uneasy task in the attempt to keep the money market's trading and clearing system functioning. The central bank injected more than NT$70 billion into the market and pumped another NT$30 billion into IBFC to keep it from insolvency. Under the regulations, a bill finance company should maintain a capital adequacy ratio of at least 5 per cent. IBFC's NT$10.6 billion losses equated to a NT$212 billion loss in CP-issuing ability. To lighten the credit crunch caused by the scandal, the central bank lowered reserve ratios by 1 per cent and eased restrictions on foreign investment in the stock market.

TAIWAN EXPERIENCE

With the existing financial problems of credit cooperatives and farmers' associations, why is Taiwan's financial system still sounder than that of other countries during the Asian turmoil era? We need to look deeply into the financial infrastructure and regulations of Taiwan to find out what Taiwan did right.

The Stock Market Bubble

When the stock market investment bubble burst in 1990, more than 90 per cent of the market participants were individual investors, who took the shocks to their old savings by a shrinking of their financial wealth. Moreover, Taiwan has fewer financial institution failures because there is a ceiling of 20 per cent net worth of bank holding for listing stocks. Traditional financial fire walls still exist in Taiwan, although in some places they have been worn thin. The banks' involvement in securities holding is limited in Taiwan. There is no fatal damage to Taiwanese financial institutions from the stock market falling as happens in Korea or Japan.

Hot Air Balloon Strategy for the Real Estate Market Bubble

The real estate market of Taiwan has never collapsed as happened in Japan. To avoid the bubble bursting, the central bank adopts a 'hot air balloon' strategy. That is, whenever there is a threat of major falls in the real estate market, the central bank will pump in more loans for first-time home buyers to boost the demand in order to keep the market afloat. The sole purpose is to let household income catch up with house prices. In Taiwan, the average house price was eight times annual household income and, after the real estate boom in the 1980s, it jumped up to 14 times. With 6 per cent average annual growth in per capita income (which is the average income growth rate of Taiwan), the household income will be around nine times the housing price within six years, provided the house price remains as it was or with a mild downward adjustment. By that time, the bubble problem will be solved. The strategy works quite well and the real estate market has kept alive, so far. The large non-performing mortgage loan has been a major headache to Japan for years, but it is not a serious problem in Taiwan. Besides, the regulations require that the risk exposure of real estate loans should be confined within the 20 per cent limit of the time deposits plus bonds issued by banks. So, even if the real estate market crashed, it would be less serious than in Japan, Thailand or even Hong Kong.

Relatively High Loan Loss Coverage Ratio

The Taiwanese financial system does not follow the Japanese main bank system, so there is no banking *keiretsu* or *chaebol* in Taiwan. Unless it has been approved by the authorities, no direct industry investment is allowed for commercial banks. The strategic loan with a favourable rate made by the bank is not guaranteed by the government and is still made at the bank's own risk. So-called 'relationship loans', which endangered banks' capital, did exist in some Taiwanese state-owned banks in the past, but on a very small scale. After the political environment changed in the 1990s, such relationship loans gradually disappeared. The credit cooperative problems have been handled quite skilfully by the authorities. Insolvent credit cooperatives have been urged to increase their capital to meet the minimum requirement, otherwise they will be merged or acquired by commercial banks. Only the farmers' association problem is yet to be solved. In Taiwan, the ratio of non-performing loans in all financial institutions has stayed around 4 per cent recently. This is very high in terms of the European standards, but comparatively low compared with most of Taiwan's East Asian neighbours. According to a Bank for International Settlements (BIS) report, the loan loss coverage ratio (loan loss reserves/non-performing loans) of Taiwanese banks was 0.42 in 1994,[3] falling behind most emerging economies. Since most loans have collateral coverage in Taiwan, the low loan loss coverage ratio has not caused any bank insolvency yet. However, this issue is not going to be ignored, especially when financial institutions become much more fragile than before. There are still weaknesses in the financial structures of Taiwan, yet the situation is improving all the time and the authorities watch very closely everything that is going on in the financial market and try to take the right measures at the right time.

Quantitative Control in Forex Market

In the foreign exchange market there are several restrictions left over from the 1987 regulations. Such restrictions might reduce the pressure of the speculative attack on Taiwan during the Asian turmoil. In order to curb the capital inflow and to ease the pressure of NT dollar appreciation during 1987–9, the central bank tried very hard to limit foreign debts, including freezing all banks' foreign liabilities and restricting Taiwanese business's ability to borrow capital from international markets by forbidding its use in the domestic market. The former constraint was gradually loosened and lifted in 1994 and the latter was eased in 1996. As a result, the cumulative external debt for Taiwanese business was only US$5billion in 1997, far less severe than in other Asian countries. Furthermore, the central bank limited banks' short selling position on foreign exchange in the spot market and restricted short selling in the foreign exchange forward market to one-third of the banks' foreign exchange position. Although the central bank allowed banks to set their own short selling limits on the spot market as required by their own risk management, the short selling restriction still limits the size of total market trading. With the abundant foreign exchange reserves, the central bank can easily influence the value of NT dollars. These measures of quantity control in the foreign exchange market, which have been criticized by the public as a barrier to liberalization, turned out to be the central bank's forward defence line against the speculators' attacks. Although it has been proved that quantitative control in the forex market is more effective than price limits, it does limit market expansion. This half-deregulated quantitative control has to be removed in the long run.

The Experience Gained from the Taiwan Strait Tension

The experience of dealing with the financial crisis during the period of tension in the Taiwan Strait is very useful for handling East Asia monetary crises, since in both incidences huge capital outflows have occurred, with the stock market plunging, and financial stress in financial institutions. When the NT dollar was attacked by speculators in July 1997, the central bank took the same stand as with Strait tension to defend the value of the NT dollar at NT$28.5 to one US dollar. However, after a loss of US$8 billion reserves within two months, with liquidity drying up in the money market and causing interest rates to be raised drastically, the authorities soon realized that this time things were different. They turned around and let the market forces decide the right currency price. Changes to the regulator's mandate are probably much more important than regulatory reform itself. This flexible attitude keeps the Taiwan economy less vulnerable to further attacks from international speculators.

FINANCIAL REFORM

With a liberalized forex control and increasing openness of the financial market, the authorities started to establish Taipei as an international financial centre in 1990. Taiwan's financial regulations have been thoroughly reviewed. There are more than 120 related regulations due to be revised in order to conform with international standards. While the laws and ordinances are under revision, an even larger scale of financial reform is being carefully mapped out for the future. The Financial Reform Task Force under the Ministry of Finance recently came up with a proposal to combine all the financial regulators in one, like the new regulatory body in Britain, the Financial Services Authority. The bank examination department of the central bank, the Bureau of Monetary Affairs, the Securities Futures and Exchanges Commission and the Insurance Regulators will all be combined into the Commission on Financial Supervision. Since the traditional fire wall is getting too thin to hold the cross-market financial activities, and financial innovation has circumvented the financial restrictions, the conflict in jurisdiction power makes regulation even more complicated. Not only should the regulating agencies be put under one roof, but also the regulations themselves should be merged and restructured. The British experience will provide a very useful reform reference for Taiwan.

LESSONS FROM TAIWAN

The Asian turmoil runs on banks, sharp currency devaluations, brokerage failures, conglomerate bankruptcy, deflation, IMF bailouts, impending recessions and so on will be over some time in the future. This will provide a very precious lesson for other emerging economies: during the process of economic development, the financial infrastructure should be placed on the same footing as the real production. Taiwan's experiences probably have something to offer for those who could make the same mistakes.

Handling of Bubbles

The crucial problem about the Asian financial crisis is the investment bubbles in the stock market and the real estate market. The power to burst the bubbles comes from the financial strength that has accumulated from strong economic growth. The reason for investment bubbles existing is that the financial market is too shallow to hold the liquid form of excess financial assets. Japan faced the bubble problem in the mid- 1980s, and it burst in 1989, when the newly appointed governor of the Bank of Japan switched to a tightened monetary policy. The stock market collapsed immediately and the real estate market followed. This created ¥50 trillion non-performing loans in the financial system, which is the root of today's Japanese financial crisis. Taiwan tightened up its monetary policy in April 1989. The lagged response of the stock market appeared in February 1990, when the TAIEX index dropped more than 9000 points but the real estate market hung on.

Increasing Market Breadth and Depth

With the Taiwan experience, the financial market should expand both in depth and breadth, increase its capacity to hold the excess financial assets demand in order to avoid a bubble appearing. The asset inflation is avoidable if the market allows more financial instruments and increases listing stocks to absorb the demand. However, if the excess liquidity is too large to hold in the local financial market, probably it is better to let capital outflow to release the pressure. This is what was done in Taiwan when the financial pressure was high due to the bubble in the real estate market. In other words, rapid financial deepening is the most important tool in dealing with financial bubbles because a larger and deeper market will always be more stable than a shallow one.

Conflicts between Internationalization and Liberalization

The openness of the capital market and abandoning of foreign exchange control is another big issue, since most developing countries try to keep capital at home and the foreign exchange policy is unfavourable to capital outflow. Authorities have been criticized for putting financial internationalization ahead of financial liberalization in Taiwan when the local financial institutions, constricted by the straitjacket of the domestic banking law, suddenly faced substantial international financial competition. Fortunately, the disorder and chaos caused in the financial market was gradually eliminated by realignment in the financial structure in the following years. Taiwan was forced to change its foreign exchange policy by the pressure of NT appreciation expectation, huge foreign exchange reserves and rapid growth of money supply. Had there been an alternative, Taiwan would have chosen deregulation in the financial sector rather than opening up to the international market. The other thing worth mentioning is that, whenever there is a big price drop in the stock market the authorities should raise the capital quota of foreign institutional investors to invest in the local market. The foreign capital will fill up the lost demand and keep the market from dropping further, since the economic fundamentals are sound in Taiwan. Opening the tap of foreign capital to balance the stock market that is full of individual investors, not only keeps a stable stock market but also achieves the goal of internationalization at the same time.

Financial Restructuring

Under reform pressure, financial restructuring should evolve at the pace of economic development. The appropriate supervision and reregulation by the monetary authorities are indispensable in financial reform. Nevertheless, this does not imply that direct credit control or market intervention should be introduced. Rather, the authorities should put much more emphasis on monitoring potential risks borne in the financial system, preventing corruption and illegal transactions inside financial institutions. The financial infrastructure, such as the trading, settlement and payment system, requires further improvement. In some Asian economics, there is more room for improvement in legal and accounting systems with respect to financial transactions, the disclosure rules for financial institutions, the improvement of bankruptcy procedures and so on. Any practice such as the hidden-loss *Tobashi* deal in Japan should be treated as a serious breach of the financial regulation. The insolvent financial institution has to suffer bankruptcy or restructuring to avoid further damage to the financial system. A further improvement in financial reform with the current globalization trend calls for the need to standardize financial tools, market structures and measures to regulate financial activities.

CONCLUSION

Transition from a policy-oriented financial system in the developing economics to an open, market-oriented financial system is a very painful process. Most Asian countries are suffering from financial structure overhaul, but after the integration of credit and capital markets to increase the trading and market depth and to merge into the world financial market, regulated under the universal code, Asian economies will be given another chance to move ahead to an even brighter future. Above all, a sound and safe financial system is the best defence against financial crises. Intensified cooperation among Asian countries to stabilize the regional intra-currency relationship is also needed. Only through a collective effort will the regional economies eventually come closer and work out their financial difficulties.

CHRONOLOGY OF TAIWAN'S FINANCIAL REFORM

8/78   US dollar forward trading started.

2/79   Shift from a fixed exchange rate system to the floating rate which was determined by the central bank and five local banks.

1/80   Private holding of foreign exchange is permitted, and exporters can open their foreign currency accounts in the banks.

3/80   The central bank gave up the daily exchange rate ceiling.

11/80   The discount rate on CDs and bank debentures was deregulated.

8/81   The real effective exchange rate index was brought into consideration for the determination of the exchange rate.

9/82   Mid-rate system adopted in the foreign exchange market.

10/83   Issuance of four mutual funds in the international financial market for foreign investors.

12/83   Offshore banking statutes enacted, allowing local banks to engage in offshore banking business.

11/84   The spread between the ceiling and floor of loan interest rates extended.

3/85   The major banks allowed to set up their own prime rate.

8/85   The interest rate restrictions on the foreign currency deposit account lifted.

Bankers' association allowed to set the range of the maximum and minimum lending rates; individual banks can freely decide the lending rates charged to their clients according to credit rating and the maturity date.

1/86   The central bank further simplified deposit rates restrictions, reducing from 12 rates to four.

5/86   Gold and silver were excluded from the foreign exchange reserves and were not subjected to the foreign exchange control statutes.

8/86   The authorities agreed to open up the insurance market and allow two foreign life insurance firms and two foreign non-life insurance firms to set up branches in Taiwan each year.

10/86   Foreign banks allowed to set up second branches in Taiwan.

11/86   Gold could be freely imported and traded in Taiwan, but subjected to import registration.

5/87   The daily short position of foreign exchange for banks limited to US$3 million and daily long position to US$20 million; also the foreign debt balance of banks frozen at the level of 13 May 1987, to release the currency appreciation pressure.

7/87   Restrictions on capital outflow removed; individuals can legally hold, purchase and utilize foreign exchange, allowing US$5 million outflow remittance and US$50 000 capital inflow per person each year.

2/88   Revised Securities Transaction Law introduced insider trading restrictions, disclosure requirement for large stockholders; allowed new brokerage firms to be established; permitted foreign securities firms' joint venture investment in local brokerage firms up to 4 per cent.

1/89   Privatization of three state-owned commercial banks announced; other state-owned enterprises to follow.

2/89   The central bank tightened up the selective credit control on mortgage lending.

4/89   The mid-rate system switched into a regular quoting system in the forex market.

6/89   Limitation of yearly capital inflow per individual raised to US$200 000.

7/89   Banking law revised, allowing new entry of private banks, abolishing interest rate limitation, setting up capital adequacy ratio in line with the BIS requirement.

8/89   Foreign exchange inter-bank call loan market established; the central bank allocated US$3 billion to set up the market as seed money, later on increased to US$6 billion and interlinked with Singapore, Hong Kong and Tokyo.

12/89   OTC market established.

8/90   Increased daily bank short sale of foreign currencies from US$3 million to US$6 million, and also increased daily bank long position from US$20 million to US$50 million.

9/90   The selective credit control on mortgage lending lifted.

12/90   Foreign institutional investors allowed to invest in the stock market, the ceiling of total inward remittance being US$2.5 billion.

2/91   TIBOR market interlinked with Singapore Asia dollar market.

11/91   The central bank lowered deposit reserve ratio by 0.5 per cent, discount rates by 0.375 per cent, a sign that the direction of monetary policy had changed from tight to loose.

12/91   First issuing of small dragon bonds from the Asian Development Bank (ADB).

10/92   Further loosening of the individual capital flow restrictions; capital outflow and inflow increased to US$5 million for individuals and capital flow for business increased to US$ 10 million.

8/94   The ceiling for foreign institutional investors' investment in the stock market increased to US$5 billion, and then, in November 1994, it increased further to US$7.5 billion.

2/95   Ceilings for foreign institutional investors' investment deleted.
Ceiling of short and long forex position unified, the amount of limits divided into four categories by size of the banks, from US$20 million to US$50 million.
The restriction on Taiwanese business borrowing capital from the international market by forbidding its use in the domestic market revised; allowing only those who will make direct investment to remit back to Taiwan.

12/95 Capital flow for business increased to US$20 million.

3/96 Foreign individuals allowed to invest in Taiwan stock market, the ceiling limit being US$5 million, but foreign individuals still have other channels to invest in the Taiwan stock market: by mutual funds and so on.

6/96 Short and long forex position limitations removed, letting the banks decide their positions according to their risk management requirement, and reporting to the central bank for supervisory purposes.

NOTES

1. Norman Yin and Ramon Moreno, 'Exchange rate policy and shocks to asset markets', *San Francisco Federal Reserve Bank Review*, January 1992.
2. Gerard Caprio, Izak Atiyas and James Hanson, *Financial Reform*, Cambridge: Cambridge University Press, 1996.
3. M. Goldstein and P. Turner, 'Banking crises in emerging countries: diagnosis and prediction', Bank for International Settlements, Working Paper No. 46, October 1966.

BIBLIOGRAPHY

Caprio, G. Jr., I. Atiyas and J.A. Hanson (1996), *Financial Reform: Theory and Experience*, Cambridge: Cambridge University Press.

Dernirguc-Kunt, A. and E. Detragiache (1997), 'The determinants of banking crises: evidence from developing and developed countries', IMF Working Paper, 106, September.

Goldstein, M. and P. Turner (1996), 'Banking crises in emerging countries: diagnosis and prediction', BIS Working Paper, No. 46.

Honohan, P. (1997), 'Banking system failures in developing and transition countries: origins and policy options', BIS Working Paper No. 39.

Kaminsky, G., S. Lizondo and C. Reihart (1997), 'Leading indicators of currency crises', IMF Working Paper 79, July.

Melick, W.R. (1996), 'Estimation of speculative attack models: Mexico yet again', BIS Working Paper No. 936.

Schaller, H. and S. van Norden (1997), 'Fads or bubbles?', Bank of Canada Working Paper 97–2.

World Bank (1993), *The East Asian Miracle: Economic Growth and Public Policy*, Oxford: Oxford University Press.

Yin, N. (1991), 'Financial reform in dynamic Asia economies', Sino-European Conference, Geneva, October.

Yin, N. (1996), 'Financial liberalisation: The Taiwan experience', paper presented at The Third Conference on Modem China, Shanghai, November.

Yin, N. and R. Moreno (1992), 'Exchange rate policy and shocks to asset markets', *San Francisco Federal Reserve Bank Review*, January.

9. Thailand's financial evolution and the 1997 crisis

Yos Vajragupta and Pakorn Vichyanond

INTRODUCTION

Thailand's financial system has been the focus of worldwide attention since the summer of 1997, when devaluation of the baht sparked a currency crisis that spread rapidly throughout South East Asia. The past two and a half decades have seen drastic and significant changes in Thailand's financial markets. Between 1972 and 1987, the adjustment in the financial system was very gradual. Because the Thai economy was not very open and external volatility as well as disturbances were insubstantial, foreign economic activities and financial conditions had only limited impact on Thailand and presented little difficulty for policy making. After 1987, however, the pace of change in Thailand's financial arena picked up dramatically. Globalization and liberalization became a primary policy objective and the government relaxed various rules and regulations to increase the flexibility of the financial system so that the Thai economy could survive and compete successfully in the international economic community. Deregulation brought about a deepening of the financial system, but enormous capital inflows during the 1990s and heightened market competition tempted Thai financial institutions to build up excessive exposure in several areas, resulting in bubble growth and deteriorating asset quality. A mounting current account deficit coincided with three other unfortunate circumstances and invited the currency speculation that forced the floating of the baht. Thailand is undertaking reforms to restore market confidence and return the country to its growth path. Thailand's experience clearly illustrates that financial liberalization is a precarious process and its past policy errors suggest precautions to guide policy in the future.

STRESSES AND STRAINS BETWEEN 1972 AND 1987

At the beginning of the 1970s, Thailand's financial system was dominated by a few sizable commercial banks whose activities were rather clustered and centrally administered. Foreign banks had only a limited role and international transfers of funds were stringently controlled and monitored. The central authority set ceilings for interest rates on both deposits and credits. The banking system was required to allocate adequate credits to 'important economic sectors' and commercial banks were obligated to buy and hold some government securities even in the absence of genuine long-term capital markets. Informal credit markets flourished alongside this restrictive formal environment.

Prior to 1987, Thai monetary authorities did not put much emphasis on the development of the financial system, although they did initiate some changes, such as establishing a repurchase market for government securities in 1979. The monetary authorities were primarily devoted to coping with the economic repercussions of external events such as the two oil price shocks and the regional conflicts in Vietnam, Laos and Cambodia. Most of the economic measures the government implemented were ad hoc responses to pressing problems. For instance, the government bailout of ailing finance companies in April 1984 was undertaken to preserve the stability of a trembling financial system. Also the increasing volatility of the US dollar led the central bank in November 1984 to switch its exchange rate policy from pegging solely to the dollar to pegging to a basket of currencies.

The Thai economy maintained a healthy average annual growth rate of 6.6 per cent from 1972 to 1987 despite rises in both inflation and the current account deficit. The policy of sustaining domestic interest rates above the inflation rate helped broaden and deepen Thailand's financial sector. The ratio of M2 money supply to GDP increased from 35.5 per cent in 1972 to 62.2 per cent in 1987, contributing to the mobilization of savings to finance the economic expansion. However, as is apparent from the large spread between deposit and lending rates, competition did not develop along with financial deepening.

A strong development momentum aimed at enlarging Thailand's industrial base pressured the central authority to accommodate industrialization and globalization by adjusting the financial system to allow greater flexibility and lower costs. A number of other factors set the stage for the acceleration of financial reform in Thailand from 1988.

Worldwide Liberalization of Trade and Services

As a participant in negotiations in the Uruguay Round and the formation of the WTO, Thailand was required to provide access to and equal treatment of foreign financial institutions. Since Thailand would gradually have to open not only its industrial and agricultural markets but also its financial markets, it was thought reasonable that the country start liberalizing its financial sector at the earliest possible moment to prepare for greater competition from abroad in the future.

European Union

The EU was in the process of unifying production, trade and finance among its member countries. Once incorporated as a single market, the EU would grant privileges to financial institutions registered in its member countries. Thai commercial banks would be at a disadvantage and could not compete effectively unless they became more efficient, flexible and dynamic.

Indochina's Market Orientation

From the end of the 1980s, Vietnam, Laos and Cambodia began moving towards a market mechanism in lieu of central planning. Recognizing the economic potential of these neighbours, Thailand felt the need to upgrade its financial structure in order to accommodate increased trade and investment between the Indochina region and the rest of the world.

Fiscal Readiness

After years of fiscal deficits, Thailand achieved its first cash balance surplus in 1988 and maintained the surplus for the succeeding nine years (Table 9.1). In addition, the country's foreign exchange reserves were more than sufficient to meet the necessary expenses. Thus the government felt ready to relax its financial regulations.

Table 9.1   Thailand's fiscal balance and international reserves

	Fiscal cash balance, % of GDP	International reserves, months of imports
1987	−1.4	4.7
1988	1.9	4.3
1989	3.2	5.0
1990	4.7	5.3
1991	4.9	5.8
1992	3.1	6.3
1993	2.2	6.8
1994	1.8	6.8
1995	1.0	6.3
1996	2.2	6.5

Source: Bank of Thailand.

FINANCIAL LIBERALIZATION, 1988–96

At the outset, Thailand had no explicit plan for financial reform and liberalizing measures were barely perceptible. Some foreign exchange controls were loosened in 1988, when foreign exchange deposits for transit passengers and credit card processing adjustments were authorized, and in 1989, when non-resident baht accounts were permitted to accommodate foreign-borrowing settlements, stock transactions and foreign investment.

The milestone that pinpointed the initiation of systematic and sustained financial reform was Thailand's acceptance of the obligations under Article VIII of the International Monetary Fund's Articles of Agreement on 21 May 1990. This resulted in the lifting of foreign exchange controls on current account transactions. (The only remaining restrictions are on capital account transactions by Thai residents for outward portfolio and property investments and for outward foreign direct investment in excess of US$10 million per person per year.) Acceptance of Article VIII marked the inception of Thailand's first three-year financial reform plan, which covered the period 1990–92. The main objective of this first plan was to enhance the efficiency of the financial system and financial resource allocation.

Another crucial episode in Thailand's financial liberalization was the establishment of the Bangkok International Banking Facilities (BIBF) in March 1993. BIBF was part of the second financial system development plan (1993–5), one of whose targets was to develop Thailand into a regional financial centre.

Together, the first and second financial reform plans involved a wide range of deregulation measures and innovations, as summarized below.

Interest Rates

In order to encourage the mobilization of domestic savings and to make the financial system more flexible, on 1 June 1989 the authorities removed interest rate ceilings on commercial banks' time deposits with maturities longer than one year. Commercial banks were required to publicize their rates. Interest rate ceilings on savings deposits (7.25 per cent) and short-term time deposits (9.5 per cent) were removed on 8 January 1992, and ceilings on loan rates (15 per cent) ended five months later on. On 1 June 1992, all interest rate ceilings were abolished for commercial banks and finance companies, as well as *crédit fonciers*. From that time, interest rates at Thai financial institutions became flexible and largely market-determined. To enhance competition and protect small borrowers, in October 1993 the central bank began requiring commercial banks to announce their minimum retail rates, based on the costs of funds, as benchmark rates for small but good-quality borrowers.

Foreign Exchange Controls

Thus far, three rounds of foreign exchange liberalization have been implemented. The aim was to keep the foreign exchange regime in line with globalization of economic and financial systems and the increased international mobility of capital. The first round, instituted in May 1990, allowed commercial banks to authorize foreign exchange transactions in trade-related activities without prior approval from the Bank of Thailand and increased the limit on foreign exchange purchases to facilitate transfers and travel expenses. Commercial banks were also permitted to remit funds for debt repayment, sale of stocks or liquidation of business within certain limits.

The second round, in April 1991, lifted most controls related to capital account transactions. However, outward direct investment above a certain limit and acquisition of foreign real estate or securities by Thai residents still needed approval from the Bank of Thailand. For the first time, unincorporated Thai entities could open foreign currency accounts provided that the funds originated abroad. Exporters were allowed to accept baht payments from non-resident baht accounts without prior approval from the central bank and to use their export proceeds to service external obligations.

The third round of foreign exchange liberalization, in February 1994, raised the limit on outward transfer of direct investment by residents, increased the limit on banknotes to be taken to countries bordering Thailand, including Vietnam, abolished the limit on travel expenses and allowed residents to use foreign exchange proceeds that originated abroad to service their external payments.

The relaxation of foreign exchange controls demonstrated two target areas. The first was a more active role for market forces. For instance, commercial banks were given more authority to approve transactions, except investments by Thai nationals in property and securities abroad. Meanwhile, regulations on foreign exchange receipts were loosened and commercial banks had more leeway to extend credits and accept deposits in foreign exchange to and from foreigners. The second was more utilization of the baht in regional trade. Foreign nationals were permitted to hold and operate non-resident baht accounts to facilitate international trade and investment.

Portfolio Management and Scope of Activities

To give commercial banks more flexibility, the central authority reduced the proportion of outstanding deposits that they were required to hold in government bonds in order to open new branches. From 16 per cent before 1988, the requirement was reduced in steps to 6.5 per cent in November 1992, and to nil in May 1993. The obligation of commercial banks to extend credits to rural borrowers was expanded to cover more related occupations and wider geographical areas. Furthermore, the definition of 'liquidity reserves' was broadened to include Bank of Thailand and state enterprise bonds, as well as debt instruments issued by financial institutions or government agencies approved by the central bank.

Commercial banks were permitted to engage in such investment banking activities as debt underwriting, dealing, fund management and financial consulting. Finance and securities companies could participate in the same activities, except financial consulting, and they could undertake leasing and mutual fund management, while qualified companies were allowed to operate foreign exchange business and/or open provincial credit offices.

New Facilities and Institutions

The Bangkok International Banking Facilities (BIBF) was established in March 1993 as a foundation for international financial services and to mobilize capital to support regional economic growth and development. BIBF may also have been formulated as a means to strengthen competition in domestic financial markets without setting up new commercial banks or finance companies. Some BIBF transactions (for example, cross-currency trading and cofinancing credit lines) receive tax privileges, while others (for example, out–in transactions) are subject to certain requirements, such as minimum amounts. In May 1994, the government decided to allow BIBF to open branches in upcountry provinces. The international orientation of Thailand's financial sector was further promoted with the establishment of the Export–Import Bank of Thailand in September 1993.

The Securities and Exchange Act passed on 16 May 1992 permitted limited companies access to direct finance by issuing common stocks and debt instruments. The Act established the Securities and Exchange Commission as an independent agency responsible for supervising capital market activities, including equities, bonds and derivatives. In 1993, the government spearheaded formation of the credit rating agency, Thai Rating and Information Services, and in 1994 private parties organized a bond dealers' club to function as a secondary debt market adding more liquidity to debt instruments.

With rapid advances in information technology, the Bank of Thailand instituted improved clearing and settlement systems that lowered transaction costs and facilitated business expansion. The BAHTNET and THAICLEAR networks were put into place to serve the needs of customers. The latest development on this front is electronic retail funds transfer through Media Clearing.

EFFECTS OF LIBERALIZATION

The drastic changes in Thailand's financial system during the 1990s affected all parties in the economy: financial intermediaries, business corporations, the government and the general public. The financial liberalization will be evaluated in terms of its impact on the expansion of the financial system, the interest rate structure and international linkages, capital market development, financial institution performance, corporate behaviour and asset quality. In addition, macroeconomic effects and policy implications will also be examined.

Financial System

Deregulation deepened the financial system to some extent. The ratio of M2 to GDP increased from 62.2 per cent in 1987 to 74.7 per cent in 1992. (The comparable ratio for Australia is 60.1 per cent, for the Netherlands 84.8 per cent, and for Singapore 101.0 percent.) In 1996, the M2 to GDP ratio stood at 79.5 per cent. Similarly, the ratio of M3 to GDP rose from 73.2 per cent in 1987 to 107.6 per cent in 1996, demonstrating the more active role of finance companies and *crédit fonciers* in tapping domestic savings (Table 9.2). The Thai financial system was broadened as well, since the number of bank branches grew from 2016 in 1987 to 3168 in 1996 and the population per branch fell from 26 721 in 1987 to 18 955 in 1996.

Interest Rate Structure

Dismantling foreign exchange controls led to greater mobility of capital across borders and decreased the spread between domestic and foreign interest rates. Both of these developments certify the growing international linkage of the Thai financial system. From 1989 to 1994, the difference between the one-month repurchase interest rate and the one-month Eurodollar plus forward premium narrowed as a result of the large volume of foreign exchange transactions (Table 9.3). Competition from foreign funds and more activities by local financial institutions drove down interest rate spreads at commercial banks. The difference between lending rates and one-year deposit rates declined from 7.25 per cent in June 1992 to 6 per cent in June 1994 and to 5 per cent in 1995. The timing of interest rate liberalization in Thailand is noteworthy. The authorities deregulated deposit rates before lending rates and liberalized lending rates when liquidity was plentiful. This timing helped reduce interest rate spreads and avoid sharp hikes in lending rates.

Although commercial banks eventually yielded to external market forces, their initial response was to differentiate among local customers. For instance, between 1990 and 1993, commercial banks lowered the prime lending rate by

Table 9.2 Thailand's major financial indicators (billion baht)

	1986	1987	1988	1989	1990	1991	1992	1993	1994	1995	1996
GDP nominal	1 133.4	1 299.9	1 559.8	1 857.0	2 183.5	2 506.6	2 834.7	3 179.5	3 634.8	4 202.8	4 689.6
% growth	—	14	20	19	17	14	13	12	14	15	11
GDP 1988 prices	1 257.2	1 376.8	1 559.8	1 750.0	1 945.4	2 111.9	2 285.9	2 481.3	2 702.1	2 941.2	3 117.7
% growth	—	9	13	12	11	8	8	8	8	8	6
M1	103	132	148	174	195	222	249	296	346	388	423
% growth	—	28	12	17	11	13	12	18	16	12	9
Relative to GDP	9	10	9	9	8	8	8	9	9	9	9
M2	672	808	956	1 207.1	1 529.1	1 832.4	2 117.8	2 507.1	2 829.4	3 310.6	3 726.7
% growth	—	20	18	26	26	19	15	18	12	17	12
Relative to GDP	59	62	61	65	70	73	74	78	77	78	79
M3	810	952	1 146.8	1 477.5	1 873.8	2 246.4	2 662.8	3 187.1	3 748.0	4 449.6	5 045.5
% growth	—	17	20	28	26	19	18	19	17	18	13
Relative to GDP	71	73	73	79	85	89	93	100	103	105	107
Financial assets	1 123.2	1 333.0	1 611.6	2 022.3	2 553.8	3 078.0	3 714.1	4 725.6	6 031.5	7 653.3	8 736.3
% growth	—	18	20	25	26	20	20	27	27	26	14
Relative to GDP	99	102	103	108	117	122	131	148	165	182	186
CB deposits	627	752	893	1 135.1	1 440.8	1 751.5	2 035.1	2 427.3	2 760.9	3 250.0	3 683.1
% growth	—	20	18	27	26	21	16	19	13	17	13
Relative to GDP	55	57	57	61	66	69	71	76	76	77	78
FC deposits	89	99	135	192	260	337	415	542	747	914	1 040.1
% growth	—	10	36	42	34	29	23	30	37	22	13
Relative to GDP	7	7	8	10	11	13	14	17	20	21	22

CB credits	543	672	853	1 110.6	1 481.9	1 789.4	2 161.9	2 669.1	3 430.4	4 230.5	4 825.1
% growth	—	23	26	30	33	20	20	23	28	23	14
Relative to GDP	48	51	54	59	67	71	76	83	94	100	102
FC credits	102	116	154	238	314	415	547	733	1 008.0	1 301.4	1 488.2
% growth	—	13	32	54	32	31	31	33	37	29	14
Relative to GDP	9	8	9	12	14	16	19	23	27	31	31
CB+FC credit/deposit, %	90	93	98	102	106	106	111	115	127	133	134

Notes: CB denotes commercial banks; FC denotes finance companies.

Source: Bank of Thailand.

163

Table 9.3   Domestic and international interest rates, 1990–96 (per cent)

		US federal funds rate (A)	One-month Eurodollar rate (B)	Bangkok inter-bank rate (C)	Bangkok–Fed funds differential (C–A)	Bangkok– Eurodollar differential (C–B)	MLR
1990	Q1	8.22	8.35	10.32	2.10	1.97	14.00
	Q2	8.20	8.35	12.02	3.81	3.66	14.50
	Q3	8.11	8.16	14.71	6.60	6.55	14.75
	Q4	7.68	8.15	14.44	6.76	6.29	16.25
	Av.	8.05	8.25	12.87	4.82	4.62	14.88
1991	Q1	6.42	6.79	13.63	7.21	6.84	16.00
	Q2	5.77	6.05	12.81	7.05	6.76	15.50
	Q3	5.56	5.79	10.70	5.14	4.91	16.00
	Q4	4.74	5.06	7.46	2.72	2.41	14.00
	Av.	5.62	5.92	11.15	5.53	5.23	15.38
1992	Q1	3.89	4.23	5.48	1.60	1.25	12.50
	Q2	3.74	3.97	7.66	3.92	3.69	12.00
	Q3	3.27	3.38	7.38	4.11	4.00	12.00
	Q4	3.05	3.43	7.24	4.19	3.81	11.50
	Av.	3.49	3.75	6.94	3.45	3.19	12.00
1993	Q1	3.06	3.19	8.15	5.09	4.96	11.25
	Q2	2.99	3.17	8.60	5.60	5.42	11.25
	Q3	3.09	3.17	6.34	3.25	3.17	11.25
	Q4	2.99	3.24	3.11	0.12	–0.13	10.50
	Av.	3.04	3.19	6.55	3.51	3.36	11.06
1994	Q1	3.21	3.36	7.24	4.03	3.88	10.13
	Q2	3.94	4.19	8.00	4.07	3.81	11.00
	Q3	4.51	4.72	7.35	2.84	2.62	11.50
	Q4	5.21	5.54	6.41	1.20	0.87	11.75
	Av.	4.22	4.45	7.25	3.03	2.80	11.09
1995	Q1	5.80	6.10	13.30	7.50	7.20	13.00
	Q2	6.00	6.10	11.10	5.10	5.10	13.50
	Q3	5.80	5.90	9.20	3.40	3.40	13.75
	Q4	5.70	5.70	10.20	4.40	4.50	13.75
	Av.	5.80	5.90	11.00	5.10	5.00	13.50
1996	Q1	5.40	5.20	7.30	1.90	2.10	13.75
	Q2	5.30	5.20	7.20	2.00	2.00	13.75
	Q3	5.30	5.20	11.40	6.10	6.20	13.50
	Q4	5.30	5.30	11.00	5.70	5.60	13.25
	Av.	5.30	5.30	9.20	3.90	4.00	13.56

Source: Bank of Thailand.

5 per cent while they reduced rates for retail clients by only 1.75 per cent. Banks exploited the weaker negotiating power of retail customers in order to compensate for reduced revenues from their prime commercial borrowers. When banks were required to adopt a minimum retail rate (MRR) based on deposit rates and operating costs, the difference between the prime rate or minimum lending rate (MLR) and the MRR decreased to some extent.

Capital Market

New capital raised in the Stock Exchange of Thailand (SET) surged from 17.5 billion baht in 1990 to 55 million baht per year in 1991–3 and to 130 billion baht per year in 1994–5. Market capitalization therefore expanded remarkably, from 29.4 per cent of GDP in 1990 to 85.9 per cent in 1995. The SET index rose from 612.9 in 1990 to a peak of 1682.9 in 1993, and settled at 1280.8 in 1995 in line with the pace of economic activities. Meanwhile, investors became increasingly diversified to include not only retail buyers but also institutional ones such as provident funds, mutual funds and insurance companies. In parallel, private debt markets captured much attention. Domestic issues of debentures rocketed from 6.3 billion baht in 1991 to 50.5 billion baht in 1995. Convertible debentures increased fourfold from 1993 to 1995.

As one consequence of the liberalization process, increasing capital mobility encouraged overseas placement. The total fixed-income instruments issued abroad rose from 58.8 billion baht in 1993 to 103.4 billion baht in 1995. On the local front, foreign investment, or net capital inflows, became exceedingly prominent in the Thai capital market. Influenced both by external factors (for

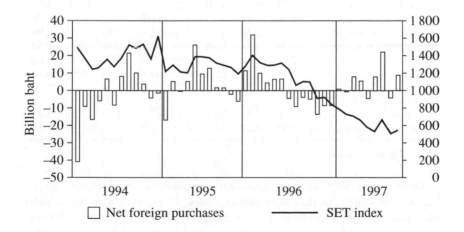

Figure 9.1   SET index and net foreign purchases

example, the Mexican financial crisis, the collapse of Barings, the depreciation of the US dollar versus the yen, and the Asian financial turmoil) and by
internal factors (such as political instability), net foreign purchases of shares
functioned as a prime mover of the SET index (Figure 9.1). Moreover, the huge
magnitude of net foreign capital flows had unrivalled repercussions on the
money market as well as on the economy as a whole.

Financial Institution Performance

Stronger competition as a result of liberalization reduced commercial banks'
share of household savings. The proportion of household savings deposited at
commercial banks declined from 73.35 per cent in 1989 to 70.71 per cent in
1993, and to 66.95 per cent in 1996, while the share of savings placed with
finance companies surged from 10.30 per cent to 14.78 per cent and 16.75 per
cent in the same period (Table 9.4). Moreover, new mutual fund management
companies organized a large number of funds to attract local savers. The picture
was the same on the credit side. The market share of commercial banks shrank
from 75.48 per cent in 1989 to 70.51 per cent in 1993, and to 67.41 per cent in
1996, while that of finance companies rose from 14.97 per cent to 19.37 per
cent, and to 20.79 per cent in the same period (Table 9.5).

*Table 9.4   Percentage share of household savings at financial institutions, by
type of institution, 1989–96*

	1989	1990	1991	1992	1993	1994	1995	1996
Commercial banks	73.35	75.14	74.40	72.22	70.71	68.64	68.36	66.95
Finance companies	10.30	10.11	11.27	13.68	14.78	16.43	16.48	16.75
Life insurance companies	2.47	2.40	2.51	2.59	2.67	2.84	2.71	2.96
Agricultural cooperatives	0.36	0.34	0.34	0.34	0.37	0.40	0.43	0.43
Savings cooperatives	2.69	2.52	2.56	2.96	3.49	3.83	4.07	4.60
Crédit foncier companies	0.15	0.12	0.14	0.16	0.18	0.17	0.15	0.16
Government Savings Bank	8.80	7.31	6.66	6.05	5.62	5.38	5.16	5.20
Bank for Agriculture & Agricultural Cooperatives	0.69	0.85	0.84	0.82	0.90	1.07	1.29	1.45
Government Housing Bank	1.19	1.21	1.28	1.18	1.28	1.24	1.35	1.50

Source: Bank of Thailand.

Greater competition as a consequence of deregulation motivated commercial
banks to economize on their operating expenses. Thai commercial banks' ratio
of operating expenses to total assets decreased from 11.06 per cent in 1990 to
9.52 per cent in 1996, resulting in a rise of net profits from 0.7 per cent of total
assets in 1989 to 1.28 per cent in 1996 (Table 9.6). Commercial banks put more

effort into fee-based income-earning activities, reflecting bank interest in additional opportunities. Their fee-based income grew from 4.16 per cent of total income in 1988 to 6.84 per cent in 1996.

Table 9.5   Credits extended by financial institutions by type of institution, 1989–96 (per cent)

	1989	1990	1991	1992	1993	1994	1995	1996
Commercial banks	75.48	74.90	73.78	71.89	70.51	69.63	68.48	67.41
Finance companies	14.97	15.64	16.74	18.21	19.37	20.46	21.07	20.79
Life insurance	0.77	0.83	0.78	0.70	0.55	0.44	0.40	0.44
Agricultural cooperatives	0.53	0.51	0.49	0.47	0.44	0.37	0.41	0.33
Savings cooperatives	2.73	2.50	2.39	2.61	2.73	2.62	2.68	2.97
Pawnshops	0.40	0.35	0.32	0.29	0.24	0.22	0.20	0.20
Crédit foncier companies	0.19	0.16	0.15	0.17	0.16	0.12	0.11	0.09
Government Savings Bank	0.41	0.58	0.61	0.61	0.82	0.66	0.64	0.79
BAAC	2.03	1.96	2.01	2.06	2.05	1.96	2.03	2.31
Industrial Finance								
Corporation of Thailand	1.02	1.07	1.08	1.20	1.23	1.16	1.24	1.44
Government Housing Bank	1.47	1.50	1.64	1.78	1.90	2.04	2.30	2.77
Small Industrial Finance								
Corporation	0.00	0.00	0.01	0.00	0.00	0.01	0.01	0.10
Export–Import Bank	—	—	—	—	—	0.31	0.43	0.45

Source: Bank of Thailand.

Nevertheless, Thai financial institutions did not catch up with the booming real sector in the late 1980s and the early 1990s. The Thai economy then was advancing at a very rapid pace, demanding more complicated financial services and instruments which could not be offered by local banks and finance companies. For instance, domestic financial institutions lagged behind in long-term project financing capability and maturity matching tactics. Unsurprisingly, in the presence of stable local currency a large number of credible corporations and agencies resorted to foreign sources of funds and financial services.

Domestic commercial banks and finance companies hardly tapped long-term deposits on variable interest rates so as to fund long-term credits. Even though there was no benchmark rate or government securities yield to refer to (because the government attained cash surplus in nine consecutive years in the period 1988–96), banks could have innovated various schemes of returns to attract long-term deposits. Owing to this shortfall and conservative attitude, bank clients depended heavily upon overdrafts, instead of long-term credits, for long-term fund uses, entailing liquidity risks to borrowers and contingent bad debt risks to original lenders. Similar maturity mismatch also prevailed when foreign credits were resorted to via BIBR. Whenever creditors doubt the creditworthiness of debtors or debtor countries, credit roll-over may not be possible, engendering liquidity shortages among borrowers, as widely experienced in the 1997 financial crisis.

Table 9.6   Performance of Thai commercial banks, 1987–96 (per cent)

	Income/Total assets	Expenses/Total assets	Net profits/Total assets
1987	9.62	8.57	0.68
1988	9.51	8.36	0.68
1989	10.75	9.54	0.70
1990	12.65	11.06	0.98
1991	12.98	11.29	0.89
1992	12.51	10.44	1.32
1993	10.62	8.46	1.44
1994	10.72	8.22	1.86
1995	12.09	9.36	1.82
1996	12.00	9.52	1.28

Source: Bank of Thailand.

What is more distressing is that domestic banks and finance companies were weak at the fundamental core. Their operating staff were rarely efficient in evaluating credit applications or project feasibility. Instead, they frequently based their decisions upon collaterals or back-up assets or connections. Worse yet, the central authority was rather deficient in examining and supervising local banks and finance companies. Consequently, Thai commercial banks' and finance companies' asset quality was largely fragile or highly vulnerable to macroeconomic disturbances. In this respect, one may conclude that financial liberalization was, to some extent, premature, as the supporting system was not yet ready to cope with drastic and rapid changes.

Corporate Behaviour

After the financial crisis several criticisms, such as the following, were raised against private corporations or business entities: excessive investment even in areas where comparative advantage or expertise was missing, too much foreign borrowing, especially without forward cover, and maturity mismatching such as short-term borrowing for long-term uses. But if all pertinent factors are examined, one can see that not all errors should be attributed to business undertakers. Normally, private businesses are profit maximizers. They were thus tempted to invest when the economy was booming and when they had easy access to cheap foreign funding in the midst of stable exchange rates, while local financial institutions did not offer them many opportunities. Therefore, though corporates' decision framework may seem imprudent with respect to allocation of capital and efficiency in capital utilization, part of the blame should be placed upon privileges given by investment promotion agencies, liberalized (foreign exchange) capital accounts under rigid exchange rates, and the weak decision framework of, as well as protracted process at, local financial institutions to begin with.

Asset Quality

Financial liberalization fuelled a spree of excessive or speculative spending and investment in several sectors of Thailand's economy. Funded largely by foreign borrowing, enterprises in these 'bubble' sectors became vulnerable to unfavourable exchange rate changes, unwillingness of creditors to roll over maturing debts, and the possibility that the business itself might flop. Negative impacts of the financial liberalization on the financial system did not emerge until the mid-1990s. Since those enterprises were also considerably accommodated by domestic commercial banks and finance companies, the asset quality of local financial institutions deteriorated to an alarming extent. For example, the non-performing loans of Thai commercial banks jumped from 8 per cent of total loans in June 1997 to 20 per cent in December 1997, and to 45 per cent in December 1998.

The course of the boom in the property market, for example, can be inferred from the data on the area of construction permitted in municipal zones (Table 9.7). From 1987 to 1988, the area under construction increased by 65.8 per cent for Thailand as a whole and for the Bangkok metropolis it almost doubled (a 98.8 per cent increase). The situation was quite different a few years later. From 1993 to 1994, the construction area declined by 5 per cent in the country as a whole and by 12.2 per cent in the Bangkok metropolis. Restrictive monetary measures implemented after mid-1995 to contain inflation drove interest rates up, putting real estate enterprises in a predicament. The construction area plunged 28.8 per cent in the country as a whole from 1995 to 1996, and it fell 37.5 per cent in Bangkok.

Lenders to these real estate firms were battered by the subsequent negative chain reaction. In 1996, commercial banks absorbed 53.7 per cent of all property credit outstanding, followed by finance companies with a 45.7 per cent share. However, for commercial banks property credits added up to only 8.8 per cent of their total credits, while property credits amounted to almost one-quarter (24.4 per cent) of total credits extended by finance companies (Table 9.8). In other words, finance companies were more vulnerable than commercial banks

Table 9.7 *Area of construction permitted in municipal zones, 1987–96 (million square metres)*

	1987	1988	1989	1990	1991	1992	1993	1994	1995	1996
Residential	7.23	12.13	15.48	20.34	19.88	18.80	21.45	24.38	23.11	16.08
% change	—	67.8	27.6	31.4	–2.3	–5.4	14.1	13.7	–5.2	–30.4
Commercial	3.82	5.73	10.39	14.04	18.24	14.30	14.05	8.06	10.71	8.12
% change	—	50.2	81.2	35.1	29.9	–21.6	–1.8	–42.7	32.9	–24.2
Industrial & other	1.05	2.20	2.63	3.85	3.21	3.13	2.52	3.70	2.95	1.96
% change	—	108.7	19.6	46.3	–16.4	–2.6	–19.4	46.7	–20.2	–33.5
Whole kingdom	12.10	20.06	28.50	38.23	41.33	36.23	38.02	36.14	36.77	26.16
% change	—	65.8	42.0	34.1	8.1	–2.3	5.0	–5.0	1.7	–28.8
Bangkok metropolis	6.84	13.59	19.37	25.86	32.71	27.24	29.72	26.11	25.38	15.85
% change	—	98.8	42.5	33.5	26.5	–16.7	9.1	–12.2	–2.8	–37.5

Source: Bank of Thailand.

to the real estate bust. In the end, when the currency crisis critically weakened Thailand's economy, 56 finance companies had to be shut down in December 1997 and four commercial banks were taken over by the government in February 1998.

Real estate was not the only sector in which bubble growth caused deterioration in the asset quality of financial institutions. There was considerable oversupply in other Thai industries as well. In 1996, supply was 192 per cent of domestic demand in the automotive industry, private hospital beds were 300 percent of demand, supply of steel bars was 150 per cent of demand, and supply of petrochemicals was 195 per cent of demand.[1] These imbalances were created in part by investment incentives offered by various public authorities, but to the extent that domestic financial institutions lent to firms in these sectors, their assets became vulnerable to the course of the bubble.

Table 9.8 Bills, loans and overdrafts of commercial banks classified by purposes (million baht)

	1995		1996		1997	
	Dec.	Share	Dec.	Share	Dec.	Share
Agriculture	158 940	3.7	164 019	3.4	161 695	2.7
Mining	24 985	0.6	24 476	0.5	36 000	0.6
Manufacturing	1 097 338	25.8	1 313 546	27.1	1 872 325	30.9
Construction	185 850	4.4	236 341	4.9	273 064	4.5
Real estate business	400 184	9.4	426 100	8.8	490 521	8.1
Imports	139 976	3.3	146 409	3.0	174 443	2.9
Exports	182 710	4.3	196 056	4.0	218 899	3.6
Wholesale and retail trade	756 799	17.8	870 225	17.9	1 037 812	17.1
Public utilities	108 106	2.5	142 751	2.9	197 128	3.3
Banking and other financial business	339 204	8.0	345 330	7.1	487 514	8.0
Services	333 296	7.8	377 839	7.8	458 037	7.6
Personal consumption	523 437	12.3	612 595	12.6	652 516	10.8
Total	4 250 825	100	4 855 688	100	6 059 956	100

Source: Bank of Thailand.

Another cause of the decline in asset quality at domestic financial institutions was financial mismanagement by Thai businesses. For example, maturity mismatching required firms to roll over debt frequently and uncovered net foreign exchange positions generated onerous burdens and great risks when exchange rates fluctuated widely. At the same time, unlisted firms that relied heavily on debt financing were highly susceptible to liquidity shortage. Overall, such business practices among borrowers lowered the asset quality of Thai banks and finance companies to a considerable extent in the mid-1990s. A final reason for the decline in the overall quality of financial institutions' assets was the increase in the proportion of small clients, who brought about greater risks, compared to large borrowers, since large borrowers have more credit access as a result of liberalization.

Macroeconomic Impacts and Policy Implications

Exchange rate stability was a major factor promoting capital inflows. Before July 1997, Thai monetary authorities were extremely conservative in their exchange rate policy. The baht had long been pegged to the US dollar. Daily fixings did not move the baht value against the US dollar to any significant extent from 1978 to 1981. Neither did the basket pegging system in use from 1984 to 1997, since the US dollar commanded the preponderant weight in the basket. (Between 1981 and 1984, the baht was fixed against the US dollar.) As a result of this exchange rate policy, foreign borrowing denominated in US dollars entailed negligible exchange risk. In the absence of a well-developed domestic debt market, the stability of the baht exchange rate, together with lower interest rates abroad, motivated private Thai businesses to tap foreign funds recklessly without hedging. To external creditors, Thailand's exchange rate stability, together with the impressive record of real GDP growth, offered appealing opportunities for interest arbitrage and speculation. The net capital inflows to Thailand rose from 8 per cent of GDP in 1990 to 14 per cent of GDP in 1995 (Table 9.9).

Table 9.9   Total net capital inflows to Thailand, 1989–96 (US$ billion)

	1985	1986	1987	1988	1989	1990
Net inflows	1.9	0.4	0.8	2.9	6.6	7.2
% of GDP	5	1	1	5	9	8
	1991	1992	1993	1994	1995	1996
Net inflows	10.6	8.1	12.6	15.8	22.8	18.1
% of GDP	11	7	1	13	14	10

Source: Bank of Thailand.

The influx of foreign capital as a consequence of financial liberalization had two crucial macroeconomic repercussions. First, it ominously magnified the momentum of the spending spree. Furthermore, given that money is extremely fungible, there was no way for the government to guarantee that the foreign borrowings were directed to productive uses. A substantial part of the run-up in stock and property prices in the first half of the 1990s was attributed to imported capital, in spite of some central bank regulations. From a macroeconomic viewpoint, foreign funds enlarged the country's current account deficits (Figure 9.2). The second repercussion was that the large volume of capital inflows, especially the short-term ones, increased Thailand's balance-of-payments vulnerability. Because of the short time frame or high mobility of their funds, foreign fund lenders were highly sensitive to changes or disruptions in conditions. Whether they would roll over or retrieve credits meant volatility to the country's balance of payments.

Financial liberalization engenders a number of policy trade-offs. Opening up the financial border means more competition and, it is hoped, more efficient use of funds, but it also reduces the autonomy of policy makers with respect to interest rates. Domestic interest rates become subject to international market pressures, while new financial instruments mean that monetary aggregates, such as M2, less accurately reflect the actual condition of the economy. For instance, in 1994, when Thailand's M2 growth fell to 12.9 per cent a year from its previous rate of 18.4 per cent, both inflation and the current account deficits were on the rise. In addition, a country cannot maintain a fixed exchange rate policy once the capital account is opened, because reserves of foreign exchange are finite. In other words, the benefit of liberal capital movement comes at the expense of exchange rate stability. Altogether, financial deregulation stimulates the degree of competition in financial resource mobilization, increases the

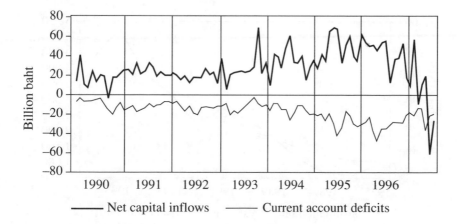

Figure 9.2   Current account deficits and net capital inflows

volatility of domestic liquidity due to foreign fund flows and compounds the difficulty of macroeconomic policy making.

INTO THE STORM

Net capital inflows perform two functions; they finance current account deficits and they fuel economic activities. Foreign capital is essential in most developing countries where foreign exchange reserves are usually insufficient to finance continuing current account deficits. But inflow of foreign capital, if excessive and not sterilized by the central bank, can engender both superfluous spending or investment (Figure 9.3) and debt service that leads to future current account deficits. Thus developing countries must handle capital inflows carefully. At the current stage of globalization, foreign capital has become virtually intractable. Its high mobility, volatility and large volumes have made it overwhelmingly powerful. Developing countries should be forewarned about reliance upon foreign capital funds: 'too little may bring about today's pain, but too much may nullify tomorrow's gain'.

Immediate Outcome

The striking appreciation of the yen and the currencies of the newly industrialized countries (NICs) that followed the 1985 Plaza Accord triggered enormous flows of capital to developing countries, including Thailand. Foreign investment helped raise Thailand's economic growth rate to over 10 per cent per year in 1988–90. The consequence was widespread speculation in both real estate and

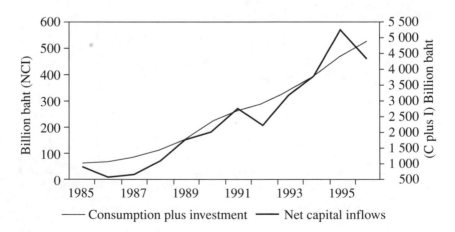

Figure 9.3   Net capital inflows and consumption plus investment

capital markets. Property prices rose to unprecedented levels, pushed by the increased capital market activities and real estate demand. The economy slowed down somewhat in the early 1990s, but the growth rate was still a robust 8.1–8.5 per cent per year (Table 9.2). The economy was reinvigorated in the second half of 1993 by a decline in world interest rates and by the commencement of BIBF. Again an influx of foreign capital fuelled both capital market transactions and property speculation.

The net inflows of capital considerably increased the supply of money in circulation in Thailand (Figure 9.4). The inflows were also clearly reflected in

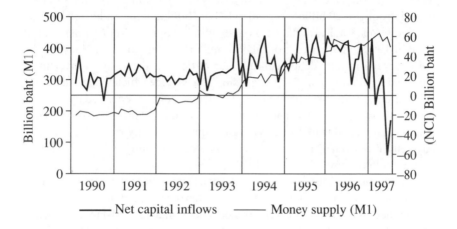

Figure 9.4   Effect of net capital inflows on money supply

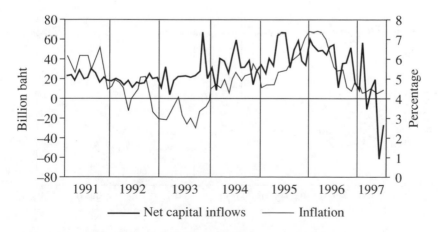

Figure 9.5   Inflation and net capital inflows

the growing extent of current account deficits and inflation (Figures 9.2 and 9.5). From a low of 3 per cent in 1993, inflation climbed to 6 per cent at the end of 1994 and peaked at 7 per cent in early 1996. In other words, while the foreign capital helped propel the pace of economic expansion, it also stoked looming macroeconomic peril.

Detrimental External Debt

The vigorous foreign borrowing that followed financial liberalization was reflected in Thailand's swelling external debt outstanding, which more than tripled, from US$29 billion in 1990 to US$94 billion in the middle of 1997. In relative terms, total external debt outstanding exploded from 34 per cent of GDP in 1990 to 59 per cent of GDP in mid-1997 (Figure 9.6). Not only did these surging foreign debts fuel the trade deficits or the savings–investment gap but they also brought about increasing debt service which worsened current account deficits in subsequent years. The vicious circle generated by external debt is shown by the fact that the proportion of Thailand's current account deficits that were due to debt service grew quite markedly from 1990. Income payments rose from 37 per cent of the current account deficits in 1990 to 50 per cent in 1996 (Figure 9.7).

Private external debt can be particularly detrimental to the current account. Private debt is typically charged at higher interest rates, for shorter maturities, and applied to riskier commercial projects than bilateral assistance or normal external borrowing by public agencies. Unfortunately, private debts predomi-

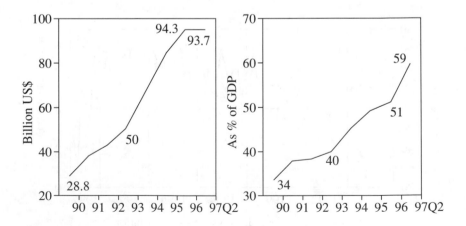

Figure 9.6   Swelling external debt outstanding

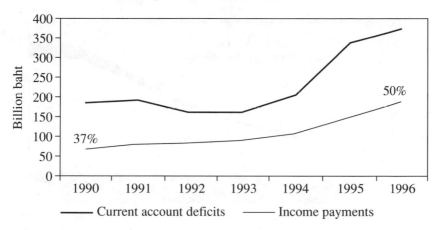

Figure 9.7   *Income payments and current account deficits*

nated in Thailand. From 1990 to 1996, the Thai government commanded a continual cash surplus, so its capital inflow was virtually nil (Figure 9.8). Almost all of these private debts belonged to the non-bank sector because Thai commercial banks were subject to limitations on their net foreign exchange positions (Figure 9.9).[2] Furthermore, the non-bank private sector's share in Thailand's external debt outstanding was not only large but also expanding, from 51 per cent in 1990 to 72 per cent in mid-1997. Given the typical time frame of private borrowers, the short-term portion of the country's external debts ballooned from 22 per cent in 1990 to 50 per cent in 1995–6 (Figure 9.10).

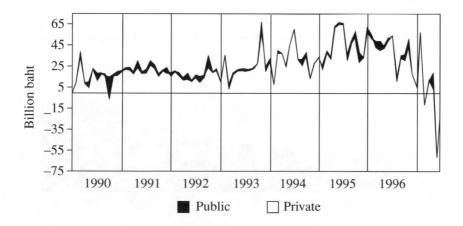

Figure 9.8   *Private and public net capital inflows*

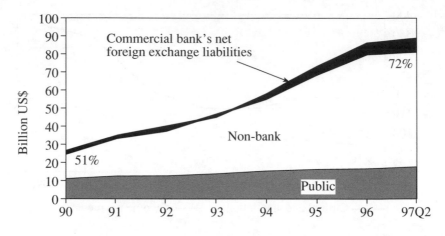

Figure 9.9   Growing external debts of the non-bank private sector

The short-term nature of the external claims put both individual borrowers and the country at risk of a liquidity shortage should creditors decide not to roll over maturing debts.

With very few controls on capital inflows,[3] Thai external debts surged ominously, even relative to the government's foreign exchange reserves. Since a sizable part of those reserves came from net capital inflows or foreign borrowings, the adequacy of these reserves should be judged by comparing them with external debt outstanding, not just months of imports. The ratio of

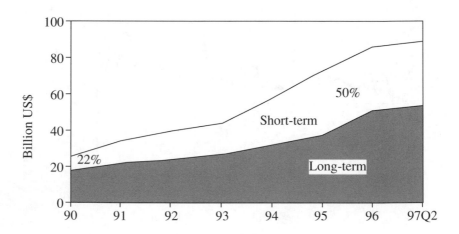

Figure 9.10   Short-term and long-term external debts

Thailand's external debts to reserves indicates extreme vulnerability. Even though the ratio of long-term debts to reserves rose only slightly, the ratio of short-term debts to reserves almost doubled, so that the ratio of long- plus short-term debts to reserves grew from 186 per cent in 1990 to 264 per cent in mid-1997 (Figure 9.11).

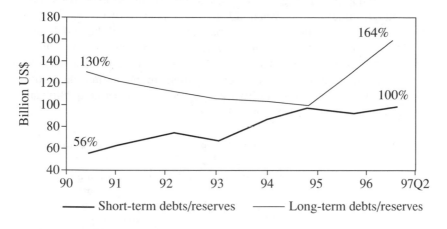

Figure 9.11   External debts/reserves ratios

Unfortunate Coincidence

The precarious spending spree financed largely by short-term private borrowing was followed by the unfortunate coincidence of four events. The first was the emergence of macroeconomic disequilibrium. Prior to 1993, Thailand had succeeded in maintaining macroeconomic stability, if stability means that the current account balance is low relative to GDP. Between 1982 and 1992, Thailand's current account deficit had reached the 8 per cent level only once, in 1990 (Table 9.10). After 1993, however, the current account deficit started to increase menacingly. In both 1995 and 1996, the external deficit surpassed 8 per cent again. Apparently, the current account deficits were pushed upwards by the powerful inflows of foreign capital (Figure 9.2). In other words, the financial liberalization and the consequent capital inflows eventually disturbed Thailand's macroeconomic stability.

Macroeconomic disequilibrium was aggravated by a second incident, the Bank of Thailand's extension of financial assistance to ailing finance companies and commercial banks in order to preserve the stability of these financial institutions during 1996 and 1997. Problems, such as excessive credit extension, non-performing loans, low asset quality, inadequate capital and loan-loss provisions, that stemmed from the liberal capital inflows, stable exchange rates, outdated rules and supervisory inefficiency were causing many Thai financial institutions to falter. The cheap and easily accessible foreign credits had spurred domestic finance firms and banks to compete among themselves for clients and this resulted in their imprudent extension of too much credit. Worse yet, supervision of financial institutions was poor in several respects including classification of non-performing assets, loan-loss provisions, financial disclosure, corporate governance, cronyism and bankruptcy laws. Worst of all were the absence of a market-oriented deposit insurance system and the widely held belief that financial institutions almost never go bankrupt or shut down. In the presence of the weaknesses in the financial sector and rising political tensions, the Bank of Thailand could not resist coming to the rescue of financial institutions that were short of liquidity as a result of poor asset quality and mismanagement between 1996 and 1997.

Table 9.10   Thailand's current account balance and domestic inflation

	Current account balance as a % of GDP	Thai–US inflation differential (per cent)
1982	−3.2	−1.0
1983	−7.8	0.6
1984	−5.1	−3.4
1985	−4.1	−1.2
1986	0.6	0.0
1987	−0.8	−1.2
1988	−2.6	−0.3
1989	−3.5	0.6
1990	−8.5	0.6
1991	−7.7	1.5
1992	−5.7	1.0
1993	−5.1	0.3
1994	−5.6	2.5
1995	−8.1	3.0
1996	−8.0	3.0

Source: Bank of Thailand.

The Bank of Thailand rescue conflicted with the appropriate strategies for restoring macroeconomic stability. The narrow scope of the repurchase market in Thailand limited the amount of sterilization that the central bank could conduct. As a result, the bailout of the financial institutions tended to enlarge the money supply. Credit injected by the Financial Institutions Development Fund (FIDF), the rescue arm of the central bank, together with the repurchase market (RP), was highly correlated with monetary base growth from September 1996 to September 1997 (Figure 9.12). The growing money supply fuelled further spending and exacerbated both the current account deficits and domestic inflation.

In addition, the central bank's frequent rescue measures signall the instability of the financial system, which shook confidence of foreign creditors to a large extent, as a sizable portion of their overseas credits was extended to financial institutions. Some creditors began to question the nation's credibility, while others started to retrieve their funds instead of rolling over.

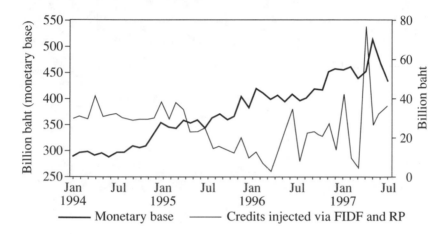

Figure 9.12   Bank of Thailand's rescue credits

The third unfortunate event occurred on the exchange rate front when the value of the US dollar began surging ahead from April 1995 onward (Figure 9.13). Between April 1995 and June 1997 the US currency appreciated by 38 per cent against the yen, from 84 to 116 yen, and by 27 per cent against the Deutschmark, from 1.38 DM to 1.75 DM. The baht value rose in tandem because it was tightly pegged to a currency basket dominated by the US dollar. Such appreciation of the baht definitely worked against Thailand's deteriorating current account deficits.

The fourth and final event occurred on the price-level front. The excess of Thai inflation over the US inflation rate began growing conspicuously from 1993 (Figure 9.14). Because the pegged exchange rate regime held the baht–dollar exchange rate virtually stable, the increase in domestic inflation caused overvaluation of the baht. The higher inflationary differential made Thai commodities less competitive in international markets if the baht did not depreciate to compensate. In fact, the currency did not depreciate at all against the US dollar in spite of the growing deficits on Thailand's current account.

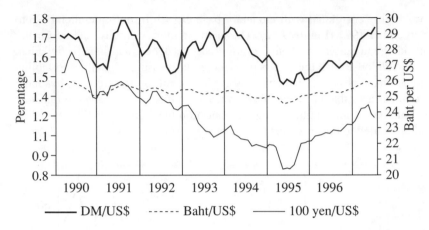

Figure 9.13   Exchange rates of the US dollar and the baht

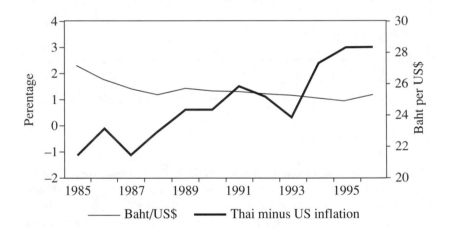

Figure 9.14   Inflation differential and baht value

Extreme Predicament

The combination of these four events – threatening current account deficits, the Bank of Thailand's assistance to ailing banks and finance firms, appreciation of the dollar and the baht, and growing excess inflation – weakened investor confidence to a large degree and caused widespread expectations in the middle of 1997 that the central bank would not defend the baht much longer. The anticipated baht devaluation triggered a flood of capital outflows to liquidate short-term foreign debts or to speculate against the baht. The capital outflows resulted in a plunge in the Bank of Thailand's foreign exchange reserves (Figure 9.15). Finally, the baht was floated on 2 July 1997.

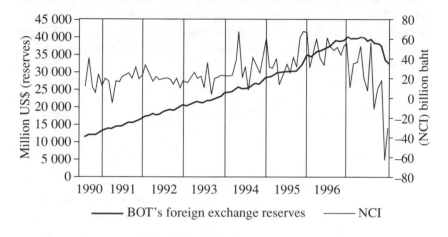

Figure 9.15   Net capital outflows and lower reserves

The outflows of capital were extreme. Daily baht transactions in foreign exchange markets in 1997 amounted to US$4 billion, or 3.6 per cent of Thailand's 4990 billion baht nominal GDP for 1997, at an average exchange rate of 45 baht per dollar. The annual turnover volume was equivalent to 950 per cent of GDP. This huge volume of capital flows drew the country's foreign

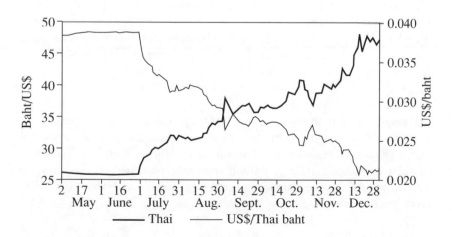

Figure 9.16   Baht exchange rates in 1997

exchange reserves down to such an extent that exchange rate flotation became an essential.

After the exchange rate was floated, the currency nosedived, from 26 baht per US dollar on 30 June 1997 to 38 on 4 September 1997 and to 47 on 31 December 1997: 45 per cent down from June (Figure 9.16). By the beginning of January 1998, the US dollar had climbed to 56 baht, but it stabilized at around 36 baht at the end of the year.

RESOLUTION AND CONSEQUENCES

Macro Aspects

The Thai monetary authorities succeeded in obtaining a rescue package worth US$17.2 billion from the International Monetary Fund (IMF) in August 1997. This aid came with a series of stringent conditions designed to rectify Thailand's economic fundamentals. Examples of those requirements are budgetary cash surplus, tight monetary policy, privatization of some state enterprises and various financial reforms, including adoption of international standards for asset classification, loan-loss provisions, capital adequacy, bankruptcy and deposit insurance.

The drastic depreciation of the baht, together with rigid IMF conditions, generated extreme economic difficulties. Higher costs of inputs from abroad led to production cutbacks and higher inflation. Tight liquidity and a heavy foreign debt burden aggravated the situation, so numerous companies opted to 'downsize' their operations, reducing employment as well as pay scales. Declining purchasing power together with the economic downturn gave rise to more bad debts and a growing number of bankruptcies, which had an adverse impact upon national credibility. Foreign capital continued to shun Thailand and new lenders hesitated because of the spread of the crisis to other South East Asian countries. This slackening stream of capital inflows exacerbated the tight domestic liquidity demanded by the IMF.

Foreign capital is an indispensable fuel for economic growth in developing countries like Thailand, and capital inflows require both confidence and stable exchange rates. In other words, Thailand's economic recuperation depends on restoring confidence on the part of international capital markets. According to a recent survey, the five main factors affecting investor confidence, in priority order, are the following:

1. political stability,
2. competence of the economic management team,

3. external account, including trade balance, current account and balance of payments,
4. efficiency and stability in the financial system, and
5. foreign exchange reserves.

Thus, to mend confidence, Thailand, and other ailing countries, must repair their macroeconomic fundamentals as soon as possible. They need to achieve a balanced fiscal budget, to reduce excess spending and to renovate weak and unstable financial systems. The ultimate target of these efforts is a manageable current account balance and inflation. In a world of rapid information technology and rational expectations, once such a target is reached, market confidence will return, together with exchange rate stability and capital inflows, which will allow for gradual reduction of domestic interest rates to facilitate further economic recovery.

Given that efficiency and stability in the financial system represents one primary factor affecting investor confidence, a promising way to buttress investor confidence is through a market-oriented deposit insurance mechanism. Deposit insurance is a controversial and intricate issue. If mishandled, it could bring about moral hazard and vicious cycles, as evidenced in several industrial countries in the past. What should be pursued simultaneously is transparency and the setting of insurance premia and/or offering insurance coverage in accordance with actual market risks. Such market-oriented deposit insurance, together with efficient examination and supervision to be conducted by the central monetary authorities, will not only upgrade the calibre of domestic financial institutions but also bolster public confidence (which is absolutely indispensable) in the financial system.

Micro Aspects

In the second half of 1997 the Thai government promulgated emergency decrees to undertake a financial restructuring package. The package had five essential elements. First, whenever there is an urgent need, the Bank of Thailand shall have authority to order a commercial bank or finance company, without having to go through a shareholders' meeting, to write down its capital below the value as stipulated by law and to allocate share increases. In addition, the Bank of Thailand, with the approval of the minister of finance, shall have power to remove directors or executives of such commercial bank or finance company and appoint replacements. The purpose of the additional authority is to allow timely intervention into inefficient financial intermediaries that experience large losses that endanger the public interest.

Second, the Bank of Thailand Act was amended to reaffirm the government's commitment to have the Financial Institutions Development Fund (FIDF) guarantee for depositors and creditors, with full financial support from the government.

Third, the Financial Sector Restructuring Authority (FRA) is established as an independent entity with the following objectives: (a) to review the rehabilitation plans of suspended finance companies, (b), to assist bona fide depositors and creditors of suspended finance companies, and (c), to administer the liquidation of finance companies which the FRA considers unable to be rehabilitated.

Fourth, the Asset Management Corporation (AMC) is set up to bid for or to purchase impaired assets of finance companies that the FRA deems not viable. The AMC is also empowered to enter a bid for good assets to support a competitive bidding process. The AMC will manage the purchased assets in order to enhance their value or will foreclose the collateral and resell them as soon as possible.

Finally, the limit on foreign ownership of shares in commercial banks and finance companies is raised from 25 per cent to 49 per cent (and in due course 100 per cent) and can be effective for up to ten years. This is to enlarge financial institutions' capital base and strengthen their management tactics.

The FRA's strategy for financial sector reform involves identifying and resolving non-viable institutions, protecting viable institutions, dealing resolutely with non-viable institutions, distributing the burden (shareholders must bear losses first, fraud and gross negligence will be pursued, wilful loan defaults will not be allowed and public sector cost will be minimized) and protecting depositors.

The FRA established the following criteria for the rehabilitation of suspended financial institutions:

- only the strong may reopen,
- strict asset classification and provisioning,
- adequate capital cushion,
- suitable ownership and management,
- maturity of borrowing from the FIDF lengthened,
- conversion of FIDF debt to equity only after write-down of existing shareholders.

On 8 December 1997 after examining the detailed status and proposed rehabilitation plans of all 58 suspended finance companies, the FRA decided to permanently shut down all but two. The FRA based its decision on the following criteria:

- capital adequacy and sources of additional capital funds,
- capability in liquidity management,

- ability to repay debts to FIDF,
- reliability or trustworthiness of executives.

Both depositors and creditors of the 56 defunct finance companies are provided with a government guarantee, whereas the shareholders may claim the excess of assets over liabilities. The monetary authority aims to segregate the 'good' and 'bad' assets of the defunct finance companies. The 'good' assets will be handled by one or two new 'good' banks, to be set up in the near future, while 'bad' assets will be sold to and managed by the newly established AMC.

The Thai authorities' clear-cut approach to resolving the problem of questionable finance firms will contribute to the revival of faith or confidence in Thai financial institutions because (a) it removes the uncertainty concerning the 58 suspended finance companies, (b) it allows only finance companies with adequate capital and good-quality assets to continue operations, (c) it provides for sufficient liquidity and accommodates the reliable debtors of defunct finance companies by turning over good assets to be managed by new commercial banks, and (d) it will protect the benefits of creditors and shareholders through efficient management.

The alternative of entertaining various merger plans would have made the process more time-consuming and would have left core companies with the predicament of handling the dubious assets and liabilities of their merging affiliates.

At the end of 1997, the Thai government decided on a number of means to strengthen the financial system. Commercial banks and finance companies were encouraged to recapitalize to support risky assets and to adopt a dividend moratorium for 1997 and 1998. Strict loan classifications were to be adopted. Actual loan losses must be recognized, but they were made tax-deductible. Foreign capital was welcome and long-term investment was no longer limited. That channel should help enhance the capital base as well as management capabilities or technology. The central bank puts special emphasis upon the role of financial institution management.

On 31 March 1998 the Bank of Thailand tightened regulations on loan classification, provisioning and reporting standards, aiming to upgrade local financial institutions to international levels by the year 2000. With effect from 1 July 1998, the definition of non-performing assets was changed to cover loans three or more months in arrears, instead of the previous six or more months. Two new loan categories, pass and special mention, require 1 per cent and 2 per cent provisioning, respectively. Meanwhile, commercial banks must increase provisions for sub-standard loans from 15 per cent to 20 per cent, the same as for finance companies (Table 9.11). Doubtful loans require 50 per cent provision instead of the previous 100 per cent, but loss loans continue to require 100 per cent coverage.

These new standards will force local banks to increase capital by as much as 80 billion baht by the end of 1998, on top of the 129 billion baht already added. Finance companies will need 42 billion baht of new capital on top of the 20 billion baht recently added. Banks must set aside up to 100 billion baht in new provisions for loan losses, while the set asides by finance companies total 43 billion baht.

Table 9.11   Loan-loss provision requirements for commercial banks

Loan classification	Months overdue	Previous provisions	1998 system of provisioning
Pass	< 1 month	—	1%
Special mention	0–3 months	—	2%
Sub-standard	up to 6 months	15%	20%
Doubtful	up to 1 year	100%	50%
Loss	> 1 year	100%	100%

Source: Bank of Thailand.

The system adopted in March 1998 also calls for quarterly, instead of annual, audits and for credit reports to be submitted to the central bank. Loan portfolio reviews must cover at least 70 per cent of credit outstanding, including the top 100 clients and credits or commitments to related parties. The measures also demand that financial institutions tighten their lending practices and credit analysis procedures, focusing more on the borrowers' cash flow and ability to service debt, rather than on loan collaterals. Debt restructuring or renegotiations must be subject to realistic assessment of the financial viability of the clients or their projects.

On 14 August 1998 the government decided to nationalize six commercial banks and five finance companies. Some of these are merged with government banks or finance companies, while some will be sold to interested parties later on. In addition, the government offered assistance to other financial institutions in the following steps of recapitalization. If financial institutions commit themselves to comply with new loan-loss provisioning immediately, or earlier than the previous target year of 2000, they are entitled to enlarge their first-tier capital by issuing preferred shares to the government in exchange for tradable government bonds. Furthermore, as a means to motivate debt restructuring or reconciliation with problem clients, the government put forward an option to financial institutions to increase their second-tier capital by exchanging non-tradable bonds for banks' newly issued debentures, equalling the losses suffered by financial institutions in their debt restructuring. The underlying dual objective of this 14 August package is to reform the financial system so that new asset classification and loan-loss provisioning come into effect as soon as possible, while reinvigorating the economy. If financial institutions were left by themselves, they could hardly extend credits, because their huge existing non-performing loans (NPLs) have to be backed up by capital funds, which are rather scarce and whose enlargement is very difficult in the midst of the current economic depression. What should be noted is that this 14 August programme is voluntary, so the extent of participation or success of the plan depends on the discretion of financial institutions.

Later on, the central bank will announce new methods for collateral valuation and a plan to establish a deposit insurance agency. At the same time, a new bankruptcy law that contains more options and flexibility will become effective. In the short run, these moves may worsen the credit crunch, but they pave the way for an essential and appropriate financial reform. Once accomplished, the financial reform, together with improved supervision of financial institutions, will help to prevent financial turmoil in the future.

CONCLUSIONS

The strenuous effort that Thailand had to exert to restore the confidence of foreign lenders and domestic savers clearly illustrates the precariousness of the financial liberalization process. Liberalization strengthens market competition and accelerates development in the financial system, but it involves many actors and conditions that may conflict with one another. Furthermore, every party in the prevailing financial atmosphere must be both ready and willing before liberalization is undertaken.

In the first half of the 1990s foreign capital flooded the Thai financial market as a result of financial liberalization and optimistic expectations. These funds fuelled exuberant and/or speculative spending or lending, creating microeconomic imbalances among borrowing entities and disequilibrium in the macroeconomy. In order to preserve stability in the financial system, the central authority offered assistance to ailing financial institutions, despite the fact that such assistance could easily lead to moral hazard among financial executives. Later on, the excessive spending and lending aggravated the country's current account deficits and inflation to such an extent that the government finally deemed a flexible exchange rate system and an IMF-led rescue package to be inevitable: otherwise, the country's financial credibility would be endangered. In retrospect, the crisis can be largely attributed to three policy errors:

* liberalizing foreign capital flows while keeping exchange rates rigid,
* liberalizing financial institutions when they were not yet ready, and
* failing to supervise financial institutions prudently.

The inconsistency between capital account liberalization and fixed exchange rates is obvious from basic economic theory. When the supply of any commodity is allowed to vary without constraint, its price should change according to the relative size of demand and supply. Otherwise, either a glut or a shortage could arise and disturb demanders, suppliers and overall market conditions. Given the glut of capital inflows in 1996 and the first half of 1997, it should come as no surprise to hear as an excuse for not floating the baht then that it could have led to revaluation, not devaluation, which would have weakened the export sector or economic fundamentals. The key error was in not having introduced some exchange rate flexibility into the system from the time that cross-border capital flows were first liberalized. If this had been done, market participants would have taken exchange risks adequately into account and neither a capital glut nor export overvaluation would have resulted.

In this context, some may argue that, under a currency board system, such as the one in Hong Kong, a fixed exchange rate can be operated together with liberal capital flows. However, one essential prerequisite of a currency board is that the volume of monetary aggregates in circulation be in strict proportion to foreign exchange reserves. And, since Thailand cannot comply with this requirement, a fixed exchange rate can hardly coexist with liberal capital flows on a sustainable basis.

The second error, immaturity or unreadiness of domestic financial institutions for liberalization, can be damaging to each financial firm or bank and to the financial system as a whole. Local staff tended to be uneducated and/or inexperienced. They therefore could hardly perform in the increasingly competitive financial circuit. Worse yet, most domestic financial institutions did not have a well-diversified network of financial services and branches. Risks from financial liberalization were thus not spread adequately.

The third error, indiscreet supervision of financial institutions, was harmful in at least four ways during the period of financial liberalization. First, financial liberalization ordinarily leads to more competition, which increases the level of risks. New market participants who may not have enough expertise or experience to handle these risks need to be cautiously supervised. Second, some market participants may have experience, not only in business management, but also in concealing risk when reporting. Third, financial liberalization broadens the scope of financial institution activities, and some institutions may undertake new activities with which they are not familiar or in which the market is so thin that the risks are quite high. Fourth, supervisors themselves may lack skills to monitor and advise the financial institutions that are the front-runners in the liberalization.

The prevalence of financial crisis in East Asia during 1997 demonstrates that pursuing dynamic growth has become an increasingly intricate task for any developing country. Impressive growth records, though alluring to foreign creditors, often give rise to growing current account deficits that can cause creditors to worry if they become too large relative to GDP or to foreign exchange reserves. Similarly, the sentiments of local and foreign investors can also turn negative if such deficits persist too long or external debt difficulties loom large, given that most investors now command rational expectations. Once creditors become concerned about a liquidity shortage, or devaluation, or even default, they may decide not to renew or to roll over short-term loans, pressuring borrowers to (p)repay outstanding debts immediately. The decline of confidence could result in a credit squeeze, not only for those debtors but also for the central bank. The worry may spread to other debtors who opt to prepay their debts instead of carrying the risk of future exchange losses. Worse yet, such an externally financed bubble crisis can permeate to other countries in the region that have adopted similar paths of excessively debt-driven growth. Indeed, with the highly advanced modes of foreign exchange transactions, the contagion of financial crises in 1997 led to the depreciation of many East Asian currencies to record low levels (Table 9.12).

Table 9.12   Exchange rates of East Asian currencies, July and December 1997 (per US$)

	Exchange rate on July 1997	Exchange rate on 15 December 1997	Depreciation %
Indonesian rupiah	2 650	5 750	53.9
Thai baht	25.88	47.95	46.0
Korean won	880	1 564	43.7
Malaysian ringgit	2.504	3.925	36.2
Philippine peso	26.38	38.85	32.1

Source: Bank of Thailand.

In short, though foreign capital enhances the capacity of borrowing countries to grow more than they could by their own resources, it makes them vulnerable to abrupt changes in sentiment by lenders, especially when the borrowing countries are small. The widespread financial strains plaguing several Asian countries in 1997 confirm the fact that reliance on short-term 'hot money' for funding longer-term investment is inherently destabilizing, since changes in sentiment and confidence can result in quick reversals in capital flows. In other words, pinning growth on external funding means increasing fragility, because it is extremely difficult to restore business confidence once it has been impaired or withdrawn, especially within a short time frame. Successful rehabilitation depends on a number of reliable parties, large amounts of rescue funds, and a lengthy period of time.

One lesson from the Asian financial turmoil is that, without strong economic fundamentals, a well-functioning market mechanism and healthy financial institutions, hasty capital account liberalization may be overwhelmingly hazardous to the national economy. The painful yet effective path to recovery, in an era of information technology, is to rectify economic fundamentals and upgrade the status of financial institutions as recommended by the IMF, since these measures are likely to have a positive impact over the long run.

The errors of the past suggest three precautions to guide financial policy in the future. First, policy makers should steadily aim at consistency among all policy actions. When a new measure is to be implemented, related policies or regulations should be amended to avoid conflicts, even if such amendment may spark political opposition. Second, before adopting a new policy stance, policy makers should ensure that all affected parties and institutions are ready to cope with any potential or expected changes. This readiness applies to market players, market supervisors and market conditions or maturity. In the case where a participant or element is not ready, the sequencing of policy actions should be adjusted to avoid negative impact or repercussions. For instance, diversifying the system so that it includes enough foreign-owned financial institutions will help serve as a safety valve against shock waves in the course of capital account liberalization. Third, policy makers should undertake liberalization gradually in order to minimize chances of error or crisis. A gradual pace will help both players and regulators prepare themselves for the more flexible financial atmosphere. Policy makers also need to devise reliable systems to monitor complex and intricate situations. Logit and discriminant indicators devised for analysing external debt problems are examples of such early warning systems.

In summary, to survive in the current era of globalization and economic dynamism requires continual adjustment, together with the three precautions mentioned above. In other words, financial disasters or crashes can be averted only by countries that do not always yield to conservatism or political opposition.

NOTES

1. See 'The Way Out of Economic Crisis', 20 September 1997.
2. For commercial banks, net foreign exchange assets cannot exceed 20 per cent of their capital funds and net foreign exchange liabilities 15 per cent.
3. In 1995, the minimum BIBF borrowing was raised from US$500 000 t o US$2 million in order to screen out small borrowers. In 1997, a 7 per cent marginal reserve requirement was imposed on BIBF credits that have maturities under one year in order to encourage a long-term profile and reduce the degree of fund mobility in the short run.

BIBLIOGRAPHY

Duriyaprapan, C. and M. Supapongse (1996), 'Financial Liberalization: Case Study of Thailand', paper presented at the 12th Pacific Basin Central Bank Conference, 18–20 November, Singapore.

Ganjarerndee, S. (1997), 'Important Changes in Money and Banking between 1972 and 1996' (in Thai).

Pongpanich, B., S. Saicheua and T. Vachirapong (1997), 'The Way Out of Economic Crisis', paper presented at the Thailand Development Research Institute on 20 September.

Sucharitkul, C. and V. Aromdee (1994), 'Assessing Thailand's Financial Reform', paper on Policy Analysis and Assessment, Economic Research Department, Bank of Thailand (in Thai).

Thailand Development Research Institute (1997), 'Financial Volatility and Currency Speculation', paper presented to the Economic Department, Ministry of Foreign Affairs, November (in Thai).

10. Currency hedging in Asian equity markets

N. Suppakitjarak and M.F. Theobald

INTRODUCTION

The recent large currency movements in a number of Asian countries such as Malaysia, Thailand and Indonesia have once again drawn attention to the currency risk that overseas investors face when making portfolio investments in Asia. Such crises can also have the effect of reducing the benefits to international diversification as a result of the increased correlations across countries at such times (see, for example, Longin and Solnik, 1995). Increasingly, a wide range of currency hedging instruments are available, such as forwards, futures, options and swaps. Investors that use such instruments may pursue a number of potentially differing objectives. (A useful description and discussion of currency hedging techniques and strategies may be found, for example, in Clarke and Kritzman, 1996.) They may wish to buy 'downside' protection, for example, via currency options, or lock into a fixed exchange rate via the use of currency forwards or futures contracts. Some investors may use these instruments to increase currency exposure. A number of authors (for example, Eun and Resnick, 1988) have demonstrated the benefits of currency hedging.

In this chapter we will consider the impacts of the use of forward and futures contracts upon the risks and returns of individual country investments and the portfolio return moments of Asian equity portfolios from the perspectives of foreign investors whose returns are denominated in US dollars and pounds sterling. Even when considering these derivative contracts only, hedging strategies may be operationalized from a number of differing perspectives. For example, hedge ratios may be derived which generate minimum variance portfolios or, alternatively, maximize utility functions defined over the first two moments of the portfolio or position return distribution; only when the currency derivative follows a martingale process will the two hedge ratios be equivalent. A wide variety of dynamic strategies are possible, ranging from changing the hedge as the currency is at a forward premium or discount, to using GARCH (Generalized Autoregressive Conditional Heteroscedasticity) models to generate a time-series of hedge ratios (see, for example, Glen and Jorion, 1993; and Kroner and Sultan, 1993). The hedge ratios, themselves, may be determined relative to the currency being hedged or to the total portfolio returns. Black (1989), by contrast, argues in support of 'universal' hedging ratios and contends that investors should never fully hedge currency risk.

In the next section the analytic relationships between differing hedge ratios are developed; the differing empirical properties of these ratios are established in subsequent sections, using Asian equity and currency data. In general terms, the results of this chapter indicate that, while hedging using currency forwards will reduce the risks faced by international investors, the loss in returns that accompanies this risk reduction in Asian markets for the time frame used means that performance is not enhanced in mean–standard deviation space (similar results were reported in Glen and Jorion (1993), where currency hedging benefits in risk–return terms were found to be present only for portfolios containing international bonds). Only when forward currency positions are determined by maximizing a quadratic utility function are statistically significant improvements in performance detected and, even then, only for high-risk tolerance investors who are prepared to take on currency exposures.

HEDGING RELATIONSHIPS

The total return, $R(f,t)$, from holding a foreign asset will be given by

$$R(f,t) = R(l,t) + R(c,t) \qquad (10.1)$$

where $R(l,t)$ is the local return on the foreign asset, $R(c,t)$ is the foreign currency return (measured as the number of units of home currency per unit of overseas currency) and all three return variables are measured in terms of logarithmic price relatives.[1] The variance of returns on the foreign asset is then given by

$$\text{var}\,\{R(f,t)\} = \text{var}\{R(l,t)\} + \text{var}\{R(c,t)\} + 2\text{cov}\{R(l,t), R(c,t)\} \qquad (10.2)$$

where var and cov are the variance and covariance operators, respectively.

The variance of a hedged position, when a hedge ratio $h(f)$ is used to hedge the total foreign return variable, $R(f,t)$, is[2]

$$\text{var}\,\{R(h,t)\} = \text{var}\{R(f,t)\} + h(f)^2\,\text{var}\{R(d,t)\} + 2h(f)\,\text{cov}\,\{R(f,t), R(d,t)\} \qquad (10.3)$$

with $R(h,t)$ the return on the hedged position and $R(d,t)$ the return on the forward or futures contract.[3] The minimum variance hedge ratio will then be (see, for example, Ederington, 1979; Grammatikos and Saunders, 1983):

$$h(f) = \frac{-\text{cov}\{R(f,t), R(d,t)\}}{\text{var}\{R(d,t)\}} \qquad (10.4)$$

$$= \frac{-[\text{cov}\{R(l,t), R(d,t)\} + \text{cov}\{R(c,t), R(d,t)\}]}{\text{var}\{R(d,t)\}} \qquad (10.5)$$

This contrasts with the hedge ratio that is used to hedge the currency component of portfolio or position return only, $h(c)$, which is given by

$$h(c) = \frac{-\text{cov}\{R(c,t), R(d,t)\}}{\text{var}\{R(d,t)\}} \qquad (10.6)$$

and is what might be described as a 'pure' currency hedge.

The difference between the two hedge ratios derives from the $\text{cov}\{R(l,t),$ $R(d,t)\}$ term. To gain analytic insights into this difference, consider a two-factor return generating process,

$$R(l,t) = \alpha(l) + \beta(l) R(w,t) + \gamma(l) R(c,t) + u(l,t) \qquad (10.7)$$

where $R(w,t)$ is a 'world' market factor return, $\{\alpha(l), \beta(l), \gamma(l)\}$ are model parameters and $u(l,t)$ the disturbance term. It then follows that

$$\text{cov}\{R(l,t), R(d,t)\} = \beta(l)\, \text{cov}\{R(w,t), R(d,t)\} + \gamma(l)\, \text{cov}\{R(c,t), R(d,t)\}$$
$$+ \text{cov}\{u(l,t), R(d,t)\} \qquad (10.8)$$

and, if $R(w,t)$ is orthogonalized relative to both $R(c,t)$ and $R(d,t)$, and assuming that the non-systematic return component is uncorrelated with derivative returns, then

$$\text{cov}\{R(l,t), R(d,t)\} = \gamma(l)\, \text{cov}\{R(c,t), R(d,t)\} \qquad (10.9)$$

and, hence,

$$h(f) = [1 + \gamma(l)]\, h(c); \qquad (10.10)$$

that is, the difference will depend upon the currency sensitivity of the local asset returns. The impact of the differing hedge ratios upon the position variance can be established as

$$\text{var } \{R(h(f), t\} = \text{var } \{R(h(c), t)\} - \gamma(l) [2\text{cov}\{R(f,t), R(d,t)\}$$
$$- (2 + \gamma(l)) \text{ var } \{R(d,t)\}] \tag{10.11}$$

with var $\{R(h(f),t)\}$ the variance of the position using a hedge ratio $h(f)$ and var $\{R(h(c),t)\}$ the position variance using $h(c)$ as the hedge ratio. If local asset returns are uncorrelated with currency returns, that is, $\gamma(l) = 0$, then $h(f) = h(c)$ and var $\{R(h(f), t)\} = $ var $\{R(h(c),t)\}$. Jorion (1989) investigates return-generating models of this type using US industry data and finds that the currency impact is not generally strong.

The use of a forward or futures hedge will have an impact upon returns as well as risk. To evaluate the overall impact of using such hedges within a mean–standard deviation framework necessitates the use of a performance metric such as the Sharpe ratio. If $S(f)$ is defined as the Sharpe ratio for the full hedge and $S(c)$ the Sharpe ratio for the currency hedge only, then, with deterministic $\{\gamma(l), h(c)\}$,

$$S(f) = \frac{[S(c) - \gamma(l)h(c)R(d)\,\text{var}\{R(h,c,t)\}]}{[1 + \gamma(l)h(c)[\text{var}\{R(h,c,t)\}]^{-1}\{(2 + \gamma(l)h(c)\,\text{var}\{R(d,t)\} - 2\,\text{cov}\{R(f,t), R(d,t)\}]^{\frac{1}{2}}}$$

$$\tag{10.12}$$

Effectively, the sign of the difference between the two Sharpe ratios will depend upon the currency sensitivity, $\gamma(l)$, and the derivative return, $R(d)$.[4]

DATA AND RESEARCH DESIGN

Monthly price data were extracted for nine Asian countries from the Datastream database, the nine countries being Australia, Hong Kong, Indonesia, Japan, Malaysia, the Philippines, Singapore, Taiwan and Thailand. The major stock market indices available on Datastream were used from each of these countries. Forward contract rates were generated from spot rates and respective interest rates by the 'covered interest rate parity' theorem on a monthly basis. Euro-currency short-term interest rates were used for Japan and Singapore, while one-month inter-bank rates were used for the other seven countries.

The hedging strategies employed were both dynamic and ex ante in nature, in that hedge ratios were estimated using 60 months' data and then that hedge was put on in the following month.[5] A rolling series of hedge ratios was generated by moving the whole process ahead one month. In this way a series of hedged (and, indeed, unhedged) monthly returns were generated for the period from 1 January 1991 to 31 August 1996.

Hedge ratios were estimated using a straight currency hedge (equation (10.6)) and a forward currency hedge across both the equity and currency components (equation (10.5)).[6] As a number of institutions restrict[7] the hedge to the range {0, −1} we also investigate the performance of this constrained hedge. The moving window of data used in generating the rolling series of hedge ratios will contain data from the 1987 Crash period; as a consequence, we run our data and evaluate the hedges, out of sample, both with and without data for the October–December 1987 period. Hedge ratios were also estimated by maximizing quadratic utility functions with varying risk aversion parameters. Hedging at both the individual country level and the Asian portfolio level is analysed in both US dollar and pound sterling terms to investigate how the domicile of the investor affects the hedging efficiency. The overall performance of the hedging strategies in mean–standard deviation space is evaluated by using the Sharpe ratio. The test statistic developed in Glen and Jorion (1993) for evaluating the statistical significance of the difference between two Sharpe Ratios is then used to evaluate the statistical significance of the results.

SINGLE COUNTRY HEDGING

Table 10.1 contains details of the average values of the rolling series of hedge ratios estimated using 60 months prior data over the period 1 January 1991 to 31 August 1996 at the individual country level. With the exception of Hong Kong and Indonesia,[8] the currency only hedge ratios ($h(c)$, equation (10.6)) are generally very close to −1 (that is, a simple reverse hedge) for both US dollar investors and, particularly, pound sterling investors. The inclusion or exclusion of data from the Crash period did not affect the currency hedge ratios; constraining the hedge ratio to the range {0, −1} similarly had no significant impact. The currency plus stock hedge ratios ($h(f)$, equation (10.5)) are usually greater than one in absolute terms, indicating a positive comovement between the stockmarkets and currencies, on average. The generally larger (in absolute terms) hedge ratios for dollar currency plus stock hedging relative to sterling is consistent with equity markets being more strongly related to the dollar (and the US economy), although, for some countries, such as Singapore, the reverse is found to be the case. The full hedges are more sensitive to the Crash period data, as would be anticipated, and constraining the hedge ratio on the range {0, −1} has more impact for these hedges.[9]

More important insights into the hedging process can be gleaned by considering the risks and returns associated with the varying hedging strategies. Table 10.2 contains the monthly returns and risks (standard deviations), from the perspective of US and UK investors, for unhedged single country portfolios, fully hedged single country portfolios (that is, a hedge ratio of −1), the currency

Table 10.1 Average hedge ratios for the 1991–6 period

| | Currency only hedge (equation (10.6)) | | | | Currency plus stock hedge (equation (10.5)) | | | |
| | Unconstrained | | Constrained | | Unconstrained | | Constrained | |
	Including Crash	Excluding Crash	Including Crash	Excluding Crash	Including Crash	Excluding Crash	Including Crash	Excluding Crash
US dollars								
Australia	−1.00	−1.00	−1.00	−1.00	−1.48	−1.36	−1.00	−1.00
Hong Kong	−0.78	−0.78	−0.78	−0.78	−4.32	−4.28	−0.91	−0.82
Indonesia	−0.86	−0.86	−0.84	−0.84	−1.42	−1.54	−0.76	−0.77
Japan	−0.99	−0.99	−0.99	−0.99	−1.38	−1.43	−1.00	−1.00
Malaysia	−0.96	−0.97	−0.96	−0.96	−0.21	−0.60	−0.40	−0.58
Philippines	−1.00	−1.00	−0.99	−0.99	−0.88	−0.86	−0.75	−0.73
Singapore	−0.98	−0.98	−0.98	−0.98	0.05	−0.22	−0.21	−0.25
Taiwan	−1.01	−1.02	−1.00	−1.00	2.91	2.809	0.00	0.00
Thailand	−0.912	−0.91	−0.91	−0.91	2.91	2.80	0.00	0.00
£ sterling								
Australia	−0.99	−0.99	−0.99	−0.99	−1.15	−0.97	−0.97	−0.96
Hong Kong	−0.98	−0.98	−0.98	−0.98	−1.03	−0.85	−0.94	−0.83
Indonesia	−0.98	−0.98	−0.97	−0.97	−1.25	−1.26	−1.00	−1.00
Japan	−0.96	−0.96	−0.96	−0.96	−0.99	−0.97	−0.93	−0.92
Malaysia	−0.97	−0.97	−0.97	−0.97	−1.33	−1.33	−1.00	−1.00
Philippines	−0.98	−0.98	−0.98	−0.98	−1.26	−1.22	−0.98	−0.96
Singapore	−0.98	−0.98	−0.98	−0.98	−1.56	−1.40	−1.00	−1.00
Thailand	−0.97	−0.97	−0.97	−0.97	−1.68	−1.57	−1.00	−1.00

199

only hedged portfolios (using $h(c)$ as the hedge ratio) and the currency and stock hedged portfolios (using $h(f)$ as the hedge ratio). In general, hedging, irrespective of type, reduced portfolio returns since, on average, the dollar and pound-denominated forward returns were positive, as were the average currency returns in these two currencies, with the latter, on average, being greater than the former. While individual country risks were reduced irrespective of the hedging method employed from a UK perspective, US dollar risks were not reduced in all strategies for Malaysia and Singapore and were reduced for no strategy in the case of Thailand. In the case of Thailand, this is apparent in Table 10.1, where the dollar hedge ratios were strongly positive for the currency plus stock hedge, indicating that an exposure to the dollar was optimal rather than a reverse position[10] (the constrained $h(f)$ strategy will effectively be an unhedged strategy for Thailand). In general, the individual country risks are lower in both currencies when stock plus currency hedges ($h(f)$) are used relative to currency only hedges ($h(c)$), reflecting the extra covariance dimension that is incorporated in the risk-minimization procedures in the case of the former hedge ratio. While there is evidence of a risk reduction due to hedging in many cases, when the various strategies are compared in terms of Sharpe ratios,[11] there is no evidence of statistically significant improvements in risk–return space; essentially, the risk reduction benefit is counteracted by the decrease in the return dimension.

Table 10.3 contains the Sharpe ratios for single country optimized positions in the stock market and the forward market for various risk aversion parameters, λ, ranging from high risk tolerances ($\lambda = 0.25$) to low risk tolerances ($\lambda = 100$). In general, the optimal forward hedge ratios implied a currency exposure, particularly at high risk tolerances, for both dollars and sterling, which became reverse hedges when Crash data were excluded from the estimating data set. The absolute value of the hedge ratio generally declined as risk tolerance declined. Similarly, Sharpe ratios declined as the risk tolerance declined, corresponding to the higher currency exposures at higher risk tolerances. Statistically significant improvements in Sharpe ratios, at high risk tolerances, occurred for Indonesia, Malaysia the Philippines and Thailand when returns were denominated in dollars; no statistically significant differences occurred for pound-denominated returns. When hedge ratios were constrained on the range $\{0, -1\}$, there were no statistically significant differences in Sharpe ratios.

In summary, then, at the individual country level, while reverse hedging will reduce position risk, the reduction that occurred in Asian country returns over the sample frame was sufficient to ensure that, in the overall risk–return domain, there was no statistically significant improvement in performance, as measured by Sharpe ratios. When a quadratic utility function is optimized over stock and forward positions, statistically significant improvements in Sharpe ratios occur for some Asian countries for investors with high risk tolerance levels.

Table 10.2 Returns and risks of various hedging strategies

US dollars	Return (%)						Standard Deviation (%)					
	Unhedged	Full hedge	Unconstrained		Constrained		Unhedged	Full hedge	Unconstrained		Constrained	
			h(c)	h(f)	h(c)	h(f)			h(c)	h(f)	h(c)	h(f)
Australia	0.44	0.24	0.24	0.15	0.24	0.24	6.67	5.59	5.59	5.42	5.59	5.59
Hong Kong	1.49	1.47	1.48	1.45	1.48	1.47	8.47	8.45	8.45	8.41	8.45	8.45
Indonesia	−0.30	−0.59	−0.55	−0.72	−0.54	−0.52	7.68	7.44	7.43	7.39	7.44	7.43
Japan	−0.11	−0.36	−0.36	−0.64	−0.37	−0.36	8.29	7.11	7.14	6.99	7.14	7.13
Malaysia	1.11	0.73	0.74	1.21	0.74	1.02	7.57	7.61	7.60	7.53	7.60	7.54
Philippines	2.18	1.29	1.29	1.19	1.30	1.42	8.87	8.67	8.69	8.64	8.69	8.65
Singapore	0.89	0.71	0.71	0.92	0.72	0.85	6.64	6.71	6.73	6.61	6.73	6.63
Taiwan	0.03	−0.13	−0.13	−0.16	−0.13	−0.10	15.19	15.02	15.05	15.01	15.05	15.05
Thailand	1.16	0.63	0.63	2.51	0.69	1.16	9.92	10.03	10.02	9.76	10.02	9.92
Pounds sterling												
Australia	0.50	0.22	0.22	0.15	0.22	0.23	7.33	5.59	5.60	5.49	5.60	5.59
Hong Kong	1.55	1.45	1.45	1.42	1.45	1.44	9.27	8.45	8.46	8.43	8.46	8.44
Indonesia	−0.23	−0.61	−0.62	−0.67	−0.60	−0.61	8.93	7.44	7.42	7.34	7.42	7.41
Japan	−0.05	−0.39	−0.38	−0.57	−0.38	−0.47	7.76	7.11	7.12	7.10	7.12	7.10
Malaysia	1.17	0.71	0.71	0.44	0.71	0.71	8.78	7.61	7.59	7.46	7.59	7.58
Philippines	2.20	1.27	1.28	0.93	1.28	1.28	10.20	8.67	8.69	8.55	8.69	8.68
Singapore	0.95	0.69	0.69	0.50	0.69	0.69	7.56	6.71	6.71	6.61	6.71	6.71
Taiwan	0.11	−0.15	−0.15	−0.52	−0.52	−0.15	15.92	15.02	15.02	15.03	14.85	15.02
Thailand	1.18	0.61	0.63	0.24	0.63	0.62	11.30	10.03	10.03	9.74	10.03	10.01

Table 10.3   Sharpe ratios for various risk aversion parameters (λ)

US dollars	Unconstrained optimal forward Sharpe ratio						
	$\lambda = 0.25$	$\lambda = 0.05$	$\lambda = 1$	$\lambda = 2$	$\lambda = 5$	$\lambda = 10$	$\lambda = 100$
Australia	0.08	0.08	0.08	0.06	0.05	0.04	0.03
Hong Kong	0.30	0.30	0.29	0.26	0.22	0.20	0.17
Indonesia	0.65	0.65	0.64	0.60	0.48	0.31	−0.05
Japan	0.08	0.06	0.02	−0.02	−0.06	−0.08	−0.09
Malaysia	0.50	0.48	0.43	0.35	0.26	0.21	0.17
Philippines	0.77	0.73	0.63	0.48	0.30	0.23	0.15
Singapore	0.19	0.19	0.20	0.20	0.18	0.17	0.14
Taiwan	0.21	0.17	0.12	0.07	0.02	0.01	−0.01
Thailand	0.92	0.93	0.94	0.94	0.81	0.62	0.30
Pounds sterling	Unconstrained optimal forward Sharpe ratio						
Australia	−0.19	−0.09	−0.05	−0.01	0.01	0.02	0.03
Hong Kong	−0.11	−0.03	0.05	0.11	0.15	0.16	0.17
Indonesia	−0.11	−0.09	−0.10	−0.10	−0.10	−0.10	−0.09
Japan	−0.24	−0.24	−0.21	−0.16	−0.12	−0.10	−0.08
Malaysia	−0.17	−0.10	−0.06	−0.01	0.03	0.05	0.06
Philippines	0.02	0.08	0.10	0.11	0.11	0.11	0.11
Singapore	−0.19	−0.14	−0.08	−0.02	0.04	0.06	0.07
Taiwan	−0.12	−0.09	−0.07	−0.05	−0.04	−0.04	−0.04
Thailand	0.03	0.06	0.05	0.04	0.03	0.03	0.03

PORTFOLIO HEDGING

Three distinct forms of international portfolio strategy were evaluated: an equally weighted asset allocation across countries (together with various currency hedges); a value weighted allocation (again with various currency hedging strategies); and a mean-variance optimized strategy, using quadratic programming across stock markets and hedging instruments. Effectively, the first two strategies entail hedging a predetermined asset allocation, while the last jointly determines the derivative position with the asset allocation. The forward hedging strategies that were employed in the previous section are analysed again at the portfolio level. In this section, additionally, futures hedging strategies using the USDX Dollar Index futures contract for dollar-denominated returns and the UK Short-term Sterling Index futures contract for the pound returns are evaluated.

The results of the differing strategies are reported in Table 10.4 in terms of Sharpe ratios. In the case of dollar returns, Sharpe ratios tend to be lower for hedged positions for both the equally weighted and value-weighted portfolios, the exceptions being the fully hedged futures cases. For UK investors, futures hedging led to improved Sharpe ratios relative to the unhedged position in all hedging strategies. By far the highest hedge ratios were achieved for the optimized positions. However, as is often the case, the mean-variance optimized portfolios necessitated taking very long positions in just a small sub-set of the various asset classes,[12] positions which are not always to the taste of most portfolio managers (Fisher and Statman, 1997).[13] For example, the optimal weights for the dollar-denominated forward strategy entailed taking equity positions in only two countries (The Philippines and Thailand) and forward currency positions in Australia, Indonesia, The Philippines and Thailand (with a very large long position in the latter, in particular).[14]

Table 10.4   Sharpe ratios for various portfolios and hedging strategies

	Equally weighted		Value-weighted		Optimized	
	$	£	$	£	$	£
Unhedged	0.085	0.086	–0.004	0.003	—	—
Fully hedged						
Forward	0.051	0.049	–0.039	–0.036	—	—
Futures	0.097	–0.106	0.005	0.015	—	—
Currency hedge, $h(c)$						
Forward	0.078	0.076	–0.065	0.075	—	—
Futures	0.086	0.025	–0.004	0.017	—	—
Currency + stock hedge, $h(f)$						
Forward	0.078	0.076	–0.065	0.075	—	—
Futures	0.085	0.068	–0.011	0.088	—	—
Optimized position						
Forward	—	—	—	—	0.302	0.300
Futures	—	—	—	—	0.136	0.177

CONCLUSIONS

A variety of currency-hedging strategies at both the country and portfolio level have been investigated in this chapter. While hedging with forward currency contracts led to reductions in risk, the corresponding decline in returns led to there being no performance improvement in mean-variance space as measured by Sharpe ratios when dynamic minimum variance hedge ratios were used. However, for high risk tolerances, statistically significant increases in Sharpe ratios were obtained when individual country positions were determined by optimizing quadratic utility functions. In general, the performance improvement was achieved by assuming currency exposures via the forward contracts.

NOTES

1. With discrete time price relatives, the relationship at equation (10.1) will hold only as an approximation, the relationship becoming less precise as the magnitude of currency or equity returns increases.
2. Strictly speaking, $h(f)$ should also have a time indicator to correspond to the data work that we conduct in the empirical sections of this chapter, since we estimate hedge ratios on a rolling time-series basis. The time indicator is not included to simplify the notation in this section.
3. The measurement of the return on a futures/forward contract varies across studies, owing to differing approaches to measuring the initial outlay. Some authors, such as Figlewski (1984), use the spot price, while others, such as Kroner and Sultan (1993), use the opening futures price. The latter return definition will be used throughout this chapter.
4. Glen and Jorion (1993) develop a test statistic to determine whether differences in Sharpe ratios are statistically significantly different.
5. There are, of course, other ways of developing dynamic strategies. For example, Kroner and Sultan (1993) use a GARCH approach, assuming constant currency/spot correlations. The strategy employed here does not impose any formal model for heteroscedasticity upon the process but does avoid the necessity of assuming constant correlations. Although OLS estimates generated by a moving window of regressions will not instantaneously reflect any potential structural changes in hedge ratios, we do find that including/excluding 1987 Crash data from our data analysis does not significantly affect the results reported in this chapter.
6. Hedging across both the currency and equity components may induce biases in the hedge ratio estimators owing to non-synchronicities between equity returns and forward returns. The impacts of such non-synchronicities are analysed in Theobald and Yallup (1997) within a stock index futures framework, additionally incorporating the impacts of differential speeds of price adjustment in the cash and derivative markets. We do not incorporate any adjustments for such effects within this chapter.
7. To prevent 'hedging' strategies becoming 'speculative' strategies via assuming large long or short currency exposures.
8. Both of which currencies have been pegged to the US dollar for periods during the estimation period, with a consequent lowering in the degree of hedging required.
9. The hedge ratios that are estimated with and without Crash data are not statistically significantly different at the 5 per cent level, using t-tests. The currency only hedge ($h(c)$) and the currency plus stock hedge ($h(f)$) are generally statistically significantly different.
10. Effectively, the reverse currency hedge, $h(c)$ is changed from close to -1 to be strongly positive in the case of $h(f)$ owing to the very strong and negative correlation between the Thai stockmarket and the dollar.
11. US and UK Sharpe ratios are computed relative to the one-month T-bill (treasury bill) in both these countries.
12. See, for example, Eun and Resnick (1988). Green and Hollifield (1992) analytically investigate this phenomenon.
13. Black and Litterman (1992) have developed international asset allocation techniques which address this problem.
14. The optimal weighting scheme will, itself, be highly sensitive to changes in the mean returns vector (see Best and Grauer, 1991).

REFERENCES

Best, M. and R. Grauer (1991), 'On the sensitivity of mean-variance-efficient portfolios to changes in asset means: some analytical and computational results', *Review of Financial Studies*, 4, 315–42.

Black, F. (1989), 'Equilibrium exchange rate hedging', *Journal of Finance*, 44, 899–908.

Black, F. and R. Litterman (1992), 'Global Portfolio Optimization', *Financial Analysts Journal*, September/October, 28–43.

Clarke, R. and M. Kritzman (1996), *Currency Management: Concepts and Practices*, Charlottesville, VA: The Research Foundation of The Institute of Chartered Financial Analysts.

Ederington, L. (1979), 'The hedging performance of the new futures markets', *Journal of Finance*, 34, 157–70.

Eun, C. and B. Resnick (1988), 'Exchange rate uncertainty, forward contracts and international portfolio selection', *Journal of Finance*, 43, 197–216.

Figlewski, S. (1984), 'Hedging Performance and Basis Risk in Stock Index Futures', *Journal of Finance*, 39, 657–69.

Fisher, S. and M. Statman (1997), 'The Mean-Variance-Optimization Puzzle: Security Portfolios and Food Portfolios', *Financial Analysts Journal*, July/August, 41–50.

Glen, J. and P. Jorion (1993), 'Currency hedging for international portfolios', *Journal of Finance*, 48, 1865–86.

Grammatikos, T. and A. Saunders (1983), 'Stability and hedging performance of foreign currency futures', *Journal of Futures Markets*, 3, 295–305.

Green, R. and B. Hollifield (1992), 'When Will Mean-Variance Efficient Portfolios Be Well Diversified?', *Journal of Finance*, 47, 1785–1810.

Jorion, P. (1989), 'The pricing of exchange rate risk in the stockmarket', *Journal of Financial and Quantitative Analysis*, 24, 373–86.

Kroner, K. and J. Sultan (1993), 'Time varying distributions and dynamic hedging with foreign currency futures', *Journal of Financial and Quantitative Analysis*, 28, 535–51.

Longin, F. and B. Solnik (1995), 'Is the correlation in international equity returns constant: 1960–1990?', *Journal of International Money and Finance*, 14, 3–26.

Theobald, M. and P. Yallup (1997), 'Hedging ratios and cash/futures markets linkages', *Journal of Futures Markets*, 17(1), February, 101–15.

11. Lessons from the financial crisis in Pacific and South East Asia

Andy Mullineux

INTRODUCTION

When the first draft of this chapter was written in late November 1997, the crisis that originated in Thailand in mid-1997 had already spread to a number of other countries in the South East Asian region (notably Indonesia) and affected most of the others. In November, South Korea, whose economy was larger than all those in the South East Asian region combined, had succumbed. In preparing the final draft in July 1998, Japan's banking sector problems, which had festered since the collapse of the 'bubble economy' in 1990, had finally reached crisis proportions. There was widespread concern that, if decisive action was not taken in Japan – banking sector restructuring, tax cuts to stimulate demand – another round of devaluations could follow those of the summer of 1997, with unforeseeable consequences. The economic slowdown in Japan, the second largest economy in the world, itself larger than all the affected countries in the region put together, was already inhibiting the necessary export-led recoveries in most countries in the Pacific and South East Asian region. Further, Japanese bank lending and FDI throughout the region was being curtailed. A revitalization of the Japanese economy through the short-term means identified above, and more thoroughgoing economic liberalization, seemed necessary to enable Japan to serve as an engine for growth to lead the region out of recession.

Another threat was also looming: a possible devaluation by China in response to its slower growth and a further devaluation of the yen. Devaluation by China would probably draw the rest of Greater China – Hong Kong, Taiwan and possibly also Singapore – into the crisis and would itself be likely to lead to a further round of devaluations in the previously affected, and perhaps other, countries in the region that had hitherto maintained their fixed exchange rates, Vietnam *inter alia*. The crisis was thus far from over, and a second round of devaluations, with associated problems for the financial sectors of the region, seemed possible. The new prime minister of Japan, Mr Obuchi, thus bore a heavy responsibility.

A world banking and financial crisis even seemed possible. Suddenly, everyone was reaching for economic history books covering the 1920s and 1930s. Presumably by chance, Kindleberger's famous study of past financial crises (*Manics, Panics and Crashes: A History of Financial Crises*) was republished in its third edition (Kindleberger, 1996).

In this chapter we consider the anatomy of the domestic financial crises in the South East and Pacific Asian countries. Problems caused by capital inflows and outflows are also outlined. Linkages between international capital flows and domestic financial fragility, the mechanism by which a domestic systematic banking crisis might have led to a regional (South East Asia Pacific) system crisis, is then considered. We will not speculate further about whether the regional crisis could be sufficiently contagious to cause a world crisis, but it should become clear by what mechanism that could arise.

Having discussed the causes of the financial crises, the chapter considers the means of curing them and then measures to be taken to prevent a future rerun of the crises.

THE ANATOMY OF DOMESTIC FINANCIAL CRISES

Much of the economic analysis of financial, and particularly banking, crises focuses on crises in a country's banking/financial system, ignoring international linkages. This is probably because, in the immediate post-1945 era, such linkages were not particularly strong. Exchange controls were, for example, widespread. The linkages have, however, become progressively stronger since the late 1960s and the terms 'globalization' and 'global capital markets' are now widely used. The current period of globalization is often compared with the pre-1900 to 1930 period. Kindleberger's aforementioned book is replete with examples demonstrating the importance of these international linkages, but more modern and model-based work on financial crises by economists[1] tends to have a narrower country-based approach. As always in Economics, there are competing theories and terminologies, but there is growing appreciation that asset-price inflation and deflation are often significant components of domestic financial crises. It is now widely accepted that this was the case in Japan in the early 1990s and subsequently in Thailand prior to the onset of the June 1997 crisis.

In fact, the property and stock market bubbles in Bangkok had burst long before June 1997, leaving the banking sector exposed to domestic bad debt problems, which the monetary authorities were slow to resolve. There is, however, some disagreement about the extent to which Malaysia, Indonesia and South Korea were also suffering from bubbles prior to contagion from the Thailand crisis in the summer of 1997. This debate, however, reveals the nature of the problem. Asset-price inflations are only undisputedly revealed to be bubbles *after* the bubble has burst. Before that, some economic and financial analysts can always be found to argue that the ever-rising asset prices are supported by fundamentals, and thus are not bubbles.

In the case of Japan, and now South Korea and many of the South East Asian countries, it has also been argued that there had been considerable overinvestment and consequently, given the underdeveloped, emerging equity capital markets in the region, overborrowing, largely from banks, but also from secondary banks, such as the finance companies in Thailand. To the extent that this is true,[2] it could reflect deficiencies in the financial system. Banks appear to be failing in their capital allocation and governance roles. They are not continuously lending to the most efficient firms. This is in part because they are making poor lending decisions, but also because their lending is often implicitly or explicitly directed by government policy initiatives or by politicians who seek to influence the direction of bank lending in pursuit of their own agenda ('crony capitalism'). Even where there is relatively little direction of lending, lack of competition in the banking sector might lead to inefficient lending.

Further, inappropriately low, often negative, real interest rates (cheap money) will generally encourage overinvestment and overlending in the presence of high domestic savings rates, especially where capital outflows are restricted (Fry, 1997). In this respect, the low nominal rates prevailing in Japan in the mid-1990s, and the capital outflows from Japan to the Pacific and South East Asian region throughout the 1990s, seem likely to have exerted a downward pressure on interest rates in Pacific and South East Asia and inflated the stock of capital driving the asset price bubble. Dollars-denominated loans could also be raised in the mid-1990s at lower interest rates than domestic currency-denominated loans. With increasingly liberalized capital accounts, large foreign currency exposures were quickly built up by private sector corporations and banks. In Thailand, for example, the borrowing was via the Bangkok International Banking Facility.

It is thus impossible to ignore the international linkages. What was special, however, was that, unlike what happened in the Latin American debt crisis of the early 1980s, the main borrowers were private sector enterprises, rather than government agencies. The closest parallel is perhaps the crisis in Chile in the mid-1980s. As in the Latin American case, however, the overlenders were major international commercial banks. This raises the issue of why the banks were willing to lend so much so cheaply, failing to charge an adequate risk premium. Moral hazard, created by the expectation of being bailed out by the governments of the recipient countries or, indirectly, by the IMF, as they had been to some extent in the resolution of the Latin American crisis, seems to have played a part in the story. Hence, once the dust has settled, it may well be that it is not just the domestic banking systems of the countries hit by the crisis (and probably others not directly affected) in the Pacific and South East Asia region that need to be restructured. The procedures for regulating and supervising international banks will probably also have to be reconsidered by the Basle Committee and the IMF.

Asset-price Inflation in Outline

Whether the source of capital is domestic or foreign, if money is cheap, that is, real interest rates are low or negative, capital begins to chase capital gains, which are available in capital (particularly equity) and property markets. There is also likely to be overinvestment in physical capital by the banks' business clients, paving the way for future bankruptcies and bad loans in the next recession.

As the capital gains begin to be realized, more and more capital is attracted to the asset markets. Banks become more and more willing to lend to 'speculators' on the basis of the collateral provided, the value of which is seemingly continuously increasing. As the banks become more willing to lend to property developers, *inter alia*, the asset prices go on up, and so too does the value of the collateral.

'Irrational exuberance', to use Alan Greenspan's now famous phrase, may be suspected; but is difficult to prove, and 'herd behaviour' is a driving force. Fund managers cannot afford to be seen to be missing out on profitable opportunities and certainly cannot afford to detach themselves from the herd, in case they are wrong. (Note the UK fund managers' underinvestment in the USA and overinvestment in Japan in 1995/6.)

It does pay, however, to panic as soon as the 'bubble' bursts, whatever the proximate cause of its doing so – financial scandal, political crisis, loss of competitiveness and so on. Those who cash their chips in first get the most for them, while those that wait in an orderly queue risk losing substantial amounts of money as asset prices fall. Once asset price-deflation takes hold, the banks find that they have overlent, since the market value of the collateral underwriting the loans no longer covers the loans extended. Property developers begin to go bust and banks' bad and doubtful debts begin to accumulate. At this stage it is clear that banks' provisioning policy is important. We will return to this point in the section on prevention of crises.

Unfortunately, the problems do not stop here, for there will be an impact on the real economy through negative wealth effects on consumption and investment. There will also be an impact through the 'credit channel', in the sense that banks will become less willing to lend because of the need to divert capital to address the emerging bad debt problem. A 'credit crunch' ensues, which leads to an increase in bankruptcy rates and a worsening bad debt problem. An 'unvirtuous' circle emerges.

At this point, 'directed' lending and traditional associations (for example, between state-owned banks (SOBs) and state-owned enterprises (SOEs) in China, and between the largest banks and the *chaebol* in South Korea) become important. If the banks tend, for whatever reason, to support the larger enterprises, then small and medium-sized enterprises (SMEs) will suffer from tighter credit rationing. Given their dependence on banks for extended finance, widespread SME failures can be expected.

The credit crunch is often exacerbated by increases in nominal interest rates. A brief review of literature on past crises, including the 1930s, would indicate that domestic interest rates should be reduced in financial crises. An increase is thus likely to be imposed from outside as the result of international linkages, such as the need to stabilize a falling exchange rate, which we turn to in the next sub-section.

Under a variable rate loan system, rising nominal interest rates make loans more difficult to service and increase banks' exposure to credit risks, which makes them yet more cautious about lending. This further increases the incidence of bad debts as more and more households and firms become unable to service their loans.

So far we have ignored depositor and shareholder responses to the increasingly evident deterioration in the banks' asset quality. In the absence of adequate deposit insurance, it is rational for depositors to panic and so, eventually, panic they will. In Pacific and South East Asia there have, so far, only been isolated incidents of 'bank runs'. However, as the case of Bulgaria in 1996 amply illustrates, a few seemingly isolated 'bank runs' can soon develop into a system-wide crisis. Panic is contagious and must be contained at all costs (while dealing with the consequences for moral hazard: see the section on crisis prevention below).

If the shareholders begin to sell shares, banks will find it costly to raise the capital necessary to cover the accumulating bad debts. Further, if, as in Japan, it is common for banks to be involved in cross-shareholding networks, declining bank share prices will undermine the assets of firms holding bank shares and, if the stock market itself begins to slide, possibly as a result of international linkages, the assets of the banks holding large equity portfolios will be further impaired. To the extent that banks hold stocks and shares as collateral, their asset price risk-exposure is further increased. If, in addition, as in Japan, banks rely on unrealized capital gains to meet the Basle capital adequacy ratios, declining share prices will eventually threaten their solvency.

International Linkages

We have already mentioned two linkages resulting from increasingly free capital flows. A truly global or regional capital market would have just one baseline, or risk-free, interest rate. Deviations from that rate would largely reflect credit and foreign exchange risks. Thus domestic rates will increasingly be influenced by rates prevailing elsewhere, particularly in the USA and Japan. Free capital movement allows money to flow in and out of country-based financial markets in response to perceived risk-adjusted returns. To the extent that perceived risks are subject to dramatic changes, the flows of capital can change abruptly. Thus, if a property and stock market bubble has been sustained by cheap money, due in part to large capital inflows, not only will the bubble be inflated further than it would have been by domestic capital alone, but also, following the bursting of the bubble, the crisis will be exacerbated by capital outflows. In the case of Thailand, given its heavy reliance on short-term borrowing through the Bangkok-based International Banking Facilities and regional 'offshore banking' centres, these outflows were substantial. However, it has also become clear that capital devoted to foreign portfolio investment (FPI) in 'emerging markets' is also very footloose and it is brought home (to the USA in the main) when the return on the perceived risk ratio declines. This happened following the Mexican crisis in December 1994/January 1995, and again following the onset of the financial crisis in Pacific and South East Asia.

Comfort is often drawn from the argument that countries in which a greater proportion of capital inflows consists of foreign direct investments (FDIs) are less exposed to outflows. This is clearly true, but if such countries are relying on the *inflows* to balance their international payments then they may be equally disappointed if the inflows suddenly dry up. This seems to have happened in the Pacific and South East Asia region, at least as far as Japanese investment in the near future is concerned. China, for example, has seen its inflow of FDI drop off substantially following the onset of the crisis in mid-1997.

A capital inflow problem tends to occur in countries which adopt a fixed exchange rate regime (peg, currency board and so on) and also attract capital inflows, which exert downward pressure on real interest rates such that a positive inflation differential with major trading partners is maintained and an appreciation of the real exchange rate results. This leads to a progressive loss of competitiveness in traditional industries and a worsening trade deficit. In the longer run, the appropriate response is to reallocate capital to higher value added sectors, such as the high-tech and the non-traded goods – largely service – sector, otherwise overinvestment in the traditional traded goods sector can easily occur. This reallocation requires an efficient allocation of capital by the financial system and investment in education and training. In the shorter run, however, pressure builds for a devaluation to restore the competitiveness of enterprises in the traded goods sector engaged in traditional industries. The trigger point for many countries appears to be a trade deficit that approaches 5 per cent of GDP, though the exact figure will depend on the foreign exchange reserve to GDP ratios. If the appropriate action is not taken (for example, widening the band of fluctuation around the peg substantially) early enough, a devaluation may well be forced by the markets, as in Thailand. Recent studies (IMF, 1998a, 1998b) have shown that domestic, foreign currency-denominated capital flight was occurring for a considerable period prior to the crisis in Thailand. Further, once the crisis ensues, the repatriation of foreign capital is commonly swelled by an acceleration of domestic capital flight.

With the onset of the crisis, the true extent of the bank bad debt problem starts to be revealed. As regards prevention, better bad debt reporting require-ments, or increased 'transparency', are clearly indicated as a means of avoiding sudden changes of perception. Political instability also seems to be an extremely important influence on capital flows (Dickinson and Mullineux, 1996; Lensink *et al.*, 2000). This was particularly evident in Poland. The outflows from Thailand and South Korea seem to have been exacerbated by the uncertainty surrounding the stability of the government. However, the key concern seems to have been over the incumbent governments' abilities to manage the economy effectively. Progress in that regard has been faster in Thailand and South Korea, which quickly replaced less reformist with more reformist governments in 1997, than in Indonesia, where public unrest preceded a change in government and uncertainty remained following President Habibie's replacement of President Suharto in May 1998.

Once the capital flight is under way, the financial crisis tends to worsen rapidly. Exchange rate depreciation increases the cost of servicing foreign currency-denominated debts. To the extent that corporations borrowed heavily in foreign currency (for example, in Thailand, South Korea and Indonesia), owing to availability and relative cheapness of the funds, they are threatened with insolvency, and will certainly face severe liquidity problems. The banks are not only exposed to their struggling corporate clients, but are themselves debtors in the international inter-bank markets; their domestic exposure is often massive by Western banking standards.

Exchange rate depreciation and loss of foreign exchange through capital flight thus exacerbates the domestic banking and wider financial crises. To stabilize the depreciating exchange rate and discourage capital outflows, it is often necessary to raise interest rates, which makes it more difficult for domestic debtors to service their debts. The domestic crisis is thus exacerbated by inter-national financial linkages.

Just as a panic involving an individual bank can lead, through panic and contagion via inter-bank exposures, to a domestic systemic banking crisis, a domestic financial crisis, through panic and contagion via international inter-bank linkages, can lead to a regional crisis, as in Pacific and South East Asia. Further, the regional crisis – especially if Japan and China succumb – could potentially become a global crisis. This could occur if the lessons contained in our economic history books, which explain what can happen if competitive devaluations beget protectionism, are not heeded. A protectionist reaction by the USA to its growing trade deficit with the Pacific and South East Asia region would, for example, be very dangerous indeed, since the worst affected countries (apart from Japan) are running trade deficits and simply must export their way back to growth. It is for this reason that the USA was urging Japan to stimulate its economy and share the 'locomotive' burden. It should be stressed, however, that a significant part of the solution entails financial sector reform.

The financial and capital account liberalization in the Pacific and South East Asian region has clearly increased the exposure of domestic banking and financial systems to the evolving 'global' capital market, but there is probably no turning back. Capital controls have been shown to be, at best, short-term instruments. Better to go forward by participating fully in the General Agreement on Trade in Services (GATS) agreement on liberalizing trade in financial services, and to restructure the domestic financial systems under the IMF's 'guidance' and with the help of IMF loans. While the banking systems are being 'restructured', or rehabilitated, an effective bank regulatory and supervisory system must be put in place to make sure systemic banking crises do not recur. Thought will also need to be given to the appropriate exchange rate policy – an Asian monetary union?

RESOLUTION

First, action must quickly be taken to protect depositors in order to prevent bank runs and limit capital flight. This was done in Japan in 1997 through a credible announcement that, effectively, deposits are 100 per cent insured.[3] It was also done, with the IMF's blessing, in Thailand and South Korea in 1997. Given the need to restore depositor confidence, as was the case in the USA in the 1930s, the establishment of a funded deposit insurance scheme is probably required to ensure credibility. It is well known that such schemes give rise to moral hazard, and also to adverse selection problems, if the premia are not risk-related and where banks are free to set interest rates competitively.[4] Risk-related premia, under which the premium rises with the risk to which depositors' funds are exposed, are essential, and only 100 per cent insurance of deposits of a reasonable size (such as one/two years' average salary, perhaps more) will reassure anxious depositors. Once the confidence in the banking system is restored, the scale and scope of deposit insurance protection could, perhaps, be scaled back, although the USA has not yet reduced deposit insurance below 100 per cent (of up to $100 000).

The next task is to tackle the bank bad debt problem. Essentially, banks are locked into lending relationships with old customers and have limited scope to develop new, more profitable, lending. Where banks' loans are collateralized, the solution is now well tried and tested. This is to set up a special state-funded bank to take control of the bad loans and the collateral and replace them with government bonds in the banks' balance sheets. This was essentially the approach adopted by the Resolution Trust Corporation, which was established in the early 1990s to resolve the 'savings and loans crisis' in the USA. A similar strategy was adopted by the Nordic countries in the early 1990s. The commercial banks, relieved of their bad debts, are then in a position to develop new, and it is hoped more profitable, lending business. There is a moral hazard issue here too, since banks may not mend their ways, expecting to be bailed out again in the future. To prevent this, shareholders and managers should, wherever appropriate, incur financial penalties. The adoption of best practice in bank regulation and supervision, discussed in the next section, is also clearly important in this respect.

But what of the cost to the taxpayer? The trick is to collect and hold the collateral underpinning the bad loans, and to sell it into a rising market. The cost to the taxpayer in the medium term may be small or negligible, as in Sweden. The solution works because the government 'buys time' and waits for the markets to recover. Commercial banks, which must regularly balance their books and generate at least some dividends for shareholders, are not afforded the luxury of waiting for the recovery. The regulators and supervisors of the international banks that provided cheap loans that were mispriced in terms of risk to the affected countries should also consider the culpability of both those banks and themselves. The 'Nordic' solution, where the recalcitrant banks were nationalized for a nominal fee, ensuring that shareholders were punished, and then restructured and reprivatized, raising money to cover the cost of the bailout, should also be considered. Thailand, in particular, has made use of this approach.

As a result of opposition from the taxpayers (voters) themselves, successive Japanese governments have failed to commit taxpayers' money wholeheartedly to a fully fledged 'bad bank solution'. Yet Japan is a democracy and the public have hitherto rejected proposals to bail out the banks. A worsening of the banking crisis in Japan (a full-blown crisis is unlikely as long as depositors remain assured) is the last thing the region needs, since this will exacerbate the regional credit crunch. It should be noted that Japanese banks are suffering not only from internal bad debts but also from bad debts arising out of their lending to the Pacific and South East Asian region. At the time of writing it appeared that the Japanese electorate had finally become convinced of the need to resolve the bank bad debt problem, in order to alleviate the associated credit crunch and allow economic growth to resume. It appears they have learnt their history lesson after all.

Thirdly, interest rates must be reduced to low positive real – or possibly negative real, at least for a period – rates as soon as possible. This will require a reduction in the political and economic risk premia and the achievement of foreign exchange rate stabilization. To reduce the risk premia, a credible economic management team must be installed. It is currently hoped that guidance received from the IMF as a result of the conditionality attached to IMF loans will help to restore confidence and credibility, thereby facilitating a reduction in interest rates. As interest rates fall, financial distress will begin to ebb as loans become more easily serviceable. In July 1998 there were signs that interest rate reductions had become possible, a year or so after the onset of the crisis, in Thailand and, following upward pressure on the exchange rate in the summer of 1998, also in South Korea.

To keep the risk premium down and to encourage a reversal of flight capital and a more general resumption of capital inflows, credible fiscal, monetary and exchange rate policies must be pursued and an effective bank regulatory and supervisory system must be put in place. The next section briefly outlines best bank regulatory and supervisory practice, which should help prevent future crises. Note also that a corollary of the above is that a country cannot slam on the 'monetary brakes' if its financial system is likely to crash as a result. A sound banking system is a necessary condition for effective monetary control. Equally, it is difficult to control inflation if the commercial banks and/or the central bank are *forced* to lend directly, or indirectly through lending to nationalized industries or parastatals, to the government. The introduction of central bank independence might thus also need to be considered as part of the institutional reform of the banking sector.

PREVENTION OF BANKING CRISES: AN OUTLINE OF BEST BANK REGULATORY AND SUPERVISORY PRACTICE

Banks should be required to hold sufficient capital to cover non-diversifiable credit and market risks, acknowledging that we live in a world of uncertainty and that hence they should err on the side of caution and 'worst case' scenarios in setting minimum risk-related capital adequacy ratios.

Depositor confidence should be assured by a funded deposit insurance scheme; which is clearly preferable to implicit insurance through 'lender of last resort' intervention at the monetary authority's discretion and ultimately the taxpayers' expense, through explicit or implicit (inflation) tax. Note also that funded schemes are usually based on premia proportional to the size of deposits, though preferably adjusted for risk exposure, and, to the extent that banks pass some or all of the costs on to depositors, the costs are borne by the depositors or shared by depositors and shareholders. Hence taxpayers in general are afforded some protection, the more so the larger the fund. Another advantage of 100 per cent deposit insurance is that the authorities can close badly run and fraudulent banks without unsettling depositors, and thereby send signals to other recalcitrants. The only constraint on closures arises in the case of banks with deposits too large to be covered by the fund ('too big to fail'). Big domestic banks probably therefore require special regulatory attention as a quid pro quo for their automatic, and otherwise free, access to the lender of last resort. Otherwise there will be a moral hazard problem.

The amount of capital that banks need to cover their risk exposures varies over the business cycle. In periods of rapid growth, as experienced by the Asian 'tiger economies' in the couple of decades before the crisis, banks can be tempted to run down capital and tend to fail to build up general loan-loss provisions against future bad loans. During drawn-out, and seemingly continuous, expansions (the business cycle persists, but people live in perpetual hope that the last recession was indeed the last *ever*), a sort of Ponzi finance starts to develop, under which banks lend to borrowers who can only possibly pay if growth continues at currently prevailing rates. Even a slowdown can make it difficult for borrowers to service loans, as in Thailand. Such developments are clearly magnified if the rapid growth period culminates in an asset price 'bubble', which bursts, again as in Thailand. Bad financial habits can thus become endemic, and when the slowdown ('growth recession') occurs and the incidence of bad and doubtful debts increases, banks are revealed to be under-provisioned. Banks should be forced to build up loan-loss reserves in good times (a buffer stock) so that they can be nourished by them in the winter of the recession. The bad and doubtful debt provisions should, therefore, display an anticyclical pattern. More commonly, banks find themselves being forced to make provisions when they can least afford to and, as a result, the credit crunch is exacerbated. However, like other (over) optimists, banks also tend to believe in the 'premature death' of the business cycle. Supervisors should adopt a pessimistic stance.

Banks should abide by overexposure and overconcentration rules. They should not lend too much to individual borrowers or sectors of the economy, otherwise the borrowers can hold the bank to ransom, because the bank cannot afford to let them fail. Mismatching by maturity and currency are major sources of risk and should be monitored carefully by supervisors. Generally, the trend is towards letting banks engage in whatever financial activities they wish, provided they have enough capital to cover non-diversifiable risks. Prohibitive and prescriptive rules are being swept away. With good cause, however, supervisors encourage diversification of lending – and, increasingly, diversification into wider financial services, that is, 'universal banking' and bancassurance – to reduce average risk. Increasingly, they also keep close watch on exposure to property, stock and futures markets, since these have been sources of numerous recent bank losses, with property market exposure causing the most frequent and biggest problems of the last couple of decades.

Increasingly, the supervisors are adopting variations on the US CAMEL (Capital Adequacy, Asset Quality, Management Quality, Expected Earnings and Liquidity) system for judging the quality of banks. Asset quality is particularly important since there is a danger that inexperienced domestic banks operating in emerging markets might effectively develop into 'pyramid schemes', attracting deposits by posting competitive interest rates and yet doing very little lending and thus not developing an asset portfolio to support their commitments to depositors. Such banks can often make a profit if they can take advantage of slow payment systems to benefit from inflation, but they face severe difficulties if inflation falls dramatically as a result of successful macroeconomic stabilization programmes (as in Brazil and Russia in the early 1990s).

Another trend is to require greater disclosure of information, or increased 'transparency', in the hope that this will create greater market discipline, perhaps by creating the opportunity for credit-rating agencies to develop and for institutional investors and other shareholders to become more active. Enhanced reporting requirements are not enough, however, since it is not just the quantity of data that matters. Quality assurance is also required. This is where the auditing process comes into play. The UK relies heavily on the auditing of company accounts, including bank accounts. The USA puts greater emphasis on on-site inspections of banks than the UK, and is probably right to do so, given the potential conflicts of interest faced by auditors, whose employing accounting firms are also trying to sell consultancy services. On-site inspections by supervisors are, however, expensive. Some countries have lists of recognized bank auditors who are required to revolve periodically so that they do not become too close to bank management. The appropriate frequency of on-site inspections is difficult to gauge.

Particular attention needs to be paid to disclosure rules relating to bad and doubtful debts, which the banks must be prevented from hiding. The US system requires disclosure of loans on which interest and principal has not been paid for so many days. The longer the period since the last payment, the greater the provisioning required. The system is scaled with various thresholds and seems eminently transferable to other countries.

With an adequate flow of rigorously audited information, a comprehensive funded deposit insurance scheme, and sufficient capital to cover non-diversifiable and non-insured (through derivatives) risks, there should be few surprises emanating from the banking sector. Exceptions might arise owing to undetected internal fraud. Hence supervisors should also ensure that 'internal controls' are adequate and that managers and traders have 'incentive-compatible contracts'. Some academics and regulators are also considering forcing the senior management of banks to enter into contracts with the regulators, with dire financial consequences for the managers if they break those contracts (see, for example, Kupiec and O'Brien, 1995). Again the idea is to achieve an incentive-compatible solution, building on the concept underlying the risk-related capital adequacy ratios recommended by the Basle Committee (which effectively 'tax' risk taking by requiring banks with more risks in their asset portfolios to hold more capital to cover those risks) that are being adopted increasingly widely in domestic banking sectors around the world. It is probable, however, that banks in developing, transition and emerging market economies should hold more capital to cover the risks they are exposed to than the minimum levels recommended by the Basle Committee.

The appropriate institutional structure for financial supervision is currently unclear. Many countries have dedicated banking commissions, which propose revisions to bank regulation and undertake supervision. In other countries these tasks are undertaken by the central bank or the finance ministry. As banks diversify, the question arises as to whether a single financial service regulator is preferable to having a number of sectorally oriented (banking, insurance, securities and so on) regulators. In the UK in 1998, responsibility for banking supervision was removed from the Bank of England, though it remains responsible for ensuring systemic financial stability, and vested in a new Financial Services Authority, which is to be made responsible for supervising the majority of the wider financial system. In 1998, Japan made a similar move, transferring responsibility for supervisory banks and security firms from the finance ministry to a new Financial Supervisory Agency. In both countries newly independent central banks were left to concentrate on setting monetary policy.

NOTES

1. See Mullineux (1990, ch. 3) for a short survey, and Davis (1992), for a much longer and deeper review of the literature.
2. The debate about whether this represents overcapacity or deficient demand is as old as business cycle theory; see Mullineux (1984, 1990) for surveys.
3. As in the USA (officially for deposits up to $100 000, but effectively for larger deposits too).
4. For example, in the US savings and loans crisis in the 1980s.

REFERENCES

Davis, E. Philip (1992), *Debt, Financial Fragility and Systemic Risk*, Oxford: Oxford University Press.
Dickinson, David G. and Andy W. Mullineux (1996), 'Currency Convertibility, Policy Credibility and Capital Flight in Poland and the CSFR', in Thomas D. Willets, Richard Sweency and Clas Wihlborg (eds), *Capital Account in Liberalising Economics*, Amsterdam: North-Holland.

Fry, Maxwell J. (1997), *Money, Interest and Banking in Economic Development*, 2nd edn, Baltimore: Johns Hopkins University Press.

IMF (1998a), *International Capital Markets. Developments, Prospects and Key Policy Issues*, Washington, DC: International Monetary Fund.

IMF (1998b), *1998 International Capital Markets Report*, Washington, DC: International Monetary Fund.

Kindleberger, Charles, P. (1996), *Manics, Panics and Crashes: A History of Financial Crises*, NewYork: John Wiley and Sons.

Kupiec, Paul H. and James M. O'Brien (1995), 'Recent Developments in Bank Capital Regulation of Market Risks', *Finance and Economic Discussion Series*, 95–51, December, Federal Reserve Board, Washington, DC.

Lensink, Robert, Niels, Hermes and Victor Murinde (2000), 'Capital Flight and Political Risk', *Journal of International Money and Finance*, 19, 73–92.

Mullineux, Andy W. (1984), *The Business Cycle after Keynes*, Brighton, UK and New York: Wheatsheaf Books and Barnes and Noble Books.

Mullineux, Andy W. (1990), *Business Cycles and Financial Crises*, Brighton, UK: Harvester-Wheatsheaf and Ann Arbor: University of Michigan Press.

12. Good governance and financial sector reform

Andy Mullineux

GOOD GOVERNANCE

The IMF survey of 14 October 1996, covering the IMF/World Bank annual meetings, emphasized the importance of 'good governance' and 'strengthening the banking sector and governance' for economic development. These themes continued to be emphasized in the October 1997 annual meetings and in announcements relating to the South East Asian financial crises that started in Thailand in May 1997 and have since spread across the South East Asian region and beyond to South Korea. Japan's growth has, of course, been inhibited by problems in its financial sector since the collapse of the 'bubble economy' in the early 1990s. If decisive action is not taken to reform the financial systems and deal with the debt problems in Pacific and South East Asia, there is a risk that the 'miracle growth' of the last couple of decades may become a thing of the past. However, the economies in the region still have much more 'catching up' to do than Japan currently has, and so high growth rates may well resume relatively quickly if prompt action is taken. In July 1998 it was still unclear whether the worst of the crisis was over. A major recession in Japan and further depreciation of the yen or indeed a devaluation by China, whose economy was showing signs of a fairly rapid slowdown, threatened to spark a further round of currency devaluations in the region. Further, the Malaysian economy appeared to be teetering on the brink of crisis, progress with economic reform in Indonesia was slow and political stability had not been convincingly re-established, and there was labour unrest in South Korea.

What is meant by 'good governance' and what is the role of the banking and the wider financial sector in establishing good governance? There seem to be at least two meanings of good governance: good (macro) governance by the state (good government), and good corporate (micro) governance. This chapter is primarily concerned with good corporate governance. It will be argued that financial institutions play a key role in the corporate governance process. A stable political and economic environment is required to enable financial institutions to operate efficiently and thereby to fulfil their governance function. In other words, good government, or macro governance, is a prerequisite for good corporate governance. We therefore dwell briefly in the next sub-section on good government, before moving on to concentrate on good governance and the financial system's role in engendering it.

What is Meant by 'Good Government'?

Broadly, good government can mean good policy formulation and execution. This involves the following: monetary, fiscal and exchange rate policies coordinated to achieve macroeconomic stability (sustainable development – steady growth with acceptably low inflation) and, perhaps, social cohesion (redistribution of income, welfare/pension provision, low unemployment). Many would add that achieving sustainable growth involves taking account of the environmental impact of the policies, especially in respect of non-renewable resources. The attainment of these objectives in turn requires adequate investment in infrastructure. Increasingly, the term 'infrastructure' is taken to mean transport, communications, utilities and so on, but also investment in human capital (education and training), which enhances living standards and contributes to 'social cohesion'. In addition, it is acknowledged that there is a need to develop an institutional structure to facilitate effective policy implementation (for example, establishment of an independent central bank and appropriate legal and regulatory structures to establish property rights, limit business liability and create efficient bankruptcy procedures). Good governance, is, however, often narrowly viewed as achieving 'cleanliness' of administration, which has an impact upon policy implementation. The IMF has recently emphasized (see IMF, 1997, for example) that widespread ingrained corruption leads to inefficiency in the allocation of resources, loss of tax revenue and a failure to achieve growth potential. It is also likely to reduce social cohesion and therefore the 'shared sense of purpose' necessary for political legitimacy. That could lead to political instability, making sound economic management difficult.

The degree of 'cleanliness' is inversely related to the incidence of bribes, sleaze, graft, nepotism, patronage, corruption, 'vote buying' or 'money politics' and so on. Such incidence seems higher in lesser-developed and emerging market economies, and the term 'crony capitalism' has been coined to describe it. However, there appears to be evidence of manipulation of macro policy to 'buy votes' to win elections in OECD countries (the political or electoral business cycle). A number of developed countries have experienced declining turnouts at elections, suggesting that they are failing to engender a shared sense of purpose. In many of these countries the distribution of income has become more unequal and there is evidence of growing 'social exclusion'. Policies to address the needs of the poor may thus be required if countries are to maintain social cohesion and a healthy democratic system.

Corporate Governance

This is a highly topical issue. In the 1990s, systems of corporate governance have been critically reviewed in France, the UK and Germany and, in all three countries, changes are being introduced with government backing. The need for corporate governance arises out of the separation of ownership by shareholders from control by hired managers and the concomitant 'principal–agent' problem, which is discussed further in the second section of the chapter.

In Asia, as in Germany, a significant proportion of large businesses are privately owned family businesses. The performance of this sector of the economy has a significant influence on the performance of the overall economy and the welfare of other agents – employees, creditors (including banks), depositors (in banks), customers and so on). Further, in many Asian economies, state ownership of enterprises (often including banks) remains widespread and so the performance of the state-owned sector is also very important. Such enterprises generate special governance problems and many countries have tried to resolve them by resorting to privatization. In most European countries, the size of the state-owned enterprise sector has been, or is in the process of being, significantly reduced in that way, leading to a separation of ownership and control. Consequently, adequate corporate governance arrangements must be in place prior to privatization. We will return to the issue of privatization following the discussion in the second section of the corporate governance mechanism in the UK and Germany.

What is Good Corporate Governance?

The current debate in the UK relates largely to the strengths and weaknesses of the 'Anglo-Saxon' (UK/US) and the 'Rhinish' (Germanic) systems. The key issues are (a) shareholder versus stakeholder control, (b) short-termism, and (c) the importance of the structure of the financial sector. These issues will be discussed in the next section, which draws comparisons between the UK and German systems of corporate governance. First, however, the relationship between good governance and economic development is considered further and, subsequently, the extent to which the UK and German systems achieve their goals and can serve as models for Pacific and South East Asian economies is considered. The overall aim is to achieve a *continuously* efficient, welfare-maximizing allocation of resources. This may or may not lead to stable, non-inflationary growth; business cycles may be beneficial to growth, as may low (non-zero), but relatively stable, rates of inflation. The financial sector, as the allocator of capital, clearly has a key role to play in the process and must continue to monitor the use of capital to ensure that it is put to the best use (that is, to avoid capital hoarding by inefficient users). To do this it must be possible to remove capital from inefficient users (through bankruptcy procedures, for example) and to reallocate it to more efficient users. The banks and other financial institutions thus contribute to the corporate governance mechanism by monitoring the use of capital, to ensure that it is being used efficiently, and reallocating it when necessary. Given high levels of uncertainty and information asymmetry, banks will be the most important financial institutions. As greater political and economic stability is achieved, and more good quality information is generated, the role of 'direct', market-based, finance and 'institutional investors' will increase.

In the presence of significant market failures, regulatory intervention can be justified so long as intervention genuinely improves matters. The presence of asymmetric information is commonly used to justify bank regulation, and excessive market concentration following privatization is commonly taken to justify the regulation of utilities, for example. However, governments should attempt to remove unnecessary distortions arising from taxes and subsidies and from corruption and ensure that contracts and property rights are honoured and enforceable. The legal system, including bankruptcy laws, and auditing processes, to ensure the quality of published information, are thus essential components of the institutional infrastructure.

CORPORATE GOVERNANCE AND CORPORATE FINANCE IN THE UK AND GERMANY

As noted above, a number of countries, including France, Germany and the UK, have recently reviewed their corporate governance structures (laws, customs and institutions) with a view to trying to improve the performance of domestic businesses and the economy as a whole. This is largely a response to pressures deriving from the globalization process, which *inter alia* entails increasingly free international trade and capital flows. This has confronted firms operating in alternative capitalist systems (for example, Anglo-Saxon and Germanic) with much more direct competition from firms operating in other systems. Because corporate governance systems impose constraints on firms' activities, they affect their production and capital cost structures and thus impose implicit, or regulatory, taxes on domestic firms. Given that these regulatory taxes vary across the capitalist regimes, governments in many countries are reviewing the costs and benefits of their domestic systems in order to ensure that domestic firms are not handicapped when competing in the global market.

Separation of Ownership and Control and Corporate Governance

The need for effective corporate governance arises out of the separation of ownership of businesses from their control. It is thus an issue relating to the performance of all firms in the private sector (public companies) and in the public sector (state-owned enterprises, SOEs) except privately owned, non-public, small and medium-sized enterprises (SMEs), where ownership and control rest with the manager-owners (for example, family businesses).

In the case of SMEs, their governance may be influenced by debtholders, rather than shareholders, and the most important debtholders are commonly banks. In the case of SOEs, the ownership rests with the state, on behalf of the electorate, whose procedures for controlling management, with a view to exacting good performance from nationalized industries, have been judged lacking in many countries, being seen as political interference in management. This led to a wave of privatization, or denationalization, which gathered pace in the UK in the 1980s and subsequently spread to continental Europe, including Germany.

The hope is that privatization will improve the performance of former SOEs by exposing them to better market discipline. This seems to mean two things: discipline through competition in the product market of the privatized firms (hence the doubts about the privatization of monopolies and the need to establish regulators to intercede on behalf of consumers) and discipline through the financial markets, particularly that imposed by the new shareholders through the stock market.

Shareholder v. Stakeholder Control

More generally, UK public (private sector, publicly owned companies) are traditionally viewed as being owned by shareholders who seek to govern or control the managers in pursuit of profit maximization or maximizing the return (capital gain and dividend payout) on their shareholdings. In other words, in common with the USA, Anglo-Saxon capitalism is run in the interests of the shareholders, the owners of the (non-human) capital tied up in a business.

In contrast, Germanic or Rhinish capitalism is built around a consensual approach in which a number of stakeholders (shareholders, debtholders, consumers, management and non-management employees, the community in the locality of the enterprise, and so on) are deemed to have legitimate interests in the management decisions and the performance of enterprises.

In reality, the contrast is not so stark, and thus Tony Blair, the UK prime minister, can talk about introducing 'stakeholder capitalism' in the UK. Management of successful firms in the UK and the USA cannot afford to ignore the interests of their bankers and bondholders (debtholders), consumers, workers and the local community, and clear-thinking shareholders would not expect them to do so. Equally, even though workers are commonly represented on the supervisory boards of major enterprises, and workers' councils are widespread, German firms cannot afford to let the workers run the firm. Instead, they must balance the needs of all stakeholders. Nevertheless, in Germany the management style has been more consensus-based than in the UK, where it has become less so in the last couple of decades as the influence of trade unions has declined. It is also true that shareholders are given a higher ranking amongst stakeholders in the UK than in Germany, although there are moves in Germany to pay more attention to the wishes of shareholders. Depositors in banks form another group of important stakeholders. By choice, they are less risk-prone than individual bank shareholders, preferring to hold their savings in bank deposits, which are less risky than bank equities. Depositors will tend to prefer banks to take fewer risks and thus seek a lower return on equity, or to hold more capital, than bank shareholders would like. Perhaps because depositors are also voters and taxpayers, and outnumber individual bank shareholders, governments, even in the USA and the UK, tend to intervene by regulating banks in the interests of depositor protection and limiting the taxpayers' exposure to bank bailouts. Similar considerations led to regulation of the wider financial sector to protect investors.

Corporate Governance Structures in the UK and Germany

The organization of major corporations differs significantly between the two countries. The UK has a unitary board of directors, whilst Germany has a two-tier structure, with a management board and a supervisory board. Management boards are responsible for the day-to-day running of the firm subject to oversight by supervisory boards, on which the aforementioned worker representatives sit, along with main debtor (usually bank) representatives, who often act as chairmen (as at Daimler-Benz).

Dramatic changes, such as the adoption of two-tier boards in the UK and their abandonment in Germany, seem unlikely in the near future. In their reviews of corporate governance procedures, however, both countries are closely examining the role of institutional shareholders, who are the most important shareholders in both countries. In the UK, the dominance of institutional share-holders has continued to increase despite the massive increase in the number of small, individual shareholders (shareholder capitalism) achieved in the past couple of decades. Most shareholders hold small quantities of shares in one or two privatized (or demutualized, as with Abbey National, Halifax and other ex-building societies) companies and prefer to invest in the wider stock market via Oiecs (open-ended investment companies, formerly unit and investment trusts, which are mutual funds) or, vicariously, via pension and life insurance funds. In the USA there has been an increase in institutional shareholder, particularly pension fund, such as CALPERS, activism and there is some evidence that this is beginning to catch on in the UK.

The question thus arises, should institutional shareholders be forced to play a more active part in corporate governance? This could be achieved, for example, by forcing pension fund trustees and/or fund managers to vote publicly at shareholder meetings. Further, the role of pensioners as stakeholders needs to be borne in mind, given the progressive privatization of pensions in response to the ageing population in the UK and the USA. Germany is also likely to be following this lead, given that it faces a more serious future pension provision problem than the UK by virtue of having a less privatized pension scheme and a more rapidly ageing population.

In Germany and Japan the main institutional shareholders are the large banks. The Grossbanken's (large banks') influence often exceeds their shareholdings, as a result of proxy voting on behalf of the shareholders who commonly deposit shares with banks for safekeeping, and by virtue of their widespread representation on supervisory boards. The perceived dominant position of banks, disputed by the banks themselves, in German capitalism has periodically met with widespread public disquiet in Germany. The anti-monopoly authorities have frequently encouraged banks to reduce shareholdings, while the tax rules encourage holdings below 10 per cent of the total shares issued. Deutsche Bank (the largest) recently announced its intention to reduce large equity participations and said it could accelerate the process if the government was willing to give capital gains tax concessions (many of its shares are booked at historic cost). The return on equity in Germany is not particularly high and, as in Japan, banks feel that they can make a better return on the capital released through equity sales. The corporate governance review in Germany has also brought forth the suggestion that the large banks should significantly reduce the number of supervisory boards they allow their top bankers to sit on. This will both reduce the influence of banks and also, it is hoped, improve the diligence of supervisory board members in the wake of the high-profile supervisory failures in recent years (Metallgesellschaft, for example).

Bank Shareholding and the German Model

There is a risk that some of the strengths of the German model could be lost if banks reduce equity participation substantially. Many experts believe the strength of the German corporate governance system derives from the relationships forged between businesses and their debt and equity-holding banks. Because banks are stakeholders in both the debt and equity sense they have a strong incentive to monitor the activities of management and invest strategically in them (fostering 'long-termism'). The bankruptcy/liquidation/financial restructuring process can be dealt with more efficiently, more quickly and more cheaply, internally and economically and socially wasteful closures can be avoided.

By way of contrast, UK banks have been discouraged from building up equity stakes in non-financial enterprises and can only do so as part of a financial restructuring programme involving debt-for-equity swaps (as with Eurotunnel). The Bank of England has hitherto expected such equity participations which are allowed, up to 10 per cent of capital, under EC banking directives and common elsewhere in the EU, to be liquidated when a reasonable market price for the stock prevails. As a consequence, 'relationship banking' is less well developed in the UK and the bankruptcy/liquidation process is an external legalistic one involving various groups of creditors (banks, bondholders, shareholders) with competing claims and differing seniority with respect to their claims on the debtor company. Bankruptcy and financial restructuring proceedings are thus often long-drawn-out and costly affairs.

'Short-termism'

'Short-termism', is another alleged drawback of the Anglo-Saxon model. Pension and insurance fund managers are themselves operating at one remove from their controllers (pension fund trustees, insurance company shareholders and so on). They may, therefore, seek high dividend payments in the name of investment fund performance at the expense of long-term strategic investment in plant and machinery and research and development by the firms in which they are investing (that is, they may place a higher weight on short-term, as opposed to long-term, profitability). Incumbent managements of firms, faced with the continuous threat of takeover if institutional shareholders are not kept sweet and thus unwilling to sell their equity stakeholdings, acquiesce with high dividend payouts. Worse, merger and acquisition activity can boost the performance of investments if they result in capital gains from target company shareholdings.

An alternative view is that the short-termism effect is of minor importance and is anyway dominated by the benefits of returning capital to shareholders for reinvestment rather than having it trapped within a firm for possibly inefficient internal investment. Efficient firms with good projects can, after all, always ask shareholders or banks or bond markets for more finance, and should be forced to compete for it.

Financial Sector Convergence between Germany and the UK

The creation of a single European financial market and ageing populations are likely to lead to a convergence of the financial sectors in Germany and the UK. The dominance of German banks as institutional investors in Germany is likely to decline, partly owing to the aforementioned expected reduction in banks' equity stakeholding, but also as a result of the expected growth in institutional shareholding by insurance and pension and mutual funds in response to the ageing population, privatization of pensions and relaxation of restrictions on equity investment by pension funds and in order to increase the returns on their investments. In addition, UK banks may be allowed to become fully universal, in the German sense of combining not just commercial and securities business, but also engaging in equity participation in non-financial companies to which they lend. This is more likely to be permitted once the authority of the Bank of England is weakened after sterling's eventual participation in economic and monetary union (EMU) and if the benefits of internal resolution of bankruptcy/financial restructuring are more widely recognized.

It is thus clear that financiers have a key role to play in corporate governance and that the contrast in the approaches to corporate governance in the UK and Germany is partly a result of differing financial structures. These differences are rooted in their contrasting socioeconomic and political histories. Germany and Japan are often described as being bank-dominated economies, whilst the UK and the USA are often regarded as capital market-oriented. This is true in the field of corporate governance, as argued above, but much less so in the sphere of finance, since, even in the USA, banks remain significant suppliers of debt finance, especially to small and medium-sized enterprises (SMEs).

Recent studies (see, for example, Corbett and Jenkinson, 1994; Mayer, 1994) have shown that corporate investment in both the UK and Germany is financed primarily from retained, or undistributed, profits (internal investment) and that the main source of external finance for investment in both countries is banks lending. Share issuance actually makes a negative net contribution in the UK in years of high mergers and acquisition activity. The menu of financial sources offered to larger companies may be more varied in the UK and the USA, but SMEs remain largely dependent upon banks for external finance in both these countries, as well as in Germany, and a worryingly large, and in the 1990s a growing proportion of net investment is internally financed. The cause for concern is that capital trapped in large firms might, in terms of return on equity and job creation, be more efficiently invested in SMEs with good growth prospects. Corporate governance in the macro sense entails ensuring not only that managements use the capital they receive efficiently, but also that capital is allocated to managements that use it most efficiently. Whether the macro is a country, the European Union or the global economy is a moot point, but an efficient financial system is required for efficient corporate governance at the micro (firm) and macro levels.

SME Financing and Governance in the UK and Germany

An efficient financial sector will ensure that SMEs receive their fair share of finance. There are good economic reasons to believe that banks may ration the supply of credit to SMEs. It may be no accident that the Mittlestand became the backbone of the German economic miracle in the post-war period given the German government's proactive policy towards SMEs, via implicitly subsidized medium to long-term loans provided through the KfW (Kreditanstalt für Wiederaufbau; German state development bank) and loan guarantees. The UK has acknowledged the SME funding problem, but has acted less decisively, although in recent years loan guarantees have been raised to levels comparable to those prevailing in Germany. Given their bank dependence, we must continue to rely on well-run banks for the efficient governance of SMEs, on whose prospects it is increasingly clear we all depend.

Whither Capitalism?

We end this section with two footnotes on the issue of how much importance should be accorded to shareholders vis-à-vis other stakeholders. First, the growing share of the service sector, which is heavily populated with SMEs, in most economies increases the importance of human capital which is owned by the individual, not the shareholder. The relative importance of shareholders is thus set to wane if businesses increasingly lease equipment and contract out activities requiring capital investment.

Second, it is increasingly recognized that management and worker remuneration via share-ownership schemes should improve incentive compatibility; that is, ensure that they share the interests of other shareholders. Privatization of pensions also increases the public's stake in capitalism both at home and abroad, given foreign equity investment by the funds. The workers and pensioners are thus set to become the major shareholders. What implications does this have for either Anglo-Saxon or Germanic capitalism and stakeholder analysis, for the shareholders are also the consumer and voters? Again it should be stressed that shareholders may need special protection from abuse by those with fiduciary responsibility (fund managers and the shareholders of fund management companies) and that banks' depositors, who prefer liquid deposits to more risky investments, may need the most protection.

FINANCIAL SECTOR REFORM IN PACIFIC AND SOUTH EAST ASIA

Analysis of the transition economies in Central and Eastern Europe (Buch, 1996; Mullineux, 1995a, 1995b) demonstrates that financial sector reform, privatization of state-owned banks (SOBs) and enterprises (SOEs), resolution of the bank bad debt problem and the growth of new private sector enterprises

(SMEs) are interconnected. Until the bad debt problem is tackled, privatization of SOBs and SOEs is extremely difficult, since SOBs remain locked into a lending relationship with SOEs, making it difficult for them to lend to SMEs, and thus increasing the severity of credit rationing. Yet, if the SMEs fail to grow fast enough, the unemployment created by the restructuring of the SOEs cannot be absorbed. Further, as a consequence of the inadequacy of the bank regulatory and supervisory system, a rapid proliferation of small new private banks often leads to fraud, mismanagement and bank or 'near bank' failures. The supervisory authorities are often understaffed and the staff they have lack training and experience. It is evident that failure to tackle the bad debt problem and to reform the financial system can severely inhibit growth, as the experience of Japan in the 1990s demonstrates.

The reason for alluding to the transition economies and Japan is that many of the problems they have faced (or face!) are evident in Pacific and South East Asia. There is now a widespread bank bad debt problem, though admittedly of varying magnitude in the individual countries. There have been asset-price bubbles of varying importance in the property and stock markets of many of the countries. There is also clear evidence, particularly in South Korea and China, of banks being locked into lending relationships with increasingly poorly performing large enterprises, for example, the *chaebol* in South Korea and SOEs in China.

It also appears that many of the South East Asia countries have suffered as a result of capital account and financial sector liberalization, as the Czech Republic and, to a lesser extent, Poland did in May/June 1997 and Estonia, Poland and other countries did again in November 1997. Following capital account liberalization, a capital inflow problem often emerges, which appears to be most acute when a country is conducting a pegged exchange rate policy. Once enough speculators or market participants believe that competitiveness is being lost – doubts are often triggered by the current account deficit approaching 5 per cent of GDP – excessive capital inflows, which put upward pressure on inflation, can quickly be reversed, leading to excessive capital outflows. It should be noted that this reversal appears to be more likely when the inflows have been predominantly short-term, perhaps through international/offshore banking facilities, as in Thailand, rather than longer-term foreign direct investment (FDI) flows, as in the Czech Republic. The jury is still out on the stability of foreign portfolio investment (FPI) flows, but these appear to be unstable in the case of 'emerging markets'. The differential capital outflows from countries in the Pacific and South East Asia region relate to differences in economic fundamentals, perceived political stability, the structure of inflows (short-term, FDI, FPI) and the degree of financial openness (South Korea less than many South East Asian countries, and China even less than South Korea): see IMF (1998a).

The capital outflows lead to downward pressure in the exchange rates and the authorities commonly respond, or are encouraged to do so by the IMF, by raising interest rates. As exchange rates fall, foreign exchange debts become more expensive to service, and as interest rates rise, so too do domestic debits. The financial and corporate sector problems are exacerbated as a consequence and outflows may accelerate in response, leading to a vicious cycle. Prevention may be easier than cure, and this partly entails ensuring that the banking and financial system is stable and thus adequately provisioned against bad debt losses, well regulated and supervised.

The role of banks in promoting good governance is more complex in a system where interlocking shareholdings are common (as in Japan and many other Pacific and South East Asian countries). This is a vague concept, not to be confused with strategic shareholding. Widespread share ownership is widely regarded as inefficient because shareholders exert little influence on managers by virtue of the difficulty of coordinating their interests. Large, strategic shareholders, such as institutional shareholders, are thus helpful in concentrating share ownership, making it potentially easier for shareholders to agree a strategy and exert an influence on managers. Under interlocking shareholdings there are a relatively small number of strategic shareholders and they tend to hold significant shareholdings in other strategic shareholders (as in Japan). Conflicts of interest can easily arise and a corporate Mafia, that is, a sort of corporate brotherhood, can develop. Capital gets locked into the group, which usually includes banks and other financial institutions (as in Japan). Inefficient firms or banks are rarely allowed to fail. Instead a 'convoy system' prevails. Variants on the theme, often dominated by key, predominantly family-owned, corporations, can develop. Political influence is often bought and in the worst cases (Indonesia, under President Suharto, the Philippines under President Marcos) the families of the most powerful politicians are key players in the interlocking shareholder networks. This has been dubbed 'crony capitalism'.

WHAT LESSONS CAN BE DRAWN?

The false conclusion might be drawn from the preceding discussion that many transition and developing economies have already taken liberalization of trade and capital accounts too far and too fast and should withdraw from the WTO talks on further liberalization of the financial sector General Agreement on Trade in Services (GATS). Even if the financial sector and capital account liberalization did perhaps progress too rapidly in the past under an inadequate bank regulatory and supervisory regime, it does not follow that further liberalization would not be beneficial, following financial sector restructuring, including resolution of the bad debt problem, and the establishment of an effective regulatory and supervisory regime. Capital account liberalization brings capital inflows to supplement savings in the financing of investment and should therefore facilitate more rapid development by increasing capacity, enhancing infrastructure and enabling 'catching up' via technology transfer. The future pensioners in the OECD countries, after all, need to earn an adequate return on their investments, and yet the rates of return available in their economies are commonly relatively low. OECD countries are, by and large, natural exporters to emerging market economies.

Further, financial liberalization achieved through participation in GATS as a requirement for OECD membership (as in South Korea) should increase efficiency of domestic financial systems in response to increased competition amongst domestic banks, as well as secondary banks or finance companies, and with foreign banks. There will also be benefits from the transfer of financial know-how. Increased competition will initially put pressure on lending margins, requiring improved efficiency to maintain profitability, and the supervisors will need to be vigilant to prevent bank failures, at the depositors' expense, or the need for bailouts, at the taxpayers' expense. The structures and procedures needed to achieve this were discussed in Chapter 11, but it is clear that banks must hold sufficient capital to cover their non-diversifiable risks and must be required to build adequate loan-loss reserves as risks increase and bad and doubtful loans proliferate. Clearly, attention also has to be paid to lending practices, especially where irrational exuberance is detected in asset markets.

Where there is substantial state-ownership of financial and non-financial enterprises, privatization should be considered, as a means both of increasing competition and efficiency and of reducing demands on the state budget for subsidies and opportunities for corruption expressed as bad or well meaning, but misguided, governance. State-directed lending by banks, it should be noted, has rarely been judged successful, especially where it is directed to the government and as a result the state becomes reliant upon it for financing, with inflationary consequences. Taxes are best raised explicitly, rather than implicitly through inflation, which is a particularly distortionary form of taxation and tends to increase economic uncertainty. State-directed bank lending also creates opportunities for indirect subsidies and patronage.

It is also worth stressing that the absence of financial fragility makes it possible for governments to apply monetary restraint, that is, raise interest rates, when it becomes necessary to prevent surges in inflation. Further, monetary control can only be achieved within the context of a state budget that can be financed without recourse to excessive borrowing from the central and commercial banks. If a deficit is to be run, and is not to be financed almost entirely by borrowing from abroad or from the banking system, attention also needs to be paid to the development of domestic government bond markets.

Finally, returning to the issue of good corporate governance, what can be learnt from the European experiences discussed in the second section of this chapter? It is clear that there is no widespread agreement on best practice in this sphere, in contrast to the consensus prevailing in the field of best bank regulatory practice. However, crony capitalism is clearly unlikely to lead to the most efficient allocation of capital.

Nevertheless, capital market development has been proceeding rapidly in many countries in the Pacific and South East Asian region (see IMF, 1998b, and previous reports). Over time, as in Germany, more and more companies will issue shares on the stock market and make use of emerging domestic corporate bond markets, as well as the international capital markets, as alternatives to bank sources of debt finance. Institutional investors will become increasingly important, alongside banks, in the corporate governance process. Increased disclosure requirements and better auditing, to guarantee the quality of the information, will accelerate the process and reduce opportunities for covert payments. Many countries in the region already have funded, but often state-controlled, pension schemes. To the extent that these are privatized, the growth in the importance of institutional investors will be accelerated. The institutional investors, insurance and pension funds, will in turn provide a stable demand for government and corporate bonds and equities, adding to the liquidity and depth of the capital markets and facilitating government debt management. In Poland, privatization revenues are to be used to help ease the transition to private funded pension provision arising out of the need for the younger working generation both to provide for their own pensions and to maintain those currently drawing on the non-funded state pay-as-you-go pension schemes. This approach could fruitfully be investigated, though the ageing population problem is much less acute in Pacific and South East Asia than it is in Poland. It is, however, notable that the ageing problem is particularly acute in Japan, and is also a considerable problem in China, partly owing to China's successful birth control policy.

Financial systems in the Pacific and South East Asia region can be expected to converge on the emerging international norm. Given greater exposure to the increasingly globalized capital markets as a result of capital account liberalization, participation in the GATS agreement on trade in financial services, and following the reforms made necessary by the recent financial crises, the convergence may well be rapid. In the evolving world financial system, direct finance through capital markets is becoming increasingly important, and so too are institutional investors and investment fund managers in general. A consequence of all this is that corporate governance systems can also be expected to converge. The judgment of investors on the performance of the managers of enterprises will become increasingly important, as has their judgment on the performance of the managers of economic policies in transition and developing countries with emerging markets, as countries in the Pacific and South East Asia region have recently discovered.

Perhaps the domestic and global financial markets have already become the ultimate arbiters of good micro and macro governance.

REFERENCES

Buch, Claudia M (1996), *Creating Efficient Banking Systems: Theory and Evidence from Eastern Europe*, Tübingen: J.C.B. Mohr (Paul Siebeck).

Corbett, J. and T. Jenkinson (1994), 'The Financing of Industry 1970–89: An International Comparison', *Discussion Paper No 948,* Centre for Economic Policy Research, London.

IMF (1997), 'Why Worry about Corruption?', *Economic Issues 6*, International Monetary Fund, Washington, DC.

IMF (1998a), *International Capital Markets: Developments, Prospects and Key Policy Issues*, Washington, DC: International Monetary Fund.

IMF (1998b), *1998 International Capital Markets Report*, Washington, DC: International Monetary Fund.

Mayer, C. (1994) 'The Assessment: Money and Banking: Theory and Evidence', *Oxford Review of Economic Policy*, 10(4), 1–13.

Mullineux, Andy (1995a), 'Banking Sector Restructuring, Debt Consolidation and Small and Medium-sized Enterprise Financing in Transition Economies', *International Finance Group Working Paper, IGFW P-95-05,* University of Birmingham.

Mullineux Andy (1995b), 'Progress with Financial Sector Reform in Six Transforming Economies', *International Finance Group Working Paper, IGFWP-95-04*, University of Birmingham.

13. Governance, human capital, labour and endogenous growth in Asia–Pacific: a comparative study

A. Bende-Nabende, J.L. Ford and S. Sen[1]

INTRODUCTION AND LITERATURE REVIEW

The role of governments in fostering economic growth is an issue of continuing interest. Within the UK this interest has manifested itself in terms of public–private partnerships, where private sector finance and technology is used to support infrastructural investment traditionally considered to be the domain of the state. In Pacific–Asian economies it was commonly believed that state intervention was kept to a minimum and that the private sector took a dominant role in promoting economic growth. This idea is now known to be a fallacy (see Wade, 1990); an active state created the preconditions for economic growth, which was then achieved by continuing 'collaboration' between the public and private sectors. Similar to the role of corporate governance in the case of a single industrial organization, the state provided macro governance that was required for the country as a whole (the macro-economy) to grow faster. As the World Bank (1997) so succinctly puts it: 'It is not a question of state or markets. Each has a large and irreplaceable role.'

However, the precise role of the state is not always clearly understood. As a provider of pure public goods, such as national defence, political stability, democratic participation or non-inflationary macro environments, the government can play a major role in economic development. Clearly, Pacific–Asian countries show evidence of such provision of pure public goods. However, there are not many such 'goods', nor are they easy to measure or commonly quantifiable. To give specific examples of non-rival and non-excludable public goods in these countries would be relatively difficult, except in the case of military expenditures. For other state-sponsored activities, including education, health or pension provision, the private sector or the household has the potential to contribute, and clearly it will do so if excluded. If we wish to measure the impact of the government on economic activity, it would be difficult to do so under a pure public good paradigm.

This chapter takes an alternative route. It assumes a congestion model of government activity where the public sector contributes towards the productivity of the private sector by relieving 'congestion' defined in the broadest sense. The following could be potentially rivalrous, but mostly non-excludable, goods whose benefits are collectively consumed but which are subject to crowding. Examples are public recreational facilities or subsidized transport or congested roads. But we also include in this broad category those goods which are potentially excludable but mainly non-rivalrous in character, because these can also suffer from crowding which reduces the productivity of the private sector. Examples include state schools, national universities or public health care. All of these need to be provided by the government and contribute to economic growth. An efficient government, or one with macro governance, will be able to increase economic growth through the optimum provision of such 'public goods'.

The optimum way to deal with the empirical measurement of the effects of macro governance is to look at the impact of functional distributions of government expenditure on economic activity. Traditional models have looked at government expenditure (activity) in aggregate; however, this begs the question regarding the relative efficiency of state provision in relieving congestion. These traditional models cannot distinguish between different types of congestion relief, given the disparate nature of government services (for example, in health, education and transport), and the aggregate effect becomes relatively meaningless. By breaking down aggregate government spending into its functional categories, we provide more precise estimates of the effects.

The next section provides a simple endogenous growth model, giving a core theoretical justification for the empirical results. A discussion of the measurement of the variables, data sources and limitations, econometric experimentation and notation is presented in the third section. The empirical findings are examined in the fourth section, while comparative diagnostics are the subject of the fifth. The final section presents concluding remarks.

THEORETICAL MODEL

The purpose of this model is to give a theoretical justification to the empirical study of the role of governments in affecting economic growth. The econometric estimates, in the next sections, seek to measure the impact of various categories of government expenditures on the level and rate of growth of the national product. The theoretical model, which follows, provides the rationale for such a relationship.

Assume a simple production function, for the ith good, of the AK type (Rebelo, 1991), capable of generating endogenous growth in the macroeconomy.

Essentially, such a model takes us back to Harrod's conception of a fixed input–output technology-driven growth model.

$$y_i = Ak_i. \tag{13.1}$$

The productivity factor A depends on numerous sources of technical progress (Barro and Sala-i-Martin, 1995). Since we are concentrating on the role of governments, let us assume a congestion model where A depends on the ratio of government expenditure (G) to aggregate output (Y). Alternatively, following Turnovsky (1995) we could have constructed a more complicated model where A depends on the ratio of government (public sector) capital stock to private sector capital stock. However, this adds to the complexity of transitional dynamics, since we need to follow the time path of two separate capital stocks. Our core model avoids this complication by concentrating on steady-state equilibrium.

$$A = A\left(\frac{G}{Y}\right) \quad A' > 0, A'' < 0. \tag{13.2}$$

Note that all the i sectors of the economy are affected equivalently by government expenditures since G has a public good element to it and therefore the ith sector cannot be excluded from benefiting from the presence of a government. However, the role of the public sector is not to create a pure public good which is totally non-rivalrous and non-excludable. Rather, its presence supports the private sector and enhances its productivity. The private sector can produce the same goods as the government does: it can construct roads, have private transport systems, provide health care and create schools and universities. However, the presence of a government sector reduces 'congestion' and creates new capacity in these areas in the process enhancing productivity in the national economy.

The form of the function demonstrates that, for a given G, if Y increases (with increased aggregate capital stock) then the economy is subject to congestion; the level of public services available to each and every ith sector is reduced, which in turn lowers productivity $A(.)$ and reduces output y_i. Alternatively, G has to rise with respect to aggregate private capital stock (or aggregate output) for there to be an increase in productivity. This relative increase in G will in turn raise the output–capital ratio. Summing up (13.1) and using (13.2):

$$Y = \sum y_i = A\left(\frac{G}{Y}\right) \sum k_i \tag{13.3}$$

$$Y = A\left(\frac{G}{Y}\right)K. \tag{13.4}$$

The household's behaviour is simple: maximizing an infinite horizon utility functional depending on consumption $c(t)$ and having an aggregate rate of time preference ρ.

$$\text{Max: } \int e^{-\rho t} u(c(t)) dt. \tag{13.5}$$

Households are subject to an aggregate asset constraint where the rate of return on capital is given by r. Assume that population growth is zero (since it does not influence endogenous growth rates). Then the Keynes–Ramsey equation gives the following condition for the household's optimization problem:

$$x = \left(\frac{1}{a}\right)[r - \rho]$$

$$\left(a = -\left[\frac{u''}{u'}\right]c, \text{ the elasticity of the marginal utility function}\right); \tag{13.6}$$

x is the rate of growth of consumption. In the steady-state equilibrium of an endogenous growth model, x is the common growth rate of aggregate consumption, output (Y), private capital formation (K) and government expenditure (G).

From (13.4), the rate of return on capital or the marginal product of capital (MPK) is:

$$r = MPK = A\left(\frac{G}{Y}\right). \tag{13.7}$$

However, this government expenditure has to be financed by taxing or borrowing from the private sector. Assume that Ricardian equivalence holds, so that in steady state we can work with balanced budgets. Since steady state requires G and Y to grow at the same rate, $G/Y = g$ is constant and this is also the rate of taxation (τ).

From (13.7), the net of tax MPK is therefore:

$$(1 - \tau)r = (1 - \tau)A\left(\frac{G}{Y}\right). \tag{13.8}$$

Given $\tau = \left(\dfrac{G}{Y}\right) = g$, we get:

$$(1 - g)r = (1 - g)A(g). \qquad (13.9)$$

Adapting the Keynes–Ramsey formula to take account of taxation, the growth rate of the economy (x) is given by:

$$x = \left(\frac{1}{a}\right)\left[(1 - g)A(g) - \rho\right]. \qquad (13.10)$$

The growth rate is dependent on the share of government expenditure in GDP; alternatively, it can also be defined to be dependent on the tax rate or government revenues.

The sign of the impact effect, $[dx/dg]$ is ambiguous. This is because tax, $\tau = g$, reduces the post-tax rate of capital's return $[r(1 - g)]$ and, on the other hand, increases productivity since $A' > 0$.

The derivative of x with respect to g is:

$$\frac{dx}{dg} = \left(\frac{1}{a}\right)\left[(1 - g)A' - A\right]. \qquad (13.11)$$

Clearly, x could have a maximum depending on the elasticity of the A function and the value of g.

In the empirical model we estimate parameter values, which gives the impact of sectoral distribution and functional categories of government expenditure on the level of income in the economy. In other words, we are concerned, not with the quantity, but with the quality of government expenditure and how each category affects economic development. This is consistent with our paradigm of congestion, since those categories such as health, education and transport are there to relieve the private sector of congestion and increase its productivity. This simple model therefore captures the essence of the role of government and macro governance in developing economies.

However, the foregoing model is analysed in the context of growth rates, while the econometric estimates are in level terms. One way to reconcile the two would be to use lagged values of the endogenous variable (GDP), but severe data limitations prevent us from losing degrees of freedom. We therefore discuss briefly another method of modelling the impact of government spending on output, emphasizing the concept of congestibility.

The alternative formulation, which also explicitly models congestion, is to use the production function approach more broadly. Here output of each household–firm (agent) is made a function of its capital stock, labour force and human capital. Using lower-case letters to denote the microeconomic unit of production, and upper-case letters to denote aggregates, the production function of the representative agent is given by:

$$y = k^{\alpha} l^{\beta} h^{1-\alpha-\beta}. \tag{13.12}$$

Let there be N such agents so that

$$y = \frac{Y}{N}, \quad k = \frac{K}{N}, \quad l = \frac{L}{N}, \quad h = \frac{H}{N}. \tag{13.13}$$

Assuming symmetry, summing over all agents (that is, substituting for y, k, l, h in (13.12) by using (13.13)), we get the aggregate production function

$$Y = K^{\alpha} L^{\beta} H^{1-\alpha-\beta}. \tag{13.14}$$

Taking growth rates of (13.13), we get the following dynamic equation:

$$\frac{\dot{Y}}{Y} = \left[\alpha\left(\frac{\dot{K}}{K}\right) \right] + \left[\beta\left(\frac{\dot{L}}{L}\right) \right] + \left[(1-\alpha-\beta)\left(\frac{\dot{H}}{H}\right) \right] \tag{13.15}$$

(a dot, as in for example $\dot{Y}$, means a time derivative dy/dt).

Now consider the amount of public service available to each agent as z, which is derived from aggregate public expenditure G. The congestion equation follows Turnovsky (1995):

$$\left(\frac{Z}{G}\right) = \left(\frac{k}{K}\right)^{q}. \tag{13.16}$$

The parameter q gives the degree of congestion. When $q = 0$ we get a pure public good; each economic agent receives the services available from the total G (national defence, for instance). When $q = 1$, we have proportional congestion; the amount of public service received by a single agent is proportional to the capital stock it holds as a ratio of aggregate capital stock.

Taking time derivatives of (13.16),

$$\left(\frac{\dot{z}}{z}\right) = \left(\frac{\dot{G}}{G}\right) + q\left[\left(\frac{\dot{k}}{k}\right) - \left(\frac{\dot{K}}{K}\right)\right].$$ (13.17)

In equilibrium, the growth rate of the private use of the public service (z) is proportional to the growth of the individual agent's capital stock (k). Thus:

$$\frac{\dot{z}}{z} = q\frac{\dot{k}}{k}.$$ (13.18)

Substituting (13.18) into (13.17), we derive the relationship between growth rates of aggregate capital stock (K) and aggregate government expenditure (G). Therefore

$$\frac{\dot{G}}{G} = q\frac{\dot{K}}{K}.$$ (13.19)

Replacing (13.19) in (13.15),

$$\frac{\dot{Y}}{Y} = \left[\frac{\alpha}{q}\left(\frac{\dot{G}}{G}\right)\right] + \left[\beta\left(\frac{\dot{L}}{L}\right)\right] + \left[(1-\alpha-\beta)\left(\frac{\dot{H}}{H}\right)\right].$$ (13.20)

Integrating differential equation (13.20) by parts we derive an alternative measure of the production function now dependent on government services, labour and human capital:

$$Y = G^{\alpha/q}L^\beta H^{1-\alpha-\beta}.$$ (13.21)

The log-linear version of (13.21) is the form in which the equation is estimated in the next sections. Given our previous discussion, we use different elements of G (health, education, infrastructure) to measure the role of macro governance. The exponential parameter for G in the production function now represents a composite index reflecting the marginal product of capital and the degree of congestibility. However, it should be noted that the productivity coefficient α is reduced by the rate of taxation τ, since the private sector has to finance government services. Hence the elasticity measure of the impact effect of government spending on the level of national output is:

$$El = (\alpha/q)(1 - \tau).$$ (13.22)

Equation (13.22) informs us that the higher the marginal product of capital, the lower is congestion; the lower the tax rate, the higher the impact of government expenditures on income levels. This squares with intuition, and the purpose of the empirical estimates is to give more precise data-based numerical values to the different sectoral impact effects. We estimate a log-linear version of (13.21) using alternative definitions and variable specifications of G, reflecting macro governance.

MEASUREMENT OF VARIABLES, DATA SOURCES AND LIMITATIONS, ECONOMETRIC EXPERIMENTATION

The theoretical model is perfectly general, but the proof of the pudding is in the eating. Hence the econometric analyses will give us a more specific idea of the role of government expenditure and macro governance on aggregate output and its growth. Most importantly, how we disaggregate, or indeed aggregate, government expenditure categories will affect our analyses. The countries chosen for analyses are Taiwan, Singapore, Malaysia, Thailand, Indonesia and the Philippines. We take fairly standard, IMF-based, functional categories of government expenditure as our independent variables. Since the theoretical models assume long-run balanced budgets, and the fact that Pacific–Asian economies have not run up substantial budget deficits, unlike Latin American countries, we should also consider tax revenues as productive determinants of growth. Finally, we need to account for the traditional Keynesian view that aggregate government expenditure, or even government consumption per se, has demand effects and could contribute positively to economic growth. Although our model is supply side-based, it would be interesting to observe these 'Keynesian effects'.

The first set of government-related variables (proxy for G in equation (13.21)) are various categories of tax revenues. Government incomes enhance the ability of the state to relieve congestion and create the conditions necessary for endogenous growth. The second set of variables are government capital formation and consumption; these are at the first level of disaggregation, but they emphasize an important difference. Government capital formation is expected to relieve congestion and is directly applicable to the model in the previous section; government consumption either has demand effects or simply enhances employment or social welfare. The third set of variables are the classic functional categories such as education, health, public services and social services. These work in conjunction with human capital and labour force to enhance productivity and possibly create higher growth. A positive impact in these variables provides a firm indication of congestion relief in terms of the broadest definition of capital (that is, combining physical and human capital). Finally, we also utilize two aggregates (called G1 and G2) to reflect part-Keynesian and part-supply-side effects on output and growth. The first aggregate is the sum of government consumption and capital formation, which tells us the aggregate impact of congestion relief, but could be contaminated by demand-side factors. The second is the sum of all the individual functional categories, and reflects factors which could enhance human capital productivity overall.

Measurement of Variables

The following notation has been used:

TTAX	= total tax,
ITAX	= indirect tax,
DTAX	= direct tax,
L	= Labour,
HS	= human capital,
GCF	= government capital formation,
GC	= government consumption,
GEPS	= government expenditure on public services,
GEHS	= government expenditure on housing and social amenities,
GEH	= government expenditure on health,
GEES	= government expenditure on economic services,
GEE	= government expenditure on education,
GED	= government expenditure on defence,
GESW	= government expenditure on social security and welfare,
G1	= aggregated government spending index, = *GC* + *GCF*,
G2	= aggregated government spending on human capital, = *GEPS* + *GEHS* + *GEH* + *GEES* + *GEE* + *GED* + *GESW*.

It is worth mentioning some special issues. In order to enable proper comparison between the different countries, the level of GDP and the level of the respective types of government activity are measured in constant per capita US dollars. The measurement of the variable government consumption includes spending on defence and non-capital expenditure on education, which most researchers normally exclude.[2] Expenditure on economic services includes road networks, other communication networks, water, gas and electricity services, and so on that facilitate the production and distribution process of goods and services. The defence variable includes both capital and recurrent expenditure on defence, and public order and safety.

For labour input, we use total annual hours worked by employees (without considering variations in worker quality or in effort). This is obtained by first multiplying the number of employees by the average weekly hours worked in the non-agricultural sectors,[3] and then converting this into annual man hours by multiplying by 52 (weeks). Data of average weekly hours were not available for Indonesia. Thus we opted to make an estimation of 48 hours per week, basing it on the figures of the neighbouring countries. Human capital is often measured by designing an index of employment experience and the level of education achieved by the employees. This is then aggregated into the level of human capital for a given period. Since it has been beyond the scope of this study to compile such an index, we have decided to use an accepted proxy measure. In measuring human skills, focus is restricted to formal secondary school education for simplicity, ignoring the contribution of primary and higher education, and investment in health. The study assumes that the knowledge and skills so acquired in secondary education enable individuals to practise an occupation that can form the foundation of a well-conducted life. The variable human capital is thus proxied by the annual number of students enrolled for secondary education. This surrogate is often used to measure the average human capital level.[4] A higher secondary school enrolment means a higher accumulation of human skills. Thus, if an increase in the level and hence quality of human skills increases the level of GDP, an increase in the level of secondary school enrolment should stimulate the level of GDP.

Data Sources and Limitations

The data for Indonesia, Malaysia, the Philippines, Singapore and Thailand for GDP, government consumption, indirect taxes and population have been obtained from the World Bank data series diskette. The figures for total taxes, indirect taxes, government capital formation, and government expenditure on education, defence, economic services, health, housing and amenities, social security and welfare, and public services were obtained from the *Government Finance Statistics* yearbook. The numbers of people employed and the average weekly working hours were obtained from the *Yearbook of Labour Statistics*; and those for secondary school enrolment were extracted from the *UNESCO Statistical Yearbook*. The data for Taiwan were extracted from the *Taiwan Statistical Data Book*.

Some data were not available for some countries (mainly Singapore and Taiwan) and the data availability period varied not only between countries but between the different variables as well. Thus data availability restricted the estimation periods. As mentioned earlier, the average weekly hours worked were only available for the non-agricultural sectors. This may have had an influence on the final results, particularly for those countries which have strong agricultural sectors.

In order to eliminate or reduce the impact of serial correlation, multi-collinearity, contemporaneous feedback and heteroscedasticity, the following precautions have been taken. *Unit root* tests to find stationarity have been carried out and have demonstrated that most variables are non-stationary in their logarithm levels, but stationary in their first differences.[5] Furthermore, in order to ensure an efficient estimation, a series of tests including LM (Lagrange multiplier), CUSUM (cumulative sum (of the residuals)) and CUSUM of squares have been undertaken. The LM test for the Philippines indicated some evidence of serial correlation when GDP was estimated as a first difference. The GDP variable was therefore converted into second differences in order to eliminate this. The equations are estimated by use of the ordinary least squares (OLS) technique. However, the instrumental variables technique has also been employed for purposes of capturing contemporaneous feedback. In deciding upon the instruments, it became apparent that the human capital variable could be the source of causation effects. A given country's previous year's wealth is likely to influence the development of its human capital in the most immediate future period. Similarly, a given level of a country's human capital also influences its future levels of human capital. Lagged GDP and lagged human capital were therefore treated as instruments for the human capital variable. These, together with the labour force and the physical capital under investigation, then comprised the complete set of instrumental variables.

The data available had two major limitations. Firstly, most of the data available for the countries under study were consistently available over a period of only 26 (or fewer) years. Secondly, the six countries under study were too few to allow a cross-section analysis. Because of this sample size limitation, an attempt was made to boost the sample size by employing a pooled time-series model. For purposes of ensuring an unbiased estimation, an analysis of variance (ANOVA) test was employed to test for the stability (homogeneity) of the pooled data (see Maddala, 1992, for details on this test). The summary results presented in Table 13.1 illustrate the different combinations that exhibited similar characteristics of the production function. In the ANOVA test, all computed values that were significant up to the 10 per cent level were rejected.[6]

Econometric Experimentation for Human Capital

The human capital surrogate may require a gestation period before imparting any influence on the level of GDP.[7] This might be best captured by moving averages, or some lag value with a moving average (to capture any trend). Alternatively, it may be captured by some lag value on the proxy variable itself. In order to ascertain the proper relationship, we first undertook an investigation of

Table 13.1   Pooled series F-test results summary

Physical capital	Indonesia	Malaysia	Philippines	Singapore	Taiwan	Thailand
TTAX	*	*	*	*	*	X
ITAX	*	*	X	*	*	X
DTAX	*	*	*	*	*	X
GCF	*	*	*	*	*	X
GC	*	*	*	*	*	X
GEPS	*	*	*	*	N.A	*
GEHS	*	*	*	N.A	N.A	X
GEH	*	*	*	*	N.A	*
GEES	*	*	*	*	*	X
GEE	*	*	*	*	*	X
GESW	N.A	X	X	X	*	*
GED	*	*	*	*	*	*
G1	*	*	*	*	*	X
G2	*	*	*	X	X	*

Note: * represents homogeneous combinations; and N.A represents data not available.

partial regressions between the human capital proxy (up to the seventh lag) and GDP, and between the moving average of the human capital proxy (up to the seventh level)[8] and GDP for the respective countries under investigation. The best results were then selected for use in the estimation.[9] For instance, the best fit for Indonesia, the Philippines, Singapore and Taiwan was concomitant with lag 6, while that for Malaysia was lag 7, Thailand was lag 4 and the pool was lag 5.

EMPIRICAL FINDINGS

In the empirical analysis, we keep replacing the physical capital component of the production function, from equations such as (13.12) or (13.14) with that represented by the government activity under investigation, but retain the human capital and labour components. In other words, we estimate equations such as (13.21) which reflect the role of government (macro governance) in development. We need not emphasize that we appreciate and therefore do not rule out the important role played by private capital. However, the central purpose of this chapter is to investigate the impact effect of government activity on private capital formation and hence on economic development as evidenced by GDP.

The empirical results reported in the respective tables show the results generated by both the OLS and instrumental variable techniques. We chose to discuss the results generated by the instrumental technique since it takes care of causality. For space-saving purposes, we only provide a summary of the results generated by the OLS and instrumental variables techniques. The detailed results can be supplied upon request.

Revenue

Indirect tax

The coefficients and significance levels for indirect tax are reported in Table 13.2. Indirect tax is positively related to GDP and significant for Indonesia, Malaysia, Thailand, Taiwan and the pool. That for the Philippines and Singapore, although positively related, is statistically insignificant. Thus an increase in the level of indirect taxation in Indonesia, Malaysia, Thailand, Taiwan and the pool significantly increases their levels of GDP. These results probably suggest that the degree of impact indirect taxes exert on the level of GDP is influenced by the GDP size and, hence, the size of the tax base.

Table 13.2   Indirect tax: coefficients and significance levels

Country	Estimation technique	Variable			n
		ITAX	*HS*	*L*	
	OLS	0.371***	−2.3*	−0.172	
Indonesia	INST	0.318**	0.579	−0.1	26
	OLS	0.162**	−0.107	0.478**	
Malaysia	INST	0.32***	−0.074	0.543	19
	OLS	0.056	−0.562	0.576	
Philippines	INST	0.075	2.909	0.873	27
	OLS	0.55***	0.53	0.386	
Singapore	INST	0.261	−0.917	1.293	18
	OLS	0.372***	−0.162*	0.087	
Thailand	INST	0.318***	−0.502†	0.221	26
	OLS	0.0512***	−0.448***	0.319	
Taiwan	INST	0.513***	−0.468*	0.331	26
	OLS	0.326***	−1.36***	−0.117	
Pool	INST	0.394***	−0.662***	0.16	89

Notes: Levels of significance: *** 1%, ** 5%, * 10% and † marginally insignificant at 10%; OLS = ordinary least squares and INST = instrumental variables.

Labour is positively related to GDP for all the countries except Indonesia. However, it is consistently statistically insignificant. Human capital is positively related to GDP in Indonesia and the Philippines, but negatively related to GDP in the other countries, although significant only for Taiwan and the pool. We find this behaviour of human capital, particularly that of Taiwan, rather strange. There is a possibility that the human capital surrogate is not a proper representation. Alternatively, it is suggesting that secondary education enrolment draws manpower from the pool of the productive labour force, thus eroding productivity and, hence, the level of GDP.[10]

Direct tax

The results for direct tax presented in Table 13.3 suggest a negative, albeit insignificant, relationship with GDP for Malaysia and Thailand. However, those for the other countries, including the pool, are significantly positively related to the GDP level. These results are concomitant with the tax base observation highlighted above. Human capital for the pool remains significant and negatively related to GDP, but insignificant for the other countries, although also negative for Thailand, Singapore and Taiwan. This time labour force for the pool is significantly positively related to GDP.

Table 13.3   Direct tax: coefficients and significance levels

Country	Estimation technique	Variable			n
		DTAX	*HS*	*L*	
	OLS	0.33***	−2.117*	−0.159	
Indonesia	INST	0.306***	0.629	−0.101	24
	OLS	−0.011	0.282	0.565*	
Malaysia	INST	−0.277	4.713	−1.7	17
	OLS	0.108*	−0.478	0.169	
Philippines	INST	0.116**	0.654	0.34	24
	OLS	0.361***	0.006	0.885*	
Singapore	INST	0.309**	−0.591	1.078	18
	OLS	0.008	−0.248†	0.101	
Thailand	INST	−0.042	−0.948	0.377	26
	OLS	0.29***	−0.5*	0.748	
Taiwan	INST	0.289***	−0.38	0.685	22
	OLS	0.27***	−1.22***	−0.093	
Pool	INST	0.171***	−0.547**	0.446***	109

Notes: Levels of significance: *** 1%, ** 5%, * 10% and † marginally insignificant at 10%; OLS = ordinary least squares and INST = instrumental variables.

Total tax

The direction of the relationship of the total tax variable (Table 13.4) is quite similar to results for the direct tax function. For instance, total tax is positively related to the GDP level for all the countries, but insignificant for Malaysia and Thailand. The human capital proxy is once more negative and statistically significant for Taiwan and the Pool. However, it is insignificant although positively related to GDP for Indonesia, the Philippines and Singapore, and negatively related for Malaysia and Thailand. The statistical significance of labour remains restricted to the pool, while the negative relationship remains restricted to Indonesia.

Table 13.4 Total tax: coefficients and significance levels

Country	Estimation technique	Variable			n
		TTAX	*HS*	*L*	
	OLS	0.358***	−2.256*	−0.169	
Indonesia	INST	0.325***	0.415	−0.11	24
	OLS	0.241***	−0.242	0.718***	
Malaysia	INST	0.3	−0.781	0.879†	23
	OLS	0.06†	−0.409	0.169	
Philippines	INST	0.069*	0.536	0.325	24
	OLS	0.624***	0.527	0.055	
Singapore	INST	0.543**	0.402	0.366	22
	OLS	0.342***	−0.126	0.139	
Thailand	INST	0.216	−0.625	0.3	26
	OLS	0.564***	−0.401*	0.371	
Taiwan	INST	0.563***	−0.433*	0.384	23
	OLS	0.29***	−1.32***	−0.095	
Pool	INST	0.296***	−0.622**	0.393***	119

Notes: Levels of significance: *** 1%, ** 5%, * 10% and † marginally insignificant at 10%; OLS = ordinary least squares and INST = instrumental variables.

The revenue results are consistently significant for Indonesia, Taiwan and the pool. Their 1997 GDP levels of 214.6 and 283.6 billion US dollars, respectively, make Indonesia and Taiwan the two largest countries in the group. The results therefore demonstrate that the significance of the level of taxation on the level of GDP is influenced by the size of the tax base.

General Government Services

Government expenditure on education
The results illustrating the impact of the level of government expenditure on education on the level of GDP are presented in Table 13.5. They suggest a negative but insignificant relationship for Malaysia. Government expenditure on education is, however, positively related to GDP for all the other countries, although insignificant for Singapore. Human capital is this time significant for only Thailand and the pool, and labour remains significant for Singapore, Taiwan and the pool.

Table 13.5   Expenditure on education: coefficients and significance levels

Country	Estimation technique	Variable			n
		GEE	*HS*	*L*	
	OLS	0.412***	−2.485*	−0.177	
Indonesia	INST	0.354**	0.488	−0.105	23
	OLS	0.061	0.09	0.668***	
Malaysia	INST	−0.036	1.078	0.362	22
	OLS	0.306**	−0.406	−0.386	
Philippines	INST	0.348**	1.289	−0.201	24
	OLS	0.313**	−0.462	1.165*	
Singapore	INST	0.16	−1.395	1.697***	22
	OLS	0.143	−0.29**	0.154	
Thailand	INST	0.358**	−0.716*	0.411	26
	OLS	0.048	−0.6*	1.042*	
Taiwan	INST	0.035***	−0.295	0.943****	23
	OLS	0.362***	−1.27***	−0.109	
Pool	INST	0.106***	−0.68**	0.302*	117

Notes: Levels of significance: *** 1%, ** 5%, * 10%; OLS = ordinary least squares and INST = instrumental variables.

Government expenditure on public services
Table 13.6 is a presentation of the results for the impact of the level of government expenditure on public services on the level of GDP. Government expenditure on public services is positively related to GDP for Indonesia, the Philippines, Thailand and the pool, but negatively related for Malaysia and Singapore. However, it is statistically significant for only Indonesia, Singapore and the pool. The negative relationship for Singapore suggests that an increase

in the level of expenditure on public services negates GDP. The human capital surrogate remains statistically significant for Singapore, Thailand and the pool. Labour, on the other hand, retains significance for Singapore.

Table 13.6   Expenditure on public services: coefficients and significance levels

Country	Estimation technique	Variable			n
		GEPS	*HS*	*L*	
	OLS	0.318**	−2.06	−0.147	
Indonesia	INST	0.282**	1.067	−0.078	23
	OLS	−0.057	0.181	0.568**	
Malaysia	INST	−0.123	1.351	0.165	22
	OLS	0.119	−0.381	−0.097	
Philippines	INST	0.15†	0.628	0.012	24
	OLS	−0.067	−0.766	2.064**	
Singapore	INST	−0.143**	−2.09**	2.847***	22
	OLS	0.037	−0.265*	0.181	
Thailand	INST	0.049	−0.811*	0.413	23
	OLS	0.286***	−1.696***	−0.096	
Pool	INST	0.158***	−1.104*	0.221	114

Notes: Levels of significance: *** 1%, ** 5%, * 10% and † marginally insignificant at 10%, OLS = ordinary least squares and INST = instrumental variables.

Government expenditure on defence
The impact of the level of government expenditure on defence on the level of GDP is reported in Table 13.7. Government expenditure on defence is significantly positively related to GDP in the countries at a lower level of economic development (less democratic?). However, it is negatively related (insignificantly, though) to the level of GDP in the more developed countries (more democratic?). Human capital is once more significant for Thailand and the pool, and labour is significant for only Singapore, Taiwan and the pool.

Government expenditure on health
The results on the impact of the level of government expenditure on health on the level of GDP are reported in Table 13.8. Government expenditure on health is positively related to GDP in all the countries except Singapore. However, it is significant for only Indonesia, the Philippines and the pool. Human capital is once more significant for Thailand and the pool, and labour is significant for only Singapore.

Table 13.7   Government expenditure on defence: coefficients and significance levels

Country	Estimation technique	Variable			n
		GED	*HS*	*L*	
Indonesia	OLS	0.41***	−2.42*	−0.178	
	INST	0.355**	0.615	−0.1	23
Malaysia	OLS	0.084	0.03	0.66***	
	INST	0.123	0.97	0.37	23
Philippines	OLS	0.09	−0.42	−0.028	
	INST	0.1**	0.64	0.147	23
Singapore	OLS	0.22	−0.25	1.6**	
	INST	−0.28	−2.9	2.2***	22
Thailand	OLS	0.21	−0.29**	0.09	
	INST	0.25*	−0.65*	0.21	23
Taiwan	OLS	−0.008	−0.5	1.1*	
	INST	−0.001	−0.25	0.9*	26
Pool	OLS	0.3***	−1.1***	−0.09***	
	INST	0.086***	−0.48***	0.34***	142

Notes: Levels of significance: *** 1%, ** 5%, * 10%; OLS = ordinary least squares and INST = instrumental variables.

Table 13.8   Government expenditure on health: coefficients and significance levels

Country	Estimation technique	Variable			n
		GEH	*HS*	*L*	
Indonesia	OLS	0.388***	−2.349*	−0.184	
	INST	0.339**	0.305	−0.119	23
Malaysia	OLS	0.071	0.106	0.648***	
	INST	0.022	1.069	.366	22
Philippines	OLS	0.282***	−0.657	−0.427	
	INST	0.266**	0.566	−0.228	24
Singapore	OLS	0.27**	0.293	1.158*	
	INST	−0.089	−2.093	2.25**	22
Thailand	OLS	0.143	−0.29	.154	
	INST	0.24	−0.888*	0.409	23
Pool	OLS	0.348***	−1.555***	−0.125	
	INST	0.392***	−1.096**	0.109	114

Notes: Levels of significance: *** 1%, ** 5%, * 10%; OLS = ordinary least squares and INST = instrumental variables.

Community and Social Services

Government expenditure on housing and social amenities

As illustrated in Table 13.9, the level of government expenditure on housing and social amenities is positively related to the level of GDP in Indonesia and Malaysia, but negatively related in the Philippines, Thailand and the pool. However, it is significant only in Indonesia. Human capital is in this case not significant for any country, while labour retains its significance for the pool.

Table 13.9 Expenditure on housing and social amenities: coefficients and significance levels

Country	Estimation technique	Variable			n
		GEHS	*HS*	*L*	
	OLS	0.373***	−2.214*	−0.132	
Indonesia	INST	0.339**	0.246	−0.079	23
	OLS	0.011	0.145	0.655***	
Malaysia	INST	0.013	1.009	0.408	22
	OLS	−0.034	−0.703	0.148	
Philippines	INST	−0.015	0.006	0.176	25
	OLS	−0.003	−0.262*	0.104	
Thailand	INST	−0.127	−1.137	0.356	23
	OLS	0.187***	−1.7**	−0.058	
Pool	INST	−0.0003	0.674	0.4**	70

Notes: Levels of significance: *** 1%, ** 5%, * 10%; OLS = ordinary least squares and INST = instrumental variables.

Government expenditure on social security and welfare services

Table 13.10 is a presentation of the results on the impact of the level of government expenditure on social security and welfare on the level of GDP. Government expenditure on social security and welfare, although not statistically significant, is positively related to GDP for all the countries except Singapore (the most developed). The human capital surrogate remains statistically significant for Singapore, Thailand and the pool. Labour, on the other hand, retains significance for Singapore and the Pool.

Table 13.10   Government expenditure on social security and welfare services: coefficients and significance levels

Country	Estimation technique	Variable			n
		GESW	*HS*	*L*	
	OLS	0.05	−0.006	0.67***	
Malaysia	INST	0.08	1.3	0.27	23
	OLS	0.042	−0.6	−0.14	
Philippines	INST	0.04	0.23	−0.009	24
	OLS	−0.078	−0.89	1.6**	
Singapore	INST	−0.068	−2.3*	1.95***	22
	OLS	0.14	−0.24*	0.18	
Thailand	INST	0.08	−0.82*	0.37	23
	OLS	−0.02	−0.52	1.17*	
Taiwan	INST	0.005	−0.24	0.97	26
	OLS	0.06	−0.36	0.37	
Pool	INST	0.03	−0.67***	0.41*	50

Notes: Levels of significance: *** 1%, ** 5%, * 10%; OLS = ordinary least squares and INST = instrumental variables.

Economic Services

Government expenditure on economic services
As Table 13.11 illustrates, the level of government expenditure on economic services in Malaysia and Thailand, although negatively related to the level of GDP, is statistically insignificant. That for all the other countries, however, is positively related but significant only for Indonesia, the Philippines and the pool. Human capital is significant for only Singapore and the pool, and labour retains significance in Singapore, Taiwan and the pool.

Table 13.11   Expenditure on economic services: coefficients and significance levels

Country	Estimation technique	Variable			n
		GEES	*HS*	*L*	
	OLS	0.422***	−2.383*	−0.181	
Indonesia	INST	0.357**	0.828	−0.103	23
	OLS	0.025	0.084	0.651***	

Table 13.11   continued

Country	Estimation technique	Variable			n
		GEES	*HS*	*L*	
Malaysia	INST	–0.036	1.078	0.362	22
	OLS	0.134	–0.413	–0.338	
Philippines	INST	0.168*	0.876	–0.247	24
	OLS	0.033	–0.692	1.666**	
Singapore	INST	0.073	–2.102*	1.974***	22
	OLS	–0.009	–0.263*	0.108	
Thailand	INST	–0.067	–0.877	0.357	26
	OLS	0.048	–0.6*	1.042*	
Taiwan	INST	0.035	–0.295	0.943*	23
	OLS	0.327***	–1.492***	–0.106	
Pool	INST	0.106***	–0.678**	0.302*	103

Notes: Levels of significance: *** 1%, ** 5%, * 10%; OLS = ordinary least squares and INST = instrumental variables.

Aggregate Government Activities

Government capital formation (*GCF*)

As illustrated in Table 13.12, the level of government capital formation is significantly positively related to the level of GDP for all the countries except the Philippines. The direction of the relationship with human capital is once more insignificant although positive for Indonesia, Malaysia and the Philippines, and negative for Singapore, Thailand, Taiwan and the pool. On the other hand, labour is insignificant for all the countries, although negatively related to GDP for Indonesia and Thailand.

Table 13.12   Government capital formation: coefficients and significance levels

Country	Estimation technique	Variable			n
		GCF	*HS*	*L*	
	OLS	0.416***	–2.327*	–0.197	
Indonesia	INST	0.354**	0.9	–0.116	26
	OLS	0.607***	0.249***	0.008	
Malaysia	INST	0.604***	0.205	0.031	24
	OLS	0.108	–0.562	0.396	

Table 13.12   continued

Country	Estimation technique	Variable			n
		GCF	*HS*	*L*	
Philippines	INST	0.201	4.166	0.764	25
	OLS	0.646***	−0.02	−0.183	
Singapore	INST	0.468***	−1.148	0.49	19
	OLS	0.433***	−0.024	−0.014	
Thailand	INST	0.431***	−0.03	−0.011	26
	OLS	0.238**	−0.497*	0.525	
Taiwan	INST	0.24***	−0.081	0.341	24
	OLS	0.383***	−1.16***	−0.133	
Pool	INST	0.573***	−0.157	0.127	118

Notes: Levels of significance: *** 1%, ** 5%, * 10%; OLS = ordinary least squares and INST = instrumental variables.

Government consumption (*GC*)

The results reported in Table 13.13 illustrate that the level of government consumption exhibits a positive relationship with the level of GDP (except for Singapore). Government consumption is, however, significant for only Indonesia, Thailand, Taiwan and the pool. The significance pattern indicates that countries with large GDP levels respond significantly to government consumption. The human capital surrogate is this time significant for Thailand, Taiwan and the pool. Labour, on the other hand, remains significant for Singapore, Taiwan and the pool.

Table 13.13   Government consumption: coefficients and significance levels

Country	Estimation technique	Variable			n
		GC	*HS*	*L*	
	OLS	1.535***	−0.726	−0.009	
Indonesia	INST	1.637***	0.985	0.023	26
	OLS	0.585***	−0.3*	0.564***	
Malaysia	INST	0.388	0.16	0.43	24
	OLS	0.366	−0.395	0.385	
Philippines	INST	0.396	4.676	0.891	27
	OLS	0.621**	0.369	1.119*	
Singapore	INST	−0.677	−3.685	2.837**	22
	OLS	0.302**	−0.231*	0.057	

Table 13.13   continued

Country	Estimation technique	Variable			n
		GC	HS	L	
Thailand	INST	0.269*	−0.61*	0.209	26
	OLS	0.695***	−0.069	0.936***	
Taiwan	INST	0.658***	−0.354*	0.977***	26
	OLS	1.21***	−0.514	0.003	
Pool	INST	0.756***	−0.26*	0.331***	125

Notes: Levels of significance: *** 1%, ** 5%, * 10%; OLS = ordinary least squares and INST = instrumental variables.

Aggregate government expenditure (*G1*)

As mentioned in the third section of this chapter, this variable is 'mixed' in terms of impact effect: government capital formation has supply-side effects, while government consumption is predominantly Keynesian in terms of its impact. Note again that $G1 = GCF + GC$.

Table 13.14 gives the estimated results by both methods (OLS and INST) for each of the countries in the region. This is strong support for the hypothesis that congestion-relieving government expenditures (that is, spending which produces physical capital to complement and supplement private sector capital) have a positive and significant effect. All countries in the region (except Taiwan) show this positive role. However, the impact of *GC* cannot be ignored, so there is some demand-side contamination. This demonstrates that, even in such developing countries, Keynesian multipliers are expected to be positive.

Table 13.14   G1: coefficients and significance levels

Country	Estimation technique	Variable			n
		GI	HS	L	
	OLS	0.43***	−2.338*	−0.193	
Indonesia	INST	0.358**	1.02	−0.108	24
	OLS	0.66***	0.176***	0.04	
Malaysia	INST	0.652***	−0.003	0.14	24
	OLS	0.181	−0.496	0.371	
Philippines	INST	0.882***	4.106	−0.308	25
	OLS	0.761***	0.199	−0.192	
Singapore	INST	0.53**	−0.939	0.531	19
	OLS	0.543***	−0.024	−0.037	

Table 13.14   continued

Country	Estimation technique	Variable			n
		GI	*HS*	*L*	
Thailand	INST	0.577***	0.063	−0.078	26
	OLS	0.112	−0.486	0.793	
Taiwan	INST	0.123	−0.162	0.62	24
	OLS	0.395***	−1.164***	−0.129	
Pool	INST	0.699***	0.032	0.064	108

Notes: Levels of significance: *** 1%, ** 5%, * 10%; OLS = ordinary least squares and INST = instrumental variables.

Aggregate government expenditure affecting human capital productivity (*G2*)

Note the definition: *G2* = *GEPS* + *GEHS* + *GEH* + *GEES* + *GEE* + *GED* + *GESW*. In other words, this variable is looking at the aggregate effect of all functional categories of government spending, mostly to do with human capital

Table 13.15   G2: coefficients and significance levels

Country	Estimation technique	Variable			n
		G2	*HS*	*L*	
	OLS	0.395***	−2.325*	−0.167	
Indonesia	INST	0.334**	0.819	−0.092	23
	OLS	0.066	0.029	0.623***	
Malaysia	INST	0.17	1.566	−0.21	22
	OLS	0.05	−0.662	0.334	
Philippines	INST	0.121**	1.513	0.266	24
	OLS	2.131***	4.358	−3.984	
Singapore	INST	2.511***	−4.681	−4.626	22
	OLS	0.155	−0.236*	0.167	
Thailand	INST	0.107	−0.688*	0.347	23
	OLS	0.09	−0.598*	0.998*	
Taiwan	INST	0.066	−0.304	0.902*	23
	OLS	0.278***	−0.996**	−0.088	
Pool	INST	0.096***	−0.021	0.283**	92

Notes: Levels of significance: *** 1%, ** 5%, * 10%; OLS = ordinary least squares and INST = instrumental variables.

formation (*GEE*, *GEH*) and also pure public goods protecting the security of the nation (*GED*, *GEPS*). Except for Philippines, Indonesia and Singapore (see Table 13.15), all the other countries show insignificant relationships between *G2* and GDP (growth). Whether this relatively unsatisfactory result (compared to *G1*) is due to functional aggregation or to country-specific behaviour is not clear. What is important, however, is that the pooled data set shows a strongly positive relationship.

COMPARATIVE DIAGNOSTICS

In this section, we make short comments on the response of the level of GDP to the different components of the supply side of the production function (that is, the different types of government activity, human capital and labour). We also attempt to identify any consistent pattern vis-à-vis the level of economic development (per capita income), the total wealth/size of the economy (GDP level) and/or population size.

Government Activity

Table 13.16 summarizes the different effects of alternative types of government expenditure (and revenue) on GDP levels. It uses the instrumental variables regression to account for causality and reports the outcomes from Tables 13.1 to 13.15. Apart from government expenditure on public services in Singapore, which is statistically significant and negatively related to the level of GDP, all statistically significant forms of government activity are positively related to GDP. Thus all the negative relationships are insignificant, while significant relationships are overwhelmingly positive.

Table 13.16 can be conceptually sub-divided into three parts. The first three rows give the effect of aggregate tax revenues (direct, indirect, total sum) and reflect the governments' ability to spend. The second set of rows are the different functional classification starting with *GCF* representing congestion relief at the aggregate level, continuing with *GC* possibly reflecting Keynesian effects and then looking at detailed functional distribution of government activity into all its constituent parts (all of which have the ability to enhance productivity of private sector physical capital, human capital and the labour force in general). The last two rows are the relevant aggregates, *G1* representing government consumption and capital expenditures, while *G2* is the aggregate of all functional spending.

It is clear that the pool results (taking all countries together) show a strong, positive and highly significant relationship between every aspect of government activity and economic development (as evidenced by per capita incomes). This is the strongest empirical evidence for Pacific–Asian economies of the vital importance of the state as well as macro governance. As regards the sub-sets, ability to tax and spend on productive activities seems to have a strongly positive impact on income levels in most of these countries. Similarly, *G1* and *G2* are generally strongly significant and always positive in terms of impact effects. There is little doubt that, at a regional, aggregate and pooled data set level, macro governance is vital for economic development.

Table 13.16   Summary: different types of government activities

	Indonesia	Malaysia	Philippines	Singapore	Taiwan	Thailand	Pool
TTAX	+***	+	+*	+**	+***	+	+***
ITAX	+**	+***	+	+	+***	+***	+***
DTAX	+***	−	+**	+**	+***	−	+***
GCF	+**	+***	+	+***	+***	+***	+***
GC	+***	+	+	−	+***	+*	+***
GEPS	+**	−	+	−**	N.A.	+	+***
GEHS	+**	+	−	N.A.	N.A.	−	−
GEH	+**	+	+**	−	N.A.	+	+***
GEES	+**	−	+*	+	+	−	+***
GEE	+**	−	+**	+	+***	+**	+***
GESW	N.A.	+	+	−	+	+	+
GED	+**	+	+**	−	−	+*	+***
G1	+**	+***	+***	+**	+	+***	+***
G2	+**	+	+**	+***	+	+	+***

Notes: Levels of significance: *** 1%, ** 5%, * 10% and † marginally insignificant at 10%; + or − indicates direction of relationship with GDP; N.A. = data not available.

However, there is a disparity among the countries. For instance, the level of Indonesia's GDP is stimulated by all the functional categories of disaggregated government spending (investigated) and also the relevant aggregates *G1* and *G2*. Malaysia benefits from indirect taxation and capital formation. The Philippines, on the other hand, benefits from taxation and expenditure on health, education and economic services, while the level of Singapore's GDP, although stimulated by taxation and capital formation, is negated by expenditure on public services. There is also an indication that Singapore does not benefit from the disaggregated flows. The stimulus of the level of Taiwan's GDP is derived from almost all the flows (where data were available) except government expenditure on economic services. Thailand's level of GDP derives benefits only from indirect taxes, capital formation, government consumption and expenditure on economic services. Apart from expenditure on housing and social amenities, the pool benefits from all the other forms of physical capital.

We now turn to the aggregates. With the exception of Taiwan, whose results for aggregate government activity are insignificant, we can generalize that the level of aggregate government activity (*G1*) imparts a positive stimulus effect on the level of GDP. The results for the total government expenditure on services (*G2*) which principally benefit human capital are less clear-cut.

Human Capital

The results reported in Table 13.17 indicate that the human capital surrogate is consistently positively related to the level of GDP for Indonesia, Malaysia (except when regressed with *TTAX*, *ITAX* and *G1*) and the Philippines. It is, however, negatively related to GDP and at times statistically significant for Singapore (except when regressed with *TTAX*), Taiwan, Thailand (except when regressed with *G1*) and the pool. Its significance is rather volatile and varies with the type of disaggregated government activity entered into the regression. In general, the human capital proxy does not perform well: it is prone to volatility and consequently results based upon it are not robust. We also note that this surrogate ignores the extra benefits that may be derived from training, learning-by-doing and the full education curriculum. On the other hand, it may be indicating the negative effect secondary school enrolment has on productivity by reducing the productive labour force. It is important in future research to identify a 'better' representation of human capital.

Table 13.17   Summary: human capital

	Indonesia	Malaysia	Philippines	Singapore	Taiwan	Thailand	Pool
TTAX	+	−	+	+	−*	−	−**
ITAX	+	−	+	−	−*	†	−***
DTAX	+	+	+	−	−	−	−**
GCF	+	+	+	−	−	−	−
GC	+	+	+	−	−*	−*	−*
GEPS	+	+	+	−**	N.A.	−*	−*
GEHS	+	+	+	N.A.	N.A.	−	+
GEH	+	+	+	−	N.A.	−*	−**
GEES	+	+	+	−*	−	−	−**
GEE	+	+	+	−	−	−*	−**
GESW	N.A.	+	+	−*	−	−*	−***
GED	+	+	+	−	−	−*	−***
G1	+	−	+	−	−	+	+
G2	+	+	+	−	−	−*	−

Notes: Levels of significance: *** 1%, ** 5%, * 10% and † marginally insignificant at 10%; + or − indicates direction of relationship with GDP; N.A. = data not available.

Labour

The results presented in Table 13.18 illustrate how labour is consistently positively related to GDP for Malaysia, the Philippines, Singapore, Taiwan, Thailand and the pool (except for a few isolated cases). The labour variable, although negatively related in Indonesia, is statistically insignificant. Furthermore, the results for Malaysia, the Philippines and Thailand are statistically insignificant, indicating that countries that are below a certain level of economic development may not derive productivity from their labour force. In other words, the quality of the labour force of such countries is not high enough to generate productivity gains. The results for Singapore and Taiwan, which are at a higher level of economic development, on the other hand, suggest that the productivity gains from the labour force increase as the level of economic development increases. This suggests that the *quality* of the labour force is paramount to increases in productivity. In addition, countries with higher per capita income, and advanced stages of development, may suffer from labour shortage and this could increase the productivity of labour in these countries compared to labour-surplus economies.

Table 13.18   Summary: labour

	Indonesia	Malaysia	Philippines	Singapore	Taiwan	Thailand	Pool
TTAX	−	†	+	+	+	+	+***
ITAX	−	+	+	+	+	+	+
DTAX	−	−	+	+	+	+	+***
GCF	−	+	+	+	+	−	+
GC	+	+	+	+**	+***	+	+***
GEPS	−	+	+	+***	N.A.	+	+
GEHS	−	+	+	N.A.	N.A.	+	+**
GEH	−	+	−	+**	N.A.	+	+
GEES	−	+	−	+***	+*	+	+*
GEE	−	+	−	+***	+***	+	+**
GESW	N.A.	+	−	+***	+	+	+*
GED	−	+	+	+***	+*	+	+***
G1	−	+	−	+	+	−	+
G2	−	−	+	−	+*	+	+**

Notes: Levels of significance: *** 1%, ** 5%, * 10% and † marginally insignificant at 10%; + or − indicates direction of relationship with GDP; N.A. = data not available.

Implications for Level of Economic Development and Population Size

A summary of these results is further illustrated in Figure 13.1, which presents the matrix of the level of economic development and the population size in an attempt to judge whether the stage of development affects the relationship between types of government activity and aggregate output per capita. The combined results from the production function indicate that countries at the lower end of economic development and with large populations could stimulate the level of GDP by increasing their levels of aggregate government activity (*G1*, *G2*) as well as their functional disaggregated levels (that is, spending on

		Level of economic development		
		Lower-end	Moderate	Higher-end
Population size	Lower-end			Singapore (96.3) [26 025] {3.7} *Labour* *Aggregate* *governmental activity*
	Moderate	Philippines (82.2) [1115] {73.5} *Aggregate* *government activity* *Functional* *disaggregated* *government activity*	Thailand/Malaysia (153.4) [2530]/(97.9) [4510] {60.6} {21.2} *Aggregate government* *activity*	Taiwan (283.6) [13 082] {21.7} *Labour* *(Lack of data)*
	Higher-end	Indonesia (214.6) [1065] {201.4} *Aggregate* *government activity* *Functional* *disaggregated* *government activity*	*Aggregate government* *activity*	Japan, Korea, possibly

Note: ( ) 1997 GDP in billions of US$; [ ] 1997 per capita income in US$; { } 1997 population size in millions.

Sources: Data for Indonesia, Malaysia, the Philippines, Singapore and Thailand, Bende-Nabende (1999, Table 2.1); data for Taiwan from *Taiwan Statistical Data Book, 1998*.

Figure 13.1   Matrix of level of economic development and population size

health, education, public services and national defence). On the other hand, countries at the higher level of development and with small populations are likely to stimulate their GDP levels by increasing the levels of their labour force and aggregate government activity without concern as to how this aggregate is functionally distributed. Labour shortage could be a constraint for such economies (such as Singapore). At higher levels of development (as in Taiwan) government activity is not significant in terms of impact effects and it is possible that such expenditures are welfare-enhancing rather than growth-enhancing. The sources of endogenous growth in such economies need to go beyond the role of government and macro governance. It is worth mentioning that data on Taiwan were scanty (hence Table 13.16 shows 'N.A.' in a number of places and therefore too strong a conclusion cannot be drawn). More problematic are the countries in the intermediate range such as Thailand or Malaysia. These are countries at a low or moderate level of economic development with moderate population sizes. They could stimulate their GDP levels through aggregate government activity (including government consumption); however, functional distribution and disaggregated levels of government activity seem to have low impact on their levels of GDP and development. Although the government does play a major role, it is the aggregate level rather than the distribution that seems to matter for growth.

CONCLUDING REMARKS

The objective of this study was to establish how governance in terms of the level and distribution of government activity might affect the level of GDP. We also sought to ascertain whether government activity is similar for countries in the same region. Thus we wished to capture the stimulus of respective types of government activity by identifying the different types of aggregate and disaggregated categories of government expenditure and individually regressing them, with human capital and labour on GDP per capita as an indicator of economic development.

Certain interesting observations eventually emerge. Overall, the pooled data show that government activity, in all its manifestations, has a strongly positive and significant impact on levels of GDP and hence on economic development. This is what we would expect from our endogenous growth model, since the government acts as a source of such growth, particularly for the relatively poorer economies in the region. However, the detailed empirical estimates also suggest that activity of governments in the same region does not necessarily have an impact to the same extent on the level of GDP. Rather, the country's population size and its level of economic development and, hence, the size of the economy, tend to be the dominating factor in differentiating between these countries. For instance, the results suggest that governments benefit from taxation when their tax bases are large. Populous and poorer countries gain particularly well from disaggregated and functional categories of government expenditure. When a country (such as Taiwan) becomes developed the role of macro governance is minimized. In general, therefore, government activity has the potential of generating positive stimuli in economies with moderate to high GDP levels. Labour, on the other hand, positively influences GDP levels when the country is at the higher end of development and hence its labour force is either highly skilled or scarce. The results for human capital, although indicating that countries at the lower and moderate levels of economic development do not derive benefits, were particularly disappointing for the more developed countries. This probably stemmed from the surrogate variable that was incapable of capturing the effects of learning-by-doing and training.

The role of governments in providing good governance at the macroeconomic level must not be minimized. Results reported in this chapter demonstrate that, even within the Pacific–Asian region where the market has functioned well, government activity has had an important role to play in economic development. Further research will expand the country set and attempt to generalize the observational regularities, which relate the impact effect of governance to country size and stage of economic development.

NOTES

1. The research for this chapter was supported by grant L 324 25 3010, Pacific Asia Research Programme of the ESRC, for which we express our thanks.
2. See, for instance, Barro (1991).
3. Data for the agricultural sector are not available.
4. This proxy has been recommended by J. Page (1995) in his comment on Shang Jim Wei's article, 'The Open Door Policy and China's Growth: Evidence from City Level Data', in Ito Takatoshi and A.O. Krueger (eds), *Growth Theories in Light of the East Asian Experience*, Chicago and London, University of Chicago Press, National Bureau of Economic Research. It has also been used by researchers, including Bende-Nabende and Ford (1998). We must, however, add that enrolment levels ignore the important role of training, learning by doing and the full education curriculum.
5. The detailed statistics are available upon request.
6. The details of the ANOVA test results are available upon request.
7. We envisage that output growth benefits from an individual's skills after that individual has passed through the formal learning process, qualified and then got a job on the basis of his/her qualification. We argue that this process is bound to take some time.
8. We choose to investigate up to the seventh level because secondary education in most of these countries takes six years. To this we add a settling down year. However, in practice the *average* period may be less, depending on the proportion of the students who drop out before completing their courses, but nevertheless apply the knowledge they have attained to enhance productivity.
9. Based on the adjusted R^2, F-statistic, D-W statistic and the t-statistic.
10. Remember that people who enrol for secondary school are of the age group ranging from 13 to 20 (or even more) years of age. This age group forms a productive labour force, particularly in developing countries.

REFERENCES

Barro, R.J. (1991), 'Economic Growth in a Cross Section of Countries', *The Quarterly Journal of Economics*, CVI (2), 407–43.

Barro, R.J. and X. Sala-i-Martin (1995), *Economic Growth*, New York and London: McGraw-Hill.

Bende-Nabende, A. (1999), *FDI, Regionalism, Government Policy and Endogenous Growth*, Aldershot: Ashgate.

Bende-Nabende, A. and J.L. Ford (1998), 'FDI, Policy Adjustments and Endogenous Growth: Multiplier Effects from a Small Dynamic Model for Taiwan, 1959–1995', *World Development*, 26 (7), 1315–30.

Maddala, G.S. (1992), *Introduction to Econometrics*, 2nd edn, New York: Macmillan.

Rebelo, S. (1991), 'Long-run policy analysis and long-run growth', *Journal of Political Economy*, 99, 500–21.

Turnovsky, S.J. (1995), *Methods of Macroeconomic Dynamics*, Cambridge, MA and London: MIT Press.

Wade, R. (1990), *Governing the Market: Economic Theory and the Role of Government in East Asian Industrialisation*, Princeton: Princeton University Press.

The Republic of China, *Taiwan Statistical Data Book 1998*, Council for Economic Planning and Development.

UN, *The UN Government Finance Statistics* (various years), New York: UN.

UN, *The UN Yearbook of Labour Statistics* (various years), New York: UN.

UN, *UNESCO Statistical Yearbook* (various years), New York and Paris: UNESCO.

World Bank (1997), *World Development Report*, Oxford: Oxford University Press.

14. Productivity growth analysis in the dynamic production function for selected Asian countries

Hitoshi Osaka

INTRODUCTION

East Asia's economic success followed by South East Asia's recent rapid economic growth has generated much literature. In his article, Krugman (1994) throws a controversial argument into the standard views about the growth process in the Asian newly industrialized countries (NICs) by suggesting that there has been 'no productivity growth' in their economic performance. Against the conventional wisdom for economic growth which is supposedly linked to industrialization and productivity growth in the economy, his conclusion provides two pessimistic messages: (a) no productivity growth for economic growth in the Asian NICs; and thus (b) their rapid economic success is a once-and-for-all phenomenon. We review Krugman's suggestion of no productivity growth in the selected Asian NICs as well as analysing their supply-side long-run and dynamic production functions. Prior to conclusion we test for the exogeneity hypothesis underpinning the economic theory on which our empirical analyses are based.

Our empirical analyses are comparative across four economies, Japan, Republic of Korea (hereafter South Korea), the Philippines and Thailand, for the 1960–91 period. The choice of these four economies is by no means accidental. Japan is selected as a yardstick for comparison since it is the first and biggest industrialized country among the South East and East Asian countries. South Korea is expected to show the rapid productivity growth associated with successful economic performance as a representative of the Asian NICs. Thailand and the Philippines are supposed to provide an interesting contrast with one another: Thailand as a successful country in the second generation of NICs and the Philippines as a country which has failed to develop as a NIC.

We divide the sample period of 1960–91 into three sub-periods: 1960–70, 1971–80 and 1981–91. The selection of sub-periods is rather conventional, but it may help to understand some trend changes of economic variables over the different sub-periods. Additionally, we investigate any change of economic trend after 1986. The Philippine economy, notably, is believed to be regaining its economic strength after its severe political turmoil in 1985. In the same year the Plaza Accord in New York involving the major economic powers caused the Japanese yen to soar and the subsequent massive capital inflows into the East and South East Asian economies from Japan are also well reported in economic literature.

PRODUCTIVITY ANALYSIS IN GROWTH ACCOUNTING: REAPPRAISAL OF KRUGMAN'S CRITIQUE

The mostly popular methodology for productivity growth analysis has been the growth accounting exercise. Productivity growth is estimated as the total factor productivity (TFP): it is synonymous with residuals in the growth accounting equation which cannot be simply explained by the growth of factor inputs in the aggregate production function.

Krugman (1994) arrives at the same conclusion as Young (1992, 1995) and Kim and Lau (1994). They argue that there is startlingly little evidence of improvement in efficiency for the rapidly growing East Asian economies, and their economic growth simply resulted from factor accumulation, such as the increase in labour force participation, the improvement in educational levels and the expansion of the investment rates.[1]

Growth Accounting: Methodology

We employ the growth accounting method for reassessment of Krugman's critique of no productivity growth in the Asian NICs and their followers. We use the transcendental logarithmic (translog) production function for measurement of the total factor productivity (*TFP*), which is employed by Christensen *et al.* (1980), Jorgenson *et al.* (1987) and Young (1992, 1993, 1995), and our *TFP* takes the form:

$$TFP = [\ln Q(T) - \ln Q(T-1)] - [v_K{}'(\ln K(T) - \ln K(T-1))]$$
$$- [v_L{}'(\ln L(T) - \ln L(T-1))] \qquad (14.1)$$

where

$$v_K{}' = 1/2[v_K(T) + v_K(T-1)]$$
$$v_L{}' = 1/2[v_L(T) + v_L(T-1)]$$

v_K' and v_L' denote the mean of each aggregate factor in total factor payments between two discrete time periods.

Growth Accounting: Results

The *TFP* estimates in growth accounting are summarized in Table 14.1. The averaged *TFP* estimates over the whole sample period for all countries but Japan exhibit negative signs, which possibly support Krugman's critique (1994) of no productivity growth for the Asian NICs and their followers[2] during their rapid economic growth periods. However, the periodical breakdown in Table 14.1 demonstrates that Krugman misreads the real trend of productivity growth.

The periodical *TFP* estimates offer the contrary view to the no productivity hypothesis of Krugman. *TFP* for South Korea and Thailand indicates the increasing trend over three decades. South Korea, for example, initiated its negative *TFP* in the 1960s and now its *TFP* shows the positive sign.

Contrary to South Korea and Thailand, the Philippines shows the decreasing trend of *TFP* until the mid-1980s when political turmoil was experienced. The Philippines' *TFP* was the second-largest, just behind Japan, in the 1960s and then started declining afterwards. Its *TFP* quickly recovered after 1986, which indicates 0.011 growth. Compared with other sample countries, Japan's *TFP* is mostly stable and constant over the sample period, the exception being the 1970s.

Second, concerning the factor contributions to growth, capital provides the greatest impact on GDP growth. On the average over the whole sample period of 1960–91, capital shows the largest contribution to growth across our sample countries: 65.0 per cent for Japan, 88.9 per cent for South Korea, 90.2 per cent for the Philippines and 102.8 per cent for Thailand. However, it indicates a decreasing trend over time and appears to be negatively associated with the increase of *TFP*. This may support the hypothesis of technology embodied in capital for our sample countries, as Englander and Mittelstadt (1988) and Hulten (1992), for example, empirically demonstrate for the OECD economies.[3] Capital may capture some changes of *TFP* and reduce the contribution of *TFP*. In our growth accounting, South Korea and Thailand especially show that their current rapid economic growth requires less capital factor contribution: capital embodies more technology so that the reduced capital is associated with the higher GDP growth which is substantially linked with *TFP* over time.

Third, we find that GDP growth is explained more by productivity growth in terms of *TFP* over time for our sample countries, with the exception of the Philippines. In a nutshell, we cast doubt on Krugman's hypothesis of no productivity growth for our sample countries, with the possible exception of the Philippines, which is still on the way to recovery after the revolution in the mid-1980s. *TFP* and the *TFP* contribution to GDP growth substantially indicate an increasing trend over time for the 1960–91 period.

Table 14.1   Translog TFP *index*

Japan	GDP growth	Factor contribution				TFP	
		L	(%)	K	(%)	Growth	(%)
1960–70	0.100	0.007	7.0	0.075	75.0	0.018	18.0
1971–80	0.044	0.005	11.4	0.032	72.7	0.007	15.9
1981–91	0.040	0.009	22.5	0.014	35.0	0.017	42.5
(1986–91)	0.044	0.011	25.0	0.014	31.8	0.019	43.2
Average	0.060	0.007	11.7	0.039	65.0	0.014	23.3

South Korea	GDP growth	Factor contribution				TFP	
		L	(%)	K	(%)	Growth	(%)
1960–70	0.079	0.009	11.4	0.091	115.2	−0.021	−26.6
1971–80	0.076	0.013	17.1	0.077	101.3	−0.014	−18.4
1981–91	0.089	0.013	14.6	0.052	58.4	0.024	27.0
(1986–91)	0.095	0.018	18.9	0.055	57.9	0.022	23.2
Average	0.081	0.012	14.8	0.072	88.9	−0.003	−3.7

The Philippines	GDP Growth	Factor contribution				TFP	
		L	(%)	K	(%)	Growth	(%)
1960–70	0.055	0.010	18.2	0.036	65.5	0.009	16.4
1971–80	0.057	0.014	24.6	0.051	89.5	−0.008	−14.0
1981–91	0.013	0.010	76.9	0.025	192.3	−0.022	−169.2
(1986–91)	0.033	0.008	24.2	0.014	42.4	0.011	33.3
Average	0.041	0.012	29.3	0.037	90.2	−0.008	−19.5

Thailand	GDP Growth	Factor contribution				TFP	
		L	(%)	K	(%)	Growth	(%)
1960–70	0.070	0.009	12.9	0.082	117.1	−0.021	−30.0
1971–80	0.065	0.010	15.4	0.067	103.1	−0.012	−18.5
1981–91	0.077	0.009	11.7	0.069	89.6	−0.001	−1.3
(1986–91)	0.089	0.009	10.1	0.077	86.5	0.003	3.4
Average	0.071	0.009	12.7	0.073	102.8	−0.011	−15.5

Note: L = employment, K = capital stock, *TFP* = total factor contribution, (%) = the relative share of the GDP growth.

PRODUCTIVITY ANALYSIS IN REGRESSION: THE LONG-RUN PRODUCTION FUNCTION

As we have previously indicated, the *TFP* analysis entirely relies on residuals in equation (14.1). Growth accountants have to answer one fundamental question: what does *TFP* stand for? As it is often defined, *TFP* is a residual in the equation which cannot be simply explained by the growth of factor inputs in production. On the basis of Abramovitz's notion of '*TFP* as our ignorance' (1993), growth accountants endeavour to reduce our ignorance by adding the supplementary factor inputs in the traditional Cobb–Douglas production function as, for example, Maddison (1987) does.

Consideration should also be given to restrictive assumptions which are included in growth accounting: profit maximization and constant returns to scale. In the regression analysis which is free from these assumptions, we seek the alternative measurement for productivity growth instead of the conventional estimates of *TFP* in growth accounting and examine Krugman's critique in the long-run supply-side production function. We define the industrialization variable as a proxy for technological progress and hence productivity growth. In order to assess the level of industrialization, we focus on the ratio of industrial employment to agricultural employment over time.

Industrialization for Productivity Growth: Concept and Stylized Fact

The industrial sector is assumed to be more technology-oriented, especially compared with the agricultural sector, though it is fair to say that technological development in agriculture and industry complement and reinforce one another to enhance the productivity of the entire economy. Moreover, technological development is considered to have the greater impact on productivity growth in the industrial sector, whilst it seems to be more limited in the agricultural sector because (a) the demand for food is inelastic since it is restricted by the size of population and Engel's law; and (b) agricultural production is more constrained by natural endowments such as geographical features and weather than by industrial production. Productivity growth in the industrial sector is more enhanced by technological development through economies of scale and the greater elasticity of consumption of industrial goods. Productivity growth can thus be intensified when the economy becomes more industrialized.

The close association between productivity growth and industrialization is documented by the centenary experience of the OECD countries. Table 14.2 shows the real GDP per capita for 1870 and 1979 at the 1970 US price and growth rates between these two time periods, which vary from 220.6 per cent for Australia to 1660.6 per cent for Japan. The northern European countries, such as Finland, Germany, Norway and Sweden, have grown much faster than other OECD countries during the 110 years between 1870 and 1979. Since the real GDP per capita appears to be not so different across the individual countries in 1979, the faster growth of these countries may depend on their initial level of real GDP, which suggests the convergence of the real output per capita among the OECD countries in line with neoclassical growth theory.

Table 14.2 *The growth of GDP per capita (GDPPH): the OECD economies between 1870 and 1979 at the 1970 US price ($)*

	GDPPH (1870)	GDPPH (1979)	Growth rate (%)
Australia	1 393	4 466	220.60
Austria	573	4 255	642.58
Belgium	925	4 986	439.03
Canada	619	5 361	766.07
Denmark	572	4 483	683.74
Finland	384	4 287	1 016.41
France	627	4 981	694.42
Germany	535	4 946	824.49
Italy	593	3 577	503.20
Japan	251	4 419	1 660.56
Netherlands	831	4 396	429.00
Norway	489	4 760	873.42
Sweden	415	4 908	1 082.65
Switzerland	786	4 491	471.37
UK	972	3 981	309.57
USA	764	6 055	692.54
Average	671	4 647	706.85

Note: Growth rates are calculated by the author.

Source: Maddison (1982, p. 8).

Table 14.3 indicates the change in the sectoral disposition of the labour force for the same countries. The 1870 data show that most OECD countries were broadly agrarian, with the exception of the UK and, possibly, Australia where the share of agricultural output in total output is 22.8 per cent and 30.0 per cent, respectively. On the other hand, Japan and Finland were highly agrarian and their share of agricultural output was well over 70 per cent. As time goes by, the difference of the ratio of industrial output to total output among the OECD countries is largely eroded.

Table 14.3   *The change of industrial structure in employment disposition: the OECD countries between 1870 and 1979 (%)*

	1870				1979				Growth
	AGR	DUS	SER	IND	AGR	DUS	SER	IND	(%)
Australia	30.0	38.0	32.0	126.7	6.5	30.9	62.6	475.4	275.30
Austria	65.0	19.2	15.8	29.5	10.7	40.5	48.8	378.5	1 181.40
Belgium	43.0	37.6	19.4	87.4	3.1	34.7	62.2	1 119.4	1 180.11
Canada	53.0	30.0	17.0	56.6	5.6	28.7	65.7	512.5	805.42
Denmark	51.7	N.A.	N.A.	N.A.	8.2	29.7	62.1	362.2	N.A.
Finland	71.2	9.7	19.1	13.6	11.5	33.7	54.8	293.0	2 051.00
France	49.2	27.8	23.0	56.5	8.6	35.3	56.1	410.5	626.43
Germany	49.5	28.7	21.8	57.9	6.0	44.0	50.0	733.3	1 164.81
Italy	62.0	23.0	15.0	37.1	14.6	37.2	48.2	254.8	586.84
Japan	72.6	N.A.	N.A.	N.A.	11.2	34.9	53.9	311.6	N.A.
Netherlands	37.0	29.0	34.0	78.4	5.9	31.3	62.8	530.5	576.86
Norway	53.0	20.0	27.0	37.7	8.6	30.1	61.3	350.0	827.50
Sweden	53.9	N.A.	N.A.	N.A.	5.8	32.5	61.7	560.3	N.A.
Switzerland	49.8	N.A.	N.A.	N.A.	7.4	39.3	53.3	531.1	N.A.
UK	22.8	42.3	35.0	185.5	2.5	38.5	59.0	1 540.0	730.07
USA	50.0	24.4	25.6	48.8	3.5	30.7	65.8	877.1	1 697.42
Average	48.8	27.5	23.7	68.0	7.5	34.5	58.0	577.5	975.26

Note: Growth rates are calculated by the author; AGR = the ratio of agricultural employment to total employment, DUS = the ratio of industrial employment to total employment, SER = the employment ratio of the service sector to total employment, IND = the ratio of industrial employment to agricultural employment.

Source: Maddison (1982, p. 205).

The averaged level of our industrialization variable, the ratio of industrial employment relative to agricultural employment, for OECD countries is 68.0 per cent in 1870 and 577.5 per cent in 1979, which roughly shows a tenfold growth between 1870 and 1979. From Tables 14.2 and 14.3 we observe the positive correlation between the growth of the real GDP per capita[4] and the change of the industrialization level in employment for OECD countries for the 1870–1979 period whose correlation is about 65 per cent, as illustrated in Figure 14.1.

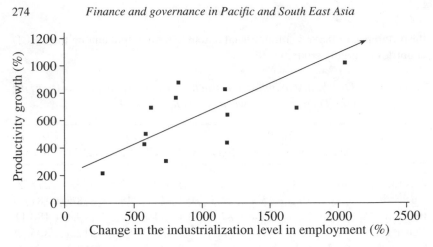

Correlation matrix (12 obs)

	GROWTH (INDUS)	GROWTH (GDPPH)
GROWTH (INDUS)	1.00	
GROWTH (GDPPH)	0.65	1.00

Note: The above figure excludes Denmark, Japan, Sweden and Switzerland, owing to lack of the relevant data in Table 14.3.

Source: Tables 14.2 and 14.3.

Figure 14.1   The change in the industrialization level in employment and productivity growth: the OECD countries between 1870 and 1979

The Augmented Cobb–Douglas Production Function

The production function used here is the logarithmic transformation of the augmented Cobb–Douglas system with the inclusion of supplementary factor inputs in production other than capital and labour:

$$Q = A \, K^{\alpha} L^{\beta} \, IND^{\gamma 1} \, EXP^{\gamma 2} \, IMP^{\gamma 3} \, DIS^{\gamma 4}$$

where

Q	= output,
A	= constant,
K	= capital stock,
L	= labour, here actual employment,
IND	= the industrialization variable, the ratio of industrial employment to agricultural employment (per cent),

EXP   = the export share in GDP (per cent),
IMP   = the import share in GDP (per cent),
DIS   = the number of workers involved in labour disputes (thousands),
α, β, $\gamma 1$, $\gamma 2$, $\gamma 3$, $\gamma 4$ = parameters of each factor input ($\alpha > 0$ and $\beta > 0$)

which can be transformed into natural logarithms:

$$\ln Q = \ln A + \alpha \ln K + \beta \ln L + \gamma 1 \ln IND + \gamma 2 \ln EXP$$
$$+ \gamma 3 \ln IMP + \gamma 4 \ln DIS$$

IND is our proxy for technological development and productivity growth. We assume that the increase of *IND* is positively associated with the industrialization level in the economy, based on the stylized fact and the conventional notion of the higher technological requirement in the industrial sector: increased employment in the industrial sector is assumed to be met by greater technological demand and hence the higher technological development and productivity growth in the economy. Two trade variables (*EXP* and *IMP*) are also included in the regressions in order to assess their impacts compared with *IND*. *IND* is our focal interest in this chapter; however, the impact of trade should also be considered since it is normally recognized as the engine of growth. We also include *DIS* as the partial adjustment of *L* (actual employment) in the production function.

Lastly, we employ the cointegration techniques for the analysis. It should be noted, however, that our sample size is limited owing to lack of data. We employ annual data for the 1960–91 period across sample countries whose sample size is not enough to produce a robust regression result. However, it should also be noted that our sample size is quite common for the regressions of productivity analysis for developing countries.[5]

Unit Roots Test

Testing for a unit root is a key advance in econometric studies. Most empirical econometric studies attempt to analyse the validity of economic theories which are generally built on the assumptions of equilibrium relationships. The time-series econometric analysis is based on the standard statistical inference procedures which require the stationarity of variables. To examine the stationarity of each variable, we use the augmented Dickey-Fuller (ADF) test (Dickey and Fuller, 1979; 1981) and the Phillips and Perron (Z) (Phillips and Perron, 1988) test: the most popular tests in the applied economic analysis. We decide the order of integration of the individual variables based on the weight of these two tests, since the test power of both ADF and Z statistics is known to be low.

ADF and Z tests generally show similar results and suggest that the order of integration is I(1) for many variables, with some exceptions. *LGDP* (GDP in log) for Japan and *LK* (*K* in log) for the Philippines may indicate they are I(2) processes.[6] Consequently, we assume these variables as I(1) in this analysis which makes our subsequent cointegration regressions more meaningful since other variables overwhelmingly indicate the I(1) property.

Cointegration Test

Consequence and methodology

The importance of the long-run relationship among variables, referred to as a cointegrating relationship, is that a regression containing all the variables will have a stationary error term even if none of the variables alone is stationary. We employ the OLS estimates in the Engle–Granger (EG) two-step modelling procedure (Engle and Granger, 1987) and Johansen's maximum likelihood method to detect the cointegrating relationship among variables: these two approaches possibly produce different results, as Dickey *et al.* (1991) and Hurn and Muscatelli (1992) discovered for their investigations into the money demand function in the USA and the UK, respectively. Two different estimates are expected to complement one another since we may not be able to get robust results owing to our limited sample size.[7] Moreover, we decide to take only one lag from each variable in our cointegration examinations since our sample size is limited.

The Johansen method (likelihood ratio test)

We initiate our test for the long-run production function with the Johansen method since it provides the useful insight for the intercorrelations among variables with the multivariate cointegrating relationships. The Johansen test, however, requires a large sample size and may not be adequate for our sample size, so that we subsequently compare with the OLS estimate of the EG approach.

Appendix I reports the details of the cointegration test by the Johansen method. All countries show the multiple cointegrating relationships. The difficult choice among the multiple cointegrating relationships is generally recognized by applied economists: assistance is often afforded by economic theory. The Cobb–Douglas production function requires $0 < \alpha < 1$ and $0 < \beta < 1$ which well fit the first rank in the cointegrating relationships for Japan and the Philippines, also supported by both trace and maximal eigenvalue tests at the 1 per cent level.

The problems arise with South Korea and Thailand, whose plausible cointegrating relationships do not exhibit reasonable values and signs. Guided by Johansen and Juselius (1992),[8] we decide to select the fifth cointegrating rela-

Table 14.4   *Cointegrating relationships: comparison between Johansen and EG methods dependent variable*: LGDP

Variable	Japan		South Korea	
	JC	EG	JC	EG
C	−4.280	−4.492	−1.773	7.783
LK	0.745	0.733	0.350	1.268
LL	0.463	0.492	0.428	−0.634
LIND	−0.017	−0.014	0.284	−0.547
LEXP	0.115	0.113	0.192	0.090
LIMP	−0.094	−0.098	−0.513	−0.561
LDIS	0.007	0.008	0.007	0.040
$\alpha + \beta$	1.208	1.225	0.778	0.634
SUM	1.219	1.234	0.748	−0.344
COINT	Yes	Yes	Yes	No
RANK	4 (1)	–	3 (5)	–
REGRES	1	5	2	6

Variable	The Philippines		Thailand	
	JC	EG	JC	EG
C	−3.979	−5.345	−0.970	0.509
LK	0.611	0.340	0.445	0.787
LL	0.335	0.512	0.136	−0.042
LIND	0.578	0.530	0.410	−0.059
LEXP	0.225	0.096	0.316	0.223
LIMP	−0.544	−0.105	−0.305	−0.217
LDIS	0.062	0.076	0.003	−0.004
$\alpha + \beta$	0.946	0.852	0.581	0.745
SUM	1.267	1.449	1.005	0.688
COINT	Yes	No	Yes	No
RANK	2 (1)	–	2 (7)	–
REGRES	3	7	4	8

Notes: JC = the Johansen cointegration test (see Appendix I); EG = the OLS estimates in the Engle–Granger approach (see Appendix II); α, β = parameter value of the factor inputs of capital and of labour, respectively; *SUM* = the sum of parameter values of all factor inputs in production; *COINT* = the existence of cointegrating relationships at the 5 per cent significance level; *RANK* = rank for the cointegrating relationships; *REGRES*: the details of statistics are available in Appendices I and II.

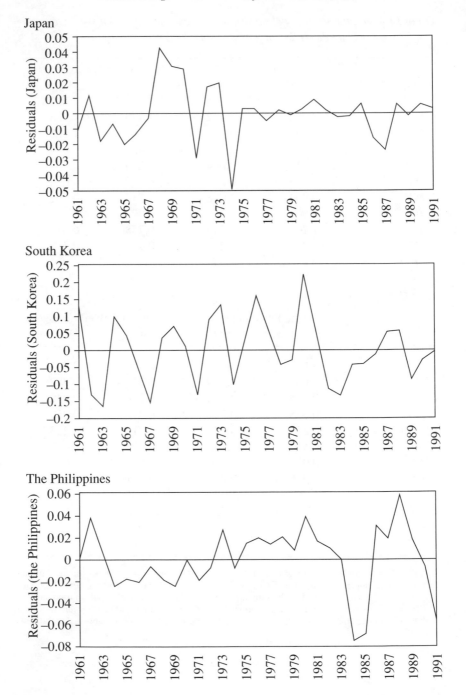

Thailand

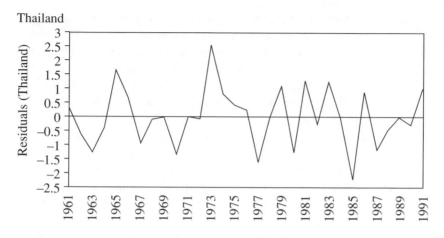

Figure 14.2   Residuals in the production function (the Johansen method)

tionship for South Korea and the seventh cointegrating relationship for Thailand, although they are not statistically robust. The statistical significance of the estimated cointegrating relationships can be best examined by the diagnostic tests. The Johansen method, however, requires a large sample size for its reliable outcomes, so that it does not have power for the relevant diagnostic tests for our estimated cointegrating relationships. Alternatively, we review visually the stationarity of residuals in the regressions in Figure 14.2. South Korea and Thailand clearly demonstrate that their selected cointegrating relationships are derived from the regressions whose residuals are stationary. However, it is not so obvious for Japan, although we can still infer stationarity. The Philippines are possibly the only country whose residuals are not stationary: this may indicate spurious cointegrating relationships. These observations are very tentative since we need a large sample of data for convincing results.

We normalize *LGDP* as –1 and exhibit the selected cointegrating relationships in Table 14.4. Our estimates provide the following important observations. First, the long-run parameter for *LK* indicates the largest value among all factor inputs in production across countries, with the exception of South Korea, whose parameter for *LL* is mostly substantial instead. Second, *LIND* demonstrates the largest supplementary impact for the production function in terms of the parameter value across countries, with the exception of Japan.[9] The test results indicate the consequence of the industrialization variable in the production function, which signifies productivity growth in those countries.

Comparison with the EG approach (OLS estimates)

We compare the estimated cointegrating relationships of the Johansen test with those of the EG approach, which are also summarized in Table 14.4 and their details are reported in Appendix II. The two sets of parameter estimates are virtually identical for Japan; and they are not too dissimilar for the Philippines. All parameters in the cointegrating relationships for Japan and the Philippines exhibit reasonable values which are less than unity with correct signs. Moreover, the returns to scale indicate 1.234 for Japan and 1.449 for the Philippines in the EG approach, and are not so different from those by the Johansen test: 1.219 and 1.267, respectively.

Japan demonstrates significant cointegrating relationships at the 5 per cent level in the EG procedure. The EG method, on the other hand, does not provide significant cointegrating relationships for the other three countries at the 5 per cent level,[10] whilst the Johansen method does provide them for all. Nonsensical results produced by the EG method can be found in particular for South Korea and Thailand, either by the unreasonable parameter value or by the wrong parameter sign: the parameters for *LK* and *LL* for South Korea (1.268 and –0.634, respectively) and that for *LL* for Thailand (–0.042), for example, are not in line with economic theory for the Cobb–Douglas production function.

In sum, the above comparison provides useful information for the cointegrating relationships estimated by the different methods: the Johansen method and the EG approach. Our cointegration analysis reveals the robust findings for Japan and the Philippines, since two different methods provide the relatively consistent results for the long-run parameter values.

DYNAMIC PRODUCTION FUNCTION IN THE ERROR CORRECTION MODEL (ECM)

We here estimate the dynamic production function in the error correction model (ECM) by using the previously measured cointegrating relationships as the error correction terms. In constructing the ECM we use only the first differences of the variables as regressors alongside the error correction term. It should be noted that the first differenced *LK* (ΔLK) is close to the current investment.[11] We compare the ECM whose error correction term is obtained by the Johansen method (model JC) with that obtained by the EG approach (model EG) in Table 14.5.

ECM with Error Correction Term by the Johansen Method: Model JC

Model JC in Table 14.5 exhibits the mixed results: all variables, for example, enter Japan's production function as significant, whilst none of variables is significant for Thailand at the 10 per cent level.

All variables indicate the reasonable parameter values with the correct sign for Japan. There are, however, two different observations between the long run and the dynamic production function for Japan: (a) the parameter value for capital stock, and (b) the sign of parameter for the industrialization variable. First, the parameter value for the differenced capital stock (ΔLK) indicates 3.280 – more than unity – and appears too large in the Cobb–Douglas system, whilst its long-run parameter shows 0.745 in line with economic theory. As we have already noted, however, ΔLK signifies current investment rather than the capital stock, so that its parameter should not necessarily be less than unity. A similar observation is found for the Philippines ΔLK (model JC (B)). However, ΔLK appears not to be statistically significant at the 5 per cent level in model JC for South Korea and Thailand.

Table 14.5   Dynamic production function: error correction model (OLS, Z by the Johansen method or by the EG approach)

Japan dependent variable: Δ LGDP (1962–91)				
Model	JC		EG	
Variable	coefficient	(SE) [prob]	coefficient	(SE) [prob]
C	−0.001	(0.004)	−0.001	(0.004)
ΔLK	3.280	**(0.235)	3.127	**(0.224)
ΔLL	0.463	*(0.213)	0.416	†(0.215)
$\Delta LIND$	0.092	*(0.040)	0.102	*(0.040)
$\Delta LEXP$	0.097	**(0.023)	0.097	**(0.023)
$\Delta LIMP$	−0.076	**(0.012)	−0.077	**(0.013)
$\Delta LDIS$	0.011	*(0.004)	0.011	*(0.004)
Z_{-1}	−1.205	**(0.103)	−1.212	**(0.104)
R^2	0.970		0.969	
F (7, 22)	100.430	[0.000]	99.196	[0.000]
σ	0.007		0.007	
DW	2.33		2.28	
RSS	0.001		0.001	
AUTO (2, 20)	0.779	[0.472]	0.540	[0.591]
ARCH (1, 20)	0.008	[0.928]	0.296	[0.593]
NORM	1.377	[0.502]	0.507	[0.776]
Xi^2 (14, 7)	0.646	[0.770]	0.580	[0.817]
RESET (1, 21)	3.128	[0.092]	2.134	[0.159]

South Korea   dependent variable: Δ LGDP (1962–91)

Model	JC		EG	
Variable	coefficient	(SE) [prob]	coefficient	(SE) [prob]
C	0.009	(0.032)	−0.004	(0.027)
ΔLK	0.380	(0.243)	1.298	**(0.292)
ΔLL	0.707	(0.422)	0.487	(0.350)
$\Delta LIND$	0.058	(0.103)	0.040	(0.085)
$\Delta LEXP$	0.034	(0.043)	0.026	(0.036)
$\Delta LIMP$	−0.196	*(0.077)	−0.310	**(0.073)
$\Delta LDIS$	0.0004	(0.004)	0.011	*(0.004)
Z_{-1}	−0.367	*(0.140)	−0.437	**(0.098)
R^2	0.390		0.579	
$F\,(7, 22)$	2.011	[0.100]	4.318	[0.004]
σ	0.031		0.026	
DW	1.96		2.54	
RSS	0.021		0.015	
$AUTO\,(2, 20)$	0.132	[0.877]	1.464	[0.255]
$ARCH\,(1, 20)$	0.515	[0.481]	1.124	[0.302]
$NORM$	2.170	[0.338]	4.358	[0.113]
$Xi^2\,(14, 7)$	1.702	[0.244]	0.137	[0.999]
$RESET\,(1, 21)$	2.131	[0.159]	7.755	[0.011]

The Philippines   dependent variable: Δ LGDP (1962–91)

Model	JC (A)		JC (B)		EG	
Variable	coefficient	(SE) [prob]	coefficient	(SE) [prob]	coefficient	(SE) [prob]
C	0.017	(0.016)	0.035	**(0.012)	0.020	(0.012)
ΔLK	2.483	**(0.633)	1.304	*(0.509)	1.087	**(0.345)
ΔLL	−0.125	(0.154)	−0.068	(0.109)	−0.041	(0.105)
$\Delta LIND$	−0.003	(0.121)	−0.046	(0.086)	−0.056	(0.082)
$\Delta LEXP$	0.127	*(0.054)	0.086	*(0.039)	0.084	*(0.036)
$\Delta LIMP$	−0.094	(0.075)	−0.102	†(0.053)	−0.056	(0.042)
$\Delta LDIS$	0.006	(0.014)	−0.001	(0.010)	−0.0003	(0.010)
Z_{-1}	−0.369	**(0.118)	−0.181	†(0.092)	−0.198	*(0.083)
DUM	–	–	−0.026	**(0.005)	−0.021	**(0.006)
R^2	0.499		0.762		0.779	
$F\,(7, 22)$	3.127	[0.019]	8.426	[0.000]	9.227	[0.000]
σ	0.032		0.022		0.021	
DW	1.04		1.40		1.34	
RSS	0.022		0.010		0.010	
$AUTO\,(2, 20)$	2.300	[0.126]	0.727	[0.496]	1.009	[0.383]
$ARCH\,(1, 20)$	0.416	[0.526]	0.591	[0.451]	0.110	[0.744]
$NORM$	1.501	[0.472]	4.174	[0.124]	4.433	[0.109]
$Xi^2\,(14, 7)$	0.213	[0.993]	0.243	[0.982]	0.147	[0.998]
$RESET\,(1, 21)$	16.172	[0.001]	0.034	[0.856]	0.088	[0.770]

Thailand   dependent variable: Δ LGDP (1962–91)

Model	JC		EG	
Variable	coefficient	(SE) [prob]	coefficient	(SE) [prob]
C	−0.017	(0.055)	−0.011	(0.019)
ΔLK	0.849	(0.522)	2.612	**(0.327)
ΔLL	0.077	(0.169)	0.001	(0.089)
$\Delta LIND$	0.018	(0.083)	−0.061	(0.044)
$\Delta LEXP$	0.041	(0.076)	0.096	*(0.035)
$\Delta LIMP$	−0.050	(0.068)	−0.195	**(0.040)
$\Delta LDIS$	0.0001	(0.005)	−0.022	(0.003)
Z_{-1}	−0.088	(0.478)	−1.033	**(0.135)
R^2	0.152		0.762	
F (7, 22)	0.565	[0.776]	10.087	[0.000]
σ	0.032		0.017	
DW	1.69		2.00	
RSS	0.023		0.006	
$AUTO$ (2, 20)	0.100	[0.906]	1.925	[0.172]
$ARCH$ (1, 20)	0.135	[0.718]	1.924	[0.181]
$NORM$	1.594	[0.451]	0.240	[0.887]
Xi^2 (14, 7)	0.238	[0.989]	0.331	[0.963]
$RESET$ (1, 21)	0.089	[0.768]	0.079	[0.782]

Notes:

JC: Z by the Johansen cointegration test.

Z for *JC*: error correction term (the selected cointegrating relationships in the Johansen test in Table 14.4).

Japan: $Z = LGDP + 4.280 − 0.745 \, LK − 0.463 \, LL + 0.017 \, LIND − 0.115 \, LEXP + 0.094 \, LIMP − 0.007 \, LDIS$.

South Korea: $Z = LGDP + 1.773 − 0.350 \, LK − 0.428 \, LL − 0.284 \, LIND − 0.192 \, LEXP + 0.513 \, LIMP − 0.007 \, LDIS$.

The Philippines: $Z = LGDP + 3.979 − 0.611 \, LK − 0.335 \, LL − 0.578 \, LIND − 0.225 \, LEXP + 0.544 \, LIMP − 0.062 \, LDIS$.

Thailand: $Z = LGDP + 0.970 − 0.445 \, LK − 0.136 \, LL − 0.410 \, LIND − 0.316 \, LEXP + 0.305 \, LIMP − 0.003 \, LDIS$.

EG: Z by the Engle–Granger approach for the cointegration analysis.

Z for *EG*: error correction term (the estimated cointegrating relationships by the OLS in the EG approach in Table 14.4).

Japan: $Z = LGDP + 4.492 − 0.733 \, LK − 0.492 \, LL + 0.014 \, LIND − 0.113 \, LEXP + 0.098 \, LIMP − 0.008 \, LDIS$.

South Korea: $Z = LGDP − 7.783 − 1.268 \, LK + 0.634 \, LL + 0.547 \, LIND − 0.090 \, LEXP + 0.561 \, LIMP − 0.040 \, LDIS$.

The Philippines: $Z = LGDP + 5.345 − 0.340 \, LK − 0.512 \, LL − 0.530 \, LIND − 0.096 \, LEXP + 0.105 \, LIMP − 0.076 \, LDIS$.

Thailand: $Z = LGDP − 0.509 − 0.787 \, LK + 0.042 \, LL + 0.059 \, LIND − 0.223 \, LEXP + 0.217 \, LIMP + 0.004 \, LDIS$.

DUM: dummy variable (time trend between 1982 and 1985 only for the Philippines).

R^2 = squared multiple correlation coefficient.

F = F–test for the null hypothesis that all the regression's coefficients are zero (excluding the intercept).
σ = equation standard error.
DW = Durbin–Watson test.
RSS = residual sum of squares.
AUTO = LM autocorrelation test.
ARCH = *ARCH* heteroscedasticity test.
NORM = Jarque-Bera normality test.
Xi^2 = White heteroscedasticity test.
RESET: Ramsey specification test.
(SE): standard error of coefficient.
[prob]: probability.
** = the 1% significance level.
* = the 5% significance level.
† = the 10% significance level.
Statistics for model JC (B), the Philippines: $F(8, 21)$, *AUTO* (2, 19), *ARCH* (1, 19) Xi^2 (16, 4), and *RESET* (1, 20).

Second, the estimated parameter for $\Delta LIND$ exhibits a positive sign for Japan though its value is small (0.092). Its parameter in the cointegrating relationships has previously indicated a negative sign (–0.017). This suggests that industrialization in employment is still the problem for the Japanese economy in the short run although Japan shows a deindustrialization trend in its long run production function.

$\Delta LIMP$ is the only significant variable in the ECM for South Korea besides the error correction term and its parameter sign is negative, as is that for *LIMP* in the long-run production function. This emphasizes that South Korea needs to reduce the import share in GDP for economic growth both in the short run and in the long run.

The initial estimate of the Philippines' production function (JC (A) in Table 14.5) shows the specification problem demonstrated by the Ramsey test, which shows 16.172 with almost 100 per cent probability. We suspect that the Ramsey specification problem for the Philippines may have some links with the severe political turmoil in the mid-1980s and decide to introduce the dummy variable in the ECM. We employ the time trend only between 1982 and 1985 (the year of the debt moratorium and the year of the severe political turmoil) on the assumption that the revolutionary pressure had increasingly damaged the Philippines' production function associated with its debt problem. Model JC (B) validates our assumption and the dummy variable negatively enters the dynamic production function in the ECM at the 1 per cent significance level without exposing any specification problems in the regression. $\Delta LIMP$ now additionally appears to be significant in model JC (B) at the 10 per cent level whilst it is insignificant in model JC (A). The parameter for ΔLK indicates 1.304, the largest among variables in model JC (B) for the Philippines' ECM whilst ΔLL, $\Delta LIND$ and $\Delta LDIS$ remain insignificant even at the 10 per cent level.

Thailand, on the other hand, does not show any consequent variables in the ECM although all parameter values appear to be reasonable. The error correction term is also insignificant in the ECM, unlike the case of other sample countries.

ECM with Error Correction Term by the EG Approach: Model EG

We here estimate the ECM with the error correction term which is derived from the cointegrating relationships estimated in the EG approach. Table 14.5 offers comparison with the ECM whose error correction term is obtained by the Johansen test. Our test results clearly exhibit the identical test results of model JC and model EG for Japan and the Philippines. However, the test results provide different observations for South Korea and Thailand: model EG indicates better statistics than model JC in terms of parameter estimates and R^2.

Comparison and Model Selection

We have two ECM models: model JC and model EG, which can be seen as two rival explanations for $\Delta LGDP$. We here select the better model, with four considerations: (a) error correction term, Z, (b) goodness of fit, R^2, (c) diagnostic tests, and (d) encompassing and non-nested hypotheses tests.[12]

Table 14.6 includes the summary for investigations for the model selection based on the above four categories. The summary table provides the consistent result for Japan and the Philippines: the better model appears to be model JC.[13] However, the results for South Korea and Thailand are more sensitive to model specification, and the choice between specifications depends upon the weighting that we give to our four statistical criteria. We mostly consider the long-run parameter values in the cointegrating relationships which enter the ECM as the error correction term. We then focus on the diagnostic tests of each ECM in order to avoid the spurious results which may underlie the other two statistics: R^2 and encompassing test. On the basis of the above considerations, we select model JC as our preferable model for all sample countries. Model EG appears to be superior to model JC for South Korea and Thailand in terms of R^2 and encompassing test results which, however, do not show the satisfactory diagnostic tests. Model EG for South Korea and Thailand, moreover, contains an error correction term whose relevant long-run parameter values are not in line with economic theory.

TESTING EXOGENEITY

The exogeneity status of variables is of crucial importance for econometric modelling. Three significant concepts for exogeneity are defined by Engle *et*

Table 14.6   Comparison and model selection (ECM)

Z (error correction term: whether it contains the reasonable parameter values for cointegrating relationships in line with economic theory)

Model	Japan		South Korea		Philippines		Thailand	
	JC	EG	JC	EG	JC	EG	JC	EG
Z_{-1}	Yes	Yes	Yes	Yes	Yes	Yes	No	Yes
PARAM	Yes	Yes	Yes	No	Yes	Yes	Yes	No
Selection	(any model)		JC		(any model)		JC	

Goodness of fit (R^2)

Model	Japan		South Korea		Philippines		Thailand	
	JC	EG	JC	EG	JC	EG	JC	EG
R^2	0.970	0.969	0.390	0.579	0.762	0.779	0.152	0.762
Selection	(any model)		EG		(any model)		EG	

Diagnostic test

Model	Japan		South Korea		Philippines[a]		Thailand	
	JC	EG	JC	EG	JC	EG	JC	EG
DIAG	No	No	No	Yes	No	No	No	No
1-STEP	No	No	No	No	(Yes)	No	No	No
CHOW	No	Yes	No	No	Yes	Yes	No	Yes
Selection	JC		JC		(any model)		JC	

Encompassing and non-nested hypotheses tests (only the F-statistics for the joint model are exhibited in this table), model 1: JC and model 2: EG

Japan				South Korea			
$1 \rightarrow 2$	$2 \rightarrow 1$	COM	TEST	$1 \rightarrow 2$	$2 \rightarrow 1$	COM	TEST
[0.673]	[0.515]	–	1	**[0.006]	[0.819]	EG	2

The Philippines				Thailand			
$1 \rightarrow 2$	$2 \rightarrow 1$	COM	TEST	$1 \rightarrow 2$	$2 \rightarrow 1$	COM	TEST
[0.208]	[0.639]	–	3	**[0.000]	[0.905]	EG	4

Model selection: summary

	Japan	South Korea	Philippines	Thailand
Z (error correction term)	(any model)	JC	JC	JC
Goodness of fit (R^2)	(any model)	EG	(any model)	EG
Diagnostic test	JC	JC	(any model)	JC
Encompassing test	(any model)	EG	(any model)	EG
Final selection	JC	JC	JC	JC

Notes:
JC, EG: as for Table 14.5. For the Philippines, JC(B) for JC.
Z_{-1}: the statistical consequence of the error correction term in the ECM at the 10% level.
PARAM: the reasonable parameter values for cointegrating relationships, which is used as the error correction term in the ECM.
Selection: the most preferred model (the selected model).
DIAG: any diagnostic problems, if found (autocorrelation, heteroscedasticity, normality and Ramsey specification problems).
1-STEP: 1-step residuals with $0\pm2\sigma$, based on the recursive estimates.
CHOW: 1-step Chow test scaled by their critical values at the 5% level at each t based on the recursive estimates.
For *DIAG*, *1-STEP* and *CHOW*, Yes = any diagnostic problems are found at the 5% significance level; No = no diagnostic problem is found at the 5% significance level; [a]for the Philippines, *1-STEP* and *CHOW* are tested for models with the exclusion of dummy variable for the period of severe political turmoil (the time trend only between 1982 and 1985) since PcGive 8.0 does not compute the recursive estimates for these models. The test results should therefore be considered as suggestive.
$1 \rightarrow 2$: the encompassing test from model 1 to Model 2.
$2 \rightarrow 1$: the encompassing test from Model 2 to Model 1.
COM: the consequent model relative to the other at around the 10% level, based on the encompassing and non-nested hypotheses tests (the joint model F-test).
[ ]: the statistical significance (p-value) for the F-test for the joint model; each model being a valid simplification of the linear union of the two models under test.
**: the statistical significance at the 1% level; *: the statistical significance at the 5% level; †: the statistical significance at the 10% level (including around the 10% level).
TEST: the relevant test number in Appendix III.
Z: the reasonable parameter values for cointegrating relationships in line with economic theory which enter the ECM as the error correction term at least at the 10% statistical significance level, with the exception of Thailand.
Selection: the model selection based on the tests.
Final selection: the final selection for the model based on the four different criteria.

al. (1983): weak exogeneity, strong exogeneity and superexogeneity. Using these definitions, researchers attempt to investigate the exogeneity status of some explanatory variables of interest to them. The method for testing the exogeneity status of *LIND* in the long-run production function is based on the likelihood ratio test suggested by Johansen and Juselius (1990, 1992).

Johansen and Juselius show that, if for some i, $\alpha_i = 0$, then ΔX_{it} is weakly exogenous for α and β in the sense that the conditional distribution of ΔX_t given ΔX_{it} as well as the lagged values of ΔX_t contains the parameters α and β whereas the distribution of ΔX_{it} given the lagged X_t does not contain the parameters α and β. The parameters in the conditional and marginal distribution are variation-independent.[14] It should be noted that the condition of weak exogeneity holds only for the case when the parameters of interest are the long-run parameters α and β. We thus test the hypothesis H_0: $\alpha = 0$ (α for *LIND*). Based on Johansen and Juselius, the likelihood ratio test for significance of this restriction is estimated:

$$-2\ln (Q: H_0) = T \Sigma \ln ((1 - \lambda^*_i) / (1 - \lambda_i)).$$

We examine model JC which is derived from the selected cointegrating relationships in the Johansen test for each sample country in Table 14.4. Considering the case for Japan, the previous cointegration tests, both of max eigenvalue test and trace test, indicate $r = 2$, so that the relevant coefficients of α_{21} and α_{22} are restricted to zero. As Appendix IV shows, the test statistic is almost nil and asymptotically distributed and therefore not significant. We thus conclude that *LIND* for Japan is weakly exogenous for β. Appendix IV exhibits the newly estimated matrices for β' eigenvectors and α coefficients under the restriction of $\alpha_{21} = \alpha_{22} = 0$. The newly estimated values of the first β' eigenvector and its α coefficient are quite close to those of the previous estimates (except the restricted α_{21} coefficient): $\beta'^* = (1.000, -0.745, -0.463, 0.017, -0.115, 0.094, -0.007, 4.280)$ and $\beta' = (1.000, -0.744, -0.479, 0.018, -0.114, 0.092, -0.008, 4.443)$; $\alpha^* = (0.272, 0.439, 0.043, 0.262, 0.024, 0.003, -0.021)$ and $\alpha = (0.263, 0.447, 0.042, 0.000, 0.020, 0.036, -0.075)$ (β'^* and α^* for the new estimates, and β' and α for the previous estimates). These close estimates can be regarded as the evidence that the α coefficient restrictions are not consequent and the concerned variable of *LIND* is weakly exogenous for β. The test results in Appendix IV demonstrate that the same can be said for *LIND* for South Korea and the Philippines, which indicates the possible exogeneity status of *LIND* in the long-run production function. Only *LIND* for Thailand suggests its endogenous property.

CONCLUDING REMARKS

We have reviewed Krugman's suggestion of no productivity growth and provided evidence for productivity growth in the selected Asian NICs and their followers by using quantitative analyses in growth accounting, cointegration test and dynamic production function. We cast doubt on Krugman's suggestion by showing the increasing trend of total factor productivity (*TFP*) over time in growth accounting for the Republic of Korea (South Korea) and Thailand. The decreasing trend of *TFP* for the Philippines eventually turns into an increasing one after recovery from the political turmoil in the mid-1980s. Moreover, the industrialization variable (*LIND*, the ratio of industrial employment to agricultural employment and the proxy for productivity growth) indicates the largest parameter value among all supplementary factor inputs in the long-run production function, especially by the Johansen method, for all sample countries but for Japan.

Finally, the exogeneity test indicates the possible exogeneity status of *LIND* in the long-run production function for all sample countries but Thailand.

APPENDIX I: DETAILS OF COINTEGRATION TEST: THE JOHANSEN METHOD

Regression 1: Japan

eigenvalue µl	loglikelihood for	rank
	625.58	0
0.999	748.07	1
0.777	771.34	2
0.617	786.21	3
0.585	799.82	4
0.476	809.83	5
0.314	815.66	6
0.069	816.76	7
−2.951e-011	—	

Ho: r = p	Max eigenvalue	95% CV	Trace	95% CV
p = 0	**245.0	46.5	**382.4	131.7
p < = 1	**46.6	40.3	**137.4	102.1
p < = 2	29.7	34.4	**90.8	76.1
p < = 3	27.2	28.1	**61.1	53.1
p < = 4	20.0	22.0	33.9	34.9
p < = 5	11.7	15.7	13.9	20.0
p < = 6	2.2	9.2	2.2	9.2

Standardized β' eigenvectors

LGDP	LK	LL	LIND	LEXP	LIMP	LDIS	Constant
1.000	−0.745	−0.463	0.017	−0.115	0.094	−0.007	4.280
−0.326	1.000	1.549	−1.268	−0.443	0.212	0.027	−14.850
−0.581	0.194	1.000	0.108	0.204	−0.116	0.016	−9.419
99.280	−25.940	−452.90	1.000	8.511	−26.540	−11.700	4571.00
5.522	−1.141	4.022	−4.638	1.000	0.050	0.130	−49.550
4.764	−2.500	−5.533	−0.410	0.365	1.000	−0.264	48.450
19.570	−19.950	−15.380	16.370	5.608	−3.782	1.000	87.850

Standardized α coefficients

LGDP	0.272	0.106	0.666	0.001	0.014	−0.018	−0.001
LK	0.439	0.012	0.238	0.000	0.002	−0.009	−0.000
LL	0.043	0.062	0.090	0.001	−0.004	0.005	0.000
LIND	0.262	0.173	−0.011	0.001	0.129	−0.016	0.000
LEXP	0.024	0.294	−3.485	−0.003	−0.095	−0.083	−0.001
LIMP	0.003	0.051	−3.462	0.004	−0.086	−0.278	0.009
LDIS	−0.021	−2.008	−9.479	0.019	−0.121	0.063	−0.013

Regression 2: South Korea

eigenvalue μI	loglikelihood for	rank
	502.80	0
0.992	576.91	1
0.830	604.34	2
0.565	617.26	3
0.536	629.14	4
0.368	636.26	5
0.242	640.55	6
0.130	642.71	7
−1.055e-013	—	

Ho: r = p	Max eigenvalue	95% CV	Trace	95% CV
p = 0	**148.2	46.5	**279.8	131.7
p < = 1	**54.9	40.3	**131.6	102.1
p < = 2	25.8	34.4	*76.8	76.1
p < = 3	23.8	28.1	50.9	53.1
p < = 4	14.2	22.0	27.1	34.9
p < = 5	8.6	15.7	12.9	20.0
p < = 6	4.3	9.2	4.3	9.2

Standardized β' eigenvectors

LGDP	LK	LL	LIND	LEXP	LIMP	LDIS	Constant
1.000	−3.429	1.511	2.744	0.300	0.594	−0.068	−15.600
−0.462	1.000	−0.787	−0.702	0.088	−0.552	0.033	9.149
−0.151	−0.163	1.000	0.150	−0.120	0.094	−0.050	−8.555
−2.553	0.441	1.963	1.000	−0.042	0.079	0.057	−15.060
−5.218	1.825	2.232	1.480	1.000	−2.678	0.038	−9.249
−6.919	17.360	−37.900	−1.754	−2.239	1.000	−0.153	318.200
138.600	−34.330	−722.50	125.000	40.380	−33.550	1.000	5890.00

Standardized α coefficients

LGDP	0.056	0.088	–0.177	–0.011	0.036	0.009	–0.000
LK	0.086	0.069	–0.070	0.003	0.020	–0.002	–0.000
LL	0.021	0.046	–0.082	–0.047	–0.009	0.002	0.000
LIND	0.061	0.204	–0.134	–0.229	0.008	–0.007	–0.001
LEXP	0.070	1.560	0.911	0.010	–0.070	0.008	0.001
LIMP	0.026	0.750	0.230	–0.118	0.153	–0.023	0.001
LDIS	0.069	–3.439	10.690	–3.594	1.742	0.032	0.008

Regression 3: The Philippines

eigenvalue μI	loglikelihood for	rank
	532.22	0
0.985	597.35	1
0.766	619.87	2
0.474	629.84	3
0.418	638.24	4
0.384	645.74	5
0.303	651.34	6
0.192	654.65	7
5.038e-013	—	

Ho: r = p	Max eigenvalue	95% CV	Trace	95% CV
p = 0	**130.3	46.5	**244.9	131.7
p < = 1	*45.0	40.3	**114.6	102.1
p < = 2	19.9	34.4	69.6	76.1
p < = 3	16.8	28.1	49.6	53.1
p < = 4	15.0	22.0	32.8	34.9
p < = 5	11.2	15.7	17.8	20.0
p < = 6	6.6	9.2	6.6	9.2

Standardized β' eigenvectors

LGDP	*LK*	*LL*	*LIND*	*LEXP*	*LIMP*	*LDIS*	Constant
1.000	–0.611	–0.335	–0.578	–0.225	0.544	–0.062	3.979
–0.540	1.000	–1.174	0.016	0.935	–0.803	–0.203	9.671
–3.039	0.625	1.000	0.391	0.946	0.951	0.237	–10.240
–0.511	2.161	–4.166	1.000	–0.421	0.500	0.263	28.630
–20.720	19.020	–16.740	–14.320	1.000	14.440	–1.431	159.400
–2.174	0.733	1.148	1.783	–2.111	1.000	–0.197	–9.468
–15.670	14.160	26.770	–56.110	–5.556	–18.060	1.000	–10.180

Standardized α coefficients

LGDP	0.115	−0.014	0.063	−0.009	−0.006	0.027	−0.000
LK	0.179	0.010	0.015	−0.003	−0.003	−0.005	−0.000
LL	0.082	0.169	0.011	0.102	−0.002	−0.004	−0.001
LIND	0.024	−0.139	0.034	0.024	0.003	−0.009	0.003
LEXP	0.050	0.002	−0.121	0.065	−0.016	0.140	0.004
LIMP	0.038	0.351	0.024	−0.054	−0.033	−0.021	0.003
LDIS	0.159	1.867	−0.127	−0.692	0.092	0.251	−0.004

Regression 4: Thailand

eigenvalue μI	loglikelihood for	rank
	498.44	0
0.996	582.45	1
0.596	596.50	2
0.566	609.45	3
0.455	618.86	4
0.405	626.89	5
0.246	631.27	6
0.152	633.83	7
5.211e-014	—	

Ho: r = p	Max eigenvalue	95% CV	Trace	95% CV
p = 0	**168.0	46.5	**270.8	131.7
p < = 1	28.1	40.3	*102.8	102.1
p < = 2	25.9	34.4	74.7	76.1
p < = 3	18.8	28.1	48.8	53.1
p < = 4	16.1	22.0	29.9	34.9
p < = 5	8.7	15.7	13.9	20.0
p < = 6	5.1	9.2	5.1	9.2

Standardized β′ eigenvectors

LGDP	LK	LL	LIND	LEXP	LIMP	LDIS	Constant
1.000	−0.808	0.163	−0.058	−0.313	0.490	0.004	−1.729
−0.944	1.000	−0.420	−0.366	0.306	−0.101	−0.004	3.610
1.704	−1.512	1.000	0.168	−0.010	−0.712	0.027	−7.553
−1.344	−1.487	5.297	1.000	−0.502	0.812	0.090	−46.380
6.284	−3.674	−3.811	−0.156	1.000	0.396	0.176	28.210
9.103	0.405	−17.320	2.111	−6.904	1.000	0.188	154.100
−229.20	133.00	40.690	122.700	94.670	−91.380	1.000	−290.20

Standardized α coefficients

LGDP	0.183	0.388	−0.046	0.041	−0.017	0.001	0.000
LK	0.267	0.107	0.029	0.005	0.003	−0.001	0.000
LL	0.084	0.097	−0.083	−0.118	0.006	0.005	0.000
LIND	0.145	0.506	−0.123	0.108	0.052	−0.006	−0.001
LEXP	0.048	0.247	0.510	−0.064	−0.076	0.012	−0.001
LIMP	0.055	0.596	0.753	−0.091	0.034	−0.005	0.000
LDIS	0.591	0.133	−2.644	−1.295	−1.328	−0.190	−0.007

APPENDIX II: COINTEGRATION TEST: THE SOLVED STATIC LONG-RUN (SSLR) EQUATION

Regression 5: Japan

1. Solved static long-run equation

$$LGDP = -4.492 + 0.733\,LK + 0.492\,LL - 0.014\,LIND + 0.113\,LEXP$$
$$\text{(SE)}\quad (1.756)\,(0.050)\quad (0.173)\quad\ \ (0.064)\quad\quad\ \ (0.028)$$
$$- 0.098\,LIMP + 0.008\,LDIS$$
$$(0.015)\quad\quad (0.004)$$

Wald Test Chi^2 (6) = 16625.0 [0.000]**

2. Analysis of the autoregressive distributed lag representation

	0	1	Σ
LGDP	−1.000	−0.263	−1.263
(SE)	—	(0.153)	(0.153)
C	−5.670	—	−5.670
(SE)	(2.410)	—	(2.410)
LK	3.210	−2.280	0.926
(SE)	(0.328)	(0.248)	(0.096)
LL	0.405	0.216	0.621
(SE)	(0.334)	(0.373)	(0.242)
LIND	0.117	−0.135	−0.018
(SE)	(0.068)	(0.062)	(0.080)
LEXP	0.117	0.025	0.142
(SE)	(0.034)	(0.026)	(0.036)
LIMP	−0.086	−0.038	−0.124
(SE)	(0.016)	(0.019)	(0.020)
LDIS	0.010	−0.000	0.010
(SE)	(0.007)	(0.006)	(0.005)

$R^2 = 0.999$ $F(13, 17) = 9466.8\ [0.000]$ $\sigma = 0.008$ $DW = 2.22$ RSS = 0.001
$AUTO = 0.420\ [0.664]$ $ARCH = 0.111\ [0.744]$ $NORM = 0.388\ [0.824]$

Regression 6: South Korea

1. Solved static long-run equation

$$LGDP = 7.783 + 1.268\ LK - 0.634\ LL - 0.547\ LIND + 0.090\ LEXP$$
(SE)   (8.541) (0.555)   (0.953)   (0.490)   (0.089)
$$- 0.561\ LIMP + 0.040\ LDIS$$
    (0.237)   (0.023)

Wald Test Chi^2 (6) = 1062.0 $[0.000]^{**}$

2. Analysis of the autoregressive distributed lag representation

	0	1	Σ
LGDP	−1.000	0.561	−0.439
(SE)	—	(0.200)	(0.200)
C	3.420	—	3.420
(SE)	(2.880)	—	(2.880)
LK	1.260	−0.707	0.557
(SE)	(0.475)	(0.388)	(0.166)
LL	0.463	−0.742	−0.278
(SE)	(0.520)	(0.458)	(0.345)
LIND	0.045	−0.285	−0.240
(SE)	(0.120)	(0.153)	(0.157)
LEXP	0.036	0.004	0.040
(SE)	(0.062)	(0.071)	(0.040)
LIMP	−0.292	0.046	−0.246
(SE)	(0.089)	(0.093)	(0.089)
LDIS	0.010	0.007	0.018
(SE)	(0.006)	(0.006)	(0.008)

$R^2 = 0.999$ $F(13, 17) = 1421.9\ [0.000]$ $\sigma = 0.030$ $DW = 2.56$ $RSS = 0.015$
$AUTO = 2.148\ [0.151]$ $ARCH = 1.262\ [0.279]$ $NORM = 6.859\ [0.032]^*$

Regression 7: The Philippines

1. Solved static long-run equation

$$LGDP = -5.345 + 0.340\ LK + 0.512\ LL + 0.530\ LIND + 0.096\ LEXP$$
(SE)   (4.656) (0.285)   (0.571)   (0.313)   (0.213)
$$- 0.105\ LIMP + 0.076\ LDIS$$
    (0.283)   (0.061)

Wald Test Chi^2 (6) = 480.2 $[0.000]^{**}$

2. Analysis of the autoregressive distributed lag representation

	0	1	Σ
LGDP	−1.000	0.619	−0.381
(SE)	—	(0.150)	(0.150)
C	−2.040	—	−2.040
(SE)	(1.460)	—	(1.460)
LK	1.870	−1.740	0.130
(SE)	(0.635)	(0.564)	(0.146)
LL	−0.058	0.253	0.195
(SE)	(0.204)	(0.164)	(0.189)
LIND	−0.033	0.235	0.202
(SE)	(0.129)	(0.135)	(0.110)
LEXP	0.121	−0.084	0.037
(SE)	(0.060)	(0.073)	(0.086)
LIMP	−0.033	−0.007	−0.040
(SE)	(0.084)	(0.071)	(0.110)
LDIS	0.006	0.023	0.029
(SE)	(0.019)	(0.014)	(0.020)

$R^2 = 0.997$ $F(13, 17) = 401.5 [0.000]$ $\sigma = 0.030$ $DW = 1.30$ $RSS = 0.015$
$AUTO = 2.191 [0.146]$ $ARCH = 0.153 [0.701]$ $NORM = 0.012 [0.994]$

Regression 8: Thailand

1. Solved static long-run equation

$$LGDP = 0.509 + 0.787 \, LK - 0.042 \, LL - 0.059 \, LIND + 0.223 \, LEXP$$
$$(SE) \quad (2.237) \ (0.120) \quad (0.262) \quad (0.080) \quad\quad (0.071)$$
$$- 0.217 \, LIMP - 0.004 \, LDIS$$
$$(0.126) \quad\quad (0.005)$$

Wald Test $Chi^2 (6) = 11075.0 [0.000]^{**}$

2. Analysis of the autoregressive distributed lag representation

	0	1	Σ
LGDP	−1.000	0.216	−0.784
(SE)	—	(0.179)	(0.179)
C	0.399	—	0.399
(SE)	(1.760)	—	(1.760)
LK	2.080	−1.460	0.620
(SE)	(0.499)	(0.458)	(0.166)
LL	0.011	−0.044	−0.033
(SE)	(0.162)	(0.156)	(0.206)
LIND	−0.047	0.000	−0.047
(SE)	(0.074)	(0.071)	(0.062)
LEXP	0.079	0.096	0.174
(SE)	(0.056)	(0.056)	(0.056)
LIMP	−0.162	−0.008	−0.170
(SE)	(0.074)	(0.063)	(0.091)
LDIS	−0.001	−0.002	−0.003
(SE)	(0.004)	(0.004)	(0.004)

$R^2 = 0.999$ $F(13, 17) = 1912.3 [0.000]$ $\sigma = 0.022$ $DW = 2.26$ $RSS = 0.009$
$AUTO = 3.339 [0.063]$ $ARCH = 0.002 [0.968]$ $NORM = 0.046 [0.977]$

Notes:
R^2 = squared multiple correlation coefficient; F = F−test for the null hypothesis that all the regression's coefficients are zero (excluding the intercept).
σ = standard error of regression.
DW = Durbin–Watson autocorrelation test.
RSS = residual sum of squares.
$AUTO$ = Lagrange multiplier autocorrelation test (F−test, 2nd order).
$ARCH$ = autoregressive conditional heteroscedasticity test (F−test, 1st order).
$NORM$ = Jarque-Bera normality test (Chi^2 test).
[**] = the statistical significance at the 1% level; [*] = the statistical significance at the 5% level.

APPENDIX III: ENCOMPASSING AND NON-NESTED HYPOTHESES TEST (MODEL JC FOR MODEL 1 AND MODEL EG FOR MODEL 2, 1962–91)

Test 1: Japan

Model 1 v. Model 2	Form	Test	Form	Model 2 v. Model 1
–0.520591	N(0,1)	Cox	N(0,1)	–0.811079
0.436499	N(0,1)	Ericsson IV	N(0,1)	0.672283
0.189864	$Chi^2(1)$	Sargan	$Chi^2(1)$	0.449517
0.182812	F(1,21)	Joint model	F(1,21)	0.438034
[0.6733]				[0.5153]

Test 2: South Korea

Model 1 v. Model 2	Form	Test	Form	Model 2 v. Model 1
–6.0989	N(0,1)	Cox	N(0,1)	–0.289411
4.05489	N(0,1)	Ericsson IV	N(0,1)	0.243747
6.84211	$Chi^2(1)$	Sargan	$Chi^2(1)$	0.0560685
9.47918	F(1,21)	Joint model	F(1,21)	0.0536567
[0.0057]				[0.8191]

Test 3: The Philippines (Model JC(B) for Model 1)

Model 1 v. Model 2	Form	Test	Form	Model 2 v. Model 1
–2.17999	N(0,1)	Cox	N(0,1)	–0.655004
1.68802	N(0,1)	Ericsson IV	N(0,1)	0.533238
1.63798	$Chi^2(1)$	Sargan	$Chi^2(1)$	0.235059
1.69195	F(1,20)	Joint model	F(1,20)	0.2264
[0.2081]				[0.6394]

Test 4: Thailand

Model 1 v. Model 2	Form	Test	Form	Model 2 v. Model 1
–123.599	N(0,1)	Cox	N(0,1)	0.138519
59.3546	N(0,1)	Ericsson IV	N(0,1)	–0.118884
15.8391	$Chi^2(1)$	Sargan	$Chi^2(1)$	0.0153657
53.9889	F(1,21)	Joint model	F(1,21)	0.0146775
[0.0000]				[0.9047]

Notes:
Cox = the Cox non-nested hypotheses test (Cox, 1961).
Ericsson IV = the Ericsson instrumental variables test (Ericsson, 1983).
Sargan = the Sargan restricted/unrestricted reduced form test (Sargan, 1964).
Joint model = the joint model F–test which checks whether each model parsimoniously encompasses the linear nesting model.

APPENDIX IV: TESTING EXOGENEITY: GENERAL COINTEGRATION TEST (A = 0 FOR LIND)

Japan

Standardized β′ eigenvectors

LGDP	LK	LL	LIND	LEXP	LIMP	LDIS	Constant
1.000	−0.744	−0.479	0.018	−0.114	0.092	−0.008	4.443
−0.203	1.000	1.666	−1.420	−0.518	0.254	0.030	−15.990
−0.641	0.205	1.000	0.156	0.232	−0.132	0.016	−9.408
−50.610	13.270	221.200	1.000	−3.270	12.500	5.719	−2232.00
38.220	−7.050	27.740	−33.860	1.000	2.780	0.818	−326.800
4.751	−2.415	−5.178	−0.592	0.245	1.000	−0.248	45.270

Standardized α coefficients

LGDP	0.263	0.098	0.647	−0.003	0.003	−0.020
LK	0.447	0.016	0.232	−0.001	0.0004	−0.009
LL	0.042	0.061	0.087	−0.001	−0.001	0.005
LIND	0.000	0.000	−0.012	−0.003	0.024	−0.017
LEXP	0.020	0.285	−3.391	0.007	−0.018	−0.088
LIMP	0.036	0.070	−3.369	−0.007	−0.016	−0.294
LDIS	−0.075	−1.994	−9.223	0.039	−0.022	0.067

log likelihood = 815.66   unrestricted log likelihood = 815.66
LR–test, rank = 6: Chi^2 ($\approx$ 0) = 0.000 [0.999]

South Korea

Standardized β′ eigenvectors

LGDP	LK	LL	LIND	LEXP	LIMP	LDIS	Constant
1.000	−3.267	1.111	2.681	0.288	0.582	−0.069	−12.210
−0.433	1.000	−0.904	−0.679	0.079	−0.524	0.030	9.997
−0.135	−0.186	1.000	0.144	−0.102	0.085	−0.043	−8.539
−2.234	−0.063	2.975	1.000	−0.003	0.091	0.055	−23.790
−5.253	1.939	1.963	1.461	1.000	−2.703	0.037	−6.912
−4.260	1.438	2.621	1.474	−0.636	1.000	0.017	−22.860

Standardised α coefficients

LGDP	0.083	0.185	−0.265	−0.121	0.039	0.067
LK	0.074	0.028	−0.048	0.059	0.019	−0.030
LL	0.021	0.048	−0.092	−0.052	−0.009	0.002
LIND	0.000	0.000	0.000	0.000	0.000	−0.136
LEXP	0.090	1.721	0.992	−0.069	−0.067	0.053
LIMP	−0.085	0.405	0.535	0.335	0.137	−0.261
LDIS	−0.119	−4.314	12.670	−3.306	1.702	−0.333

log likelihood = 640.546   unrestricted log likelihood = 640.546
LR–test, rank = 6: Chi^2 ($\approx$ 0) = 0.000 [0.999]

The Philippines

Standardized β' eigenvectors

LGDP	LK	LL	LIND	LEXP	LIMP	LDIS	Constant
1.000	−0.617	−0.319	−0.570	−0.231	0.540	−0.061	3.843
−0.593	1.000	−1.180	−0.028	0.890	−0.660	−0.167	9.601
−0.513	−0.395	1.000	0.189	−0.134	0.463	0.113	−8.564
0.050	1.338	−3.107	1.000	−0.884	0.639	0.286	20.670
2.316	−1.677	1.059	2.297	1.000	−2.895	0.150	−13.310
−8.389	6.360	−3.099	3.235	−0.961	1.000	−0.686	22.750

Standardized α coefficients

LGDP	0.116	−0.023	0.193	−0.011	0.037	0.013
LK	0.179	0.026	0.053	−0.002	0.015	−0.003
LL	0.078	0.248	0.043	0.112	0.013	−0.003
LIND	0.000	0.000	0.181	0.051	−0.033	−0.014
LEXP	0.146	−0.668	−0.647	−0.019	0.158	0.098
LIMP	0.088	0.084	−0.076	−0.108	0.227	0.008
LDIS	0.298	1.340	−0.868	−0.901	−0.424	0.177

log likelihood = 648.604   unrestricted log likelihood = 651.34
LR–test, rank = 6: Chi^2 ($\approx$ 0) = 0.001 [0.999]

Thailand

Standardized β' eigenvectors

LGDP	LK	LL	LIND	LEXP	LIMP	LDIS	Constant
1.000	−0.811	0.165	−0.054	−0.313	0.490	0.004	−1.746
−0.988	1.000	−0.400	−0.316	0.319	−0.130	−0.004	3.466
1.768	−1.544	1.000	0.140	−0.027	−0.692	0.027	−7.572
−1.422	−1.168	4.591	1.000	−0.351	0.585	0.077	−40.080
4.265	−2.600	−2.936	0.237	1.000	0.012	0.138	21.950
4.232	−0.587	−5.095	−0.259	−2.475	1.000	0.056	44.560

Standardized α coefficients

LGDP	0.196	0.453	−0.058	0.060	−0.015	0.002
LK	0.269	0.127	0.025	0.010	0.006	−0.003
LL	0.123	0.246	−0.117	−0.102	0.026	0.013
LIND	0.000	0.000	0.000	0.000	0.000	0.000
LEXP	0.010	0.116	0.540	−0.107	−0.114	0.046
LIMP	0.058	0.625	0.747	−0.104	0.044	−0.019
LDIS	−0.011	−2.034	−2.122	−2.021	−1.960	−0.585

log likelihood = 622.357   unrestricted log likelihood = 631.268
LR–test, rank = 6: Chi^2 ($\approx$ 6) = 17.823 [0.007]**

Notes:
1. The degrees of freedom as reported for the general restriction test are approximate and cannot be guaranteed to be correct for all possible restrictions.
2. The general restriction tests are based on the cointegration tests reported in Appendix I.
LR–test: likelihood ratio test.
** = 1% significance level.

APPENDIX V: DATA DESCRIPTION

1.   Growth Accounting (1960–91)

Q: gross domestic product (GDP) at the factor cost (1985 price, billion US$), taken from the *National Account Statistics* (various issues) by the United Nations.

K: capital stock (1985 price, billion US$), constructed by the perpetual inventory method,

$$K_t = I_t + (1 - \delta)^* K_{t-1}$$

where I (investment) is the gross fixed capital formation in *International Financial Statistics* (various issues) by the International Monetary Fund; δ (depreciation rate) is set to be the conventional rate of 5 per cent. K_{t-1} (initial capital stock, 1959 data) taken from the World Bank database, '*STARS*'.

L: actual employment (thousands), taken from *International Labour Statistics* (various issues) by the International Labour Organization.

v_L: labour factor share, estimated from the labour income (wages and social benefits) share in output. The relevant data are taken from *National Account Statistics* (various issues) by the United Nations.

v_K: capital factor share, ($v_K = 1 - v_L$), based on the assumption of constant returns to scale in the basic Cobb–Douglas production function.

2.   Regression (1960–91): PcGive 8.0 and PcFiml 8.0 are used for the estimation.

Q: same as the above.

K: same as the above.

L: same as the above.

IND: the ratio (%) of industrial employment to agricultural employment, calculated by the author and based on the data from *International Labour Statistics* (various issues) by the International Labour Organization.

EXP: the export ratio (%) to output (GDP), calculated by the author and based on the data from *International Trade Statistics* (various issues) by the United Nations.

IMP: the import ratio (%) to output (GDP), calculated by the author and based on the data from *International Trade Statistics* (various issues) by the United Nations.

DIS: workers involved in labour disputes (thousands), taken from *International Labour Statistics* (various issues) by the International Labour Organization.

NOTES

1. Krugman (1994, p. 71). It should be noted, however, that his conclusion is derived from literature such as Young (1992, 1993) but not from his own estimates.
2. The second generation of Asian NICs includes Malaysia and Thailand. It should be noted that Krugman (1994) has only mentioned the Asian NICs. However, we assume from his lead that his critique is also directed at other rapidly growing Asian economies, here Thailand among our sample countries.
3. Moreover, Intriligator (1992) provides a useful survey of the embodiment hypothesis of technical progress in capital.
4. The consequence of productivity growth is the enhancement of the general standard of living of a society which is conventionally considered to be synonymous with the growth of real GDP per capita. We here define the growth of real GDP per capita as being analogous to productivity growth.
5. See, for example, De Long and Summers (1991) and Thomas and Wang (1996) in the literature.
6. These test results of unit roots at various levels may be due to the small sample bias or may suggest the fractional process of integration of these variables. There has been a growing literature on the source of non-stationarity in macroeconomic series in terms of fractionally differenced time series. For example, the fractional process of integration of times series can be shown as follows:

$$(1 - L)^d y_t = \mu + \gamma t + u_t, \quad t = 1, 2, ...,$$

   If $\mu = \gamma = 0$, if u_t is an I(0) series, and if $0 < d < 1/2$, then y_t is a covariance stationary I(d) series, having autocovariances which decay much more slowly than those of an ARIMA process; in fact, so slowly as to be non-summable (Gil-Alana and Robinson, 1997, p. 245). Moreover, the fractional process of integration of time series can also be found; for example, when $1 < d < 3/2$, which might be the case in our unit roots tests. See Gil-Alana and Robinson (1997) for a recent literature survey for the fractional process of integration of time series.
7. Banerjee *et al.* (1993) argue that there is a small sample bias in the OLS estimates of cointegrating relationships, and Hendry and Mizon (1990) demonstrate the possible parameter instability in the Dickey–Fuller (DF) and ADF tests which may damage the second stage in the EG approach.
8. In their analysis for proportionality between money and income for Finland, they chose the cointegrating relationship which is not statistically supported at the conventional 5 per cent level; however, it is in line with economic theory.
9. LIND may not be appropriate as a proxy for industrialization and technological development for Japan since the decline of Japan's agricultural employment is absorbed more by the service sector than the industrial sector. Moreover, Japan is assumed to be in a different development stage (post-industrialization) from other sample countries.
10. It should be noted that neither can the statistically substantial cointegrating relationships be obtained by the change of the dependent variable in the OLS estimates in the EG approach for three countries: South Korea, the Philippines and Thailand.
11. See Appendix V for the data description.
12. This is a test, for example, of model 1 with model 2 providing the alternative to see whether model 2 captures any specific information not embodied in model 1. The converse is whether model 1 can account for all the results found by model 2 and that idea is formalized in the notion of encompassing. Moreover, a congruent undominated model should encompass (that is, account for) the empirical findings of all company models that purport to explain the given variables(s) (see Doornik and Hendry, 1994, for details). For example, the Cox and Ericsson tests examine whether the adjusted likelihood of two rival models is compatible. The Sargan test checks whether the restricted reduced form of a structural model encompasses the unrestricted reduced form including exogenous regressors from rival models. The joint model F

test, moreover investigates whether each model parsimoniously encompasses the linear nesting model. See Hendry and Richard (1989) for details.

13. PcGive 8.0 does not compute the recursive estimates with the presence of our dummy variable in any models for the Philippines. We thus conduct the recursive estimates for the Philippines without the dummy variable, which may exaggerate our test results, so they should be treated with extreme caution.

14. Johansen and Juselius (1992, p. 224).

REFERENCES

Abramovitz, M. (1993), 'The search for the sources of growth: areas of ignorance, old and new', *Journal of Economic History*, 53, 217–43.

Banerjee, Anindya, Juan J. Dolado, John W. Galbraith and David F. Hendry (1993), *Co-integration, Error-correction, and the Econometric Analysis of Non-stationary Data*, Oxford: Oxford University Press.

Christensen, Laurits R., Dianne Cummings and Dale W. Jorgenson (1980), 'Economic growth, 1947–73: an international comparison', in John W. Kendrick and Beatrice N. Vaccara (eds), *New Developments in Productivity Measurement and Analysis*, Chicago: University of Chicago Press.

Cox, D.R. (1961), 'Tests of separate families of hypotheses', in *Proceedings of the Fourth Berkeley Symposium on Mathematical Statistics and Probability, vol.1*, Berkeley: University of California Press.

De Long, J. Bradford and Lawrence H. Summers (1991), 'Equipment investment and economic growth', *Quarterly Journal of Economics*, 106, 445–502.

Dickey, D.A. and W.A. Fuller (1979), 'Distribution of the estimators for autoregressive time series with a unit root', *Journal of the American Statistical Association*, 74, 427–31.

Dickey, D.A. and W.A. Fuller (1981), 'Likelihood ratio statistics for autoregressive time series with a unit root', *Econometrics*, 49, 1057–72.

Dickey, David A., Dennis W. Jansen and Daniel L. Thornton (1991), 'A primer on cointegration with an application to money and income', *Federal Reserve Bank of St. Louis Review*, 73, 58–78.

Doornik, Jurgen A. and David F. Hendry (1994), *PcGive 8.0: An Interactive Econometric Modelling System*, London: International Thomson Publishing.

Englander, A. Stern and Axel Mittelstadt (1988), 'Total factor productivity: macroeconomic and structural aspects of the slowdown', *OECD Economic Studies*, 10, 7–56.

Engle, Robert F., and C.W.J. Granger (1987), 'Co-integration and error correction: representation, estimation and testing', *Econometrica*, 55, 251–76.

Engle, R.F., D.F. Hendry and Jean-François Richard (1983), 'Exogeneity', *Econometrica*, 51, 277–304.

Ericsson, Neil R. (1983), 'Asymptotic properties of instrumental variables statistics for testing non-nested hypotheses', *Review of Economic Studies*, 50, 287–303.

Gil-Alana, L.A. and P.M. Robinson (1997), 'Testing of unit root and other non-stationary hypotheses in macroeconomic time series', *Journal of Econometrics*, 80, 241–68.

Hendry, David F. and Grayham E. Mizon (1990), 'Evaluating dynamic econometric models by encompassing the VAR', *University of Oxford Applied Economics Discussion Paper no. 102*.

Hendry, David F. and J.-F. Richard (1989), 'Recent developments in the theory of encompassing', in B. Cornet and H. Tulkens (eds), *Contributions to Operations*

Research and Econometrics, The XXth Anniversary of CORE, Cambridge, MA: MIT Press.

Hulten, Charles R. (1992), 'Growth accounting when technical change is embodied in capital', *American Economic Review*, 82, 964–80.

Hurn, Stan and Vito Antonio Muscatelli (1992), 'Co-integration and dynamic time series models', *Journal of Economic Surveys*, 6, 1–43.

International Labour Organization (ILO), *International Labour Statistics (ILS)*, various issues, Geneva: ILO.

International Monetary Fund (IMF), *International Financial Statistics (IFS)*, various issues, Washington, DC: IMF.

Intriligator, Michael D. (1992), 'Productivity and the embodiment of technical progress', *Scandinavian Journal of Economics*, 94, S75–87.

Johansen, Soren and Katarina Juselius (1990), 'Maximum likelihood estimation and inference on co-integration with applications to the demand for money', *Oxford Bulletin of Economics and Statistics*, 52, 169–209.

Johansen, Soren and Katarina Juselius (1992), 'Testing structural hypothesis in a multivariate co-integration analysis of the PPP and the UIP for UK', *Journal of Econometrics*, 53, 211–44.

Jorgenson, Dale W., Frank M. Gollop and Barbara M. Fraumeni (1987), *Productivity and US Economic Growth*, Cambridge, MA: Harvard University Press.

Kim, Jong-Il and Lawrence J. Lau (1994), 'The sources of economic growth of the East Asian newly industrialised countries', *Journal of the Japanese and International Economics*, 8, 235–71.

Krugman, Paul (1994), 'The myth of Asia's miracle', *Foreign Affairs*, 73, 62–78.

Maddison, Angus (1982), *Phases of Capitalist Development*, Oxford: Oxford University Press.

Maddison, Angus (1987), 'Growth and slowdown in advanced capitalist economies: techniques of quantitative assessment', *Journal of Economic Literature*, 25, 649–98.

Phillips, P.C.B. and Pierre Perron (1988), 'Testing for a unit root in time series regression', *Biometrika*, 75, 335–46.

Sargan, J.D. (1964), 'Wages and prices in the United Kingdom: a study in econometric methodology', in P.E. Hart, G. Mills and J.K. Whitaker (eds), *Econometric Analysis for National Economic Planning, vol. 16 of Colston Papers*, London: Butterworth Co.; reprinted in D.F. Hendry and K.F. Wallis (eds) (1984), *Econometrics and Quantitative Economics*, Oxford: Basil Blackwell, and in J.D. Sargan (1988), *Contributions to Econometrics, vol.1*, Cambridge: Cambridge University Press.

Thomas, Vinod and Yan Wang (1996), 'Distortions, inventions and productivity growth: is East Asia different?', *Economic Development and Cultural Change*, 44, 265–88.

United Nations (1981, 1992), *World Tables*, Baltimore: Johns Hopkins University Press.

United Nations *International Trade Statistics*, various issues, New York: United Nations.

United Nations *National Accounts Statistics*, various issues, New York: United Nations.

Young, Alwyn (1992), 'A tale of two cities: factor accumulation and technical change in Hong Kong and Singapore', *NBER Macroeconomic Review 1992*, 13–54.

Young, Alwyn (1993), 'The tyranny of numbers: confronting the statistical realities of the East Asian growth experience', MIT, unpublished paper.

Young, Alwyn (1995), 'Tyranny of numbers: confronting the statistical realities of the East Asian growth experience', *Quarterly Journal of Economics*, 110, 641–80.

15. The impact of FDI on the economic growth of the ASEAN-5 economies, 1970–94: a comparative dynamic multiplier analysis from a small model, with emphasis on liberalization

A. Bende-Nabende, J.L. Ford and J.R. Slater

INTRODUCTION

Research by classical economists[1] focused on the importance of factors of production in improving efficiency and productivity within an economy. Neo-classical economists including Solow (1957) and Denison (1985) changed this focus by introducing the concept of convergence in their models. However, these models were undermined by the assumption of diminishing returns to capital, which meant that the growth of output could not be accounted for adequately by the growth of inputs, thereby raising the question as to whether the long-term per capita growth would be determined by an *exogenous* factor, such as technical progress.

Much recent research has been devoted to the formulation of models in which the key determinants of long-run growth are endogenous, leading to the creation of the 'new' or 'endogenous' growth theory.[2] However, the first endogenous models had deficiencies,[3] which prompted researchers including Van der Phoeg and Tang (1992), UNCTAD (1992), Barro (1991) and Levin and Renelt (1992) to investigate the potential role in the economic growth process of a combination of factors. These embrace such factors as improvements in the quality of the economy's labour, improvements that emanate from better health, more education and greater access to training (that is, human resources development), technological change, international trade and government policy.

In the recent past, it has been hypothesized that foreign direct investment (FDI) has also been making an increasingly important contribution to the economic growth of developing host countries through its positive spillover effects on the above mentioned factors.[4] However, the empirical investigations have remained minimal. Moreover, their analyses have been based upon structural forms of the models and, hence, on the 'static' effects.[5]

In view of this, we present an empirical dynamic analysis which permits us to use the *multiplier* methodology. We investigate the dynamic effects of the impact of policy on FDI and, hence, its spillover–effects variables, and consequently on the economic growth process of the ASEAN-5 economies. We seek to find out what effect a change in policy *vis-à-vis* the level of economic development has on (a) the decision-making process of the foreign investors, (b) the speed of the spillover process, (c) the magnitude of the multiplier effects, and (d) the degree of the relocation of production. However, for space-saving purposes, we put emphasis on one policy variable – *liberalization* – and offer only a remark or two about the other policy variables: much of the information concerning them is provided in the appendices.

The chapter is, therefore, organized as follows. The next section briefly outlines the model and hypotheses, while our methodology is the subject of the third section. The empirical results are presented in the fourth section whose sub-sections cover in turn, the impact of liberalization multipliers on FDI, on human skills, on employment, on new technology transfer, on international trade, on learning-by-doing, and on the growth of output, ending with a summary of the impact of the other policy variables' multipliers. Concluding remarks summarizing the principal findings are the focus of the fifth section.

THE MODEL AND HYPOTHESES

Our model is founded upon the hypothesis that the growth of real per capita domestic output is a function of FDI, and since FDI has been positively associated with spillover effects that lead to human resources development, new technology transfer, capital formation, expansion of international trade, and learning-by-doing in developing countries, then the growth (Gr) of real per capita domestic output is a linear function of these variables.[6] For instance:

$$Gr_t = [FDI_t, HS_t, EMP_t, TT_t, IT_t, LD_t]^7 \qquad (15.1)$$

We hypothesize further:

1. The response of transnational companies (TNCs) to policy liberalization is expected to take place in the period *after* liberalization, particularly for the less developed countries, indicating that the TNCs need to build confidence and certainty about the liberalization process through a 'wait and see'

response. This is based on the assumption that the TNCs need to prove that what the policy makers propose is actually implemented before making any financial commitments.

2. The speed of the spillover process may *slow down* as the level of economic development increases owing to the more involving interaction effects of the policy variables on the spillover effects variables and then on real per capita GDP growth.

3. The magnitude of the multiplier effects should *increase* as the level of economic development increases owing to the higher influence of the spillover effects.

4. The dynamic changes in the sources of comparative advantages are expected *increasingly* to promote the relocation of production as the level of economic development increases.

The variables on the right-hand side of equation (15.1) are taken to be endogenous and so six equations have been developed to explain them. The general state of the proposed structural relationship is provided in Appendix II, where the dependent variables are in the top row and the independent in the first column. The expected signs of the coefficients are also illustrated in the table.

A Brief Discussion of the Hypothesis

Foreign direct investment: FDI capital inflows increase the quality and quantity of the host country's stock of physical capital, increase domestic savings and the investment/GDP ratio, and reduce the host country's foreign exchange burden, a combination which may lead to economic growth. The hypothesis tests the impact of FDI on economic growth. FDI capital inflows are measured as an annual percentage ratio of net FDI inflows to GDP.

Human skills (HS): education and training lead to acquisition of skills, facilitate the diffusion of technology, promote entrepreneurship and hence raise productivity and, therefore, stimulate economic growth. The hypothesis tests the impact of human skills on economic growth. The variable human skills is, for simplicity, proxied by the annual number of students enrolled for secondary education.[8] A higher secondary school enrolment means a higher accumulation of human skills. Thus, if higher-quality human skills means higher economic growth, higher secondary school enrolment should lead to higher economic growth.

Employment (EMP): employment increases personal income, which may lead to higher consumption and hence demand, generates skills in the process of learning-by-doing and facilitates the diffusion of technology which promotes productivity. These factors collectively stimulate economic growth. The hypothesis tests the impact of employment on economic growth. Employment is proxied by the annual labour force employed by the manufacturing sector.

New Technology Transfer (TT): new technology improves the efficiency of production, product quality and range, and induces competition and, hence, improves factor productivity, which stimulates economic growth. The hypothesis tests the impact of the transfer of new technology from the developed to the developing economies on the latter's economic growth. In the absence of data on the expenditure on R&D, which is a good proxy for technology, annual imports of machinery and equipment as a percentage ratio of GDP are used as a proxy. We assume that technology is transferred through the importation of new capital goods and equipment, and components and parts, in which it is embedded.

International Trade (IT): international trade eases supply constraints of the host country, promotes competition and innovation, and increases demand for the host country's products, which helps to reduce the shortage of foreign exchange and, therefore, to improve its balance of payments position and, hence, stimulate economic growth. Export expansion is expected to stimulate the demand for factor inputs (which may result in import expansion as well) and enlarge the scale of operations. The hypothesis tests the impact of international trade on economic growth. International trade is proxied by total annual exports of goods and services as a percentage ratio of GDP.

Learning-by-doing (LD): learning-by-doing leads to experience. When a process is endlessly repeated, the direct cost of manufacturing a unit of the good is expected to decline as a result of increased productivity. That is, scale economies result from savings which result from accumulated learning which accompanies repetition. The hypothesis tests the impact of learning by doing on economic growth. Learning-by-doing is proxied by annual manufacturing value added as a percentage ratio of GDP.[9]

The notation used for the eight exogenous variables is GP = government policy (liberalization), MS = domestic market size, RWR = relative wage rates, IF = infrastructure, PS = personal savings, GE = government expenditure on education, XR = foreign exchange rates, and T = time trend.

We should point out with regard to government policy (GP or liberalization) and the measurement of the other exogenous variables that FDI can be induced by positive liberalization of policy, as seen by TNCs. This includes FDI policy and trade policy liberalization. Under FDI policy liberalization, the policy package includes ownership policies, taxes/subsidies (including tariffs and transfer payments), convertibility of currency (including limits on dividends, and royalties and fees), price controls and performance requirements (such as export, local content and foreign exchange balancing abilities). Trade policy liberalization, on the other hand, involves the reductions of restrictions and tariffs on the merchandise being traded and therefore making the country in question more open and easier to trade with.[10] Positive liberalization as seen by the TNCs is expected to have a positive impact on FDI inflows by allowing a freer flow of goods and services and, hence, freer participation of TNCs. It leads to a freer movement and a larger volume of international trade and, hence, goods and capital products in which new technology is embedded. Liberalization has been proxied by exports plus imports (less exports of mining and quarrying, and imports of fuel – to remove the aggregate influence of oil) as a percentage ratio of GDP. This proxy is commonly used to measure the level of openness of the economy.[11] The data sources are presented in Appendix I.

THE IMPACT, INTERIM AND TOTAL MULTIPLIER METHODOLOGY

Much as the theoretical simultaneous system of equations in the model consists of the specified explanatory variables, the 'dynamism' of these explanatory variables is expected to vary slightly from country to country owing to the different country-specific characteristics. In order to get the true relationships between the explanatory variables and the dependent variables, first, scatter diagrams were observed, followed by an investigation of the partial regressions of each individual relevant explanatory variable on the respective dependent variables. The best combinations were then selected for use in the analysis by looking at the adjusted R^2, F-statistic, D-W statistic and the t-statistic. That is to say, the determination of the lags was a matter of empirical manipulation based on the criteria of goodness of fit and of statistical significance of the relevant coefficients. The experimentation was then extended to the single seven equations and estimated using the OLS technique, and then to the model and estimated using the 3SLS technique.

The lag structure for the growth equation demonstrates that FDI has an immediate impact on the Philippines but is lagged for Indonesia (4), Malaysia (4) and Singapore (5).[12] *HS*, which was significant only for Malaysia, has a four-year lag, while *EMP* has no lag for the more developed Malaysia and Singapore, but is lagged for the less developed Indonesia (4) and the Philippines (1). *TT* takes a 5 period lag in the least developed Indonesia and in the most developed Singapore, but is immediate (or almost immediate) in the moderately developed Malaysia (0) and Thailand (1).[13] *IT* has a 1 period lag for all the countries except Indonesia, where it has no lag. The lag length for *LD* in general increases as the level of economic development increases. The equation for *FDI* shows that, as the level of economic development increases, the lag structure of *Gr* and *RWR* decreases, but *HS* and *IF* increase. The coefficients, signs and lag structures for the parameters estimated for the model for each country are presented in Appendix III.[14]

Experimentation was also carried out on the instrumental variables. The best set of instrumental variables for each country ended up coinciding with the set of the predefined variables both for the system and for each equation.

Unit root tests to find stationarity were carried out, and demonstrated that most of the variables were non-stationary in their levels, but stationary in their first differences. That is, they were I(1) and used as Δs for all variables except *Gr*. The system was then tested for serial correlation using the LM test, for multicollinearity, for heteroskedasticity (White's test) and for ARCH.

Each of the structural equations in the above model have served to describe part of the structure of the economy. The coefficients of the structural equations have provided tests on qualitative and quantitative prepositions of economic theory. The structural model has depicted economic mechanisms in terms of direct determinants. It has, however, been only an implicit description of the economic process. For instance, it has included current and lagged endogenous variables together with the other exogenous variables (current and lagged) on the determinant side. The endogenous variables have themselves been accounted for in other structural equations.

However, the reduced form of such a system is not suitable for the calculation of the effects of exogenous changes on the behaviour of the endogenous variables when there are lagged endogenous variables. This requires the construction of a *final form* which is capable of describing the current endogenous variables in terms of current and lagged exogenous variables and disturbances, obtained by a repeated elimination of all lagged endogenous variables from the reduced form.

The final form method is a dynamic system that is able to make forecasts of current endogenous variables over a period of time when it is provided with observed values of exogenous variables over this period and values of lagged endogenous variables for only the first year of the period. In successive periods it can draw upon its own past forecasts to provide values for the remaining predetermined variables. In this way, it is capable of providing effects of what Goldberger (1959) has called *impact, interim* and *total* multipliers.[15]

Impact multipliers express that part of the response of endogenous variables to changes of predetermined variables which occurs in the first year. Interim multipliers, on the other hand, describe the effect of exogenous changes during a given later time, while total multipliers describe the total effect of an exogenous change from the current time to the very end (that is, until its effects become zero).

Derivation of the Final Form[16]

If the reduced form of a structural model is denoted by

$$y_\alpha = d_0 + D_1 y_{\alpha-1} + D_2 x_\alpha + D_3 x_{\alpha-1} + \varepsilon_\alpha, \tag{15.2}$$

where:
y_α is the vector of endogenous variables in period α,
x_α is the vector of exogenous variables in period α,
d_0 is the L-element vector of constant terms in reduced form,
ε_α is the L-element vector of error terms in reduced form, and
D_1, D_2 and D_3 are matrices of multiplicative reduced-form coefficients (D_1 being square and D_2 and D_3 being of the same order),

then the effect of an exogenous change on an endogenous variable in the same period is determined by the appropriate element of the matrix D_2 in equation (15.2). Replacing $y_{\alpha-1}$ with the left-hand side of (15.2) lagged one period shows that matrix D_3 does not provide the effect one period later because of the indirect effect via the term $D_1 y_{\alpha-1}$, that is, the equation becomes:

$$y_\alpha = (I + D_1)d_0 + D_1^2 y_{\alpha-2} + D_2 x_\alpha + (D_1 D_2 + D_3)x_{\alpha-1}$$
$$+ D_1 D_3 x_{\alpha-2} + \varepsilon_\alpha + D_1 e_{\alpha-1}. \qquad (15.3)$$

Applying this substitution s times and assuming that in the limit $s \to \infty$ gives:

$$y_\alpha = (I + D_1)^{-1}d_0 + D_2 x_\alpha + \sum D_1^{t-1}(D_1 D_2 + D_3)\, x_{\alpha-t} + \sum D_1^t \varepsilon_{\alpha-t}, \quad (15.4)$$

which is a vector equation known as the final form of the equation system. Isolation of the matrices gives the following successive coefficient matrices of the final form:

$$D_2 \quad D_1 D_2 + D_3 \quad D_1(D_1 D_2 + D_3) \quad D_1^2(D_1 D_2 + D_3) \ldots D_1^{t-1}(D_1 D_2 + D_3). \qquad (15.5)$$

The impact multipliers are described by the elements of matrix D_2, that is, the immediate (current) effect of exogenous changes. The elements of the third matrix, $D_1(D_1 D_2 + D_3)$ $D_1^2(D_1 D_2 + D_3) \ldots D_1^{t-1}(D_1 D_2 + D_3)$, describe the interim multipliers, that is, the effect during given later periods. Adding all the matrices of the sequence (15.2) gives the total multiplier effects of the system which, after some algebra and rearrangement, can be represented by

$$G = (I - D_1)^{-1}(D_2 + D_3), \qquad (15.6)$$

where G is the matrix of total multipliers; and I is an identity matrix.

EMPIRICAL ANALYSIS

As mentioned in the preceding section, in order to economize on the degrees of freedom when experimenting with the dynamic specifications of the equations, only those regressors that had significant coefficients in the structural model have been retained.[17] This has meant that the determinants of the respective endogenous variables have varied across countries owing to the different individual country-specific characteristics. It has also meant, therefore, that the exogenous and hence *policy* variables, as they will be referred to in this chapter, have similarly varied across countries. This implies that the structure of the final forms of the models for the countries under study has also differed slightly, with some of the policy variables appearing/accounting for some endogenous variables for some countries and not appearing/accounting for others.

The hypothesis and, therefore, the model that has been developed in the structural analysis have been designed to capture the impacts of FDI and, hence, its spillover effects variables, on real per capita GDP growth. Since all the variables in the growth equation have been treated as endogenous, it implies that the policy variables only have an effect on real per capita GDP growth indirectly via the spillover effects variables. This means that there is need to understand, first, how these variables affect the spillover effects variables and, then, to link that effect to real per capita GDP growth. The fact that the spillover effects variables are a direct consequence of FDI also means that there is need to understand first how the relevant policy variables directly affect FDI before identifying the indirect effects of other policy variables via the other endogenous variables. In this context, therefore, it is logical that the policy multiplier effects are first analysed for FDI, followed by the spillover effects variables *HS*, *EMP*, *TT*, *IT* and *LD*, and then, finally, that the indirect effects on real per capita GDP growth are assessed. For space-saving purposes, we choose one policy variable, liberalization (*GP*) and trace its multiplier effects on FDI, followed by its effects on the spillover effects variables, that is, on all the endogenous variables, and finally on the growth of output. The detailed results for liberalization multipliers are presented in Appendix IV.[18]

As the analysis has been conducted using first differences, a multiplier impact in this case is described by a *rate of change* or an *acceleration*; that is, it measures the acceleration or rate of change of the endogenous variable that results from a percentage change in a change in the policy variable. This means that positive multiplier values show acceleration effects, while negative values represent deceleration effects.

The Impact of Liberalization Multipliers on FDI

The multiplier effects of liberalization on FDI vary across the countries. The analysis shows the effects of both current and lagged liberalization. These effects are reported in Tables 15.1 and 15.2, and Figures 15.1 and 15.2.[19]

Current liberalization

The multipliers show that current liberalization has an immediate effect for Malaysia, Singapore and Thailand – the more advanced, more politically stable and more open economies – and a lagged effect for Indonesia (–2) and the Philippines (–1), the less advanced, less politically stable and less open economies. This is indicative of the confidence (or lack of confidence) and, hence, certainty (or uncertainty) these conditions create for the investment climate. It demonstrates that, once the political situation is stable, and the environment conducive to foreign investment, FDI responds immediately to liberalization; otherwise, the investors pursue the hypothesized 'wait and see' strategy as they monitor the situation.

Table 15.1   Impact of liberalization multipliers on FDI

Year	0	1	2	3	4	5	6	Total
Indonesia	0	0	0.722	0	0	0	0	0.722
Malaysia	13.52	5.447	–4.802	0.158	–0.0474	0.0012	–0.00047	14.2775
Philippines	0	0.14157	0	–0.01801	0	–0.00393	–0.0022	0.118873
Singapore	–2.934	–179.3	0.079	4.853	–0.00297	–0.13139	0.0001	–177.427
Thailand	98.620	30.355	0	0	0	0	0	128.975

The immediate impact of liberalization on FDI is greatest for Thailand, followed by Malaysia and Singapore. In Thailand, a percentage increase in a change in liberalization almost doubles the rate of growth of FDI inflows (that is, it accelerates by 99 per cent) in the first year, but reduces to 30 per cent in the second year and then peters out thereafter. This is not surprising since Thailand is currently regarded as one of the most attractive countries for FDI in South Asia because of its comparative advantage stemming from a private enterprise economy, plentiful cheap labour and positive attitudes towards foreign investment. For Thailand, therefore, liberalization causes an acceleration effect which is spread over two years, but with the heaviest impact in the initial year.

For Singapore, a percentage increase in a change in liberalization creates an immediate deceleration of FDI inflows of about 3 per cent, followed by another deceleration of 180 per cent in the second year. A possible explanation for this behaviour is that based on the reorganizational type of investment that leads to the relocation of production and that has been associated with the 'flying-geese' type of development and the 'billiard-ball' shifts in FDI within the region;[20] and rationalization of investment from outside the region and, hence, the international division of labour in the ASEAN-5 economies.[21] It has to be noted that it is almost the same TNCs that are operating in the ASEAN and South Asian region as a whole, particularly those that are using the region as a centre for sourcing production. Since the human capital in Singapore is highly skilled and undergoes refresher skills training courses from time to time, it is capable not only of handling fairly sophisticated production processes and, hence, sophisticated machinery and equipment, but also of adopting the new processes and technology very fast. This has made Singapore's production process very dynamic, involving continuous upgrading and/or replacement of old machinery in a bid to produce the high-tech, high-value added goods that are more competitive in the global market place.[22] When liberalization takes place, the TNCs in Singapore take it as an opportunity to relocate the current production to the neighbouring less developed countries, where the quality of manpower is lower, the infrastructure is less sophisticated and the production processes require the use of less sophisticated machinery and, hence, where this combination of factors is suitable for the type of production processes, and where they are regarded as 'modern', much as they are deemed 'obsolete' in Singapore. The production process is then modernized by installing new and more sophisticated machinery, which itself is probably relocated from Japan and the other more developed countries where it has become obsolete vis-à-vis these countries' factor endowments, but nevertheless can provide efficiency gains for the TNCs when utilized in Singapore. This process may involve the physical removal and transfer of old machinery and equipment. Instead of all the old machinery and equipment being made redundant and, hence, incurring unnecessary expenses in purchasing similar sets for use in the less developed countries, some of it is physically transferred to the country(ies) at a higher level in the value chain of the international division of labour (for this case, the ASEAN-4[23]) where the quality of manpower and infrastructure is on a par with such machinery and production process.

The transfer is initiated in the first year but the highest rate of transfer is experienced in the second year, probably after all the foundations (location decisions and so on) have been laid in the first year. This relocation process is finalized in the second year. Most of the new investment which can be described as relocation of investment from Japan and the other developed countries then starts in the third year (probably on the same site) and is accomplished in the fourth year; hence the positive acceleration impact of 5 per cent.[24] This time lag also gives management ample time to train their staff in the new production techniques. The presence of new technology and a skilled labour force increases efficiency, which in turn increases productivity and generates profits. This prompts further relocation of production in the fifth and sixth years in preparation for reinvestment involving machinery upgrading in the seventh year. This cycle continues until the impact fades out. The total effect is, however, negative: a deceleration of FDI inflows by about 180 per cent. This is not surprising because whatever gets relocated, particularly in the first two years, is most likely the *accumulated investment* (that is, all the investment prior to liberalization whose production processes and, hence, machinery and equipment are regarded as *obsolete* insofar as Singapore's current sources of comparative advantage dictate) whereas the new investment that comes in as new and more sophisticated machinery and equipment is, *ceteris paribus*, a standard liberalization responding inflow. This means that the massive deceleration effects experienced during the first two years outweigh the acceleration effects experienced later on.

In Malaysia, the immediate impact is an acceleration of 13.5 per cent but this reduces to 5 per cent in the second year and then decelerates by 5 per cent in the third year. A possible explanation for this is based on a concept similar to that of Singapore. The fairly dynamic nature of the comparative advantage which Malaysia currently possesses has meant that it has also started relocating production to countries above it in the value chain of the international division of labour (rationalization of investment to the less developed countries in South Asia and reorganization of investment within the ASEAN) like Singapore, but to a lesser extent. A percentage increase in a change in liberalization accelerates the inflow of new investment in the first two years, probably as a result of production relocation in Japan and the Asian NIEs, as discussed above. After the new investment, which is based on its *current* sources of comparative advantage, has been established, the 'obsolete' processes are relocated to the less developed countries, resulting in deceleration effects in the third year. The new investment then generates profits which are reinvested in the fourth year,

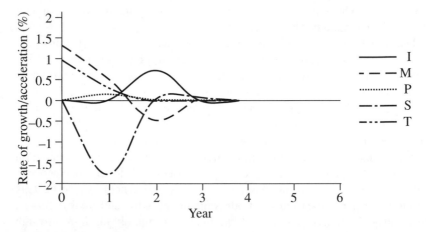

Notes: The following format has been used: M ÷ 10, S ÷100 and T ÷100; I = Indonesia, M = Malaysia, P = Philippines, S = Singapore and T = Thailand.

Figure 15.1   The impact of current liberalization multipliers on FDI

and then relocation of production takes place again in year five. This cycle continues until the impact peters out.

The lag in the Philippines probably results from the political instability which creates an uncertain investment climate and introduces the 'wait and see' attitude in foreign investors. This supports Aquino and Bolanus's (1993) suggestions of the impact of political instability on FDI in the Philippines. The lag for Indonesia probably results from its erratic way of handling foreign investment. For instance, it has remained fairly closed relative to other ASEAN countries and has been hostile to foreign investment whenever its economy has been booming. The results for Indonesia and the Philippines support the proposed 'wait and see' hypothesis. This suggests that the business investment decision process takes longer when dealing with politically unstable and foreign investment-hostile host countries. In Indonesia, however, the multipliers suggest further that, once the investors are certain that the policies have come to stay (that is, after studying/observing the environment for two years), the investment is made as a 'one-off'; that is, it comes as a lump sum, the investors having had enough time to plan and strategize. The results are similar for the Philippines, although the deceleration effects that follow after the third year suggest successive small-scale production relocation to the countries above it in the international division of labour – probably the neighbouring less developed countries in South Asia.

There is one notable difference between the behaviour of the multipliers between Singapore and the ASEAN-4. Whereas a percentage increase in a change in liberalization first leads to relocation of production and deceleration of FDI inflows in Singapore, followed by acceleration effects, the opposite happens in the ASEAN-4 economies. This probably suggests that, whereas the ASEAN-4 have alternative locations for new investment, Singapore is limited by its geographic size, so that there is need first to create room for new investment, thus warranting an initial relocation of production (reinforced by government policy).

Lagged liberalization
The multiplier effects of liberalization on FDI are not only confined to current liberalization, but include that made in the previous years as well. The results for Indonesia, Singapore and Thailand, for instance, show that lagged liberalization continues to have an impact on FDI inflows. For Indonesia, for example, whereas current liberalization creates effects in the third year, liberalization of two years earlier has an effect in the second year. For Thailand, liberalization of the previous year has an effect in the second year and that of two years earlier has an effect in the third year. For Singapore, a percentage increase in a change in liberalization of the previous year creates an accelerated multiplier effect of 5 per cent in the second year. Further observation of Singapore's results inter-

estingly reveals a pattern of effects both in magnitude and direction of liberalization of the previous year (starting in year two) similar to that of current
liberalization starting in year four onwards. That is, Singapore's lagged liberalization also has two-yearly acceleration and deceleration cycles which reflect
the investment, relocation and reinvestment activities which have been observed
under current liberalization.

Table 15.2   Impact of liberalization (lagged) multipliers on FDI

Year	0	1	2	3	4	5	6	Total
Indonesia (–2)	0	0.32109	0	0	0	0	0	0.32109
Singapore (–1)	0	4.802	–	–0.013	2.2E–5	0.0035	–	4.67498
Thailand (–1)	0	9.4254	0	0	0	0	0	9.425
Thailand (–2)	0	0	31.05	0	0	0	0	31.05

Notes: The cells represented by – show the direction of the insignificantly small multipliers; the
figures in parentheses show the year lag specifications of the determinant variable in the structural
model.

The different impacts of the respective liberalization from current to previous
years suggests that the determination of FDI (that is, investment decision
making) is not based on one particular liberalization package alone. Rather, it
is a result of the combined effects of all the packages put together. A liberalization package of one year may produce negative multiplier effects, but then
these may be neutralized or even dominated by positive multiplier effects that
result from liberalization packages stemming from other years, or vice versa.

The results demonstrate that the impact of liberalization varies across
countries. Whereas the impact is immediate in the more developed, politically
stable and foreign investment-friendly economies, there is a time lag in those
economies which are less developed, politically unstable and have an element
of hostility to foreign investment. They further reveal a high impact in those
economies that are politically stable, are consistently revising their liberalization policies and have very positive attitudes towards foreign investment. They
also reveal that, whereas liberalization in the less developed countries is
attracting FDI in a lump sum, in the more developed countries it is leading to
relocation of production, thus creating investment, relocation and reinvestment
cycles. Further, the results suggest that the already prevailing high levels of
FDI and the limited geographic size of Singapore, combined with its higher
level of economic development and its sources of comparative advantage, have
created a multiplier pattern that differs from the ASEAN-4, which are geo-
graphically relatively large but relatively less developed.

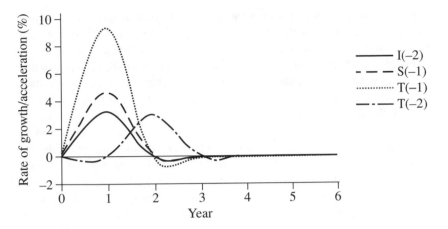

Notes: The following format has been used: I(−2) × 10 and T(−2) ÷ 10; I = Indonesia, S = Singapore and T = Thailand.
The figures in parentheses show the year lag specifications of the determinant variable in the structural model.

Figure 15.2   The Impact of lagged liberalization multipliers on FDI

The Impact of Liberalization Multipliers on Human Skills

The effect of liberalization on *HS* comes indirectly via FDI. A percentage increase in a change in liberalization causes an immediate acceleration of *HS* by 0.8 per cent for Singapore which falls to 0.0009 in the second year and then decelerates for the next three consecutive years, as can be observed in Table 15.3 and Figure 15.3.

Table 15.3   Impact of liberalization multipliers on HS

Year	0	1	2	3	4	5	6	Total
Indonesia	0	0	0	0	0	0	0	+
Malaysia	0	0	0	0	0	0	0	0
Philippines	0	0	0	0.19194	−0.04982	−0.02442	0.00634	0.108079
Singapore	0.8038	0.00091	−0.00073	−0.04445	−3E-5	0.0012	+	0.760656
Thailand	0	0	0	0	0	0	0	0

Notes: The cells represented by + or − show the direction of the insignificantly small multipliers.

A possible explanation is that liberalization attracts FDI which creates jobs (through the loosening of laws where there are tight labour markets) and, hence, employment opportunities. Its desire for certain skills also encourages people to go for further training. The mere fact that people get employed and therefore get involved in the production process improves their skills. For instance, staff may be sent on refresher courses such as industrial training in the more developed countries in order to make them better able to handle such production processes when they are installed in their factory. These are short-term courses which improve the quality of the existing labour force almost immediately. Such skills are then passed on to the other employees once the new production process is implemented. After two years, however, there is relocation of production and installation of newer and more sophisticated/mechanized production processes needed for the production of higher value-added products (as described under the effect of liberalization on FDI). These production processes, however, require the use of a smaller but highly skilled labour force. The mechanization therefore leads to job losses and creates a pool of unemployed people. The human capital becomes redundant or idle and its skills start to deteriorate. After three years, however, the new, efficient and more productive production process generates profits large enough to warrant rein-vestment. This reinvestment creates jobs once more, employs more people and improves their skills. This also prompts more relocation of production, leads to more job losses and negates *HS* once more. This cycle is repeated until its impact fades out. The total effect is a positive 0.8 per cent, suggesting that lib-eralization improves HS over a period of time.

The three-year time lag in the Philippines probably results from its political instability, as discussed earlier. The impact in the initial year is an acceleration

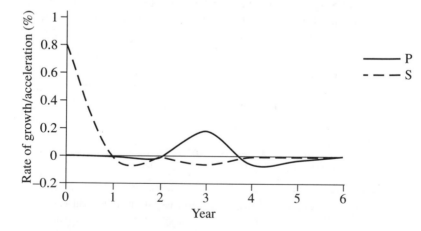

Notes: P = Philippines, and S = Singapore.

Figure 15.3 The impact of liberalization multipliers on HS

of *HS* by 0.2 per cent, followed by two-year deceleration effects and then another acceleration effect in the seventh year. An explanation for these cyclical fluctuations is the same as that for Singapore. The total impact that results from a percentage increase in a change in liberalization is an acceleration of *HS* by 0.1 per cent. The multipliers for Malaysia and Thailand show a zero effect. Those for Indonesia are also zero, but the total multiplier is positive, though negligibly small.

The results provide evidence that liberalization has an overall positive impact on *HS*. The impact is, however, more significant in the more developed countries.

The Impact of Liberalization Multipliers on Employment

The significant results for the liberalization multipliers reported in Table 15.4 and Figure 15.4 are for a significantly developed *vis-à-vis* a moderately developed country. The effect of liberalization on *EMP* comes indirectly via FDI.

Table 15.4   Impact of liberalisation multipliers on EMP

Year	0	1	2	3	4	5	6	Total
Indonesia	0	0	0	0	0	0	0	+
Malaysia	4.1759	6.0711	−1.483	0.04895	−0.01465	0.00037	−0.00015	8.79851
Philippines	0	0	0	0	0	0	0	0
Singapore	65.177	0	−1.7644	−107.82	0.04777	2.9186	−0.00179	−41.5151
Thailand	0	0	0	0	0	0	0	0

Note: The cells represented by + or − show the direction of the insignificantly small multipliers.

In Singapore, a percentage increase in a change in liberalization accelerates *EMP* by 65 per cent in the initial year, but falls to zero in the second year, and then decelerates by 1.8 per cent and by 108 per cent in the next two years before it starts accelerating again. These two-yearly cycles are continued until the impact peters out. A possible explanation for the behaviour of the multipliers is that liberalization leads to capital investment which creates job opportunities and therefore employment, as described above. Once the required labour force has been employed in the first year, there is no demand for extra labour in the second year. Two years from the time of investment, however, some production is relocated and some people are laid off. In the fourth year of establishment the relocation is completed. This no doubt involves transferring most of the labour-intensive production processes, and retaining and/or installing capital-intensive production processes which require limited but highly skilled manpower. This leads to a deceleration of *EMP* by about 110 per cent. Gains from the efficiency and productivity attained from the new production system generate profits that are reinvested, thus creating more jobs and employment in the fifth and sixth years. This cycle is repeated until it peters out. The total effect is, however, negative, implying that the dominantly labour-intensive production techniques are relocated and replaced by dominantly capital-intensive production ones.

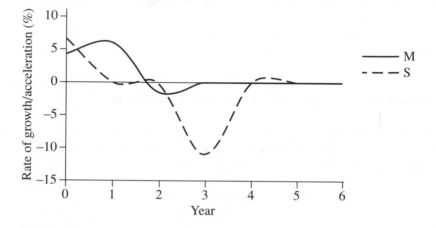

Notes: The following format has been used: S ÷ 10; M = Malaysia and S = Singapore.

Figure 15.4   The impact of liberalisation multipliers on EMP

The pattern and explanation are similar for Malaysia. The acceleration effect on *EMP* is highest in the first two years (4 and 6 per cent, respectively), but falls and decelerates by 1.5 per cent in the third year. It then fluctuates with one-yearly cycles thereafter until the effect fades out. This suggests that there are one-yearly cycles of mechanization/machinery upgrading. The total effect is positive owing to the high acceleration impacts in years one and two that outweigh the deceleration effects that are experienced later. This implies that, even though the production processes in Malaysia were upgraded from time to time, they maintained fairly labour-intensive production techniques.

These results suggest that liberalization in the more developed countries attracts FDI which creates jobs and high employment in the initial period, but this is negated by high levels of unemployment that result from the mechanization of the production process that follows the relocation of production to the less developed countries. This is driven by the desire to produce higher value-added products and is probably facilitated by the availability of a combination of high-quality human skills and infrastructure. However, for the moderately developed countries, where these two factors are of a lower quality, the overall effects are positive, since the production processes maintain the use of labour-intensive techniques. Liberalization therefore leads to labour-intensive production techniques and, hence, employment in the moderately developed countries, and to capital-intensive production techniques and, therefore, job losses (unemployment) in the more developed countries, but it has almost no effect on the less developed countries. The results also demonstrate that the impact of the multipliers increases as the level of economic development increases.

The Impact of Liberalization Multipliers on New Technology Transfer

The multipliers presented in Table 15.5 and Figure 15.5 show a one-off impact for Indonesia, Malaysia and Thailand, the largest being for Malaysia and Thailand, where a percentage increase in a change in liberalization accelerates *TT* by about 30 per cent. The one-off response has implications for the type of production prevalent in these economies, where the production activities are characterized by assembly and sourcing (to a lesser extent) which require unsophisticated machinery which, once installed, can serve in the short run without replacement. This means that such simple machinery and, hence, technology can be imported in one go.

In Singapore and the Philippines, however, the effect takes a number of years before fading out. The multipliers for the Philippines show a one-year lag probably due to the 'wait and see' attitude discussed earlier. The investment is made half-heartedly in the initial year, then the situation is monitored for another two years and finally, when the investors attain confidence in the system, the rate at which investment is made in the fifth year almost doubles the initial rate. Thereafter, there is some noticeable relocation of production which takes with it some of the existing technology before the impact fades to zero.

Table 15.5   Impact of liberalization multipliers on TT

Year	0	1	2	3	4	5	6	Total
Indonesia	0.30042	0	0	0	0	0	0	0.30042
Malaysia	31.357	0	0	0	0	0	0	31.357
Philippines	0	0.13506	0	0	0.21508	0	–0.02736	0.31566
Singapore	12.188	0.01373	–0.01101	–0.67394	–0.00046	0.01824	+	11.5339
Thailand	28.965	0	0	0	0	0	0	28.965

Note: The cells represented by + or – show the direction of the insignificantly small multipliers.

The situation for Singapore is slightly different. A percentage increase in a change in liberalization accelerates *TT* by about 12 per cent in the first year. The effect is, however, only marginal in the second year (0.01 per cent), which is probably the result of the importation of components and parts required for the initial production but whose value is rather small when compared with the initial capital investment. Its effect, however, decelerates for the next three years and the deceleration is highest in the fourth year when it is about 0.7 per cent. A possible explanation for this behaviour is that liberalization attracts FDI inflows and leads to new investment of capital which comes in as new technology; that is, in the form of new machinery and equipment. Once this machinery and equipment has been installed in the first year and the components and parts delivered in the second year, the old production processes are relocated. This relocation, which involves the transfer of some of the old machinery and equipment, erodes the country's stock of technology even if such technology may be regarded as 'obsolete' *vis-à-vis* its current sources of comparative advantage. This therefore leads to a net loss of technology and, hence, creates the deceleration recorded. Over time, the new and more efficient and more productive production processes then generate profits which are reinvested in newer technology in the seventh year. This cycle is repeated until the impact peters out. The total effect is positive for all the countries, suggesting that liberalization leads to the transfer of new technology from the more developed to the less developed countries.

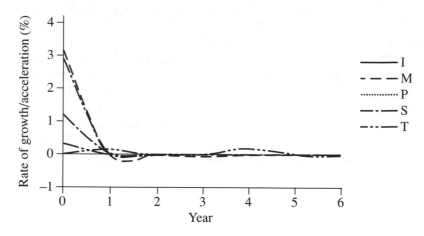

Notes: The following format has been used: M ÷ 10, S ÷ 10 and T ÷ 10; I = Indonesia, M = Malaysia, P = Philippines, S = Singapore and T = Thailand.

Figure 15.5   The impact of liberalization multipliers on TT

The results demonstrate that liberalization attracts investment which comes with new capital and, hence, new technology in the form of new machinery and equipment, components and parts. They also show that the transfer of new technology occurs immediately in the politically stable economies, but there is a 'wait and see' strategy in the politically unstable economies; and even when transfer does come, it is relatively small and is followed by a period of monitoring before the final larger inflow is accomplished. The results further reveal that the magnitude of the multipliers, and the relocation of new technology, increase as the level of economic development increases.

The Impact of Liberalization Multipliers on International Trade

The results presented in Table 15.6 and Figure 15.6 show that a percentage increase in a change in liberalization creates a one-off acceleration impact on *IT* for Indonesia (0.7 per cent) and Malaysia (43 per cent), but a sequential movement for the Philippines and Singapore. They suggest that, when liberalization attracts new investment that is aimed at producing for the export market, its effect on *IT* is immediate. This is probably because it utilizes better machinery in the production process and, therefore, benefits from its efficiency and productivity. The results further demonstrate that the new investment attains its optimum production capacity in the first year.

Table 15.6 Impact of liberalization multipliers on IT

Year	0	1	2	3	4	5	6	Total
Indonesia	0.72782	0	0	0	0	0	0	0.72782
Malaysia	43.212	0	0	0	0	0	0	43.212
Philippines	0.57573	0	0.14872	0	−0.01892	0	−0.00413	0.70061
Singapore	5.8667	0	0	−0.41881	0	0	0	5.8667
Thailand	0	0	0	0	0	0	0	+

Note: The cells represented by + show the direction of the insignificantly small multipliers.

For the Philippines, the prolonged effects are probably a result of uncertainty created by the political instability discussed earlier. The fluctuations that follow after the fourth year are, however, a result of the investment, relocation and reinvestment cycles discussed below.

The more economically advanced Singapore offers a fairly similar pattern, but an almost tenfold magnitude. A possible explanation is that liberalization results in very large initial investment and, therefore, more efficient production techniques. The combined effect of the presence of a highly skilled labour force, sophisticated infrastructure and the efficient production techniques boosts productivity, which consequently boosts *IT*. For instance, a percentage increase in a change in liberalization accelerates *IT* by about 6 per cent in the initial year. Once the maximum output capacity and, therefore, productivity have been attained, however, they stay at that level and do not change in the next two years. Production is then relocated to other countries in the fourth year, followed by installation of new machinery. This transition process, however, disrupts productivity in two ways. First, the relocation of production creates unemployment, as discussed earlier. Second, when the new production techniques are introduced, the labour force, skilled as it is, still takes time to familiarize itself with them before it fully adopts them. These two factors then make the labour force less productive. Efficiency and productivity fall in this transition period and the value of exports also falls. This creates the negative impact recorded. However, once the new techniques have been mastered and more people employed, efficiency and productivity increase and consequently create a positive impact, though only marginally. The cycle continues at a decreasing rate until it peters out. The total effect is positive.

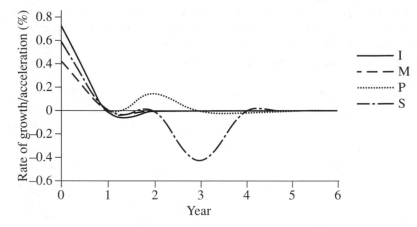

Notes: The following format has been used: M ÷ 100 and S ÷ 10; I = Indonesia, M = Malaysia, P = Philippines and S = Singapore.

Figure 15.6   The Impact of liberalization multipliers on IT

The results suggest that liberalization encourages new investment, which promotes productivity, particularly in the production activities geared for the export market. They also demonstrate that the multiplier effects increase as the level of economic development increases.

The Impact of Liberalization Multipliers on Learning-by-Doing

The impact of liberalization on *LD* is indirect and comes through its effects on FDI and *TT*. The results presented in Table 15.7 and Figure 15.7 show that there is a one year time lag for the Philippines probably due to the uncertain investment environment. It is, however, immediate for Malaysia, Singapore and Thailand. There is a one-off acceleration of *LD* by 15 per cent for Thailand that results from a percentage increase in a change in liberalization. The pattern for Malaysia, the Philippines and Singapore is similar though the Philippines' occurs with a one year lag.

Table 15.7 Impact of liberalization multipliers on LD

Year	0	1	2	3	4	5	6	Total
Indonesia	0	0	0	0	0	0	–	+
Malaysia	0.19519	0.28377	–0.06932	0.00229	–0.00068	1.7E–5	–	0.411251
Philippines	0	0.01995	0	–0.00254	0	–0.00055	–0.00031	0.016752
Singapore	7.5739	0.00853	–0.00684	0.07944	–0.00029	0.01134	+	7.16755
Thailand	15.219	+	0	0	0	0	0	15.2194

Note: The cells represented by + or – show the direction of the insignificantly small multipliers.

A possible explanation for the behaviour of the multipliers is that liberalization attracts FDI, which brings along capital in the form of machinery and equipment which contain new technology that provides the basis for learning-by-doing. It also creates jobs and, therefore, employment, thereby giving opportunity to individuals to learn by doing. The initial acceleration of *LD* that results from a percentage increase in a change in liberalization is high for Singapore (7.6 per cent) resulting from the impact of liberalization on *EMP* (65 per cent), *TT* (12 per cent) and *HS* (0.8 per cent).[25] By contrast, that for Malaysia is 0.2 per cent in the initial year but reaches its maximum of 0.3 per cent in the second year. This also results from the effect of liberalization on *TT* (31 per cent) and *EMP* (4 per cent) but not *HS*, implying that the relatively less skilled labour force needs more time to learn the new skills and production techniques and their application on the new technology; that is, it is an indication of a less skilled labour force that is less capable of adopting new methods and techniques of production. For Malaysia, the Philippines and Singapore, there is relocation of production after two years. This involves the transfer of some machinery and, therefore, loss of technology, and loss of jobs and employment, which results in the deterioration of human skills. These factors collectively cause a negative effect on *LD* in the third year, for various reasons. For instance, the loss of technology negates the basis for learning-by-doing, the unemployment created means that the labour force becomes idle and, therefore, less capable of learning anything new, and the deterioration of human skills reduces their capability to adopt any new ideas and concepts. The profits generated by the more efficient and more productive production techniques are then reinvested in new machinery and equipment and, hence, new technology. This creates new jobs and employment, improves the quality of human skills, and promotes *LD* once more. This pattern continues until it fades out. The total impacts are positive for each country.

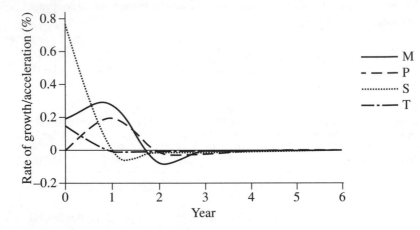

Notes: The following format has been used: P × 10, S ÷ 10 and T ÷ 100; M = Malaysia, P = Philippines, S = Singapore and T = Thailand.

Figure 15.7   The impact of liberalization multipliers on LD

The results demonstrate that the effect of liberalization on *LD* that comes indirectly from its combined effects on FDI and hence *EMP*, *TT* and *HS* is an overall effect of stimulating *LD*. They further suggest that *LD* is also affected by the investment, relocation and reinvestment cycles, particularly in the more developed countries.

The Impact of Liberalization Multipliers on Real Per Capita GDP Growth

The impact of liberalization on real per capita GDP growth is attained indirectly through FDI, *TT* and *IT*. The results reported in Table 15.8 and Figure 15.8 show that the initial impact is immediate for Indonesia, Malaysia, Singapore and Thailand, but lagged for the Philippines, probably owing to its uncertain investment environment. The immediate impact is greatest for Malaysia, followed by Thailand.

For Singapore, a percentage increase in a change in liberalization accelerates real per capita GDP growth by 0.06 per cent in the first year, resulting from its impact on *IT* (6 per cent), *TT* (12 per cent), *EMP* (65 per cent), *LD* (7.6 per cent) and *HS* (0.8 per cent) but negated by FDI (–3 per cent). This reaches a maximum of 3.8 per cent in the second year when the positive indirect effect via the spillover effects variables outweighs the negative effect via FDI. However, it falls and decelerates in the next two years owing to the predominant negative effects of *HS*, *EMP*, *TT* and *IT* before growing and accelerating once more in the fifth and sixth years, when the combined indirect effects via these variables become positive. An explanation for this behaviour is that liberalization attracts *FDI* which brings with it capital in the form of new technology, creates new jobs and employment, improves the quality of human skills, improves productivity and international trade, and introduces an environment that promotes learning-by-doing. The combined effects of all these factors boost the productivity of the economy and, therefore, stimulate real per capita GDP growth. The production relocation that comes in the third and fourth years leads to a loss of technology, to the loss of jobs and employment, to the deterioration of human skills, to a fall in productivity and, hence, in *IT*, and to a decline in *LD*, as has been discussed under the impact of liberalization on the spillover effects variables above. This causes a decline in the entire economy's productivity and consequently negates the real per capita GDP growth process. The new and more efficient and, therefore, more productive production techniques then generate profits which are reinvested. This reverses the above effects and stimulates the growth process once more. These cycles are repeated on a two-yearly basis until the effect fades out. The total impact is an acceleration of the growth of real per capita GDP by 3.7 per cent.

Table 15.8   Impact of liberalization multipliers on real per capita GDP growth

Year	0	1	2	3	4	5	6	Total
Indonesia	–0.07258	0	0	0	0	0	0	–0.07258
Malaysia	31.232	–27.534	0.90879	0.02719	0.0069	–0.0027	4.7E–5	4.33923
Philippines	0	0.02186	0	–0.00278	0.00463	–0.00061	–0.00093	0.023289
Singapore	0.06168	3.7697	–0.00167	–0.10204	4.5E–5	0.00276	–	3.73036
Thailand	5.4131	1.6661	0	0	0	0	0	7.07924

Note: The cells represented by – show the direction of the insignificantly small multipliers.

In Malaysia, a percentage increase in a change in liberalization accelerates real per capita GDP growth by 31 per cent in the initial year followed by a 28 per cent deceleration in the next year. The initial impact is a result of the combined impact of liberalization on *TT* (31 per cent), *IT* (43 per cent), FDI (14.5 per cent), *EMP* (4 per cent) and *LD* (0.2 per cent). The negative effect that follows can also be explained by the negative effects of the relocation of production, and the cyclical fluctuation observations by the investment, relocation and reinvestment described above.

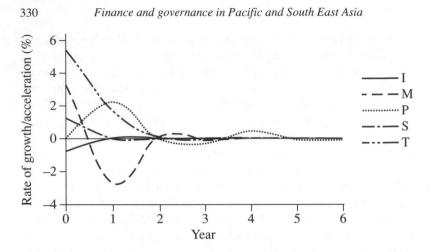

Notes: The following format has been used: I × 10, M ÷ 0 and P × 100; I = Indonesia, M = Malaysia, P = Philippines, S = Singapore, T = Thailand.

Figure 15.8   The impact of liberalization multipliers on real per capita GDP growth

In Indonesia there is a one-off effect resulting from its impact on *IT* (0.7 per cent) and *TT* (0.3 per cent). The cause of the negative effect is not quite clear but might be the predominant negative effect *IT* has had on real per capita GDP.[26] In the Philippines, a percentage increase in a change in liberalization accelerates the growth process by 0.02 in the initial year, but this falls and decelerates by 0.003 per cent in the fourth year. The predominant negative direct effect of FDI and indirect effect of *LD* cause a negative effect in the fourth year. Thereafter, the results follow the two-yearly fluctuations that come from investment, relocation and reinvestment. For Thailand, the impact multiplier acceleration of 5 per cent is transmitted mainly through its effect on FDI (99 per cent), *TT* (29 per cent) and *LD* (15 per cent), and the effect in the second year mainly results from the effect via FDI (30 per cent).

Further observation reveals that the effects of the liberalization multipliers on FDI, *EMP* and *LD* for Malaysia follow the same pattern and that, starting from the second year, a decrease/increase of the multipliers of these variables in year *t* similarly causes a decrease/increase of real per capita GDP growth in year *t* + 1, demonstrating that it takes one year before the full impact is absorbed by the growth process. Singapore is slightly different, in that the pattern, not surprisingly, is dominated by FDI; that is, a decrease/increase of FDI in year *t* causes a decrease/increase of real per capita GDP growth in year *t* + 2. The effect for the Philippines and Thailand however, is, instantaneous in that it is transmitted in the same year: the pattern of the multipliers effects on FDI in year *t* is the same as that on real per capita GDP growth in year *t*.[27] This demonstrates that the spillover process takes a shorter time (is faster) in the less developed countries than in the more developed countries.

With the exception of Indonesia, the results provide evidence suggesting that liberalization leads to real per capita GDP growth. They further suggest that the highest positive effects occur in the first two years when new investment is made, and the negative effects occur when investment is relocated; and that the spillover process slows down as the level of economic development increases. They also demonstrate that the multiplier effects increase as the level of economic development increases.

We make a remark on what appears to be an inconsistency in the multipliers for Singapore (see Appendix IV, Table AIV.4). The multipliers depict deceleration effects of liberalization on FDI, but acceleration effects on the other endogenous variables during the first two years. This would appear to be impossible in elementary terms, that is, *HS*, *EMP*, *TT*, *IT* and *LD* should not accelerate when FDI is being relocated (decelerating). However, according to the clarification presented in note 24, this is possible. Whereas liberalization causes the rate of relocation to exceed the rate of new investment, hence, imparting a net *deceleration* effect on FDI during the first two years, there is a net *acceleration* of (a) new technology transfer because the new investment (machinery and equipment) has a higher content of new technology as compared to that which is eroded away through the relocated production (machinery and equipment); (b) human skills because extra skills are attained through training in preparation for the new production process, and also through learning on the job during the initial exposure to the new technology; (c) employment because new and more skilled personnel more conversant with the new production process (technology) are hired (although in the long run more people are made redundant, as seen earlier); (d) learning-by-doing because the new technology offers new and more opportunities for learning-by-doing than the relocated technology; and (e) international trade because the above factors, *TT*, *HS*, *EMP* and *LD*, promote productivity and hence international trade.

The Impact of other Policy Variables on the Endogenous Variables

The results for *RWR* demonstrate that lower *RWR* encourage inward FDI flows (except for the Philippines) which creates jobs and employment, and further suggest that its effects are greater in economies which have more advanced sources of comparative advantage, particularly a highly skilled labour force, linked to it. Those for *IF* demonstrate that it attracts FDI, which eventually leads to job creation and employment. This improves productivity and promotes international trade, and creates an opportunity for learning-by-doing. It also facilitates the process of technology transfer, which in turn facilitates the rate at which the spillover process is achieved and, hence, the rate at which productivity promotes the growth process.

GE has a total positive effect on human skills and learning-by-doing undoubtedly because it has an immediate consequence for skill and, therefore, ability/capability improvement, though this comes after a time lag which is influenced by the duration of the education/training process. Its total impact on the other variables is, however, negative, suggesting that, in the short run, investment in formal education takes too long to act as an attraction for FDI, since in the short run it draws people from the potential labour force, reduces the stock of human capital available for productive activities and lowers productivity and therefore acts as a disincentive for FDI and consequently the growth process.

The results indicate that *PS* are reinvested, but the type of investment in which they are put is influenced by the level of economic development of the country. In the less developed countries where the *PS* are controlled by the business community, they unsurprisingly reinvest in small-scale labour-intensive industries. The limited employment and mechanization these businesses offer lead to the deterioration of human skills and learning-by-doing, negate the transfer of technology and collectively reduce productivity and, hence, create a negative impact on the growth process. For the more developed countries, however, where the *PS* are made by the working elite group that is aware of the benefits of investing in the improvement of human skills, they are invested partly in the improvement of the stock of human capital, which generates a positive impact that comes after a time lag which is influenced by the duration of the education/training process.

The results also suggest that the impact of *XR* on FDI is influenced by the countries' levels of economic development and their ability to handle macro-economic controls and, whereas an increase in *XR* causes a lump-sum inflow of FDI to the less developed countries, it encourages relocation of production in the more developed ones. *XR* create good terms-of-trade which attract FDI, increase productivity and boost *IT* and hence the growth process.

CONCLUDING REMARKS

The multiplier methodology has brought to light the dynamic effects of the impact of policy on FDI and its spillover effects variables and the consequent economic growth process of the ASEAN-5 economies. The findings that have been explained by the reorganization of investment and the relocation of production that has been associated with the 'flying-geese' type of development and 'billiard-ball'-style shifts in FDI within the region, and rationalization of investment from outside the region, and consequently the international division of labour, have demonstrated that:

- whereas the impact is immediate in the more developed, politically stable and foreign investment-friendly economies, there is a time lag (a 'wait and see' strategy) in those economies which are less developed, politically unstable and have an element of hostility towards foreign investment;
- the speed of the spillover process slows down as the level of economic development increases;
- the relocation of production increases as the level of economic development increases;
- the magnitude of the multiplier effects increases as the level of economic development increases.

APPENDIX I   DATA SOURCES

Output Indicator: Per Capita GDP

The values have been extracted from the World Penn Tables (Mark 5.6) retrieved from the data base via the website. They were originally in 1985 prices but have been converted to 1987 prices to make them compatible with the other data. The chain index RGDPCH is used because its growth rate for any period is based upon international prices most closely allied to the period.

FDI

Indonesia, Malaysia and Philippines: the World Bank data series diskette.
Singapore: the figures for Singapore have been supplied by the Statistical Bureau of Singapore.
Thailand: the figures for Thailand have been supplied by the Central Bank of Thailand.

Human Skills: Secondary School Enrolment

Mitchell, B.R. (1982), *International Historical Statistics: Africa and Asia*, London: Macmillan.
The Government of Indonesia, *Indonesia Statistical Yearbook*, various years, Jakarta.
The Government of Malaysia, *Malaysia Statistical Yearbook*, various years, Kuala Lumpur.
The Government of the Philippines, various years, *The Philippines Statistical Yearbook*, Manila.
The Government of Singapore, *The Yearbook of Statistics*, various years, Singapore.
The Government of Thailand, *Statistical Yearbook*, *Thailand*, various years; *Thailand Bulletin of Statistics*, various years.
UN, *UNESCO Statistical Yearbook*, various years, New York and Paris: UNESCO.

Employment: Manufacturing Employment

Indonesia, Malaysia, the Philippines and Singapore: employment index (1987=100) from the World Bank data series diskette and actual figure for 1987 from the Asian Development Bank (1994), *Key Indicators of Developing Asian and Pacific Countries, 1994*, Singapore and Oxford: Oxford University Press.
Thailand: actual employment figures from the Asian Development Bank (1994), *Key Indicators of Developing Asian and Pacific Countries, 1994*, Singapore

and Oxford: Oxford University Press; UN, The UN *Yearbook of Labour Statistics*, various years, Geneva: ILO.

New Technology Transfer: Imports of Machinery and Equipment

Annual data for imports from the World Bank data series diskette, and percentage share of machinery and equipment in imports from UN, *The UN International Trade Statistics Yearbook*, various years, New York: UN.

International Trade: Exports of Goods and Services

Annual exports from the World Bank data series diskette.

Learning-by-Doing: Manufacturing Value Added

Annual data from the World Bank data series diskette.

Domestic Market Size: GDP

Annual data of per capita GDP and population from the World Penn Tables (Mark 5.6) retrieved from the data base via web site.

Relative Wage Rates: Ratio of Real Manufacturing Earnings per Employee in US Dollars

Real manufacturing earnings per employee and exchange rates from the World Bank data series diskette.

Infrastructure: Government Expenditure on Economic Services

The annual figures for recurrent and development expenditure on economic services have been extracted from the Asian Development Bank (1994), *Key Indicators of Developing Asian and Pacific Countries, 1994*, Singapore and Oxford: Oxford University Press; UN, *The UN Government Finance Statistics*, various years, New York: UN; UN, *The UN Statistical Yearbook*, various years, New York: UN; and World Bank, *The IMF Country Surveys*, various years, Washington, DC.

Government Expenditure on Education

The annual figures for recurrent and development expenditure on education have been extracted from the Asian Development Bank (1994), *Key Indicators of Developing Asian and Pacific Countries, 1994*, Singapore and Oxford: Oxford University Press; UN, *The UN Government Finance Statistics*, various years, New York: UN; UN, *The UN Statistical Yearbook*, various years, New York: UN; and World Bank, *The IMF Country Surveys*, various years, Washington, DC; and UN, *UNESCO Statistical Yearbook*, various years, New York and Paris: UNESCO.

Personal Savings: Time and Savings Deposits

The annual figures for time and savings deposits have been extracted from the Asian Development Bank (1994), *Key Indicators of Developing Asian and Pacific Countries, 1994*, Singapore and Oxford: Oxford University Press, and UN, *The UN International Financial Statistics Yearbook*, various years, New York: UN.

Foreign Exchange Rates: Local Currency per US Dollar

Annual data from the World Bank data series diskette.

Government Policy: Exports of Goods and Services (less exports of mining and quarrying) plus Imports of Goods and Services (less imports of fuel)

Exports of goods and services from the World Bank data series diskette; exports of mining and quarrying as a percentage of exports, and imports of fuels as a percentage of imports, from UN, *The UN International Trade Statistics Yearbook*, various years, New York: UN.

APPENDIX II

Table AII   The expected direction of the relationship between the dependent and independent variables

| | Dependent variable | | | | | | |
	Gr	FDI	HS	EMP	TT	IT	LD
Gr		+					
FDI	+		+	+	+	+	+
HS	+	+		+/–	+		+
EMP	+		+		+		+
TT	+						+
IT	+			+			
LD	+		+			+	
MS		+					
RWR	–			–			
IF		+			+		
GP		+			+	+	
PS			+/–				
GE			+				
XR						+	
T							+

Notes: + and – represent results that are expected to be positively and negatively statistically significant; **Bold** = endogenous, *Italic* = exogenous.

APPENDIX III   THE COEFFICIENTS, SIGNS AND LAG STRUCTURES OF THE RELATIONSHIP BETWEEN THE DEPENDENT AND STATISTICALLY SIGNIFICANT INDEPENDENT VARIABLES

Indonesia

$Gr = 0.00429918\ FDI(3) + 0.321955\ EMP(4) + 0.1739748\ TT(5) - 0.0997275\ IT$

$FDI = -9.9521729\ Gr(2) + 50.434679\ MS(2) - 0.19703032\ RWR(4) + 0.3210925\ GP(3) + 0.5476557\ IF(3)$

$HS = 0.01807233\ FDI(5) - 0.329775\ EMP(3) + 0.5303007\ LD(1) - 7.733163\ PS(3) + 0.1818418\ GE(3)$

$EMP = 0.01683534\ FDI(5) + 0.615131\ HS(5) + 0.0291469\ IT(5)$

$TT = -0.04022893\ FDI(5) + 0.670044\ HS + 0.3004152\ GP + 0.6610141\ IF$

$IT = -3.2108447\ LD(1) + 0.7278163\ GP + 0.12256004\ XR(1)$

$LD = 0.450248\ HS - 0.532086\ EMP(1) - 0.2411879\ TT(6)$

Malaysia

$Gr = 1.669061\ FDI(3) + 0.424831\ HS(3) + 0.159328\ EMP + 0.9747873\ TT - 0.6777832\ IT(1) + 4.03523\ LD(1)$

$FDI = 0.1743949\ Gr(1) + 0.091208\ HS(6) + 13.520762\ GP$

$HS = 0.3780691\ FDI(5) - 0.038096\ EMP(4) + 9.302509\ PS + 0.195186\ GE(5)$

$EMP = 0.3088516\ FDI - 0.052082\ HS(2) + 0.01015657\ IT(1) - 4.55492\ RWR(3)$

$TT = 0.108144\ HS(4) + 31.356982\ GP + 0.4217067\ IF(1)$

$IT = 2.2164047\ FDI(5) + 43.212198\ GP$

$LD = -0.115467\ HS(2) + 0.046741\ EMP + 0.2696611\ TT(5) - 4.32\ T$

The Philippines

$Gr = 0.1543798\ FDI + 0.007411\ EMP(1) + 0.2120125\ LD(2)$

$FDI = -0.8240573\ Gr(2) - 0.032408\ HS(2) + 0.1415677\ GP(2) + 0.516371\ IF(1)$

$HS = 1.3558161\ FDI(2) + 0.030353\ EMP(3) - 2.2796717\ LD(2) + 2.9060776\ GE(5)$

$EMP = -0.078659\ HS(5) - 16.244096\ RWR(5)$

$TT = 1.5192884\ FDI(3) + 0.1350565\ GP(1) + 0.4429421\ IF(2)$

$IT = 1.3162404\ FDI(1) - 1.8853678\ LD(1) + 0.5757276\ GP$

$LD = 0.140921\ FDI - 0.009695\ HS(5) + 0.005227\ EMP(1) - 0.2959385\ TT(4) + 2.30427\ T$

Singapore

$Gr = -0.0041584\ FDI(4) + 0.000946\ EMP + 0.041329\ TT(5) + 0.64255\ IT(1)$
$+ 0.0527055\ LD(3)$

$FDI = -47.566676\ Gr + 0.018443\ HS(1) - 8.615462\ RWR(1) + 4.801516\ GP(2)$
$+ 0.4110136\ IF(4)$

$HS = -0.1139863\ FDI(3) + 0.001461\ EMP(5) + 0.106125\ LD + 0.130673\ PS$

$EMP = 0.6013299\ FDI(2) - 0.011036\ HS(3) + 11.109636\ IT - 4.152391$
$RWR(3)$

$TT = 0.3686515\ FDI(5) + 0.017075\ HS(1) + 0.00625\ EMP + 11.780416\ GP$

$IT = 0.0303126\ FDI(3) + 0.0633009\ LD(4) + 5.866697\ GP + 2.277051\ XR$

$LD = 0.486494\ FDI(4) + 0.011597\ HS + 0.004738\ EMP(5) + 0.6206686\ TT$

Thailand

$Gr = 0.0575233\ TT(1) + 0.0912475\ IT(1) + 0.3556719\ LD$

$FDI = 18.218801\ Gr + 0.043027\ HS(4) - 0.2144726\ RWR(3) + 9.425356\ GP(2)$
$+ 0.00824232\ IF(5)$

$HS = 2.287411\ FDI(4) + 0.016723\ EMP(4) + 1.316566\ LD(3) - 17.283948$
$PS(3)$

$EMP = 1.1645024\ FDI(5) - 0.051782\ HS(5) + 0.7591456\ IT(3) - 0.6907437$
$RWR(1)$

$TT = 0.019662\ EMP(1) + 28.964595\ GP$

$IT = 0.6972798\ LD(5) + 18.677598\ GP(3) + 0.7064356\ XR(3)$

$LD = 0.5267933\ FDI(3) - 0.012738\ HS(2) + 0.014297\ EMP(2) + 0.5254473$
$TT - 7.298954\ T$

APPENDIX IV   THE IMPACT, INTERIM AND TOTAL MULTIPLIERS FOR THE ASEAN-5

Table AIV.1   Multipliers: Indonesia

Year	0	1	2	DGP 3	4	5	6	Total
Gr	−0.07258	0	0	0	0	0	0	−0.07258
DFDI	0	0	0.722361	0	0	0	0	0.722361
DHS	0	0	0	0	0	0	0	+
DEMP	0	0	0	0	0	0	0	+
DTT	0.300415	0	0	0	0	0	0	0.300415
DIT	0.727816	0	0	0	0	0	0	0.727816
DLD	0	0	0	0	0	0	−	+

Year	0	1	2	DGP(−2) 3	4	5	6	Total
Gr	0	0	0	0	0	0	0	0
DFDI	0	0.321092	0	0	0	0	0	0.321092
DHS	0	0	0	0	0	0	0	0
DEMP	0	0	0	0	0	0	0	0
DTT	0	0	0	0	0	0	0	0
DIT	0	0	0	0	0	0	0	0
DLD	0	0	0	0	0	0	0	0

Table AIV.2   Multipliers: Malaysia

Year	0	1	2	DGP 3	4	5	6	Total
Gr	31.2317	−27.5336	0.908785	−0.27191	0.006899	−0.0027	4.69E−05	4.33923
DFDI	13.5208	5.44665	−4.80172	0.158488	−0.04742	0.001203	−0.00047	14.2775
DHS	0	0	0	0	0	0	0	0
DEMP	4.17591	6.07108	−1.48302	0.048949	−0.01465	0.000372	−0.00015	8.79851
DTT	31.357	0	0	0	0	0	0	31.357
DIT	43.2122	0	0	0	0	0	0	43.2122
DLD	0.195186	0.283769	−0.06932	0.002288	−0.00068	1.74E-05	−	0.411251

Table AIV.3 Multipliers: The Philippines

Year	0	1	2	3	4	5	6	Total
				DGP				
Gr	0	0.021855	0	–0.00278	0.004634	–0.00061	–0.00093	0.023289
DFDI	0	0.141568	0	–0.01801	0	–0.00393	–0.0022	0.118873
DHS	0	0	0	0.19194	–0.04982	–0.02442	0.006338	0.108079
DEMP	0	0	0	0	0	0	0	0
DTT	0	0.135057	0	0	0.215082	0	–0.02736	0.31566
DIT	0.575728	0	0.148724	0	–0.01892	0	–0.00413	0.70061
DLD	0	0.01995	0	–0.00254	0	–0.00055	–0.00031	0.016752

Table AIV.4 Multipliers: Singapore

Year	0	1	2	3	4	5	6	Total
				DGP				
Gr	0.061683	3.76965	–0.00167	–0.10204	4.52E–05	0.002762	–	3.73036
DFDI	–2.93407	–179.295	0.079442	4.85352	–0.00297	–0.13139	0.000103	–177.427
DHS	0.803782	0.000905	–0.00073	–0.04445	–3E–05	0.001203	+	0.760656
DEMP	65.1769	0	–1.76435	–107.815	0.047771	2.91857	–0.00179	–41.5151
DTT	12.1878	0.013725	–0.01101	–0.67394	–0.00046	0.018243	+	11.5339
DIT	5.8667	0	0	–0.41881	0	0	0	5.8667
DLD	7.57392	0.008529	–0.00684	0.079442	–0.00029	0.011337	+	7.16755

Year	0	1	2	3	4	5	6	Total
				DGP(–1)				
Gr	0	0	0	0.002733	0	–7.4E-05	+	0.002661
DFDI	0	4.80152	–	–0.12998	2.2E-05	0.003519	–	4.67498
DHS	0	0	0	0.00119	0	–3.2E-05	–	0.00116
DEMP	0	0	0	2.8873	0	–0.07816	1.32E-05	2.81121
DTT	0	0	0	0.018048	2.03E-05	–0.00049	–	0.017592
DIT	0	0	0	0.011216	0	0	0	–
DLD	0	0	0	0	1.26E-05	–0.0003	–	0.010932

Table AIV.5   Multipliers: Thailand

	DGP							
Year	0	1	2	3	4	5	6	Total
Gr	5.4131	1.66614	0	0	0	0	0	7.07924
DFDI	98.6202	30.3551	0	0	0	0	0	128.975
DHS	0	0	0	0	0	0	0	0
DEMP	0	0	0	0	0	0	0	0
DTT	28.9646	0	0	0	0	0	0	28.9646
DIT	0	0	0	0	0	0	0	+
DLD	15.2194	+	0	0	0	0	0	15.2194

	DGP(−1)							
Year	0	1	2	3	4	5	6	Total
Gr	0	0	0	0	0	0	0	0
DFDI	0	9.42536	0	0	0	0	0	9.42536
DHS	0	0	0	0	0	0	0	0
DEMP	0	0	0	0	0	0	0	0
DTT	0	0	0	0	0	0	0	0
DIT	0	0	0	0	0	0	0	0
DLD	0	0	0	0	0	0	0	0

	DGP(−2)							
Year	0	1	2	3	4	5	6	Total
Gr	0	0	1.70428	0	0	0	0	1.70428
DFDI	0	0	31.05	0	0	0	0	31.05
DHS	0	0	0	0	0	0	0	0
DEMP	0	0	0	0	0	0	0	0
DTT	0	0	0	0	0	0	0	0
DIT	0	18.6776	0	0	0	0	0	18.6776
DLD	0	0	+	0	0	0	0	+

NOTES

1. Such as Adam Smith (in 1776), Thomas Malthus (in 1798), David Ricardo (in 1817), Ramsey (in 1928), Frank Knight (in 1944) and Joseph Schumpeter (in 1934).
2. See for example, Romer (1986), Lucas (1988) and Grossman and Helpman (1991).

3. For instance, they assigned a comparatively large role to only one or two factors and either ignored the remaining factors or held them constant, and failed to make allowance for improvements in the quality of the labour force and so understand its contribution to output growth.

4. On the importance of FDI in this context see, ILO (1977, 1981 and 1994), Hall (1991), Georgion and Weinhold (1992), UN (1992), Chudnovsky (1993), Lucas (1988), Cantwell (1994), Franko (1994), Mansfield (1994), Manson (1994), Pina (1994), World Bank (1995b), Chou (1995), Hamad (1995), OECD (1995) and Wei (1995).

5. See for example, UNCTAD (1992), Wei (1995), Balasubramanyam *et al.* (1996), and Bende-Nabende *et al.* (1997).

6. This hypothesis is a variant of that developed by the Transnational Corporations and Management Division of the United Nations Department of Economic and Social Development. See UN (1992, p. 250).

7. The investigation of the effects of capital formation has been omitted from this study because of the sample size limitations.

8. This proxy has been recommended in the absence of quantified data of the human stock by Page (1995). Otherwise, human capital would be computed using an index that attaches weights to the different levels of academic qualification and practical experience, and then aggregating the values.

9. It is apparent that FDI is not the only important factor that is expected to explain the economic growth of the developing economies. Other factors such as domestic (private and public) investments may also have a significant influence on the explanatory variables discussed, and factors such as domestic (private and public) consumption and investment may have a significant influence on growth. The empirical analysis, therefore, does not rule out these possibilities, but instead tries to propose an independent special role of FDI, which these other important factors could not play. In the absence of data that are capable of directly capturing the FDI activities alone, aggregate figures which also capture effects of the other important factors have been employed and this has introduced a constraint on the analysis.

   Given the growing importance of the services sector in the developing countries, its effect, particularly on employment, and hence on learning-by-doing and human skills development, is also growing. It is, therefore, more appropriate to include data on all the sectors, or at least include data of the services sector. Inconstancies in the availability of such data have, however, prompted us to use the figures provided by the manufacturing sector. A similar situation is experienced during the computation of relative wage rates (see exogenous variables, Appendix II).

10. For an account of the relevant changes in the liberalization of FDI policy and of the liberalization of trade policy in these economies, see for instance, Lim and Pang (1991) and GATT, *Trade Policy Review* (respective countries, various years).

11. The following points regarding the measurement of the other exogenous variables should be noted: (a) *domestic market size*: is proxied by annual real GDP in 1987 prices; (b) *relative wage rates*: in the computation of relative wage rates, the real manufacturing earnings per employee for the country under study have been converted into US dollars and compared with those for Japan over the period under study; (c) *infrastructure*: government annual expenditure on economic services, which by definition includes transport and communication, electricity, gas and water, industry and agriculture, as a percentage ratio of GDP have been used as a proxy for infrastructure. This proxy was chosen because the data on actual expenditure on infrastructure alone were not consistently available for all the countries under study; (d) *personal savings*: the level of personal savings has been proxied by the end of year annual amount of time and savings deposits in commercial banks as a percentage ratio of GDP; (e) *government expenditure on education*: the actual annual government recurrent and capital expenditure on education as a percentage ratio of GDP is used to measure this variable; (e) *foreign exchange rates*: this is measured as an annual average of the exchange rate between the local currency and one US dollar.

12. The figures in parentheses are lag periods.

13. The concepts of 'least', 'moderate', 'most', 'more' and 'less' developed countries often referred to hereafter are used comparatively with respect to the ASEAN.

14. We retained only those regressors that were significant in order to economize on the degrees of freedom.
15. There are other techniques, such as the *cointegration* methodology, that are used to investigate the dynamic impacts of an economic model. The preference for the *multiplier* methodology in this chapter has been mainly influenced by our desire to investigate the effects of the exogenous (policy) variables on the endogenous variables, and by the sample size limitation.
16. For a more detailed derivation, see Theil (1971, pp. 463–4).
17. It then follows, *technically*, that the multipliers of the insignificant and, hence, omitted regressors are zero in all the cases. This has therefore introduced a constraint on the analysis since, theoretically speaking, these multipliers (though based on statistically insignificant regressors) do exist and are thus *not* equal to zero. This explains why there are no multipliers for some countries for certain variables.
18. Appendix IV reports the impact, interim and total liberalization multipliers for only the original seven endogenous variables. The other variables that were created during the analysis as a result of the lag structure of the determinant variables have been omitted. The multipliers are also reported only up to the seventh year. Those for the years after have been omitted because either they are negligibly small or they are equal to zero. The multipliers for the other policy variables can be obtained on request.
19. The figures in this analysis are based on annual figures but are designed to look as if they are based on quarterly figures.
20. The concept of the 'flying geese' was first put forward by Akamatsu (1962). It entails the relocation of industry (production) and FDI from countries at a higher level of economic development to those at lower levels, resulting in more efficient use of production factors, growth and a higher level of industrialization for both groups. Recipient countries utilize their surplus labour and accumulated capital, technology and management skills, advancing their industrialization. Investing countries redirect excessive labour from 'sunset industries' to 'sunrise industries', thereby moving to an even higher level of industrialization.

    According to Fukushima and Kwan (1993), whereas the 'flying-geese' type of economic development occurs at the macro (country) level, the 'billiard-ball' style shifts in FDI and production occur at the micro (industry) level, with the transfer of technology and international division of labour between the developed and the developing countries arising from a shift in production of one product after another to developing countries as the industry in the developed countries struggles to establish a new relationship based on international division of labour by developing new technologies and introducing new products.
21. We consider these concepts as the most appropriate for the explanation of the effects of FDI and its spillover effects variables in this region, especially given that our study proposes an independent specific role of FDI and that the economies in this region have benefited significantly from this kind of industrial growth. Consequently, most of the explanations that follow are based on these concepts.
22. This is one of its strategies in its 'Second Industrial Revolution' programme.
23. The ASEAN-4 are Indonesia, Malaysia, the Philippines and Thailand.
24. Since reference is made to the relocation and investment (reinvestment) cycles in the remaining sections of the chapter, we present a clarification to avoid possible misunderstanding of the explanations. For simplicity, we have referred to the relocation and investment periods as distinct periods. In practice, what happens (and what the multipliers are indicating) is a continuous process of relocation and investment. However, there are times when the acceleration of relocation exceeds that of inward investment (hence a net deceleration effect, which we refer to as *relocation*, for simplicity); similarly, there are times when the acceleration of inward investment exceeds that of relocation (hence a net acceleration effect which we refer to as *investment*, for simplicity). Similarly, the multipliers for the spillover variables report the net effects. For instance, a deceleration (acceleration) effect on employment does *not* imply that the people are *strictly only* losing (getting) employment; rather, it means that the rate at which the people are getting unemployed (employed) exceeds that at which they are getting employed (unemployed).
25. See Appendix IV.

26. This may be explained by the fact that the economic boom that resulted from international trade based primarily, though not exclusively, on oil could have been misappropriated. In a report by the World Bank (1995a, Figure A3, p. 73) on the Middle East and North Africa, the graphs for the real oil price and GDP growth show that the two are oppositely related; that is, GDP growth rates have been lowest during the times when the real oil prices have been highest, for example during the 1973/74 and 1979/80 oil booms. For countries where crude oil dominates the value of exports, these export values also follow the trend of prices and are consequently also negatively related to the growth of GDP. The World Bank (1995a, p. 21) offers the following general explanation: 'Countries that consume rather than save the windfalls and that invest the windfalls disproportionately at home rather than reduce their foreign debt or invest abroad can penalise themselves three ways. They adopt an unsustainable pattern of consumption. They obtain low returns on investment and fail to diversify their assets. And they tend to suffer from "Dutch disease", where the real exchange rates appreciates and the growth of tradables is stunted, compromising the role international trade can play as an engine of growth and innovation for the whole economy.'

27. See Appendix IV.

REFERENCES

Akamatsu, K. (1962), 'An Historical Pattern of Economic Growth in Developing Countries', *The Developing Economies*, 1, 17–31.

Aquino, T.G. and B.B. Bolanus (1993), 'Foreign Direct Investment Inflows and Political Stability in the Philippines', in *The New Wave of Foreign Direct Investment in Asia*, Singapore: Nomura Research Institute of Southeast Asian Studies.

Asian Development Bank, (1994), *Key Indicators of Developing Asian and Pacific Countries*, 1994, Singapore and Oxford: Oxford University Press.

Balasubramanyam, V.N., D. Sapsford and M.A. Salisu (1996), 'Foreign Direct Investment and Growth: New Hypothesis and Evidence', Discussion paper EC7/96, The Management School, Lancaster University.

Barro, R.J. (1991), 'Economic Growth in a Cross Section of Countries', *The Quarterly Journal of Economics*, CVI (2), 407–43.

Bende-Nabende, A., J.L. Ford and J.R. Slater (1997), 'The Impact of FDI and Regional Economic Integration on the Economic Growth of the ASEAN-5 Economies, 1970–1994: A Comparative Analysis from a Small Structural Model', University of Birmingham, Department of Economics Discussion Paper, no. 97–13.

Cantwell, J. (1994), 'The Theory of Technological Competence and its Application to International Production', in J. Cantwell (ed.), *The United Nations Library on Transnational Corporations, Transnational Corporations and Innovatory Activities*, Vol. 17, London: Routledge.

Chou, J. (1995), 'Old and New Development Models: The Taiwanese Experience', in Ito Takatoshi and A.O. Krueger (eds), *Growth Theories in Light of the East Asian Experience*, Chicago and London: University of Chicago Press and National Bureau of Economic Research.

Chudnovsky, D. (1993), 'Introduction: Transnational Corporations and Industrialisation', in D. Chudnovsky (ed.), *The United Nations Library on Transnational Corporations, Transnational Corporations and Industrialisation*, Vol. 11, London: Routledge.

Denison, E.F. (1985), *Trends in American Economic Growth, 1929–1982*, Washington, DC: The Brookings Institution.

Franko, L.G., (1994), 'Trends in Direct Employment in Multinational enterprises in Industrialised Countries', in P. Enderwick (ed.), *The United Nations Library on Transnational Corporations, Transnational Corporations and Human Resources*, Vol. 16, London: Routledge.

Fukishima, K. and C.H. Kwan (1993), 'Foreign Direct Investment and Regional Industrial Restructuring in Asia', in *The New Wave of Foreign Direct Investment in Asia*, Singapore: Nomura Research Institute of Southeast Asian Studies, pp. 1–39.

Georgion, G.C. and S. Wienhold (1992), 'Japanese Direct Investment in the US', *The World Economy*, 15(6), 761–78.

Goldberger, A.S. (1959), *Impact Multipliers and Dynamic Properties of the Klein-Goldberger Model*, Amsterdam: North-Holland.

Grossman, G.M. and E. Helpman (1991), 'Trade, Knowledge Spillovers and Growth', *European Economic Review*, 35, 517–26.

Hall, S. (1991), 'Marketing Barriers Facing Developing Country Manufactured Exports: A Conceptual Note', *The Journal of Development Studies*, 27(4), 137–50.

Hamad, K. (1995), 'Comment', in Ito Takatoshi and A.O. Krueger (eds), *Growth Theories in Light of the East Asian Experience*, Chicago and London: University of Chicago Press and National Bureau of Economic Research.

ILO (1977), *Social and Labour Practices of Multinational Enterprises in the Petroleum Industry*, Geneva: ILO.

ILO (1981), *Multinationals' Training Practices and Development*, Geneva: ILO.

ILO (1994), 'Multinationals' Training Practices and Development', in P. Enderwick (ed.), *The United Nations Library on Transnational Corporations, Transnational Corporations and Human Resources*, Vol. 16, London: Routledge.

Levin, R. and D. Renelt (1992), 'A Sensitivity Analysis of Cross-Country Growth Regression', *American Economic Review*, 82, 942–63.

Lim, L.Y.C. and P.F. Pang (1991), *Foreign Direct Investment and Industrialisation in Malaysia, Singapore, Taiwan and Thailand*, Paris: OECD.

Lucas, R.E. (1988), 'On the Mechanics of Economic Development', *Journal of Monetary Economics*, 22, 3–42.

Mansfield, E. (1994), 'Technology and Technological Change', in J. Cantwell (ed.), *The United Nations Library on Transnational Corporations, Transnational Corporations and Innovatory Activities*, Vol. 17, London: Routledge.

Manson, R.H. (1994), 'An Introduction Based on an Overview of the Literature', in P. Enderwick (ed.), *The United Nations Library on Transnational Corporations, Transnational Corporations and Human Resources*, Vol. 16, London: Routledge.

Mitchell, B.R. (1982), *International Historical Statistics: Africa and Asia*, London: Macmillan.

OECD (1995), *Foreign Direct Investment, Trade and Employment*, Paris: OECD.

Page, J. (1995), 'Comment on Shang-Jin Wei', in Ito Takatoshi and A.O. Krueger (eds), *Growth Theories in Light of the East Asian Experience*, Chicago and London: University of Chicago Press and National Bureau of Economic Research, pp. 100–104.

Pina C. (1994), 'Direct Employment Effects of MNEs in Developing Countries', in P. Enderwick (ed.), *The United Nations Library on Transnational Corporations, Transnational Corporations and Human Resources*, Vol. 16, London: Routledge.

Romer, P.M., (1986), 'Increasing Returns and Long Run Growth', *Journal of Political Economy*, 94(5), October, 1002–37.

Solow, R.M. (1957), 'Technical Change and the Aggregate Production Function', *Review of Economics and Statistics*, 39 (3), 312–20.

The Government of Indonesia, *Indonesia Statistical Yearbook*, various years, Jakarta.

The Government of Malaysia, *Malaysia Statistical Yearbook*, various years, Kuala-Lumpur.
The Government of the Philippines, *The Philippines Statistical Yearbook*, various years, Manila.
The Government of Singapore, *The Yearbook of Statistics*, various years, Singapore.
The Government of Thailand, *Thailand Bulletin of Statistics*, various years, Bangkok.
The World Penn Tables (Mark 5.6), retrieved from data base on web site.
Theil, H. (1971), *Principles of Econometrics*, Amsterdam and London: North-Holland.
UN, *The UN Government Finance Statistics*, various years, New York: UN.
UN, *The UN International Financial Statistics Yearbook*, various years, New York: UN.
UN, *The UN International Trade Statistics Yearbook*, various years, New York: UN.
UN, *The UN Statistical Yearbook*, various years, New York: UN.
UN, *The UN Yearbook of Labour Statistics*, various years, Geneva and New York: UN.
UN, *UNESCO Statistical Yearbook*, various years, New York and Paris: UNESCO.
UN (1992), *World Investment Report 1992, Transnational Corporations as Engines of Growth*, New York: UN.
UNCTAD (1992), *World Investment Directory 1992, Vol. 1, Asia and the Pacific*, Division of Transnational Corporations and Investment, New York: UN.
Van der Phoeg, F. and J.G. Tang (1992), 'The Macroeconomics of Growth: An International Perspective', *Oxford Review of Economic Policy*, 8(4), 15–28.
Wei, Shang-Jin (1995), 'The Open Door Policy and China's Rapid Growth: Evidence from City-level Data', in Ito Takatoshi and A.O. Krueger (eds), *Growth Theories in Light of the East Asian Experience*, Chicago and London: University of Chicago Press and National Bureau of Economic Research, pp. 73–98.
World Bank (1995a), *Global Economic Prospects and the Developing Countries*, Washington, DC: Oxford University Press and The World Bank.
World Bank, (1995b), *The World Development Report 1995, Workers in an Integrating World*, Washington, DC: Oxford University Press and The World Bank.
World Bank, 'The World Bank data series', on a diskette.

16. Investment, finance and firms' objectives: implications for the recent experience of South East Asian economies

D.G. Dickinson

INTRODUCTION

One of the most active areas of research in financial economics is the investigation of the importance of financial structure in determining firms' behaviour. The impact of financial structure has, of course, been a very fertile area of research since the seminal 1958 paper by Modigliani and Miller (MM) which argued that financial structure did not matter. Numerous papers since then have demonstrated reasons why the MM proposition does not hold and hence why financial structure is important. The most recent explanations have relied upon introducing asymmetric information and agency problems into the problem, in the process emphasizing how different sorts of financial asset can be used as control devices on managers' behaviour.

This chapter considers this issue by examining how such problems have affected investment decision making by firms in a number of South East Asian economies, some of which have recently experienced major financial sector and currency crises. It argues that the interaction between macroeconomic conditions and the (in)ability of financial markets to provide appropriate corporate control mechanisms has been central to the causes of the financial/currency crisis.

Early work on currency crises highlighted the unsustainability of large fiscal deficits in countries which were attempting to hold to a pegged exchange rate regime (for example, Krugman, 1979). Later analysis (which was focused, for example, on explaining the problems of the ERM in 1992) used the idea that currency crises can be self-fulfilling, in the sense that they occur because that is what is expected. The driving force behind such models is the fact that the foreign exchange market displays multiple equilibria (see, for example, Ozkhan and Sutherland, 1995).

The ideas developed in this chapter point towards an explanation for currency crises based on private sector deficits due to high levels of fixed capital formation, financed by capital inflows (mainly in the form of short-term debt). It will be argued that this choice of finance creates problems, because of a lack of control over the actions of managers, so that the investment undertaken is not determined according to value maximization principles and hence asset prices (including the exchange rate) fall significantly as expected returns decline. If the high levels of investment have been financed by foreign currency borrowing then the realization of a sudden collapse in asset values will generate the potential for a currency crisis.

Thus we can have a high investment/high debt regime where the economy is growing strongly, financed by foreign currency loans flowing into the domestic banking system, which then lend on to enterprises. This equilibrium is dependent on a credible pegged exchange rate regime, sustained by high real growth and the consequent expected real returns necessary to service the domestic loans, financed by inflows of capital. Continuation of the capital inflows will ensure that the external value of the currency is maintained. However, if the returns on investment decline, this equilibrium is no longer sustainable. The banking sector will suffer a crisis as firms are unable to service their debts and as a result the flow of international capital into domestic banks will stop. An alternative low investment/low debt equilibrium would emerge where the economy is growing more slowly, with investment financed mainly by domestic savings perhaps with some limited (direct) foreign investment.

Thus poor lending/investment decisions during the high investment/high debt phase generate the conditions necessary for a switch to the low investment/low debt regime. One of the consequences of this switch in regime is the collapse of the pegged exchange rate regime because of the drastic fall in the capital inflows which have been sustaining it. But this allows for speculative attacks on the currency since market operators will recognize that a currency devaluation must take place in the future (note that such a scenario can also encourage international investors to favour short term lending which itself will increase the possibility of any currency crisis). Speculation brings forward the date at which the collapse occurs, but is not responsible for the failure of the peg to hold.

The financial environment can be even tougher in the short run (and hence imply significantly greater costs from the collapse of the currency than outlined above) for a number of reasons. If monetary policy is directed towards protecting the exchange rate through increases in interest rates then firms will find their financial position deteriorating with increasing probability of bankruptcy (the IMF has been criticized extensively for forcing this policy on economies such as Thailand when the crisis first hit and putting healthy enterprises into severe financial difficulties as a consequence). Furthermore, the failure of firms to meet their debt obligations leads banks to cut back on lending as they attempt to build loan-loss provisions. This would have particularly severe effects when the regulation of banks has been lax and hence loan-loss provisions have been inadequate. Additionally, the banking system cannot meet its foreign currency obligations as a result of the exchange rate collapse. International financiers may overreact to this default and cut back even on profitable investment. Finally, the collapse of asset (stock and property) markets, which typically are overvalued during the high investment regime as a result of bubbles (the price of assets do not reflect the present value of future income stream), creates further problems as firms and banks find that the value of loan collateral drops dramatically (this point is discussed in Edison *et al.*, 1998). These effects worsen the banking crisis considerably and this has knock-on effects on the currency.

The explanation of the currency/banking crisis given above relies on the observation that investment returns are not sustained and highlights the reason as a lack of appropriate corporate governance. The rest of this chapter investigates this issue for the East Asian economies affected by the crisis. Therefore, we do not consider what we have highlighted as the short-run costs of the crisis, although much of the discussion of the Asian crisis in the literature (for example, about the role of the IMF, of the impact of liberalization of capital markets, concerning the role of speculators) has been about the short-run consequences of the collapse of the pegged exchange rate regime.

The chapter is divided into four main sections. In the next section we consider the arguments which have been used to explain the failure of the MM propositions and what such failure implies for optimum financial structure. The third section considers how the interaction between firms' decision making and financial structure is influenced by external events, in particular the overall macroeconomic environment, in the context of the recent experience of a number of East Asian economies. The impact that this has on firms' and financial market behaviour is considered. The fourth section considers the recent developments in the financial structure of firms in South East Asian economies and discusses how corporate control mechanisms (or the lack of them) have been a cause of the problems recently faced. This section contains analysis of sectoral data as well as econometric estimation of investment functions using a panel of firm-level data. A final section summarizes the results of the chapter and considers the policy implications.

FINANCIAL STRUCTURE AND THE BEHAVIOUR OF FIRMS

In making investment decisions firms should increase capital stock until the value of the firm is maximized. In a world without distortions (such as differential taxation, capital market imperfections or bankruptcy costs) the way in which that investment is financed is immaterial to the optimum level of capital stock. This was the argument put forward by Modigliani and Miller (1958) in their seminal work. The essential intuition is as follows. Suppose that the firm finances itself through equity issue (normalized at one) only, so that it has a value V representing the discounted value of future earnings. Now let a proportion be financed by debt rather than equity. Then the value of the shares is $V - I$ where I is the discounted value of the payments on the debt. In other words the value of the firm is independent of the choice of financial structure. The reason is that, alternatively, an individual investor could have borrowed to finance purchase of, say, all of the shares and would have received the value of V but would be required to pay interest equal to I, so that the net worth of the transaction is $(V - I)$. The two situations are identical, when capital markets are perfect. As MM showed (Modigliani and Miller, 1963) this argument can take into account the tax deductibility of interest payments, and the increased probability of bankruptcy as more debt is issued, without destroying the basic intuition. The result is extremely powerful, with enormous implications for corporate finance but, of course, as is well known, is dependent on assumptions which are not likely to hold in practice. In particular, the problem of asymmetric information and the resulting agency problems, imperfections in the capital markets and positive bankruptcy costs work to cause the breakdown of the MM result. Hence, if we are to find significant effects of financial structure on firms' decisions, we will have to look to these three key areas for explanation. We now turn to this issue.

When we consider decision making in firms we must recognize that those who make the decisions often have superior information compared to those who own the firm or are creditors to it. This creates a number of alternative possibilities. Thus there is a potential moral hazard problem that managers may not act in the best interests of the owners. By keeping the level of debt to a minimum and, consequently, ignoring profitable investment, managers can retain greater control over the firm's cash flow (this is the free cash flow hypothesis proposed by Jensen, 1986). Even if there is no conflict between managers' and owners' interest, financial structure may still be important in the presence of asymmetric information. Ross (1977) has pointed out that there is an incentive for firms to increase debt since it can be taken as a positive signal about the firm (the risk of insolvency is greater for poorly performing firms who will therefore reduce their debt). Kraus and Litzenberger (1973) showed that a firm's value decreases with increase in debt because of positive bankruptcy costs and an increase in probability of bankruptcy as debt increases. Alternatively, Jensen and Meckling (1976) argue that, since managers will work in the interests of owners (shareholders), they have an incentive to choose high-risk (and high-return) projects as debt increases. Thus agency costs for debt holders (incurred from monitoring or imposing restrictive covenants) increase as debt increases. Another argument for an additional cost of external finance is due to Myers and Majluf (1984), who point out that investors will only use publicly available information in setting the terms of finance for firms. Hence the cost of external finance may be too high, causing a rejection by managers of projects with positive net present values. There is an incentive for firms to use internal finance for investment and then debt, rather than equity, the so-called 'pecking order' model of finance.

In addition to the advantages of using internal finance, there may be particular biases towards types of finance at various stages of development. A firm has an incentive to acquire a reputation as a good borrower so as to benefit from lower borrowing costs in the future (see Diamond, 1991). Firms' behaviour in their early life is constrained by the incentive effects of reputation acquisition and banks may be the predominant sources of external finance since they are the main source of credit history (reputation). Another feature to take into account is the fact that transactions costs on financial assets are not homogeneous. Equity issue for small (immature) firms is a relatively expensive process because of lump-sum costs. Hence there is a bias against equity finance for these enterprises, which consequently rely either on debt (bank finance) or internally generated funds (but note contrary evidence reported by Singh, 1994).

A further issue is the differential taxation treatment of bonds and equities. Two ideas relevant here are the effects of taxation on firms and their owners, respectively. Whilst early work (Miller and Modigliani, 1963) argued that a corporate tax implies that the value of the firm is an increasing function of debt, later work by Miller (1977) showed that taxation has no effect on individual firm financial structure when personal taxation is also taken into account. Later research (such as De Angelo and Masulis, 1980) has shown, however, that tax can make a difference particularly when attention is paid to depreciation and other tax shield schemes.

To summarize, therefore, we can find a number of reasons why financial structure is important. These are the results of agency problems, where the objectives of managers and owners may diverge or where those of debt holders and equity holders are in conflict. The existence of capital market imperfections where, for example, asymmetric information can create an incentive for internal funds rather than external funds and bonds rather than equity also provides a mechanism whereby the MM proposition does not hold. In addition, there is a preference for bank-based finance in the early stages of development. Finally, the tax system can also create incentives for equity rather than debt or vice versa.

In the case of the economies most affected by the Asian financial crisis, we can highlight a number of features which have particular relevance. Firstly, there will be reliance on banks, since financial systems tend to be underdeveloped.

Thus debt holders (banks) will need to be aware of the potential conflicts in interest between them and the owners of the firm. In particular, there may be incentives for firms to undertake relatively risky investment in order to make high returns or to follow other objectives (such as growth maximization) rather than enhancing the value of the firm. Beyond the existence of agency problems, because of asymmetric information, it can also be argued that the institutional and general economic environment played a role in the failure of proper corporate governance procedures (on related issues for the OECD countries, see, for example, Alonso and Iturriga, 1997). It is this issue which we now consider.

THE EXTERNAL ENVIRONMENT AND THE FIRM'S FINANCIAL STRUCTURE

The discussion so far has emphasized problems, internal to the operation of the firm, which may cause the failure of the MM propositions. We now turn to consider the way in which the external environment can affect the sort of monitoring procedures which banks should carry out. We will proceed by identifying how the factors identified above are influenced by the general institutional and economic environment and then draw conclusions as to how significant the external environment is likely to be.

Firstly, we consider the overall health of an economy. At a time when the economy is growing strongly, whilst the agency problems identified above still exist, their impact is likely to be reduced. The main reasons are that the level of bankruptcy costs, and the probability of incurring them, will fall. To justify this assertion, note that bankruptcy costs relate to the additional costs imposed by having to liquidate the assets of the firm. But the ability to sell assets is a function of the state of the economy and we would expect that the discount necessary to find a buyer would fall as the economy grows strongly, for two reasons. Firstly, the risk premium will reduce, since the probability of market expansion exceeds that of contraction; secondly, the market for capital goods will be relatively liquid, reducing the liquidity premium. In addition, as the general well-being of the economy increases, the probability of individual firm bankruptcy declines (but note that this does not necessarily imply that bankruptcies themselves decline, since this depends on the number of new projects (enterprises) created). Furthermore, we have identified that monitoring can reduce agency problems. But part of the cost of monitoring is information gathering. In a strongly growing economy there are incentives to reduce this activity since the benefits of acquiring information are reduced as bankruptcy probability falls, while the costs of gathering information will not and, indeed, could rise, if a growing economy implies creation of new opportunities.

Secondly, we can consider the impact of the institutional structure of the financial system and, more generally, the economy. We have already noted that, in the early stages of development, firms will tend to use banks as the main providers of external finance. Economies with relatively underdeveloped and protected financial markets (which invariably means great emphasis is placed on the banking system and debt instruments), therefore may, in fact, be providing what amounts to an optimal financial structure. However, such economies are also likely to have wealth and power concentrated in a small number of powerful individuals or families. As a result, inappropriate business relationships may arise. For example, managers/owners of the firm may enter into relationships with banks which rely more on personal contacts and mutual benefits than on a realistic assessment of business potential. This can become even more apparent when there is cross-ownership (between banks and enterprises), as may happen in economies with highly concentrated wealth distribution or where such an ownership structure has been a feature of the development of their financial system. The problems will be further exacerbated when regulatory and supervisory agencies develop too slowly and hence are unable to provide an appropriate level of monitoring of the banking system. The situation will be made even more complicated when political power is too closely connected with industrial/commercial interests. The opportunities for crony-capitalism are much greater when there is not a clear dividing line between the political, financial and industrial sectors.

A third issue which arises from the nature of financial development is the limited forms of financial assets which are available. This creates the potential for greater instability in the face of shocks. For example, because of the lack of assets to diversify risks there may be more emphasis placed on short maturity assets and holding assets over short periods of time. This increases the risks which firms face, since they are exposed to the possibility that finance will not be renewed at maturity and this may encourage them to go for projects which are more speculative but which may deliver higher returns more quickly. In addition, there is less incentive for debt holders to monitor properly the actions of the firm, since the planning horizon is shortened as debt maturity declines. The lack of variety in domestic financial assets also creates a need to look to foreign markets for investment finance. We can identify two effects from this. Firstly, the risks associated with unexpected currency changes increase; secondly, foreign holders of domestic financial assets are unlikely to monitor, either as effectively or at as low a cost, as domestic holders. Indeed, they may pass this responsibility on to the local banks by lending to them directly. But if the local banks are not undertaking their proper monitoring responsibilities this will not improve governance.

The fact that domestic financial markets are underdeveloped, and that this leads to reliance on international capital markets and on shorter-dated assets, also creates problems should a financial crisis occur. If the lending is predominantly short-term then the pace at which the problems arise can be very fast and create significant difficulties for a properly worked-out debt restructuring (note that Radelet and Sachs, 1998, have criticized international agencies for failing to assist in this process). Furthermore, if the debt is backed by foreign currency borrowing, the situation evolves at a very fast pace. By attacking the currency, speculators are able to force the issue as a collapse of the pegged exchange rate regime triggers the banking sector problems which result from the poor lending decisions made in the good times.

There are other risks associated with high levels of capital inflows at a macroeconomic level. The nominal (insofar as it can) and real exchange rates (through domestic price inflation) will appreciate and distort resource allocation (towards the non-traded sectors and towards those industries which rely on imported products, such as raw materials). This resource misallocation (which can generate a price bubble in real estate and will cause some industries to prosper which would not be profitable at the long-run equilibrium exchange rate) will eventually need to be corrected and will result in exchange rate adjustment which, when linked to the short-term borrowing in foreign currency and the high-risk investment which it has financed, creates an increased risk of a financial crisis.

Beyond the (lack of) action of financial markets, another area of concern relates to the role of the government sector. It is well recognized that it is important for markets to be given as much freedom as possible to promote economic efficiency. Hence when governments interfere in the provision of finance for industrial investment they interfere with market mechanisms in two ways. Initially, such directed investment may result in funds being transferred into less productive sectors than would be found in a free market. In addition, the government may increase total investment beyond its optimum level, thus generating intertemporal inefficiencies. Beyond this, however, we can argue that such direct intervention creates distortions in the control mechanisms. Firms' managers may find that they can ignore the constraints which debt might impose upon them. Secondly, the very act of government intervention will reduce the incentive to monitor. Holders of debt may well expect the government to underwrite the debt (this point is emphasized by Krugman, 1998).

The above discussion has highlighted that the agency problems, which may lead firms to behave in non-optimal fashion, are greater in fast-growing economies with limited financial sector development. Hence it is especially important for such economies to have a properly functioning legal and regulatory framework within which the consequences of such inefficiencies can be resolved and to ensure that their costs are kept to a minimum. Unfortunately, this has not been in place for the Asian economies most affected by the financial crisis. Not only have the regulatory and legal systems been unable to prevent the impact of the agency problems discussed above, they have also been found wanting in responding to the crisis once it had hit. If investors had recourse to the law, and the regulators had imposed effective control, the problems would have been tackled earlier and their real effects would have been reduced. It cannot be argued that the crisis was not inevitable. It was the local environment in which firms, banks, regulators and government operated which interacted with the external environment to create an unsustainable situation. This highlights a crucial point, that the effects of financial structure are influenced by the external environment both in macroeconomic and in institutional terms. If financial sector development lags behind that in the real economy it is important to ensure that proper legal and regulatory safeguards are in place to prevent the worst consequences of such underdevelopment.

We conclude this section with a summary of the key propositions forthcoming from the discussion above.

1. If an economy grows quickly, it is likely that bankruptcy costs will fall and the benefits from monitoring will also decline, since the probability of bankruptcy will fall. Hence firms may be financed to overinvest and are not properly controlled by debt holders.
2. A debt-based financial structure may be optimal for economies with a lack of mature firms. However, this has implications for monitoring and a consequent control over the activities of firms and these activities may not operate effectively when the financial and industrial sectors are too closely linked and when regulatory agencies do not operate effectively.
3. A further implication of a lack of financial development is that opportunities for effective risk diversification are not available. This may force investors to favour shorter maturity assets and hence create a potentially more volatile financial sector environment. Thus shocks to the system will have greater and quicker-acting effects.
4. Demand for funds for investment will go into international capital markets when domestic financial markets are underdeveloped and the economy has adopted liberal policies towards the capital account. As a result of this, the real exchange rate will appreciate, causing resources to be misallocated, going into sectors which are relatively protected from the effects of appreciation such as real estate and those for which imported products are more important.
5. The involvement of the government in directing investment funds, the existence of cronyism and corrupt activities and a lack of appropriate regulation of the financial sector will also imply that financial markets do not play their proper role in controlling the actions of firms and significantly exacerbate the problems identified above.

6. Although the lack of financial sector development interacts with the economic environment to create conditions conducive to a financial crisis, it is not argued that such a crisis is inevitable. Regulation of the financial sector becomes crucial to avoid the worst excesses of the agency problems identified and a well-functioning and transparent legal framework provides the private sector with a mechanism for dealing with the problems created in an efficient manner. If these are not in place then the adverse consequences and resulting costs of the lack of control over firms can increase very significantly. Furthermore, inappropriate macroeconomic policies (particularly with regard to pegging of the exchange rate) also play their part in creating conditions for a crisis to occur.

In the last two sections we have introduced a number of ideas to explain why the Asian financial crisis occurred. The main driving force behind these arguments is that failure of corporate governance mechanisms led to excessive investment being undertaken. We now turn to consider the evidence for this assertion.

AN ANALYSIS OF INVESTMENT, CAPITAL STRUCTURE AND FIRMS' OBJECTIVES FOR COUNTRIES IN SOUTH EAST ASIA

In this section we consider the recent experience of Pacific and South East Asian economies with regard to financial structure and discuss the implications of the observed developments for the analysis of the recent crises in the region. Our analysis takes the form of analysing a panel data set of firms from the crisis-hit countries. We use the following abbreviations for the countries we study; I: Indonesia, K: South Korea, M: Malaysia, TA: Taiwan, TH: Thailand. The data are taken from Datastream; the details of the data used are given in the appendix. The choice of South East Asian economies allows us to compare the differences between economies in the region which have been affected to varying degrees by the 1997 financial crisis.

We start with some basic features of firm financial structure and performance. Firstly, we report the proportion of equity to total assets (see Figure 16.1). This is an average across 1992–6. This provides an immediate insight into the financial structure which firms choose. However, it may be that it is less a choice than a forced decision as a result of a lack of financial development, where the stock market does not really play a significant role in the allocation of capital.

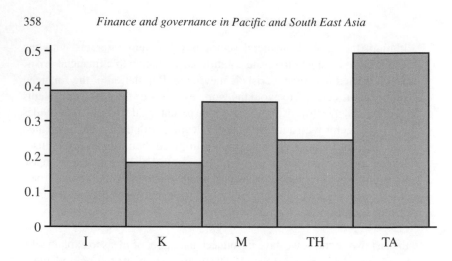

Figure 16.1   Equity as a proportion of total assets

It is clear from the figure that the economies considered have rather variable use of equity markets. That Taiwan has a relatively developed financial market is indicated by the importance of equity financing. Note also that the figures do not change very much over the period (not shown). There is not a significant change in attitude towards financial structure over time. In developed countries we may observe the following comparable figures (see Alonso and Iturriga, 1997: Germany (0.24), Japan (0.30), UK (0.44), USA (0.41)). Hence the economies in this study have had a financial structure more like Germany or Japan than the USA or UK. But in order to consider this further we should investigate other features of financial structure.

One aspect we have considered as important is the relative share of debt which is short-term. Figure 16.2 shows the proportion of debt with less than a year to maturity relative to total debt.

Here we may observe that, for all the economies studied, the proportion of short-term debt seems to be high. However, for comparison, note that for developed economies the figures are not so different, except in the market-based systems: Germany (0.69), Japan (0.69), USA (0.43), UK (0.62). But, as we have argued above, the level of short-term debt, allied to a volatile macro-economic picture, may create particular problems and increase the probability of a crisis taking place.

Another way of looking at the issue of short-term debt is to consider how its use has changed over the data period. In Figure 16.3 we show what has happened.

Interestingly, there has been some decline in this ratio over the data period, which suggests that action was being taken to reduce the amount of short-term debt, although it is at a high level through the whole of the period. We now

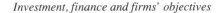

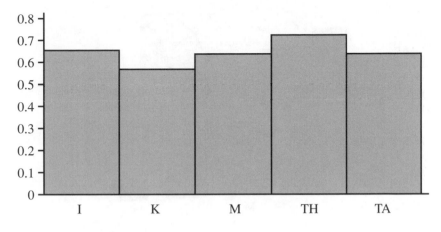

Figure 16.2   Short-term debt as a proportion of total debt

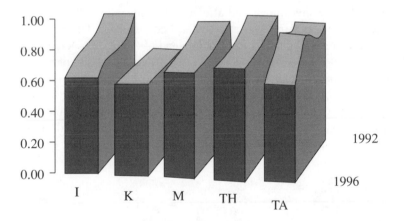

Figure 16.3   Time path of short-term debt ratio

consider what the investment performance of firms has been. Figure 16.4 shows the relative investment rates for the five economies.

It is clear that all the economies examined had relatively high investment rates. What is more, these rates have been sustained for a longer period of time than is evident from the data set we have used. Hence our sample of firms confirms that these economies were indeed high investment economies. But an issue we should consider is the profitability of such investment. Figure 16.5 shows the trends in return on assets.

Hence we may note that all of the economies, apart from Korea, seemed to be earning similar returns on their assets. The low figures for Korea illustrate

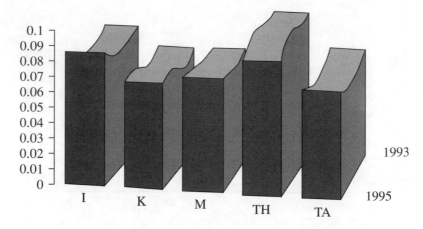

Figure 16.4   Change in short-term debt ratio

that much of the overinvestment had already taken place by 1993 and the financial performance of firms was affected as a consequence. Of interest is the decline in the return on assets towards the end of the period, potentially signalling that problems were looming for investors. Note that the sort of returns experienced are not out of line with those seen in developed countries. For example, we may note the following figures: Germany (0.058), Japan (0.066), USA (0.075), UK (0.096). Typically, those economies with more market-oriented financial systems have required a higher return on assets, indicating the effects of financial markets on firm performance.

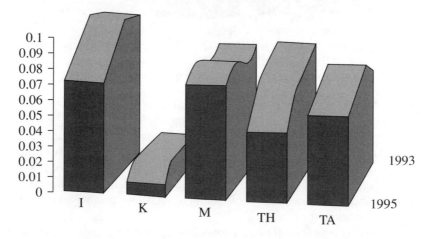

Figure 16.5   New assets as a proportion of total assets

We have a general picture of firms in these economies which have had high investment, respectable but declining returns on assets and a relative lack of equity finance (except for the case of Taiwan). Although we cannot illustrate this with data, it should also be noted that increasing reliance on foreign currency bank borrowing was also a feature of these economies (again with the exception of Taiwan). Whether this constitutes a case for claiming that the financial structure encouraged excessive investment is not clear, but further investigation of the relationship between financial structure, investment and return on assets should throw more light on this issue.

We now consider the relationship between various balance sheet measures for firms in different sectors by calculating sectoral averages over the five years 1992–6. In particular, we are interested in the extent to which sectors with more debt undertake more investment or, equivalently, whether increased investment is associated with higher amounts of debt. Furthermore, we want to investigate the extent to which increased investment is associated with reduced return on assets and higher sales growth. Such an association would be indicative of agency problems, with investment directed towards sales growth rather than value maximization.

The rationale for using sectoral averages is that sector-specific variations do not dominate. By taking sector averages we are removing a lot of 'noise' at the individual firm level. But by focusing on sectors we are also able to use more information that is in the data than would be the case if we used economy-wide averages. Using cross-country data will tend to reduce the importance of sector-specific effects incorporated into the data as long as sectors behave differently across countries. Comparing data in a specific sector across the different countries in the sample shows no particular pattern. The appendix contains more information on the data we have used and their sectoral composition.

The first issue we consider is the relationship between debt and the level of fixed assets. It can be argued that, the higher proportion of fixed assets, the greater the risk to the firm and hence the lower the debt ratio which is optimal. Thus a situation of increasing leverage in industries with higher fixed assets could signal potential vulnerability should economic circumstances deteriorate. Figure 16.6 shows the pattern for countries where it exists.

Looking at all countries in the sample, we do not observe any specific relationship. However, when we look at individual countries, for all except Korea there appears to be a positive relationship. This implies that, should there be a liquidity crunch, companies would find it more difficult to survive. Note, however, that the relationship is not very strong, except in Taiwan, where doubling fixed assets (relative to total assets) is associated with an approximate doubling of the debt to asset ratio. The probability of a liquidity crisis is a function not only of the liquidity of assets but also of the maturity structure of debt. Hence we consider next the ratio of short-term debt to total debt and its relationship to the level of fixed assets to total assets (see Figure 16.7).

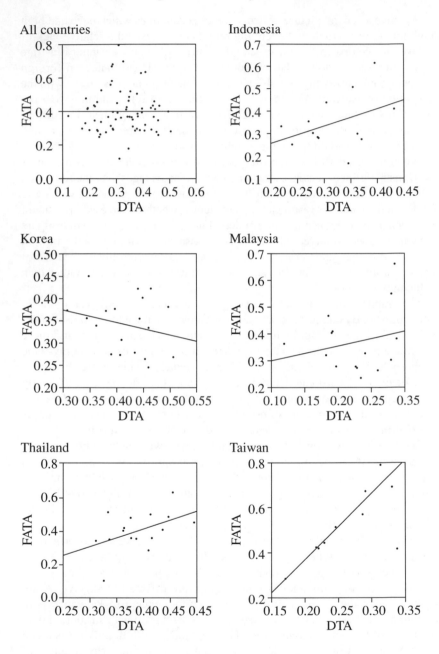

Figure 16.6   Relationship between debt/total assets (DTA) and fixed assets/total assets (FATA)

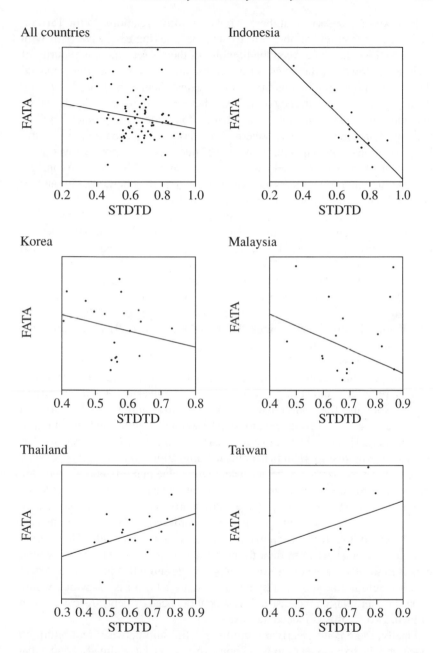

Figure 16.7   Relationship between fixed assets/total assets (FATA) and short-term debt/total debt (STDTD)

Here we may observe that there is only a positive relationship for Taiwan. The other economies do not seem to have been taking excessive risks with regard to the balance between the liquidity of their assets and the maturity of their debt. However, this does not mean that they would not suffer financial distress should economic conditions turn against them. One issue is whether the debt is in foreign currency or not. Another relates to their ability to sustain operations in the face of deteriorating market conditions. The problems will be particularly acute if firms have overinvested prior to the economic downturn. We have argued above that this may well be due to poor corporate governance brought about by excessive debt. One way of examining this issue is to consider whether high investment rates are associated with high debt ratios, although of course this does not imply causality. See Figure 16.8.

We may observe that there appears to be a positive relationship between the acquisition of new assets and leverage when we take all countries together. However, this relationship is not particularly strong and therefore we also consider individual countries. For Indonesia, Malaysia and Thailand, it is clearly positive, while for Taiwan and Korea we observe a negative relationship. Therefore there does not appear to be a consistent interaction between investment and increases in debt. The following figures provide some further insight into the processes at work. Firstly (see Figure 16.9) we examine the relationship between the ex post real return on assets, real sales growth and investment across all countries.

By inspection, the relationship between investment and real sales growth is both more precise and stronger than that between investment and real rate of return. Note also that individual countries all show similar trends (although there does not seem to be any relationship between investment and rate of return in Thailand). This is evidence that increasing the size of firms was regarded as an objective more important than value maximization. Of course, it is possible for growth maximization to be consistent with value maximization in the long run, but if firms are pursuing growth maximization then we would expect to see a clear impact in the event of economic downturn. We have highlighted above that firms may face a liquidity problem if economic conditions deteriorate once high levels of investment (in pursuit of growth) have been made. They would have to rely on short-term debt to meet their obligations. Hence we would expect to see a negative relationship between sales growth and short-term debt which would not be matched by an increase in debt to assets (which would happen if there was an increase in investment financed by debt). As can be seen in Figure 16.10, this is indeed the case.

Finally, there is no clearly discernible relationship between real return on assets and the fixed asset ratio (see Figure 16.11). We have already argued that the development of capital-intensive industries is high-risk and consequently we would expect the return to reflect the higher risk. This does not seem to

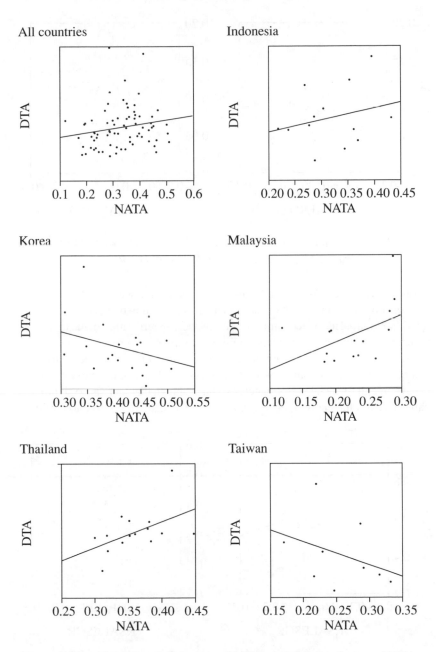

Figure 16.8   New assets/total assets (NATA) and debt/total assets (DTA)

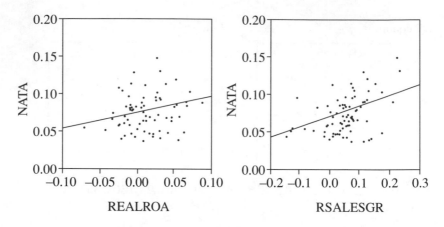

Figure 16.9   Investment (NATA) against real rate of return (REALROA) and real sales growth (RSALESGR) for all countries

have been the case; indeed, for Thailand and Indonesia, we observe a negative relationship. In addition, we observe that sales growth is negatively related to fixed asset ratio. Hence economic conditions were deteriorating in the industries which would have most difficulty coping with the problems.

To summarize, we have examined certain features of firms' financial structure in a number of the economies of South East Asia and related them to investment behaviour and financial performance. We have shown that there is no significant pattern across the economies in terms of the use of debt relative to equity to

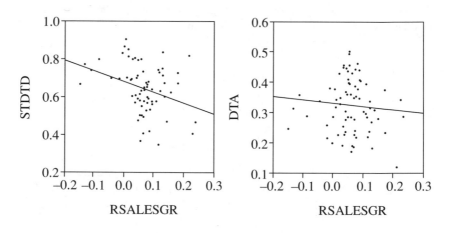

Figure 16.10   Short-term debt/total debt against real sales growth and debt/total assets against real sales growth for all countries

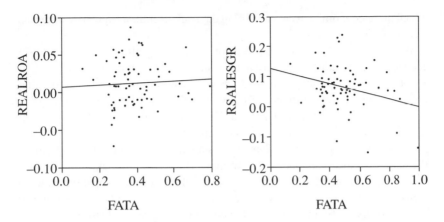

Figure 16.11   *Fixed assets/total assets against return on assets and real sales growth for all countries*

finance investment, although we may note that all the economies except Taiwan seem to rely more on debt than on equity. Similarly, we do not see an obvious trend in use of short-term debt and, indeed, observe that Taiwan seems to rely more on short-term debt to finance investment, in that sectors which invest more also have more short-term debt. There does appear to have been a reduction in short-term debt to total debt over the period, but we have also noted that there is an increased need to build short-term debt in sectors which are experiencing low or negative sales growth. This is clearly a liquidity rather than investment effect. The rate of investment is uniformly high during the period, although the return on assets is declining and, in the case of Korea, unacceptably low. We have also been able to establish that high investment has taken place in capital-intensive industries. This is a risky strategy, since a deterioration in economic conditions will have greater effects in industries with large amounts of illiquid assets. Further analysis of the performance of the corporate sector has thrown up a number of results. Firstly, we do find that investment is positively associated with real returns, as would be expected if the firm is value-maximizing. However, there appears to be a stronger relationship between investment and real sales growth which, while not inconsistent with value maximization, does suggest that firms may have been more interested in growth than in return to capital. This observation is supported by the fact that firms are having to increase short-term debt in the face of low sales growth. Hence they have not properly taken account of the risks of the increased investment which has been undertaken. The further observation that capital-intensive industries have not yielded higher returns on assets and also have experienced the lowest sales growth is further indication of the overall risks to which these economies were subjecting themselves if their high growth regime were to falter.

We now turn to consider a more formal investigation of the investment decision by estimating a standard neoclassical investment model. However, we adapt it to take account of the analysis we have highlighted above. We then estimate this model, in its empirically testable form, for three of the Asian currency crisis economies: Thailand, Korea and Malaysia (data availability restricted the choice, as amplified in the appendix).

Firstly, we construct a version of the standard value maximization model. We start with the basic optimizing framework. A firm, in making investment decisions, is assumed to maximize the value of the firm, an objective which is consistent with the objectives of the owners of the firm who are assumed to have well-diversified portfolios. Because the value of the firm is dependent upon future as well as current conditions, under the assumption of risk neutrality the managers of the firm should maximize the expected value. The expected value of the firm at time t is given by $V(t)$, where we take the simplest assumption that all investment is financed through debt (although a mixture of retained earnings and debt would be permissible as long as the costs of internal and external sources of finance are the same). We can write $V(t)$ as

$$V(t) = E_t \left[\sum_{i=0}^{\infty} \left\{ p(t+i)Y(t+i) - w(t+i)N(t+i) - p^I(t+i)I(t) - C_t\big(I(t+i)\big) \right\} \beta^i \right],$$

$$(16.1)$$

where $p(t + i)$ is the price of output, $Y(t + i)$ is output, $w(t + i)$ is the wage and $N(t + i)$ is labour input, $p^I(t + i)$ is the price of capital goods and $I(t + i)$ is the level of investment, where the index $(t + i)$ is time period. $C(.)$ is the investment adjustment cost function, while β is the rate of discount. The valuation is conditional on expectations formed using information at time t (E_t). The firm operates under the following dynamic equation for the capital stock:

$$K(t + i) = (1 - \delta)K(t + i - 1) + I(t + i), \qquad (16.2)$$

where K is the capital stock and δ is the rate of capital stock depreciation.

Forming the Langrangean, we have

$$L = E_t \left\{ \sum_{i=0}^{\infty} \beta^i \left[\begin{array}{l} \{P(t+i)Y(t+i) - w(t+i)N(t+i) \\ -p^I(t+i)I(t+i) - C_t\big(I(t+i)\big)\} \\ +\lambda(t+i)\big(-K(t+i) + (1-\delta)K(t+i-1) + I(t+i)\big) \end{array} \right] \right\} \qquad (16.3)$$

and hence the conditions for optimization are as follows:

$$\frac{\partial L}{\partial N(t+i)} = 0 = E_t\left\{P(t+i)F_2\big(K(t+i),N(t+i)\big) - w(t+i)\right\} \quad (16.4)$$

$$\frac{\partial L}{\partial I(t+i)} = 0 = E_t\left\{-p^I(t+i) - C_t'\big(I(t+i)\big) + \lambda(t+i)\right\} \quad (16.5)$$

$$\frac{\partial L}{\partial K(t+i)} = 0 = E_t\left\{\beta^i\left\{P(t+i)F_1\big(K(t+i),N(t+i)\big) - \lambda(t+i)\right\} + \lambda(t+i+1)(1-\delta)\beta^{i+1}\right\}.$$

$$(16.6)$$

In addition, we have the transversality condition which imposes a zero capital stock in the indefinite future. The first condition sets the marginal product of labour equal to the real wage (it is assumed that labour can be adjusted costlessly), the second condition sets the marginal revenue of investment to its marginal cost (including adjustment cost). The third condition ensures that capital is allocated optimally over the time by equating the marginal benefits of an incremental change in the capital stock in the current and future periods.

From the above models we must obtain an explicit expression for the investment function which can be empirically implemented. One method is the q-theory pioneered by Tobin (1969). Alternatively, we will use the dynamic structure of the optimization problem to solve (the Euler equation approach). We use equation (16.5) to solve for $E_t(\lambda(t+i))$ and hence $E_t(\lambda(t+i+1))$ which can be substituted into equation (16.6), yielding a difference equation in $I(t+i)$ and $I(t+i+1)$. This equation can be used to solve for the optimal investment path as long as the expected value of the shadow price of capital $(E_t(\lambda(t+i)))$ for the current $(t+i)$ period can be determined. This problem is usually approached by finding suitable instruments with which to forecast the future profits of the firm, rather than resort to stock market valuation.

The estimated form of the Euler equation is derived from the basic value-maximizing model by imposing rational expectations and assuming a quadratic adjustment cost function of the form:

$$C\big(I_{t+i}, K_{t+i-1}\big) = \frac{a_0}{2}\left[\frac{I_{t+i}}{K_{t+i-1}} - a_1\right]^2 K_{t+i}. \quad (16.7)$$

In addition, the production function is assumed linear homogenous in capital and labour and it is also assumed that labour always receives its marginal product. We also can control for imperfectly competitive markets in which firms sell their product (in this case, the price of the product is a function of sales) and also for increasing probability of bankruptcy as the use of debt increases. This yields an empirical specification:

$$\left(\frac{I(t)}{K(t)}\right) = b_0 + b_1\left(\frac{I(t-1)}{K(t-1)}\right) + b_2\left(\frac{I(t-1)}{K(t-1)}\right)^2 + b_3\left(\frac{\Pi(t-1)}{K(t-1)}\right)$$

$$+ b_4\left(\frac{Y(t-1)}{K(t-1)}\right) + b_5\left(\frac{B(t-1)}{K(t-1)}\right)^2 + b_6 R(t) + u(t) \quad (16.8)$$

(see Bond and Meghir, 1994 for details of this derivation). Note that $\Pi(t)$ is cash flow at time t, while $Y(t)$ is output at time t. $R(t)$ is the user cost of capital, which for a panel data set of firms we allow to vary across firms. This introduces a firm-specific effect. As discussed in Bond and Meghir (1994) the appropriate estimation technique when firm-specific effects may be correlated with the error term is to rewrite the variables using the 'orthogonal deviations' transformation and estimate using generalized methods of moments. This is the technique used here with lagged variables as instruments in the GMM estimation.

In addition, we wish to consider whether behaviour deviates from this value maximization model. To consider this issue we adopt the technique of creating sub-samples of the data set using particular variables as indicators of the potential for departures from optimization behaviour. Note that we have identified that firms may pursue sales growth rather than value maximization. Hence we use sales growth to test the importance of this. We have also investigated two further variables which have been identified as having influence on firm decision making: the first is the debt/asset ratio. The second is the fixed assets ratio. However, our analysis does not find a significant effect of these latter two variables and we do not report the results.

As a first step, we report in Table 16.1 the results of applying our base model, as in equation (16.8). In addition to allowing the user cost of capital to vary across firms, we also include variation across time by introducing a time dummy. Note that the coefficients are defined and signed as follows in the context of the appropriateness of the model (see Bond and Meghir, 1994): $b_1 > 1$; $b_2 < -1$; $b_3 > 0$; $b_4 < 0$; $b_5 < 0$.

Hence failure of these coefficients to satisfy these restrictions can be seen as failure of value maximization. For example, a finding of $b_1 < 1$ can indicate that firms are using a negative discount rate, itself a sign of deviation from value maximization principles. Note that this observation would be supported if b_2 were also positive. As Bond and Meghir point out (this is the focus of their study) the coefficient on cash flow (b_4) will be positive if firms operate under financial constraints.

Table 16.1 Estimation results for basic investment equation

Parameter	Korea	Thailand	Malaysia
b_1	−0.2704 (−6.38)	0.490 (3.98)	−0.66 (−1.89)
b_2	0.00513 (16.77)	−0.085 (−11.48)	−0.000148 (−1.24)
b_3	0.00292 (15.66)	0.0044 (0.623)	0.342 (9.39)
b_4	0.00275 (10.40)	−0.00274 (−0.098)	−0.1108 (−1.82)
b_5	−0.000244 (−1.89)	0.178 (3.86)	0.00501 (8.88)
Sargan test	0.261	0.244	0.275
Data period	1991–6	1992–6	1993–6
No. of firms	507	149	163

Notes: The figures shown in brackets are *t*-values. The test is the Sargan test of overidentifying restrictions implied by the instruments used. The value reported is the probability of the test statistic taking the value found. For Korea and Thailand we used lags $(t − 3)$ or greater as instruments since the Sargan test failed for $(t − 2)$ lags. However, we used $(t − 2)$ or earlier for Malaysia since data were limited and the Sargan test was satisfactory.

It is clear from these results that our basic model does not perform particularly well. There are incorrect signs and also lack of significance for a number of the key coefficients. Only for Thailand do we find reasonable correspondence to our theoretical specification, but note the positive effect of debt, which is not consistent with value maximization. For Korea, the results indicate a lack of value-maximizing behaviour as well as evidence of financial constraints. For Malaysia, the model does not perform well. We now consider the version of the model which allows for difference in behaviour between firms with high and low sales growth. The specification is shown below in equation (16.9):

$$\left(\frac{I(t)}{K(t)}\right) = b_0 + b_1\left(\frac{I(t-1)}{K(t-1)}\right) + b_2\left(\frac{I(t-1)}{K(t-1)}\right)^2 + b_3\left(\frac{\Pi(t-1)}{K(t-1)}\right)$$

$$+ b_4\left(\frac{Y(t-1)}{K(t-1)}\right) + b_5\left(\frac{B(t-1)}{K(t-1)}\right)^2 + b_6 R(t)$$

$$+ b_{10} * SG + b_{11} * SG *\left(\frac{I(t-1)}{K(t-1)}\right) + b_{12} * SG *\left(\frac{I(t-1)}{K(t-1)}\right)^2$$

$$+ b_{13} * SG *\left(\frac{\Pi(t-1)}{K(t-1)}\right) + b_{14} * SG *\left(\frac{Y(t-1)}{K(t-1)}\right)$$

$$+ b_{15} * SG *\left(\frac{B(t-1)}{K(t-1)}\right)^2 + u(t). \tag{16.9}$$

Here *SG* is a dummy variable which is set equal to one for high-growth firms and zero otherwise. Details of how we determine the setting of this dummy variable are contained in the appendix. The results of estimating the model represented by equation (16.9) are given in Table 16.2 below. The results reported are indicative of significant differences between the behaviour of firms according to the past performance of sales growth. This is, of itself, suggestive of a divergence from value maximization principles. However, we can consider this hypothesis in more detail by examining the precise nature of the results.

Table 16.2   Estimation results when firms are sorted according to sales growth

Parameter	Korea	Thailand	Malaysia
b_1	−0.062 (0.12)	0.663(1.17)	0.215 (0.66)
b_2	0.00852 (2.15)	−0.202 (−2.01)	0.00045 (4.31)
b_3	0.40 (1.16)	0.016 (3.83)	0.077 (3.2)
b_4	−0.023 (−1.11)	0.165 (4.55)	−0.435 (−7.42)
b_5	0.0027 (1.62)	−0.0087 (−0.34)	0.00066 (0.77)
b_{11}	1.44 (3.41)	−0.649 (−0.87)	−0.766 (−1.95)
b_{12}	−0.023 (−6.74)	0.249 (2.44)	0.003 (2.5)
b_{13}	−0.00138 (−0.48)	−0.033 (−5.07)	0.184 (0.58)
b_{14}	0.0635 (2.97)	−0.094 (−2.42)	0.318 (4.96)
b_{15}	−0.0033 (−2.23)	0.025 (0.96)	0.011 (5.37)
Sargan test	0.84	0.42	0.561
Data period	1991–6	1992–6	1993–6
No. of firms	507	149	163

Taking the case of Korea first, it may be noted that the parameter estimates are considerably different from those of the base model reported in Table 16.1. For firms which have low sales growth (less than 15 per cent in the previous year) we do not find much explanatory power from the model. In other words, these firms are not apparently engaged in value-maximizing behaviour. However, for the firms with high sales growth the model is reasonably consistent with estimates. Thus $b_1 > 1$ (although $b_2 < 0$ it is not $< −1$). The lack of significance of b_3 is of no real concern but cash flow appears with a positive coefficient, indicating the firms are investment maximizers subject to a financing constraint. The negative sign for b_5 is also consistent with the theoretical model, indicating that firms do attempt to control for the risks of bankruptcy from debt finance. However, together the results suggest that Korean firms will experience problems if there is a sudden deterioration in economic conditions and hence a greater proportion of firms fall into non-optimizing behaviour.

Moving on to Malaysia, we have already noted that the basic model does not perform well. When we control for sales growth, we find similar results. For low sales growth firms, then, the estimated coefficients do not suggest consistency with the theoretical model. That b_1 is not significantly different from zero suggests that firms are effectively using a negative discount rate, a result supported by b_2 being significantly positive. However, b_4 does not indicate the presence of financial constraints for this category of firms. For the high sales growth firms we find that the basic model still lacks explanatory power. The combined effect of $I(t-1)/K(t-1)$ is now negative, while that of $(I(t-1)/K(t-1))^2$ is positive. It may also be noted that these firms suffer from financial constraints, as indicated by the sign of b_4. Furthermore, we also find that b_5 is positive, indicating excessive risk taking by these firms. Hence, if these results are taken together, there appears to be significant deviation from value-maximizing behaviour in the case of Malaysia.

Finally, we turn to Thailand. For low sales growth firms we find a lack of consistency with our basic model. The parameter b_1 is not significantly different from zero, while the parameter b_2 is negative but significantly different from minus one. A negative discount rate is a possible reason. Firms in this category also seem to experience financial constraints. For firms with high sales growth we find that the results for the coefficients on $I(t-1)/K(t-1)$ and $(I(t-1)/K(t-1))^2$ are similar and suggest deviation from the optimizing model. We may also note that the coefficient on $Y(t-1)/K(t-1)$ is now negative and inconsistent with the theory. Thus this term must be picking up some other, possibly expectational, effect. Furthermore, we find that the term on cash flow is now no longer inconsistent with the theory.

To summarize, the results of estimating our investment model indicate behaviour at variance with value maximization. In addition, we find significant differences between firms which we have classified as high-growth and one which is low-growth. This is further evidence that firms are pursuing strategies at variance with standard optimizing behaviour and potentially indicative that sales growth may well figure as an objective which firms are following. This hypothesis is supported by earlier results from examining sectoral data. We also have evidence that cash flow is important for high-growth firms (although not in Thailand, where it is important for low-growth firms). One interpretation of this result is that finance has not been very effectively directed, or, at least, has not been appropriately priced when taking account of the risks involved. Although high-growth Korean firms do seem to recognize the risks of debt finance generally, we do not seem to see much evidence for this across the other economies or indeed for low sales growth firms in Korea.

POLICY CONCLUSIONS

This chapter has considered the way in which financial markets can impose constraints on firms' behaviour and hence the way in which financial structure matters. It has highlighted the fact that macroeconomic and institutional factors can interact to prevent the appropriate constraining influence over the actions of firms, particularly with regard to investment. It has argued that the problems experienced by a number of the former 'tiger' economies of South East Asia can be attributed to a failure to recognize that macroeconomic policy decisions, a lack of financial development and liberal policies towards capital inflows can work together to create an unsustainable economic and financial environment, as evidenced by excessive investment which does not add value and indeed may be value subtracting. In this section we consider what lessons for policy can be gleaned from these arguments.

Firstly, we need to examine the lessons for macroeconomic policy. To begin, we consider the difficulties which are created by pegging an exchange rate at times of substantial capital inflows. This would be clearly unsustainable if such inflows were financing fiscal deficits (the original argument for a currency crisis). But the experience of the Asian financial crisis has been to demonstrate that a private sector investment boom, financed by capital inflows, can rapidly destroy the credibility of a pegged exchange rate, particularly when that investment is directed into sectors which are not likely to sustain the economy in the long run. Secondly, asset price inflation is a cause of concern for policy makers when this is fuelling an already overheated economy. Such an environment is not sustainable and will eventually collapse (probably through a forced floating of the exchange rate). The resulting impact on the economy will be significantly worse if there has been a bubble economy prior to the collapse. Then we will see significant balance sheet problems for the banking sector brought about by bad loans and collapsing asset and real estate prices. As we have discussed, the problem with a pegged exchange rate is that it does not allow national monetary policy to adjust to domestic economic circumstances. Policy makers should be aware of this danger and the potential for fuelling a bubble economy.

Whilst these macro-policy lessons are clear from the analysis in the chapter and have been well documented elsewhere (for example, Radelet and Sachs, 1998) they are not the central theme of the arguments presented. These are related to the structure and performance of the financial sector. The main thrust of the chapter is that an important role for policy is to ensure that financial markets can play their proper role. There are two aspects to this which can be brought out of the analysis of this chapter. One relates to the interaction between macroeconomic behaviour and the financial system. The second relates to ensuring that the financial system operates in an efficient manner and, importantly, that firms are appropriately controlled by their owners and creditors.

Considering the first issue, we have already mentioned that the impact of the exchange rate regime can have a major effect on the risks which the economy faces. Thus high levels of capital inflows can be very beneficial. But they also bring with them increasing potential for instability and volatility. One of the lessons of the Asian financial crisis can be seen to be a failure of macroeconomic policy makers to properly assess the risks of the strategies they were pursuing. The most obvious example of this is the continued maintenance of the pegged exchange rate even when it was becoming clearly unsustainable. A further example is the lack of action to control an asset price and real estate bubble (which was of itself related to the desire to preserve the exchange rate regime). In a similar vein, our analysis of the actions of firms and of their sub-optimal behaviour also suggests that more attention should be paid to the financial performance of the corporate sector. More analysis of the way in which macroeconomic policy is conducted and how it responds to the effects of high growth on private sector behaviour is required to prevent the sort of problems which have been behind the Asian financial crisis.

Beyond this is the development of a proper institutional and regulatory structure in which the financial system operates. Many issue have been flagged as being important. Confidence in the operation of these markets will, of course, have taken a severe beating as a result of the crisis. Hence it is important to re-establish this confidence by improving regulatory control and ensuring that operations are much more transparent than before. There is a danger that attempting to achieve stability by withdrawing domestic financial markets from the global system (as Malaysia has done) will be both ineffective and potentially damaging to the overall development of the domestic economy. The sort of policy adopted by the Thai government, of letting the markets sort the problems out as much as possible, and trying to bring new management and ideas into the financial sector, is much more likely, in the longer term, to be successful, although it carries with it short-term (economic and political) risks which the international community should do its best to minimize by providing financial support.

In terms of restoring confidence in the financial system and ensuring that it plays a full role in the future development of the economy, there are two clear problems which need to be confronted. Firstly, it is necessary to sort out the consequences of the banking sector crisis. One of the recent disturbing trends in a number of the crisis-hit economies is that, as their real economy recovers, they have been seen to be dragging their feet in this regard. It is very important, however, to continue with the reform process. This means closing down those institutions which are beyond rescue and recapitalizing those which can survive. Of course this may mean attracting foreign capital and such inflows may be forthcoming only reluctantly. Hence re-establishing confidence of domestic and foreign investors is vital in the short term. In order to achieve this, and also to promote long-term development, it is crucial to re-establish a proper functioning legal framework. It is not the case that the laws were not in place in these economies, more that they were not applied in an open and even-handed way. This applies particularly to the regulatory system. It has to be recognized that regulation of the financial sector has not been properly undertaken and, as a consequence, there has been the potential for corruption. An overhaul of the regulatory system is required, with the possibility that the regulatory authorities are re-established. It is becoming normal in developed financial markets for regulation of financial services to be brought under one umbrella organization. It may be sensible for this to be seriously considered as part of the regulatory changes which are required in the crisis-hit economies.

Beyond this it is necessary to consider how financial market development can be encouraged so that a more balanced financial structure can emerge. Of course, the role of the government is limited in this respect. Firstly, tax systems often imply favourable treatment of bank lending relative to other forms of finance. Hence any distortion should be corrected. As an intermediate stage it may also be desirable to use the tax system to favour other non-bank sources of finance, such as corporate bonds. The development of stock markets should also be given priority, itself not necessarily easy given that many firms are in a fairly parlous financial state. Transparency of financial accounting is an obvious requirement of a properly functioning stock market. In addition, companies should be required to provide basic information about the way that they are run. For example, it is now standard practice to provide information on the size of the board, the age of directors and compensation packages (at least in the aggregate). But information about individual pay of directors, their equity holdings (particularly in related enterprises or in the financial sector) and the role and identity of non-executive directors (if they exist) and whether they are members of other boards of directors, would also assist in making corporate decision making clearer. The role of cross-shareholdings is a particularly important issue when this involves potential conflicts of interest (for example, when banks and firms hold each other's equity). So is the link between the corporate sector and political parties. Information on donations above a certain level should be routinely included in company statements.

In order to promote the development of a stock market is it important to establish the confidence of the individual investor. A thorough review of the legal framework with a view to promoting (small) investor protection should be undertaken. Some of the measures outlined above, designed to make corporate decision making more transparent, will assist in this regard. It is also very important to ensure that the rule of law is upheld. One way of doing this would be to set up an independent watchdog which has the sole aim of monitoring the legal framework governing investment in financial assets, with a view to highlighting any anomalies and irregular behaviour. Such agencies exist in developed financial markets. A further mechanism for promoting a more open system of corporate governance would be to establish a set of rules which firms would be expected to follow in reporting to, and taking account of the interests of, their shareholders. The issue of corporate governance is one which is increasingly being examined in developed economies with a view to ensuring that powerful interests do not ride roughshod over minority groupings. One suggestion has been to give more powers to non-executive directors as monitors of the company performance. It has also been suggested that executive pay should be related to profitability and not to volume of sales or company size (for more discussion, see Dimsdale and Preveser, 1994). The role of stake-holders has also been highlighted (these can include a company's workforce, its customers and the general public). Whilst each of these recommendations has been devised in the context of developed stock market systems, they reflect a general concern that the creation of financial institutions and markets is not a sufficient condition for efficient allocation of capital. It has been argued that lack of financial development has been one of the causes of the problems seen in South East Asia, but a general recommendation to promote financial development will not solve the problem. These markets must work properly and using the experience of the developed economies (for example) can help in making this happen.

Overall, then, the policy conclusions of this analysis are that the crisis which has affected a number of Asian economies over the last two years is not evidence of a failure of international capital markets, but of domestic financial markets, regulation and policy. If the result of the crisis is to bring forth a strengthening of the regulatory system, a broadening of financial structure, the creation of a clear and properly applied legal framework, increasingly transparent and responsive corporate governance mechanisms, then it is likely that the 'tiger' economies will once again rear their heads and resume their hunting down of economic opportunities afforded to them in the global economic jungle.

APPENDIX

In this appendix we provide details of the data which have been used in the fourth sections of the chapter. The details of firms' performance (balance sheet and income statement) have been taken from Datastream. The period varies from 1993–6 for the analysis of sectoral data while for estimation of the investment equation it depends on the country. Thus for Korea we have 1991–6, for Thailand 1992–6 while for Malaysia we have 1993–6. The variables (with their Datastream codes in brackets) used are total equity and reserves (305); total debt (1301); borrowing with a maturity of less than a year (309); total fixed assets (net of depreciation) (339); total new fixed assets (435); pre-tax profit (154).

The choice of data reflects availability. For example, we represent cash flow in terms of pre-tax profit rather than of operating profit with addition of depreciation allowance. Similarly, we use total debt to represent loan capital. Both of these approximations will be suitable for the particular countries studied. Also we do not attempt to calculate the capital stock using the perpetual inventory method since we have a short time period and hence the approximation implicit in the use of balance sheet data should not be too imprecise.

Table A.1   Sectoral analysis

	I	K	M	TH	TA
Agriculture	37	39	114	106	0
Chemicals	34	249	45	48	52
Construction	57	543	214	115	82
Distribution	15	52	39	52	0
Diversified	0	159	101	0	0
Electronic	14	399	25	56	110
Food	31	238	56	123	31
Household	0	130	0	97	0
Medical	29	229	0	0	0
Metallurgy	0	30	0	0	0
Motors	32	167	19	34	17
Oil	11	48	27	23	0
Paper	44	75	27	87	
Printing	0	68	0	42	11
Retail	45	171	19	39	0
Telecommunications	29	22	24	29	0
Textiles	81	412	25	142	59
Transport	14	97	24	29	27

For the sectoral analysis the industries are Agriculture; Chemicals; Construction; Distribution; Diversified; Electronic; Food; Household Products; Medical/Health Products; Metallurgy; Motors; Oil and Minerals; Paper and Packaging; Printing and Publishing; Retail; Telecommunication; Textiles; Transport. The coverage of industries across different countries varies, reflecting the relative importance of that sector as well as data availability. Table A.1 reports the number of firms on which data are available at some time over the data period for each country (I=Indonesia, K=Korea, M=Malaysia, TH=Thailand, TA=Taiwan) .

When estimating the investment function we have used sample selection on the basis of sales growth. In order to maintain consistency between countries we have used sales growth of 15 per cent annually as our trigger value. For all firms which have experienced sales growth better than this value in the previous year, we assign a value of one to the SG dummy. For all firms which have less than this growth rate, we assign a value zero. Table A.2 indicates how our sample is split.

Table A.2   Number of firms which meet growth target (total number of firms in brackets)

	1994	1995	1996
Korea (507)	212	320	287
Malaysia (163)	77	95	78
Thailand (149)	64	76	68

REFERENCES

Alonso, P. and F. Iturriga (1997), 'Financial system models, corporate governance and capital investment in OECD countries: Some stylised facts', *European Investment Bank Papers*, 2(2), 69–95.

Bond, S. and C. Meghir (1994), 'Financial policy and Investment', *Review of Economic Studies*, 61, 197–222.

De Angelo, H. and R. Masulis (1980), 'Optimal capital structure under corporate and personal taxation', *Journal of Financial Economics*, 7, 3–29.

Diamond, D. (1991), 'Monitoring and reputation: The choice between bank loans and directly-placed debt', *Journal of Political Economy*, 99, 680–721.

Dimsdale, N. and M. Preveser (1994), *Capital Markets and Corporate Governance*, Oxford: Clarendon Press.

Edison, H.J., P. Luangaram and M. Miller (1998), 'Asset bubbles, domino effects and "lifeboats": Elements of the East Asian crisis', *International Finance Discussion Paper Series, Federal Reserve Board*, no. 606.

Jensen, M.C. (1986), 'Agency costs of free cash flow, corporate finance and takeovers', *American Economic Review*, 76, 323–9.

Jensen, M.C. and W. Meckling (1976), 'The theory of the firm: Managerial behaviour, agency costs and ownership structure', *Journal of Financial Economics*, 3, 305–60.

Kraus, A. and R. Litzenberger (1973), 'A state preference model of optimal financial leverage', *Journal of Finance*, 28, 911–22.

Krugman, P. (1979), 'A model of balance of payments crises', *Journal of Money, Credit and Banking*, 11, 311–25.

Krugman, P. (1998), 'What happened to Asia', mimeo, MIT.

Miller, M.H. (1977), 'Debt and taxes', *Journal of Finance*, 32, 261–75.

Modigliani, F. and M. Miller (1958), 'The cost of capital, corporation finance and the theory of investment', *American Economic Review*, 48, 261–97.

Modigliani, F. and M. Miller (1963), 'Corporate income taxes and the cost of capital – a correction', *American Economic Review*, 53, 433–43.

Myers, S. and N. Majluf (1984), 'Corporate financing and investment decisions when firms have information that investors do not have', *Journal of Financial Economics*, 4, 187–221.

Ozhkan, F.G. and A. Sutherland (1995), 'Policy measures to avoid a currency crisis', *Economic Journal*, 105, 510–19.

Radelet, S. and J. Sachs (1998), 'The onset of the East Asian financial crisis', *NBER Working Paper Series*, no. 6680.

Ross, S.A. (1977), 'The determination of financial structure: the incentive-signalling approach', *Bell Journal of Economics*, 8, 23–40.

Singh, A. (1994), 'How do large firms in developing countries finance their growth?', *Finance and the International Economy*, 8, Oxford: Oxford University Press.

Tobin, J. (1969), 'A general equilibrium approach to monetary theory', *Journal of Money, Credit and Banking*, 1(1), February, 15–29.

Index